# GREEK
## ARCHAEOLOGY

# GREEK
# ARCHAEOLOGY
## A THEMATIC APPROACH

# CHRISTOPHER MEE

**WILEY-BLACKWELL**

A John Wiley & Sons, Ltd., Publication

This edition first published 2011
© 2011 Christopher Mee

Blackwell Publishing was acquired by John Wiley & Sons in February 2007. Blackwell's publishing program has been merged with Wiley's global Scientific, Technical, and Medical business to form Wiley-Blackwell.

*Registered Office*
John Wiley & Sons Ltd, The Atrium, Southern Gate, Chichester, West Sussex, PO19 8SQ, United Kingdom

*Editorial Offices*
350 Main Street, Malden, MA 02148-5020, USA

9600 Garsington Road, Oxford, OX4 2DQ, UK

The Atrium, Southern Gate, Chichester, West Sussex, PO19 8SQ, UK

For details of our global editorial offices, for customer services, and for information about how to apply for permission to reuse the copyright material in this book please see our website at www.wiley.com/wiley-blackwell.

*Library of Congress Cataloging-in-Publication Data*
Mee, C. (Christopher)
  Greek archaeology : a thematic approach / Christopher Mee.
      p. cm.
  Includes bibliographical references and index.
   ISBN 978-1-4051-6734-5 (hardcover : alk. paper) – ISBN 978-1-4051-6733-8 (pbk. : alk. paper)   1. Greece–Antiquities.   2. Material culture–Greece–History–To 1500.   3. Excavations (Archaeology)–Greece.   4. Historic sites–Greece.   5. Greece–Civilization–To 146 B.C.   I. Title.
  DF77.M47 2011
  938–dc22

                                                                    2010038167

A catalogue record for this book is available from the British Library.

Set in 10.5 on 13 pt Minion by Toppan Best-set Premedia Limited

For Cathy, Matthew, and James

# Contents

# List of Figures

# List of Maps

# List of Tables

# Acknowledgments

There are many friends to whom I am indebted for their assistance and advice, notably John Camp, Bill Cavanagh, Christos Doumas, Don Evely, Matthew Fitzjohn, David Gill, Paul Halstead, Gina Muskett, Graham Oliver, Matt Ponting, Tony Spawforth, George Vavouranakis, and Todd Whitelaw. I am especially grateful to Jenny Doole for her splendid illustrations.

I would like to thank my colleagues in the School of Archaeology, Classics and Egyptology at the University of Liverpool for their support and also the students on whom many of the ideas in this book have been inflicted. Cathy Morgan and the staff at the British School at Athens provided the ideal environment to finish it off. It has been a pleasure to work with everyone at Wiley-Blackwell, in particular Haze Humbert, Galen Smith, Sue Leigh, and Jennifer Speake.

I owe so much to my wife Christa for her help and encouragement. The book is dedicated to our children, Cathy, Matthew, and James, who have ensured that my enthusiasm for those piles of stones is always kept in perspective.

# List of Abbreviations

EC    Early Cycladic
EH    Early Helladic
EM    Early Minoan
MC    Middle Cycladic
MH    Middle Helladic
MM    Middle Minoan
LC    Late Cycladic
LH    Late Helladic
LM    Late Minoan

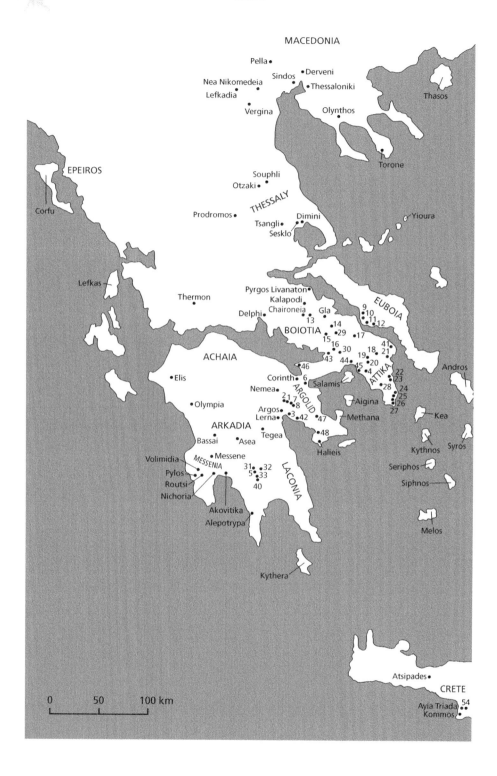

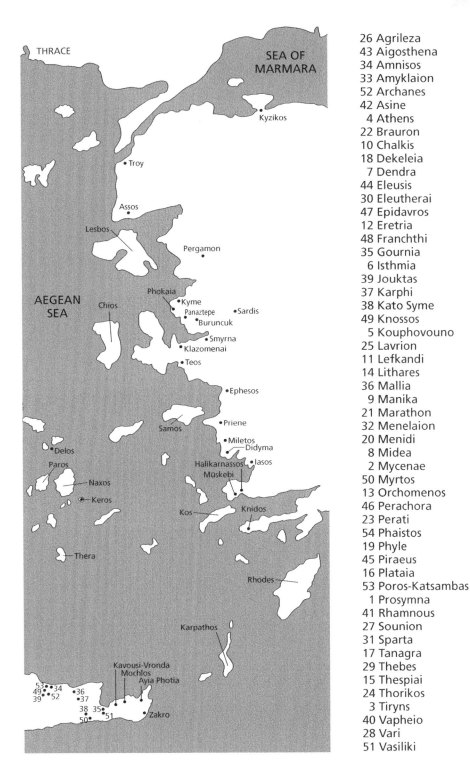

26 Agrileza
43 Aigosthena
34 Amnisos
33 Amyklaion
52 Archanes
42 Asine
 4 Athens
22 Brauron
10 Chalkis
18 Dekeleia
 7 Dendra
44 Eleusis
30 Eleutherai
47 Epidavros
12 Eretria
48 Franchthi
35 Gournia
 6 Isthmia
39 Jouktas
37 Karphi
38 Kato Syme
49 Knossos
 5 Kouphovouno
25 Lavrion
11 Lefkandi
14 Lithares
36 Mallia
 9 Manika
21 Marathon
32 Menelaion
20 Menidi
 8 Midea
 2 Mycenae
50 Myrtos
13 Orchomenos
46 Perachora
23 Perati
54 Phaistos
19 Phyle
45 Piraeus
16 Plataia
53 Poros-Katsambas
 1 Prosymna
41 Rhamnous
27 Sounion
31 Sparta
17 Tanagra
29 Thebes
15 Thespiai
24 Thorikos
 3 Tiryns
40 Vapheio
28 Vari
51 Vasiliki

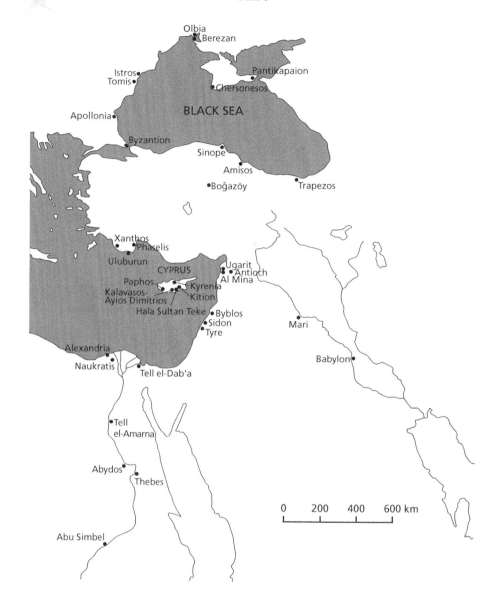

Olbia
Berezan
Istros
Tomis
Pantikapaion
Chersonesos
Apollonia
BLACK SEA
Byzantion
Sinope
Amisos
Boğazöy
Trapezos
Xanthos
Phaselis
Uluburun
CYPRUS
Ugarit
Antioch
Al Mina
Paphos
Kyrenia
Kalavasos-
Ayios Dimitrios
Kition
Hala Sultan Teke
Byblos
Sidon
Tyre
Mari
Alexandria
Naukratis
Babylon
Tell el-Dab'a
Tell
el-Amarna
Abydos
Thebes
Abu Simbel

0     200    400    600 km

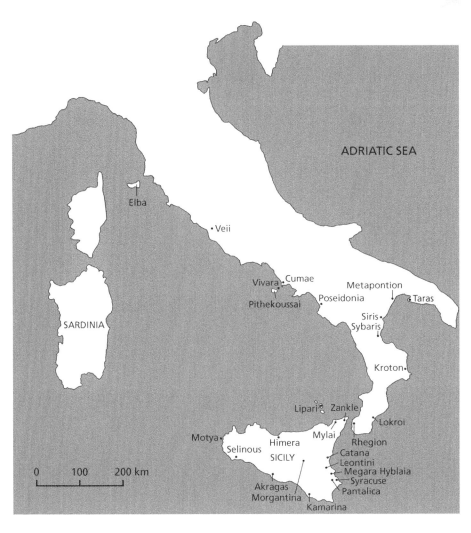

ADRIATIC SEA

Elba

• Veii

Vivara • Cumae       Metapontion
Pithekoussai   Poseidonia            • Taras
                        Siris •
                        Sybaris

SARDINIA

                                    Kroton •

                    Lipari  Zankle
                               • Lokroi
            Motya •        Mylai
                 Selinous      Rhegion
                 Himera    Catana
                 SICILY    Leontini
            Akragas        Megara Hyblaia
            Morgantina      Syracuse
                 Pantalica
                 Kamarina

0    100    200 km

CHAPTER 1

# Introduction

## Across the Great Divide

The Greek archaeology discussed in this book bridges two quite distinct and often divergent academic disciplines, which are differentiated primarily on a chronological basis. Aegean archaeology covers the prehistoric period, particularly the Bronze Age. Classical Greek archaeology has traditionally focused on the Archaic, Classical, and Hellenistic periods but now reaches back into the Early Iron Age. As a result the gap between Aegean and Classical archaeology has been significantly reduced, though certainly not closed. The reason is a second major difference, the availability of written sources and the implications that this has had for the way that the disciplines have developed. Late Bronze Age texts do provide evidence, especially about the economy. Nevertheless, they are limited in number and restricted in the range of information they record. Therefore we can only understand these societies through their material culture. There is no such problem in the Classical period. Indeed, since so much was written down, the remit of archaeology has been rather narrow, with an emphasis on the study of art and architecture. Yet the Classical Greek texts that have survived seldom mention most cities and do not document the Archaic period reliably, while the Early Iron Age is prehistoric or at best proto-historic. Archaeology can obviously make a more positive contribution than has been the case in the past.

Recently there has been a rapprochement between Aegean and Classical Greek archaeology. Developments in survey archaeology have provided much of the impetus for this, directly or indirectly, because these projects are diachronic, that is they investigate the way that landscapes were settled and exploited through time.

*Greek Archaeology: A Thematic Approach*   By Christopher Mee
© 2011 Christopher Mee

The archaeologists involved will often be period specialists but they share their expertise. Survey projects are also interdisciplinary and require environmental scientists to explain how a landscape was formed and has been transformed, historians to study documentary sources, and anthropologists to look at more recent practices and provide a comparative perspective. Most archaeologists find that survey broadens the mind.

My enthusiasm for survey archaeology is based on direct experience and partly explains the time span covered in this book. Another reason is that as an undergraduate I studied Classics but my doctoral thesis was on the islands of the eastern Aegean in the Bronze Age and my most recent field project has been the excavation of a Neolithic site in Laconia. Moreover, I teach Aegean and Classical Greek archaeology, so although I am well aware of the disciplinary divide, I do not believe it is insurmountable. Nor do many of the archaeologists who now work in Greece because they share similar aims and use the same methods and theoretical frameworks. Differences still exist, but not the mutual incomprehension that once split the two disciplines.

It is therefore curious that the end of the Bronze Age remains such a barrier. Aegean prehistorians seldom stray into the Early Iron Age, while Classical Greek archaeologists may take account of the period after the destruction of the Mycenaean palaces but do not venture into the more remote past. There are good reasons for this, not least the volume of evidence, but I believe that a longer-term perspective would be beneficial. The point is not to demonstrate continuity, though some practices and traditions were maintained. This is particularly true of agriculture. The crops and livestock of a Bronze Age and Classical farmer were much the same. Neolithic potters had mastered many of the techniques which were perfected in fifth-century Athens. Of greater interest is the process of change. Given that the physical environment remained essentially constant, why did societies in Greece adapt and behave differently? The reasons for this become clearer over a time span of millennia and subtler rhythms can be detected. Consequently this book takes account of developments between the start of the Neolithic and the end of the Hellenistic period, from approximately 7000 to 100 BC. The Mesolithic and Palaeolithic periods have not been covered because the introduction of agriculture had such profound consequences for the way that people lived. The focus on change would certainly have justified the inclusion of the Roman period as well but I felt that to do this would have compromised the level of detail.

Greek archaeology is a geographically movable feast. The prehistoric Aegean is often rather narrowly defined as the central and southern Greek mainland, the Cyclades, and Crete. The northern Aegean and the west coast of Turkey tend to have a more peripheral role. The Classical Greek world is one that constantly expands. It covers the whole of the Aegean in the Early Iron Age, then follows the Greeks who settled in Italy, Sicily, the Black Sea, and Africa, and finally crosses Asia after Alexander in the Hellenistic period. I have attempted to follow these shifts, though inevitably there is a focus on the southern Aegean.

As the title implies, the book is structured thematically, though each chapter is arranged chronologically. The reason for this is to try to break away from the periodicization of Greek archaeology. I believe that the emphasis on themes provides a clearer indication of developments over time and also of the way that these have been studied and interpreted. It is salutary to move away from a period-specific mentality and take a broader perspective.

Chapter 2 on Settlement and Settlements has a dual role. For those who are not familiar with Greek archaeology, there is an overview of each period. Then the settlement pattern is analyzed, mainly on the basis of the evidence from surveys. The Architecture of Power considers the way that monumental architecture was used to symbolize authority. The case studies reveal subtle variations in the exercise and expression of power. Status, as well as social conventions and practical considerations, determined the design of many of the houses discussed in Residential Space. The Countryside looks at how agriculture was practiced and the implications that this had for the environment, settlement, and society. Technology and Production focuses on pottery and metalwork, which provide us with a longer-term perspective than other types of artefact on the process of innovation and the extent of specialization. Trade and Colonization examines the movement of goods and people overseas. The different forms of exchange are discussed and the evidence for settlement, as well as the identity and motivation of those involved. The role of conflict is assessed in Warfare. The types of weapons and fortifications show how combat developed on land and at sea. Death and Burial looks at the evidence from cemeteries to see what we can deduce about the way that societies were structured and their beliefs. Sanctuaries, votives, and ritual practices are the main themes in Religion.

## Chronology

Time is a fairly fluid concept in archaeology and there is some flexibility in most chronologies. Even if a relative sequence has been established, absolute dates can vary, as we will see. The major subdivisions—Neolithic, Bronze Age, Iron Age—are based on developments in tool technology but it is pottery which provides the chronological framework for Greek archaeology. On most sites more pottery will be found than any other type of artefact. The shapes evolve continuously and also the decoration. Stylistic analysis can detect quite subtle changes over relatively short periods of time, particularly in the case of the pottery produced in sixth- and fifth-century Athens. Any stylistic sequence must be correlated with and should derive from well-stratified excavation levels. One problem is residuality in that there will almost invariably be some earlier pottery in any context on a settlement site and sanctuary deposits tend to be even more mixed. Graves can be closed contexts, though not if tombs were reused, which was a common practice in Minoan Crete and Mycenaean Greece. Even a single grave may contain heirlooms. Nevertheless it has been possible to define good relative sequences for key sites in most periods. It is obviously an advantage when a pottery style has a wide circulation. There is not

**Table 1.1**   The relative and absolute chronology of the Neolithic period

| | |
|---|---|
| Early Neolithic | 6700–5800 |
| Middle Neolithic | 5800–5300 |
| Late Neolithic | 5300–4500 |
| Final Neolithic | 4500–3200 |

much localized variation in Mycenaean pottery for example. If a number of different pottery styles coexist, they have to be synchronized, usually through their presence together at a particular site. A chronology built on broken pottery sounds inherently fragile but has proved remarkably robust. The main outlines are as follows.

The Neolithic period was originally divided into Early, Middle, and Late phases. Then it was noted that some sites apparently practiced agriculture but did not use pottery, so an Aceramic phase was added at the start. However, reservations have been expressed about this and it is not included in table 1.1. A Final Neolithic phase has been recognized as well when metals first appear. Middle Neolithic pottery styles share a number of similarities and can be correlated. At other times there is more diversity.

Three is definitely the magic number in the Bronze Age. Greece, Crete, and the Cyclades are differentiated as Helladic, Minoan, and Cycladic respectively. The Early, Middle, and Late subdivisions are loosely based on the Egyptian Old, Middle, and New Kingdoms. Each of these subdivisions has three phases—I, II, and III—which can sometimes be further refined. As table 1.2 indicates, the sequences for Greece, Crete, and the Cyclades more or less coincide, though there are some anomalies, especially at the start of the Late Bronze Age. Pottery styles do develop at different rates and the imposition of a chronological framework on this process can be a rather arbitrary exercise. In parts of Greece no EH III pottery has been found. Does this mean that there were no sites at that time or that the EH II pottery style continued? Because of dissatisfaction with the pottery based chronology, a complementary scheme has been devised for Crete: Prepalatial = EM I–MM IA, Protopalatial = MM IB–II, Neopalatial = MM III–LM IB, Final Palatial = LM II–IIIA1, and Postpalatial = LM IIIA2–C.

The period after the end of the Bronze Age has been characterized as a Dark Age, though this term is now used less than Early Iron Age, which does not have such negative connotations. There were a number of different pottery styles, centered particularly on Athens, Euboia, and Crete. The Submycenaean, Protogeometric, Early Geometric, Middle Geometric, and Late Geometric sequence in table 1.3 is based on the phases defined for the Early Iron Age pottery from Athens, which can be tied in with the other regional styles. The Archaic period effectively starts with the appearance of the Near Eastern-influenced Protocorinthian style. In due course this evolved into the Corinthian style, which was widely exported and copied. Then Athens became the major production center for decorated pottery once again with the black-figure and red-figure styles. The Classical period conventionally starts

**Table 1.2**   The relative and absolute chronology of the Bronze Age Aegean

| Greece | Crete | Cyclades | Low/High |
|---|---|---|---|
|  |  |  | 3200 |
|  |  |  | 3100 |
| EH I | EM I | EC I | 3000 |
|  |  |  | 2900 |
|  |  |  | 2800 |
|  |  |  | 2700 |
|  |  |  | 2600 |
| EH II | EM II | EC II | 2500 |
|  |  |  | 2400 |
|  |  |  | 2300 |
| EH III | EM III | EC III | 2200 |
| MH I | MM IA | MC I | 2100 |
| MH II | MM IB | MC II | 2000 |
|  | MM II |  | 1900 |
| MH III | MM III | MC III | 1800 |
| LH I | LM IA | LC I | 1700 |
| LH IIA | LM IB | LCII | 1600/1700 |
| LH IIB | LM II |  | 1500/1600 |
| LH IIIA1 | LM IIIA1 | LC III | 1400/1400 |
| LH IIIA2 | LM IIIA2 |  | 1300 |
| LH IIIB | LM IIIB |  | 1200 |
| LH IIIC | LM IIIC |  | 1100 |
| Submycenaean | Subminoan |  | 1000 |

**Table 1.3**   The relative and absolute chronology of the Iron Age

| Protogeometric | 1050–900 |
|---|---|
| Early Geometric | 900–850 |
| Middle Geometric | 850–760 |
| Late Geometric | 760–700 |
| Archaic | 700–480 |
| Classical | 480–323 |
| Hellenistic | 323–146 |

with the Persian invasion in 480 BC and finishes with the death of Alexander in 323 BC. This marks the transition to the Hellenistic period which ends when the Romans took control of Greece in 146 BC. The chronology of the Classical and Hellenistic periods is derived primarily from pottery deposits in the Athenian Agora.

The duration of each of the Neolithic phases has been calculated from radiocarbon dates, though not as accurately as table 1.1 implies. Each of the dates given there has a range of at least ±50 years. The absolute chronology of the Early Bronze

Age is also radiocarbon-based. For the Middle and Late Bronze Age, synchronisms with Egypt and the Near East can be used as well. These synchronisms take the form of datable Egyptian or Near Eastern artefacts in secure Aegean contexts or Aegean artefacts in securely datable Egyptian or Near Eastern contexts. Many of the imported items found in the Aegean were valuable and could have remained in circulation for some time. The Minoan and Mycenaean pottery which was traded in the eastern Mediterranean would generally have had a shorter period of use, and it has proved possible to work out quite precise dates for each phase. However, there is a major controversy about the eruption of Thera and the destruction of Akrotiri. The imported Cretan pottery from the destruction levels is late LM IA and so the date derived from the synchronisms with Egypt would be around 1525 BC. The samples from Akrotiri which have been radiocarbon dated are much earlier, mainly late seventeenth century. No compromise seems possible and so a high and a low chronology have been devised for the crucial period at the start of the Late Bronze Age. Consequently I have preferred to give relative rather than absolute dates. We can say with certainty that Akrotiri was destroyed in LM IA but this could be some time in the seventeenth, sixteenth, or fifteenth centuries. Greater accuracy is possible with dendrochronology, for example in the case of the ship which sank at Uluburun off the southern coast of Turkey. The tree-ring date for brushwood from the wreck is 1307 +4/−7 BC which fits well with the calibrated radiocarbon date of 1304 ±33 BC.

Dendrochronology has shown that the amount of radiocarbon in the atmosphere fluctuates. It is therefore necessary to correct the radiocarbon age of a sample in order to determine the calendar date. This is done with a calibration curve based on tree-ring samples which have been radiocarbon dated. Unfortunately the curve is not a smooth line but oscillates and occasionally flattens out. The result can be a lack of precision and this is a problem in the period after 1000 BC. So the few available radiocarbon dates do not provide a chronological framework for the Early Iron Age, and furthermore we do not have good synchronisms because trade was disrupted at that time.

Once historical events can be identified archaeologically, the sequence of pottery styles theoretically has some fixed points but this is rarely straightforward. Thucydides (6.3–5) gives foundation dates for the Greek colonies in Sicily and Italy. His list starts with Naxos in 734 BC (see chapter 7). The first question we must ask is whether Thucydides, who wrote his history in the fifth century BC, really knew the date of events 300 years in the past. If we assume that he did, is it likely that the earliest Greek pottery found at these sites came with the colonists rather than later? There may also have been trade before they arrived. Clearly allowance must be made for these factors and their implications for the chronology of Corinthian pottery in particular.

After the battle of Marathon in 490 BC the Athenians buried their dead in a tumulus which has been partially excavated. The black-figure and red-figure sherds mixed with the bones should be early fifth century. In 480–479 the Persians captured and sacked Athens. Once they had left, the Athenians returned and cleaned up the city. Sculpture and pottery in pits on the Acropolis and wells in the Agora has been linked with this operation, though there could be some later material as well. Thucydides (3.104) says that the Athenians purified the sacred island of Delos in the winter of 426/425. All burials were removed and reinterred in a pit on Rheneia. The latest pottery from this pit presumably dates from shortly before the purification but obviously many of the burials were much earlier. In 348 BC Philip II captured Olynthos and enslaved the population. This should give us a terminus ante quem for the imported Athenian pottery found in the houses, yet there is always the possibility of some reoccupation, even after such a major destruction. These are just some of the historical events which have been used as fixed points but they do underline how careful we must be.

Inscriptions on pottery can sometimes be dated. In the fourth century the names of officials occasionally appear on the oil amphorae given as prizes in the Panathenaic Games at Athens and in some cases their year of office is known. The names of officials were also stamped on the handles of transport amphorae from Rhodes and Knidos.

The chronology of Greek coins is well established but the number in circulation was limited and they were obviously valuable. Consequently they are not a particularly common find and may have been in use for some time, so they do not necessarily provide an accurate date for a context.

## Bibliographical notes

See McDonald and Thomas 1990 for a historical account of the development of Aegean archaeology and Dyson 2006 for Classical archaeology, Greek and Roman. The chapters in Cherry et al. 2005 reflect on the current state of Aegean archaeology as a discipline. Shanks 1996, Morris 2000 and 2004, Whitley 2001, and Snodgrass 2007 present a range of views about the nature and future of Classical archaeology.

Warren and Hankey 1989 set out the relative chronology of the Bronze Age Aegean and the synchronisms with Egypt and the Near East. Shelmerdine 2008 and Tartaron 2008 review the debate about the eruption of Thera, which is examined in detail in the papers in Warburton 2009. See Snodgrass 1971 and Dickinson 2006 for the Early Iron Age. Sparkes 1991, Biers 1992, and Whitley 2001 discuss later Greek chronology and the archaeological identification of historical events.

# CHAPTER 2

# Settlement and Settlements

## Introduction

There has never been any doubt where certain sites were located because they had kept their ancient names and were still inhabited when early travelers went to look for them. But many of the sites whose names were known from written sources proved more elusive and had to be identified from their ruins, inscriptions, or coins. So these travelers pioneered archaeological prospection in Greece and their accounts of what they saw provided a first impression of the distribution of sites across the landscape. In the nineteenth and twentieth centuries this basic framework was filled in by archaeologists who undertook extensive surveys which often covered entire regions. Local information and an eye for likely locations led to the identification of thousands of sites and a much better knowledge of the prehistoric period in particular. Of course the scale of these surveys meant that some sites were bound to be missed and this led to the introduction of more intensive methods. Survey projects began to use teams of field walkers spaced no more than 10 to 20 meters apart to ensure that even small sites would be recognized. They also recorded sites of every period so that the long-term settlement history of the region could be reconstructed. Although some of the sites have architectural remains, what the survey archaeologists usually find is a scatter of pottery sherds, tile fragments, or chipped stone. These small sites can easily be buried by alluviation, destroyed by erosion, or ploughed out, so no survey can provide a complete record of what was once there. But over time we do see some significant changes, which this chapter will examine. We will also look at the layout of settlements and what this implies.

*Greek Archaeology: A Thematic Approach*   By Christopher Mee
© 2011 Christopher Mee

## Neolithic Greece

Prior to the introduction of agriculture and hence the start of the Neolithic period, there were very few sites. Though some may have disappeared as a result of the rise in sea level after the end of the last Ice Age, the Palaeolithic and Mesolithic population of Greece appears to have been tiny. For example, it has been estimated that only one or two hundred people lived in Epeiros in the Upper Palaeolithic. By the Hellenistic period this region had several hundred thousand inhabitants. It was the replacement of the hunter-gatherer lifestyle by domesticated livestock and cultivated cereals that made this much higher population density possible. Most of the new agricultural practices ultimately came from the Near East but it is still not clear whether they were brought by migrant farmers or adopted by local Mesolithic communities, and some combination of these two models is also a possibility.

The availability of light and well-watered soils that were ideal for cultivation made Thessaly particularly attractive, and the number of settlements expanded rapidly in the Early Neolithic period. More than a hundred sites have been identified in eastern Thessaly alone. Most are tells—artificial mounds mainly composed of the mudbrick used in the construction of the houses—which stand out in the flat landscape. The sites vary in size but average 3–4 hectares. It is difficult to extrapolate population numbers directly from the size of a settlement, since much depends on the density of the houses and the composition of each household. A figure of around 200 persons per hectare has been proposed for some later prehistoric settlements in Greece but, in the case of Thessaly, a more modest 100–300 inhabitants per site seems a reasonable estimate. So these were village communities, on average just 2.5 kilometers apart and presumably in regular contact. This pattern, once established, was remarkably stable because there were more or less the same number of Middle Neolithic sites in eastern Thessaly, most of which were in the same location as their predecessors.

Sesklo is often cited as the classic Middle Neolithic Thessalian settlement. There is a tell with quite spacious detached houses, partly surrounded by a wall which may have been structural rather than defensive but did separate the acropolis from the lower settlement, known as the polis. In the lower settlement occupation was discontinuous and the houses formed tighter clusters. Other differences between the acropolis and the polis have been noted and suggest divisions within the community, which may not be strictly hierarchical but could indicate some inequality. Although it was once thought that the population may have been 3,000–4,000 at this time, a much lower figure now seems more likely, given the rather fluid pattern of settlement in the polis.

Whereas northern Greece was quite densely settled in the Neolithic period, the southern mainland and the islands look distinctly underpopulated, despite a number of intensive surveys which would have found sites if they still existed. Some have undoubtedly been destroyed but it does appear that there was a real north–south divide. The obvious explanation for this is that conditions in southern Greece were less favorable for early farmers: the soils were not as fertile and the rainfall was lower. Yet the Peloponnese could certainly have supported more communities, since the distance between sites is often 20 kilometers or more. Nor is it the case that the villages in the south were larger than their counterparts in Thessaly. At Kouphovouno in Laconia the surface distribution of Middle Neolithic pottery gives a figure of around 4–5 hectares for the size of the settlement, which is comparable with Thessalian sites. Although environmental considerations must have been a factor when people decided where to live, it is clear that social choices were just as important.

In the Late and more especially the Final Neolithic period there is a gradual shift. In eastern Thessaly the number of sites rose in the Late Neolithic period and then decreased dramatically in the Final Neolithic. Meanwhile in southern Greece and many of the islands this is a period of expansion, often into rather marginal environments, that is places where the poor quality of the soil and the low rainfall would have posed considerable risks. This may have been facilitated by developments in the way that animals were exploited, with more use of their "secondary products," such as milk, wool, and manure. Sheep and goats could graze on land which was unsuitable for cultivation and the sites that were now occupied do suggest a greater reliance on pastoralism. But this does not explain why the pattern of settlement changed, only how it would have been possible. Many of the new sites were not in optimal locations, which could be taken as an indication that people lived there because they had to. However, population pressure can hardly be the only explanation at a time when site numbers were still comparatively low. There was evidently an element of choice and one that may have made communities more interdependent.

## Early Bronze Age

The Neolithic–Early Bronze Age transition implies that there had been a major technological change, namely the replacement of stone tools by metal implements. However, this was a protracted process because some knowledge of metallurgy is already evident in the Final Neolithic period and stone tools were still widely used in the Early Bronze Age. Moreover, it was some time before bronze alloys were produced and most of the metalwork is made of copper. The same slow pace also characterizes the spread of settlement in southern Greece. The expansion in the Final Neolithic period is not seen everywhere. Moreover, some of the sites are rather ephemeral scatters of chipped stone tools and may not have been permanently occupied. It is only in the Early Bronze Age that the new pattern becomes firmly established, and the data from survey projects show this clearly. For example, in the southern Argolid there were just four Late Neolithic sites and over 30 of Early Bronze Age date. The Laconia Survey did not record any Late Neolithic sites but the Early Bronze Age figure is again around 30. On Melos in the Cyclades Neolithic settlement is questionable, whereas 25 Early Bronze Age sites have been found. In many other regions the sequence is broadly comparable.

More sites does not necessarily mean a higher population if the average size of settlements decreased. In southern Greece the Neolithic was a period of nucleation with quite large sites located some distance apart. One possibility is that these communities had now fragmented, which would be a rational choice since scattered households could exploit the resources that were available more efficiently. Many Early Bronze Age sites are small, less than $2500 \, m^2$, and have been interpreted as farmsteads, so we have some evidence that this was the case. Yet there were larger settlements as well. In the southern Argolid farmsteads constitute one tier in a hierarchy which also includes settlements of 1–2 hectares and a few villages of 5 hectares or so. A similar pattern can be seen in the Mesara in southern Crete, where Phaistos was the dominant settlement in a three-tier hierarchy of farmsteads, hamlets, and villages. Phaistos was more or less the same size as Knossos at this time, around 5 hectares, but both of these sites would expand rapidly when the first palaces were built early in the second millennium. Some settlements may have experienced this type of expansion already. The estimate for Thebes is 20 hectares and over 50 hectares for Manika on Euboia.

What does the existence of these site hierarchies imply? In the case of the southern Argolid it has been noted that settlement size and the range of artefact types correlate, with greater diversity on the larger sites. This inequality is indicative of a more developed level of social organization and the evidence of differential wealth, for example in tombs on Crete, supports this conclusion. However, it was particular individuals in the larger settlements who would have enjoyed a higher status, whether inherited or attained. It does not mean that the sites in the upper tier of the hierarchy necessarily exercised direct control over those lower down, though some form of economic dependency is likely. Simply by virtue of their size, the major sites must have dominated exchange relationships, which then reinforced their position. Yet sites would also have been linked by a web of social networks. So it should not be assumed that the hierarchies had a political basis, even if this was the case subsequently.

Few Early Bronze Age sites have been extensively excavated, with the exception of Myrtos on Crete (figure 4.3). Sometimes the center of the site has been cleared but the layout of the settlement remains uncertain. This is true of Lerna (figure 3.2), otherwise one of the most informative mainland Greek sites, where the House of Tiles stands alone. Later construction activity has often destroyed earlier levels, for example at Knossos and Phaistos when the palaces were laid out. Some sites are under modern cities, such as Thebes, and can only be investigated opportunistically rather than systematically. However, at Lithares in Boiotia a substantial proportion of the carefully planned settlement has been excavated (figure 2.1). In the final phase of occupation there was an east–west street, which varies in width from 1.7 to 3.5 meters and has been traced for over 60 meters. This was lined by houses, neatly built single-story structures. They were not particularly spacious but most have several rooms.

Lithares is one of many mainland Greek settlements which were abandoned toward the end of the Early Bronze Age. Most survey projects have recorded a decrease in the number of sites. Although there is some variation, the Middle Bronze

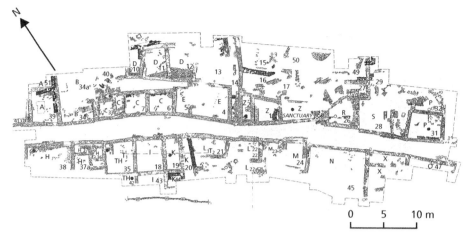

**Figure 2.1**   Plan of Lithares

Age is a period when settlement was much more restricted and it is not the case that sites were larger than before, so population levels must have declined quite dramatically. Was this a sudden event or a gradual process? Here a digression on the type of pottery found by surveys is necessary, since this is how the sites are dated. Surface sherds are usually not as numerous and are much more abraded than the pottery from excavations. They are therefore more difficult to date precisely. Indeed it has been suggested that some of the lows in survey data reflect the fact that the pottery of that period is not particularly distinctive. However, this is not true of the Middle Bronze Age, so the reduction in site numbers is undoubtedly real. Nevertheless, another pottery-related factor adds a further complication. The settlement density peaks in EH II when a common style of pottery was in use throughout southern Greece and much of the Aegean. In EH III there is greater diversity and in fact this style is seldom found in the southern Peloponnese. It is of course possible that there were no sites of this period in Laconia and Messenia. Alternatively, the previous pottery style may have continued in use. So the chronology of this decrease in site numbers remains uncertain, which makes it difficult to explain.

The fact that some sites, such as Lerna, were destroyed at the end of EH II and then experienced major cultural changes led to the hypothesis of an invasion. However, where there is evidence of destruction, this does not always occur at the end of EH II. Moreover, some cultural continuity is now accepted and there is a realization that the changes need not indicate a new population. Consequently the invasion hypothesis is no longer regarded as particularly plausible and we must seek an alternative explanation for the reduction in the number of settlements, though there is as yet no consensus on this.

A glance at the Cyclades suggests a similar sequence of events in the Aegean. For example, the Melos Survey recorded 14 definite Early Bronze Age sites but only two of Middle Bronze Age date. However, this is a case of nucleation because the scattered Early Bronze Age farmsteads were replaced by a dominant settlement at Phylakopi. This process is replicated on a number of the other islands. Nucleation had obvious advantages, such as greater security, and would also have facilitated inter-island exchange. The downside was the greater distance that people would have to travel to their fields. So there may have been some pressure to change. On Crete a reduction in site numbers is evident after EM II, though the scale of the decrease is difficult to gage because the EM III pottery style is not well defined. Nevertheless, it would appear that much of the countryside was deserted and that there was settlement nucleation.

## Palatial Crete

This nucleated settlement pattern is particularly apparent in MM IA. There were relatively few settlements in the Mesara in southern Crete, no doubt because Phaistos was now a 27-hectare town and must have drawn in much of the population from the countryside. Knossos and Mallia also expanded rapidly and this is significant because these were the three sites where the first Minoan palaces were constructed in late MM IA/early MM IB, the start of the Protopalatial period. This development coincided with and may well have been spurred by a further growth in their size, which is estimated as 75 hectares or more in the case of Knossos and 55 hectares for Phaistos. This implies a population of several thousand. Moreover, we also see a sharp increase in the number of sites, for example in the Mesara where there were just seven in the MM IA period but 38 dated MM IB–II. These newly founded settlements include villages and hamlets as well as farmsteads.

Because of reconstruction in MM III–LM I, our knowledge of the first palaces is rather limited but their basic range of functions can be deduced (the architectural characteristics of the palaces will be examined in more detail in chapter 3). The central court is their most distinctive feature and this was presumably used for public ceremonies, some of which may have been religious. Knossos and Phaistos also have a west court with circular stone-lined pits, possibly granaries. The storage of agricultural produce was certainly important and the existence of administrative documents written on clay tablets in the Hieroglyphic and Linear A scripts indicates that some of this was redistributed. The palaces supported specialist craftworkers, as well as other dependents such as officials. There is also evidence that food was prepared and consumed. A residential role seems likely but we cannot be certain that the palaces were actually royal residences. They may have functioned primarily as administrative, economic, and ceremonial centers.

Unquestionably the palaces were powerful institutions but how much control did they exercise? Just north of the first palace at Mallia was the Agora, an open square which measured 30 by 40 meters with storage magazines for olive oil. Further west was the complex known as Quartier Mu. This consisted of two large houses with reception, residential, and store rooms. Fallen from the upper floor were administrative documents. Annexes housed workshops for a sealstone engraver, a potter, and metalworkers. There is still speculation about the relationship of the palace, the Agora, and Quartier Mu but, if they were independent and not integrated, then this would suggest rival power bases. Factional competition between groups of elite families is one of the theories put forward for the higher level of social complexity that is now apparent. Competition is also a key feature of what is known as peer polity interaction and explains why sites on Crete share so much in common. Especially between rivals imitation can be the sincerest form of flattery.

It is generally agreed that this period marked the first appearance of states that controlled territories. Sites were now bound together politically in a way that had not been the case before. The size of these territories is less certain and no doubt it would have fluctuated over time. Some believe that central Crete was carved up between Knossos, Mallia, and Phaistos; others envisage a mosaic of power centers.

Knossos, Phaistos, Mallia, and a number of other sites were destroyed at the end of MM II. The cause of these destructions is uncertain but, culturally at least, there is continuity and in due course the palaces were reconstructed. At Knossos the palace eventually covered around 20,000 m$^2$ and the settlement also expanded (figure 2.2). The surface distribution of MM III–LM I pottery gives a figure now assessed as at least 100 hectares for the Neopalatial town. Some of the zone around the palace was used for public or official activities, and important individuals also resided here. In the next zone of detached houses the population density may have been around 250 persons per hectare. Further out the houses were more densely packed together and the estimate here is up to 450 persons per hectare. The houses around the edge of the town were more isolated and on the outskirts there were cemeteries. With a population in excess of 20,000 in MM III–LM I, Knossos was a sizable community by any standards.

The growth of Knossos in the Neopalatial period is not paralleled elsewhere. In the Mesara the number of sites increased initially and then leveled off or decreased slightly. Phaistos also contracted in size and it is not clear whether the palace was fully operational. Around Mallia settlement was much sparser and there is no evidence of nucleation, since the town did not expand. One explanation for this variability could be political domination by Knossos. If southern Crete was under Knossian control in LM I, the decline of the palace at Phaistos and the development of the nearby villa at Ayia Triada as an administrative center would make sense. Nor could Mallia have competed against such a powerful neighbor. It seems unlikely that Knossos ruled the whole of Crete but the economic repercussions of this expansionist policy may have been felt more widely.

A case in point is Gournia on the bay of Mirabello in eastern Crete, a completely excavated Late Minoan town of around 4 hectares (figure 2.3). The houses were built close together and their modest size suggests that they were occupied by single families. On top of the hill was the much larger "palace." The use of this term has been questioned because there is no central court, though some of the architectural features do suggest an aspiration for the palatial lifestyle. An ambitious local ruler could well have profited from the fact that Gournia was so strategically placed on major land and sea routes.

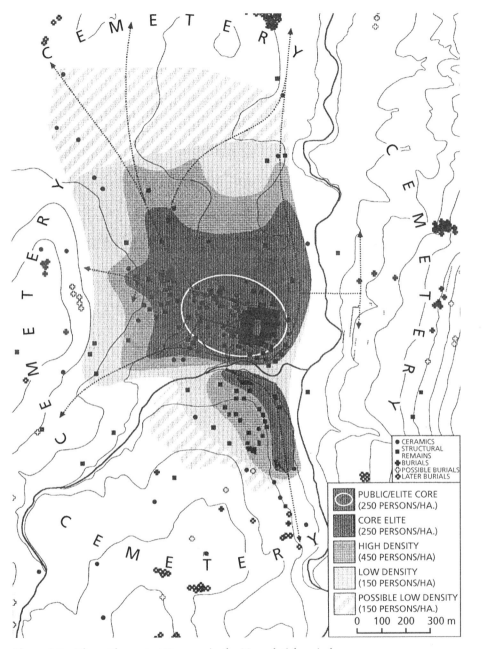

**Figure 2.2**  The settlement at Knossos in the Neopalatial period

**Figure 2.3**   View of Gournia

   The good times eventually came to an end in LM IB when Gournia, like most
sites on Crete, was destroyed. Once again there is speculation about the cause of
these destructions. In their aftermath the Mycenaeans evidently took control of
Knossos because the palace administration now used the Linear B script, which
Michael Ventris deciphered as an early form of Greek, whereas the Hieroglyphic
and Linear A texts were in a different language. Should the Mycenaeans be held
responsible for this trail of devastation? The weapons in their graves certainly suggest
that they were warriors but it is questionable whether they could have launched a
successful attack unless Crete had been weakened and this may have been the case.
One possibility is that the major centers had suffered as a result of the eruption
of the Thera volcano in LM IA. Although this was well before the LM IB destructions, the impact on agriculture and consequently on the Minoan economy could
have been catastrophic. Competition for resources may have led to warfare, a situation which the Mycenaeans exploited, and they remained on Crete until the final
destruction of the palace at Knossos, probably in LM IIIA.


## The Cyclades

The Thera eruption buried and consequently preserved the settlement at Akrotiri
on the south coast of the island. Like Pompeii, Akrotiri is a site frozen in time. The
depth of the volcanic ash makes it difficult to estimate the size of the town but there

are indications that it may have been around 20 hectares. If so, only a fraction of the site has been excavated. Much reconstruction took place early in LC I after a major earthquake. The result was an irregular network of streets and squares with some detached houses and others built in blocks (figure 2.4). Certain architectural features clearly originated on Crete, and Akrotiri takes on a decidedly Minoan veneer at this time. As Thera would have been the first port of call for ships that sailed north from Crete, this is not a great surprise. However, it may be significant that there were other small sites, possibly farmsteads, scattered across the island. This is reminiscent of Crete whereas elsewhere in the Cyclades, for example on Melos and Kea, the highly nucleated settlement pattern, which was established early in the Middle Bronze Age, had not altered. By the start of the Late Bronze Age Phylakopi on Melos was a fortified town with a regular grid of narrow streets and blocks of small houses (figure 2.5). In some respects Phylakopi resembles Akrotiri but there were also major differences and this may well reflect the nature of their relationship with Crete. Kolonna on Aigina is another important island site of this period and has an impressive sequence of fortifications (figure 8.4). There is also a Middle Bronze Age shaft grave in which a warrior was buried, and it may be no coincidence that funerals of this type were soon a feature of mainland Greece.

## Mycenaean Greece

As we have seen, there was a reduction in the number of sites on the mainland towards the end of the Early Bronze Age and the situation did not improve in the Middle Bronze Age, at least not at first. Sites of this period, such as Asine and Lerna in the Argolid, were not particularly large and their architecture is generally unimpressive. In comparison with Crete and the Cyclades, mainland Greece was decidedly the poor relation. The poverty and isolation can be exaggerated, though study of the skeletons from Middle Helladic cemeteries suggests that life was fairly grim for most of the population. However, many survey projects have noted an expansion in settlement late on in the period. The fact that some abandoned sites were now reoccupied underlines this impression of a gradual recovery.

How does this tie in with the other major development on the mainland, namely the sudden increase in disposable wealth, which is epitomized by the spectacular finds from the grave circles at Mycenae? Elsewhere in the Peloponnese—in the Argolid, Laconia and Messenia—many individuals were given lavish funerals in the period which spans the end of the Middle Bronze Age and the start of the Late Bronze Age. This emphasis on their high status when they died was no doubt intended to ensure that their heirs enjoyed the same privileges. Yet the scale of the expenditure also indicates a fiercely competitive environment. Where this additional wealth came from is not immediately obvious. Warfare is one possibility, though it is questionable whether so much plunder could have been acquired locally or even from overseas. Trade is an alternative option and it has been suggested that the mainland supplied Crete with some high-value commodity, such as metals or

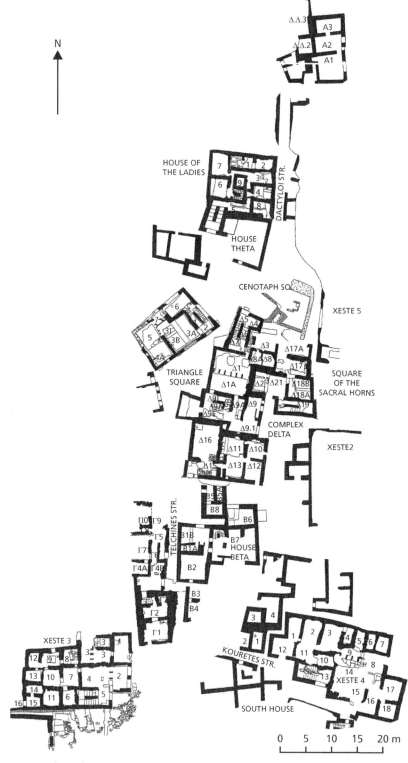

**Figure 2.4** Plan of Akrotiri

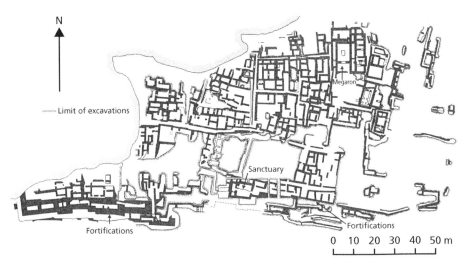

**Figure 2.5**   Plan of Phylakopi

horses. There was a new social order but the transition from the much simpler level of organization in Middle Helladic communities must have been protracted. It seems that authority could now be inherited, though factional competition between elite groups was common.

What impact do these changes have on the archaeology of Early Mycenaean Greece? One problem is that we are heavily reliant on the evidence from the graves. On many of the major sites, such as Mycenae, the architectural remains of this period have largely been destroyed by later construction activity. There is also a suspicion that the Mycenaeans lived rather modestly, since they died so expensively. Although we do not know as much as we would like about Early Mycenaean settlements, their location is informative. A case in point is the Nemea valley, north of Mycenae, which was neglected for much of the Middle Helladic period but had now been resettled. As the valley tends to flood, this may have required drainage works which would make the involvement of Mycenae even more likely. Clearly there was some territorial expansion and, as we have seen, the Mycenaeans soon turn up on Crete. Yet it is doubtful whether fully fledged states had materialized at this stage. In Messenia, for example, a number of separate centers can be identified from the distribution of elite tombs.

It was not until LH IIIA that the first Mycenaean palaces were built, though most of our information comes from their LH IIIB successors. The best-preserved palace is at Pylos in Messenia (figure 3.5), which also has the largest mainland archive of Linear B texts (see chapter 3 for a detailed discussion of Pylos). They tell us that there was a ruler, the wanax, and that the palace was an administrative center. The olive oil in the storerooms was used in the manufacture of perfume, just one of the industries that the palace supervised. State officials kept detailed records of economic transactions and ensured that taxes were collected. The hospitality budget must have

**Figure 2.6**   View from Mycenae

been generous, to judge from the size of the wine magazine. Perhaps religious festivals provided the justification for these feasts. Survey around the palace at Pylos has
found evidence of settlement over an area of 20 to 30 hectares. Because there may
well have been gaps between the houses, it is difficult to extrapolate a figure for the
population. Geophysical prospection has revealed a section of what could be a fortification wall. How much of the town this would have protected is uncertain.

At Mycenae massive fortifications were built over the course of the LH IIIA–B
periods (figure 8.13). Much of the citadel was occupied by the palace, a highly visible
symbol of the dominant position that the ruler enjoyed, with a superb view (figure
2.6). As residential space within the fortifications was limited, most of his subjects
must have lived in the houses around the citadel, though even here there were subsidiary annexes of the palace in which oil, ivories, and other goods were stored. At
30 hectares or so the settlement was slightly larger than Pylos. The regular layout
of a Cretan or Cycladic town would not have been feasible because of the uneven
terrain and so the houses were built on terraces.

For the size of the territories controlled by these palaces, the Linear B texts from
Pylos have again proved invaluable. The tablets indicate that there were two provinces, the Hither and the Further, each of which was subdivided into administrative
districts. Study of the place names suggests that the provinces were located in
western and eastern Messenia respectively. So the whole of the southwestern
Peloponnese was evidently ruled from Pylos when the texts were written at the end
of the LH IIIB period and it is thought that this had probably been the case for

some time. At an earlier stage, perhaps in LH IIIA, the two provinces may have been independent and were then unified, the culmination of a process which had started in the Early Mycenaean period.

Similar territories could be envisaged for each of the other palaces, though the Argolid presents a problem because there is Tiryns as well as Mycenae. It seems unlikely that these two palaces were enemies, given their close proximity. They must surely have cooperated and may have been bound together politically. The growth of Mycenae and Tiryns had repercussions throughout the Argolid. We have already noted the increase in site numbers in the Nemea valley and other surveys have found that this was a period of expansion on a scale which is not matched in Laconia and Messenia for example.

The Argolid was certainly very powerful but even in LH IIIB there are hints that trouble lay ahead. Though the destruction of some of the houses outside the citadel at Mycenae could have been accidental, the fortifications were subsequently extended and the water supply secured. Similarly at Tiryns the fortifications were strengthened. Overseas trade, a key component of the palace economy, may have been affected, which implies widespread instability. Then at the end of LH IIIB many sites across Greece were destroyed by fire. Some, for example Pylos, were never rebuilt. Others, such as Mycenae and Tiryns, were still occupied, though the palaces went out of use, together with the administrative system they had maintained and the Linear B script. It would be several centuries before literacy returned in the form of the alphabet. This list of casualties suggests that it was the elite who suffered most but, as we shall see, the destructions had consequences for every sector of Mycenaean society.

Given the scale of the collapse that followed, there has been considerable debate about the cause of these destructions and a number of possibilities have been suggested. External agency was an early favorite, one theory being an invasion from the north by speakers of Dorian Greek, but attempts to link various cultural innovations with their arrival have not proved persuasive. The Sea Peoples appear in Egyptian records around this time and were clearly a serious threat, though we have no evidence that they were active in the Aegean. Alternatively, the explanation could be warfare between Mycenaean states. Then there are natural causes—earthquakes, a deterioration in the climate, and epidemics have been cited. A distinction does need to be made between the event or events that triggered this disaster and the reasons why the system then collapsed so completely. An enemy attack, for example, would not have had this effect unless the Mycenaeans were already vulnerable. One suggestion is that the palace economies had become overstretched. Any additional pressure could have resulted in greater competition for resources, which simply exacerbated the problem and ultimately destabilized Mycenaean society.

In the immediate aftermath of the destructions, in early LH IIIC, some communities enjoyed a measure of prosperity. Sites around the Aegean may have profited from the opportunity to establish new trade networks. At Tiryns there was reconstruction on the citadel and in the town, which was still as large as it had been in LH IIIB, around 25 hectares. However, the modest structure built on the ruins of the palace suggests a very different form of authority. It also seems likely that the size of Tiryns is actually a sign of insecurity because people had evidently come here from elsewhere in the Argolid. Survey projects in the northeastern Peloponnese have recorded a sharp decrease in the number of sites in LH IIIC. Because surface pottery of this period is not especially diagnostic, the exact sequence of events is unclear but it seems that there was widespread abandonment of sites at the end of LH IIIB and those that do continue into LH IIIC did not survive for long. The pattern is the same in Laconia where the destruction of the Menelaion precipitated a similar collapse. A reduction in the size of the population has also been documented in Messenia. Some moved away, presumably out of necessity rather than choice, and apparently settled in Achaia, Attica, or even overseas. However, migration was only a temporary solution because every region eventually experienced some measure of depopulation.

Crete may have suffered less than the mainland, perhaps because there had been no palaces for some time, but even here many new sites were established in easily defensible locations. The motive for this need not simply have been a desire for security, though this was surely a factor. Karphi in eastern Crete is a classic example of this type of site (figure 2.7). The blocks of stone houses recall earlier Cretan architectural traditions and suggest a greater degree of continuity.

The collapse of the Mycenaean palace system transformed Greece. There were political, social, and economic repercussions, as well as major cultural and technological changes. It is difficult to appreciate what this meant at the level of the individual but warfare and violence must have been a common experience. Deprived of the protection that the palaces had provided, many left their homes, a momentous decision which was fraught with risk and, in a period of such instability, could they really feel confident that the situation would ever improve?

## The Early Iron Age

The centuries that followed have often been described as the Dark Age of Greece, a period of recession which decisively separated the Mycenaean past from the Classical future. It was because so much less was known about the later eleventh, tenth, and ninth centuries that the term Dark Age seemed particularly appropriate. However, the darkness has been partially dispelled as a result of recent archaeological research, so a more neutral label is needed. One alternative is Protogeometric for the period 1050–900 and Geometric for 900–700, since these were the main styles of pottery and provide the chronological framework. But the term preferred here is Early Iron Age because it does highlight a significant technological change.

The introduction of iron metallurgy will be explored in more detail in chapter 6, but some points should be emphasized. We have seen that the conversion from stone to copper and then bronze tools was very protracted. By contrast, once the Greeks had learned how to work iron, probably from Cyprus, it became the metal of choice within a century or so. This sudden enthusiasm for iron was not

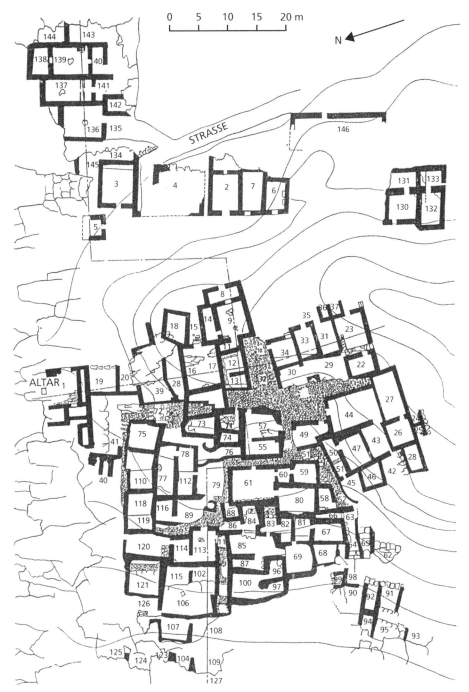

**Figure 2.7** Plan of Karphi

necessarily prompted by an appreciation of its technical superiority. The first iron swords were not significantly better than the bronze swords they replaced. However, iron did have one obvious advantage. Unlike copper and tin, which were imported, iron ores were available locally. As trade with the eastern Mediterranean was disrupted in the eleventh and tenth centuries, this has led to the hypothesis that the use of iron took off rapidly because bronze was in short supply. Yet there was still some bronze in circulation, so the attraction of iron may have been what it represented, a higher-status metal which quite possibly symbolized a break with the past.

This search for a new identity is implicit in the treatment of the dead. Mycenaean practices were certainly not uniform but, in the palace period, inhumation in a tomb which was used for several generations of the same family is fairly standard. Signs of change can be detected in LH IIIC and intensify at the start of the Early Iron Age. The conservatism of some regions may reflect a conscious link with the past but more generally we find a mixture of old and new practices, with cremation of the dead as well as inhumation and more single graves. There is greater regional variation than before, which could be an assertion of independence. However, variation is also a feature in some communities and underlines the social tensions which were present at this time.

The dead loom large in the story of Early Iron Age Greece because so much less is known about where they lived. It is extraordinary how few sites of this period have been reported by survey projects. For example, there is no evidence of settlement in the Laconian countryside, even though Sparta was founded in the tenth century. This does not rule out activities which have left no trace, such as pastoralism, but permanently occupied sites would produce some datable pottery. Most of the population of Greece was probably based in nucleated settlements such as Athens, which had been an important Mycenaean center but now becomes much more prominent. Unfortunately there is not much left of Early Iron Age Athens except for cemeteries. These were scattered around the Acropolis in a way that is repeated at other sites, such as Argos and Tiryns. One interpretation of this is that each cemetery served a separate group of families who lived nearby, so settlement would have been clustered.

The most extraordinary structure built in this period was the so-called "Heroon" at Lefkandi on Euboia. The settlement centered on the Xeropolis headland where recent excavations have shown that occupation continued through the Early Iron Age. The cemeteries were some distance away and included Toumba where the "Heroon" was found (figure 3.7a & b). It was built in the early tenth century and is exceptionally large, almost 50 meters in length. A man and a woman had been buried in the central room, so the "Heroon" could have been constructed as their mausoleum. Alternatively this was where they had lived and became their tomb when they died. These theories will be examined in chapter 3, but it is generally agreed that the man must have been the ruler of Lefkandi. After a short time the "Heroon" was partially dismantled and covered by an enormous earth mound which became the focal point for a cemetery.

The "Heroon" is so far unique, but it foreshadows a trend for greater differentiation in the treatment of the dead. It is not so much the external appearance of the tombs that is elaborated but rather the fact that some graves are much richer. This is true of late tenth- and early ninth-century burials in the Toumba cemetery at Lefkandi, which are provided with more metalwork than had been customary and this includes gold jewelry. Near Eastern and Egyptian imports were particularly valued. In Athens and elsewhere burials with weapons become more common in the ninth century (figure 9.11). These individuals may have achieved a higher status through their military prowess but in Athens there were also some rich graves of women whose position in society was probably determined at birth or when they married. So the most plausible interpretation of these competitive practices is that they reflect the progress toward a more hierarchical social structure.

## The Eighth Century

Although this is still the Early Iron Age, eighth-century Greece merits a separate section because many of the developments that started in the ninth century now intensify and other significant changes occur.

In a chapter on settlement and settlements it may seem odd to begin with burials but they do highlight an important phenomenon. From the middle of the eighth century the number of graves in Athens increased sharply. This is also the case in Attica, so it cannot be explained as a drift from the countryside into the town. The simple explanation is that there had been a comparable increase in the size of the population, at a rate which would have been remarkable. However, it has been pointed out that the proportion of child burials is now much higher and this suggests that practices had changed. In the ninth century formal burial may have been a privilege. Those who did not have this entitlement were probably buried in shallow graves or exposed. As a result they are archaeologically invisible. In the eighth century the restrictions had perhaps been lifted. It is questionable whether the treatment of the dead was now truly democratic but the social pressures that led to this change must have been considerable.

One source of pressure may have been population growth. From the location of the cemeteries, it would appear that Athens had expanded and at the same time the number of sites in Attica multiplies from 15 in the ninth century to 50 by the end of the eighth. So paradoxically settlement becomes more nucleated and dispersed. Surveys have recorded a similar revival elsewhere. In the southern Argolid many sites were reoccupied or newly established in the eighth century and the Berbati valley was also resettled. However, the only eighth-century activity in the Laconian countryside was at cult sites, even though it was around this time that Sparta began the conquest of Messenia. In the Cyclades rural settlement has been noted on Melos but not on Kea.

The need for security was evidently greater on the islands, perhaps because of piracy. The main Bronze Age settlement on Melos had been at Phylakopi on the coast. Ancient Melos, which now became the capital, was a more defensible site. Zagora on Andros is a headland with steep cliffs on three sides and a fortification wall was built to protect the only approach (figure 2.8). As there is no water supply

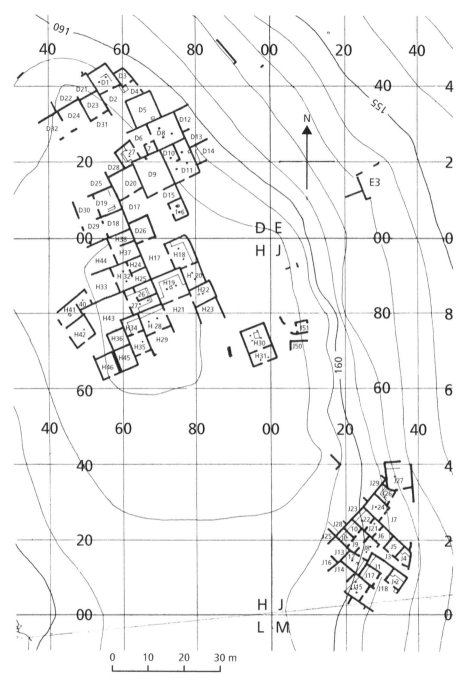

**Figure 2.8** Plan of Zagora

or easy access to good agricultural land, it is quite understandable that the site was only occupied until around 700 BC. Stone was readily available and this was used to construct the houses which have consequently survived well. The sanctuary on the summit of the headland was the focal point of the settlement. Around this were blocks of houses, laid out in a way that looks carefully planned.

Attention has focused on developments in the eighth century because this may have been a critical period in the rise of the polis. "City state" is not a particularly good translation of "polis," though it does emphasize the point that these were notionally independent polities. From later written sources and inscriptions we know that there were hundreds of poleis, mainly concentrated in eastern Greece and around the Aegean. In western and northern Greece, federal states were more common. In a polis city and countryside were politically unified, so they were territorial states and also communities of citizens.

The adoption of the alphabet in the eighth century may be one consequence of the rise of the polis but it would be some time before any historical documents were written. So we can only say for sure that poleis existed by the sixth century. Nevertheless the size of some eighth-century settlements, such as Athens, Argos, and Knossos, is suggestive, even if they were not yet fully urbanized. Moreover the expansion into the countryside could be an indication of territoriality. As we have seen, there is some variation in the scale of rural settlement. In Laconia the only eighth-century activity is at cult sites but this is significant precisely because of the way that sanctuaries were used to stake out territories.

Greek religion was not invented in the eighth century. Even if continuity from the Mycenaean period is questionable, some sanctuaries had already been established in the tenth and ninth centuries but now they proliferate. Usually it is a sudden increase in dedications that signals the start of cult activity. By the end of the eighth century many sanctuaries also had temples, built in honor of the patron deity and as a symbol of civic solidarity because religion was one of the ties that bound communities together. The changes in the treatment of the dead, described above, could be another indication of greater inclusiveness. However, the evidence for an eighth-century revolution should not be overemphasized. The process may have accelerated but in many respects the polis was in a constant state of evolution.

The disruption that followed the collapse of the Mycenaean palace system had an impact on trade but Greece was not completely isolated in the tenth and ninth centuries. Raw materials and other imported items from the eastern Mediterranean still reached Lefkandi for example. Phoenician merchants were active in the Aegean in the eighth century and a Greek presence at Al Mina on the Syrian coast is suspected. The Near East was the catalyst for many of the changes that have been mentioned, such as the introduction of the alphabet, and orientalization transformed art.

The material culture of eighth-century Greece is much richer and more innovative. Consumer demand had intensified and this provided the impetus for new trade networks, particularly in the central Mediterranean where iron and other metals were available. The Phoenicians had already settled as far west as Spain, and the

Greeks could presumably see the advantages that a permanent base overseas would offer. Around 750 they occupied Pithekoussai on the island of Ischia, just off the west coast of Italy. The site could easily be defended and had harbors on either side of the acropolis. As the agricultural potential of Ischia would not have been the obvious attraction, the lure for the settlers was evidently trade. Metallurgical installations confirm that ores were processed on the island but they were not mined there and must have been imported, possibly from Etruria in central Italy, so this was a complex operation. From the number of graves that have been excavated in the cemetery, it is estimated that there were several thousand Pithekoussans. Many had come from Euboia but this was clearly a cosmopolitan community.

Later in the eighth century a colony was founded at Cumae, on the Italian coast opposite Ischia, where the agricultural resources were better as well as the commercial opportunities, and this may have prompted a drift away from Pithekoussai. Greek settlements were also established in Sicily and southern Italy. Late eighth-century foundations include Naxos, Syracuse, Leontini, Catana, Megara Hyblaia, and Zancle on Sicily. In southern Italy there were colonies at Rhegion, Croton, Sybaris, and Taras. Sometimes the settlers were drawn from a particular city in Greece, though many of these ventures were cooperative and occasionally had local support as well. However, for most of their new Sicel and Italian neighbors the arrival of the Greeks was bad news because they wanted agricultural land. A shortage of land in Greece has been seen as one of the main motives for the colonization movement but the Greek countryside does not look remotely overexploited at this time. However, this may have been a chance to acquire more land and there were other opportunities for profit because many of the colonies had excellent harbors.

The best evidence for the way these settlements were planned comes from Megara Hyblaia in eastern Sicily where a grid was laid out for the plots of land on which the eighth-century houses were built. A central space was set aside and this became the agora in the seventh century. It is significant that the dead were buried away from the settlement, a practice which starts later in Greece. Because they were new towns, the colonies did not face the same constraints as well-established settlements, which could not change their layout so easily. They consequently had the freedom and also the determination to create a different sort of civic identity.

## The Archaic Period

Colonization continued in the seventh century. In Sicily there was a move away from the east of the island with the foundation of Himera, Kamarina, Gela, Akragas, and Selinous on the north and south coasts. New colonies in southern Italy include Metapontion, Poseidonia, Siris, and Lokroi. Greeks also settled at a string of sites around the Sea of Marmara and the Black Sea: Kyzikos, Byzantion, Apollonia, Tomis, Istros, Olbia, Pantikapaion, Sinope, and Trapezos. Cyrene in north Africa was founded in the seventh century and the Egyptians gave permission for a commercial colony at Naukratis in the western Delta. Contact with Egypt revolutionized

Greek architecture and art. The Near East had already inspired an orientalizing style in pottery and metalwork. What Egypt offered was monumentality and it can be no coincidence that temples were now rebuilt in stone. The size and pose of statues is also a clear indication of Egyptian influence.

Artistically the seventh century is a dynamic period; archaeologically it is rather a puzzle in some respects. Intensive surveys show us how settlement evolved but it can be difficult to date the changes precisely. One reason for this is the low visibility of seventh-century pottery. This is a period when the most distinctive types of pottery were not particularly robust and therefore disintegrate when exposed for any length of time on the surface of a site. So there is a chance that surveys will miss seventh-century activity. This is less true of the sixth century because black glaze pottery becomes popular and is more easily identifiable. Nevertheless some broad similarities and also significant differences can be seen across Greece.

In the southern Argolid the number of sites had already increased in the eighth century. This growth continues in the seventh century with the development of a three-tier settlement hierarchy. Each area has a sizable town, subsidiary villages, and a few small farmsteads. There is also a three-tier hierarchy at Asea in Arcadia but not until the sixth century. In the Laconian countryside, where the only eighth-century sites were sanctuaries, the seventh century is just as tranquil. The situation then changes in the late sixth century when numerous small and medium-sized sites appear in quite a short space of time. Boiotia had some rural settlement in the late sixth century. The polis center of Koressos on Kea was first occupied in the seventh century and expanded in the sixth century when the evidence for rural activity is also substantial. On Kea and Melos there were few medium-sized sites and so the settlement hierarchy is two-tier, with a main town and farmsteads.

Phaistos, once the site of a Minoan palace, was a major settlement once again by the eighth century and grew appreciably in the seventh century. Between 625 and 550 the number of rural sites increased—and then they disappear off the radar. At many Cretan sites the sixth century is a complete blank. One explanation is that there had been some sort of catastrophe and this cannot be completely ruled out. However, archaeological visibility could also be a factor if, as seems possible, the material culture of Crete in the sixth century was unspectacular and conservative.

In the case of Athens it is the seventh century which is problematic. In Attica there were fewer settlements but more sanctuaries. A number of the cemeteries in the countryside also went out of use. Some movement into Athens is a possibility, though this is difficult to substantiate. Not many seventh-century burials have been excavated in the city and the contrast with the eighth century is stark. The fact that some wells were filled in has led to the suggestion that the population had actually fallen. This was certainly a period of change for Athens. It has been argued that the burial record reflects the imposition of restrictions by a more oppressive aristocratic regime. Alternatively a different set of priorities and choices may have altered the pattern of behavior. Whatever had happened, it could not be described as a steady development. Significantly, the one reasonably well-documented historical event was an attempted coup by Kylon and his supporters around 630. Clearly there were serious political

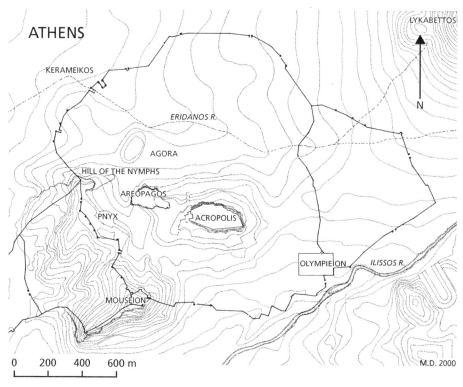

**Figure 2.9**   Plan of Athens

divisions in Athens and the situation had not improved by the start of the sixth century. Consequently Solon was given exceptional legislative powers and passed a series of laws which were designed to curb the power of the aristocracy and resolve the crisis. Although he did have some success, the conflict continued and by the middle of the sixth century Peisistratos had established himself as tyrant of Athens. Tyrants were individuals who ruled unconstitutionally but were not necessarily tyrannical. Indeed Peisistratos seems to have been well regarded. When he died in 527 he was succeeded by his sons Hippias and Hipparchos and the tyranny lasted until 510 when the Peisistratids were expelled. A brief power struggle ensued from which Kleisthenes emerged as the dominant politician and he completely reorganized the system of government. Athens now became a democratic city.

It is reckoned that the population of Athens was around 25,000 by the end of the sixth century and parts of the city were evidently built up. Nevertheless, there may still have been some open spaces. This was certainly true elsewhere, for example at Argos, Corinth, and most famously Sparta which consisted of five separate villages. Some cities, such as Megara Hyblaia, already had an agora in the seventh century but it is not certain where the civic and commercial center of Athens was originally located (figure 2.9). The site north of the Acropolis that became the Classical Agora was in use by around 500 when the square was marked off by boundary stones, and it is possible that the reforms of Kleisthenes had prompted this reorganization of the political infrastructure. No trace of an earlier agora has been found, probably because it was extremely simple. Assemblies were held in the open, and temporary stalls could be set up when the agora was used as a market. Purpose-built structures were more of a political statement than a necessity and it seems that they were not a feature of most Greek cities in the sixth century. A more vital civic amenity was a fresh water supply, which Peisistratos provided by means of an aqueduct. This fed at least two fountain houses. Another tyrant, Polykrates of Samos, was probably responsible for an even more ambitious scheme which involved the excavation of a tunnel over a kilometer in length.

Tyrants generally feel the need to impress, and Polykrates was no exception. His most grandiose project was the reconstruction of the temple of Hera. With a platform that measured 55 by 109 meters and 155 columns, this would have been one of the largest Greek temples had it been completed. However, work stopped when Polykrates was killed in 522. The Peisistratids also liked temples, though how much credit they should be given for any of the major initiatives on the Acropolis is questionable. Their pièce de résistance was the temple of Olympian Zeus, which rivaled the temple of Hera and was similarly left unfinished. Many cities, not just those ruled by tyrants, constructed monumental temples in the sixth century. They represented an enormous investment of resources by the state and, as such, were an expression of civic pride as well as an act of piety. They also provided cities with an opportunity to outdo their neighbors. Samos and Ephesos fought out their rivalry in this way and the western Greek cities were equally competitive, none more so than Selinous where six temples had been built or were under construction by the end of the sixth century. This spirit of competition is also evident in the dedications at Delphi and Olympia, the two great Panhellenic sanctuaries. So it is no accident that temples are one feature of Archaic cities that has endured.

## The Classical Period

The Greek cities were often at war with each other but it was the expansion of the Persian empire that really endangered their existence. By the end of the sixth century the cities in the east had lost their independence and the islands were being threatened. Athens was the first mainland city in the line of fire but the Persian expeditionary force which attacked in 490 BC was sensationally defeated at the battle of Marathon. Xerxes, the Persian ruler, then invaded Greece with an even larger army and navy but the Greek alliance triumphed at the battles of Salamis in 480 and Plataia in 479. The psychological impact of these victories reshaped the way the Greeks thought of themselves. Athens and Sparta emerged from the Persian Wars as the dominant Greek states, and the history of the fifth century is mainly the story of their rivalry which culminated in the Peloponnesian War of 431–404. Because Athens had built up a maritime empire of Aegean cities and the Spartans led a Peloponnesian alliance, the war was fought across the Greek world and eventually ended in defeat for Athens. Spartan supremacy was short-lived however. In the fourth century Athens revived and Thebes also grew more powerful. At the battle of Leuktra in 371 the Theban army crushed the Spartans who subsequently lost control of Messenia. Macedonia, which had played a rather marginal role in Greek politics, was now turned into a major military force by Philip II. His victory at the battle of Chaironeia in 338 effectively ended Greek independence but he was assassinated in 336 before he could take on Persia. This challenge was left to his son Alexander who had fought his way as far east as India by the time he died in 323.

The eastward spread of Greek culture was one consequence of Alexander's victories over the Persians but the correlation between the events outlined above and the archaeological record is often more subtle, especially when longer-term processes are involved. It can also be dangerous to draw general conclusions which gloss over variations that reflect particular local circumstances. Surveys have demonstrated that rural activity often intensified in the Classical period but not necessarily at the same time. In Boiotia the number of rural sites increased sharply in the fifth century and peaked in the fourth century. The survey of Thespiai revealed that this 100-hectare site was also much more densely settled in the fifth century. On Methana rural sites become more common in the fifth century, when the main urban center at ancient Methana expanded, but there were fewer in the fourth century. Meanwhile in the southern Argolid, on the other side of the Akte peninsula from Methana, the sixth-century settlement pattern does not change significantly until the middle of the fourth century when many more rural sites appear. In Laconia the level of rural activity escalated in the late sixth and early fifth centuries but this is followed by a reduction in the number of sites in the late fifth and fourth centuries. The surprise is that this decline was not reversed when Sparta lost control of Messenia after their defeat at Leuktra in 371, which should have led to more intensive exploitation of the Laconian countryside. However, independence for Messenia and the foundation of the city of Messene was followed by an increase in rural settlement around Pylos. On Melos there were fewer sites, presumably because of the Athenian attack on the island in 416. Most of the men were massacred and the women and children were sold into slavery. They were replaced by an Athenian colony which was expelled by the Spartans in 405 and the Melians who had survived were reinstated. The impact of these events was obviously dramatic but they may well have reinforced a trend that had already started and were therefore a contributory factor rather than the cause. On Crete the reduction in rural settlement in the western Mesara lasted well into the fifth century and it is only in the fourth century that activity in the countryside takes off again.

As we will see in chapter 5, it seems likely that some of the rural sites were farmsteads which were occupied on a permanent or seasonal basis. Nevertheless, most Greeks evidently lived in the city. It is reckoned that rural sites accounted for just 5 percent of the population of the southern Argolid in the Classical–Hellenistic period. The figure proposed for Boiotia is 20 percent and 25 percent for Kea. In Laconia the rural population may have been higher, perhaps 40 percent in the Archaic–Classical period. Settlement was still nucleated, though less so than had

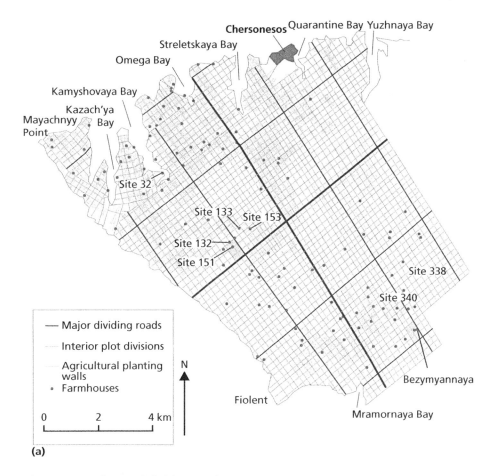

(a)

**Figure 2.10a & b**   Land divisions at Chersonesos

been the case previously. Residence on the land was obviously more efficient since farmers did not have to travel so far to their fields. They could therefore work more intensively and increase output, which would have given them greater economic independence and, potentially at least, a more influential role in the government of their cities. So this was a significant change.

An important aspect of the new agricultural regime is the evidence for the way that some cities divided up their territory. At Metapontion in southern Italy gridded plots of land were laid out north of the city. A typical plot measured 625 by 415 meters and was subdivided into six smaller units. A late sixth-century date for the introduction of this system of land division seems likely, which would coincide with a sharp increase in the number of farm sites in the part of the Metapontine territory that has been intensively surveyed. Chersonesos, a Greek colony in the Crimea, was founded in the late fifth century and in the middle of the fourth century the whole of the Herakleian peninsula was divided into plots (figure 2.10a & b). A grid of

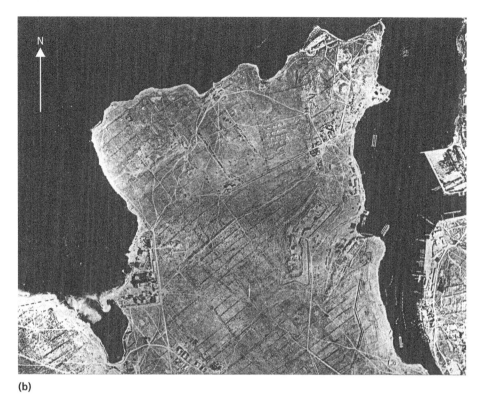

**(b)**

**Figure 2.10a & b**    (*Continued*)

paved roads lined by stone walls, still visible on aerial photographs, formed more than 400 plots which measured either 420 by 420 meters or 630 by 420 meters. Farmhouses have been identified on around a third of the plots, as well as terrace and vineyard walls. Some of the farmers presumably commuted from the city, though the local Crimean population may have provided much of the workforce.

The physical demarcation of these land divisions is echoed in many cities, most obviously where a grid plan was used in their layout. Fortification walls also created a defined space and this symbolic role should not be overlooked, even if they were primarily built for defensive purposes. Some island sites, such as Zagora on Andros, were fortified in the eighth century but mainland Greek cities must have felt more secure. Although there may have been a sixth-century circuit at Corinth, it was not until the fifth century that most cities were protected by fortifications. It is unclear whether Athens was fortified in the Archaic period or simply relied on the Acropolis as a last line of defense. After the Persian invasion the Athenians immediately started to construct a circuit which enclosed the whole of the city. Subsequently the fortification system was extended to ensure that Athens could not be cut off from the sea (figure 2.11). In the fourth century Dionysios I, the tyrant of Syracuse, built a 27-kilometer circuit which included the heights above the city. Similarly at

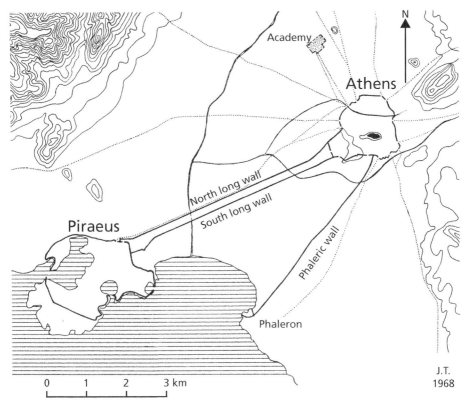

**Figure 2.11**    Fortifications of Athens and the Piraeus

Messene and Priene, the decision was taken to encircle the acropolis as well as
the town, so much of the urban space defined by the fortifications was never
developed.

Many Classical Greek cities had grown haphazardly and were not well planned.
Athens was notorious because there was such a contrast between the architectural
splendors of the Acropolis and the narrow alleys which meandered between the
houses. However, a more systematic approach can also be seen and this is associated
with Hippodamos of Miletos. He is often described as the first town planner but
precedents exist for his use of a grid plan, as early as the eighth century in the case
of Megara Hyblaia. In the sixth century, Poseidonia in Italy was laid out with broad
east–west avenues and narrower north–south streets which divided the residential
sectors into regular 35 by 300 meter blocks. A central strip of land was reserved for
the agora and the main temples. This arrangement was also followed at Metapontion.
Selinous and Akragas in Sicily had grid plans as well. So what did Hippodamos do
that was different? One puzzle is his role in the reconstruction of his home town
after Miletos was sacked by the Persians in 494. The plan of the Classical city incor-
porates features which are considered typically Hippodamian, yet it is unlikely that

he was old enough at the time to have been entrusted with this commission. Miletos occupied a rather awkwardly shaped peninsula with two main harbors which were skillfully integrated into the civic and commercial center of the city. The blocks of houses were then laid out around this. Piraeus, the port of Athens, presented a similar challenge and this was a project which Hippodamos did supervise. The difficulty here was the need to keep the military installations, commercial facilities, public amenities, and private houses separate and yet accessible. Priene is unusually well preserved and gives us a real sense of how these cities would have looked. The town, which had a population of around 4,000, was laid out below the acropolis in the fourth century. The streets form a regular grid around the civic center where the agora and the bouleuterion were located. The theater was higher up with a superb view over the Maeander valley. The only deviation from this strictly orthogonal arrangement was the stadium which had to be built at an angle because of the slope.

Athens was transformed in the Classical period. The Agora was now firmly established as the center of government with facilities for the magistrates, legislators, and administrative officials. There were also a number of shrines in the Agora, most notably the temple of Hephaistos which overlooked the square. But this was overshadowed by the newly refurbished Acropolis. Perikles, the dominant figure in Athenian politics from around 450 until his death in 429, was the instigator of this extraordinary project. The Parthenon was built first, followed by the Propylaia, then the temple of Athena Nike, and finally the Erechtheion. Although the focus was on Athens, sanctuaries in Attica benefited from this architectural bonanza as well. The Athenians also provided permanent venues for the competitions that were held as part of religious festivals. Perikles built an odeion for concerts and musical contests next to the theater of Dionysos where the plays were performed. The theater was very simple at first but was rebuilt in stone in the fourth century when the athletics stadium was also resited. This monumentalization of theaters and stadia is a regular occurrence in the fourth century and the same trend can be seen in domestic architecture as well. The Athenian politician Demosthenes complained (*Aristokrates* 207) that his contemporaries demanded much more luxurious houses than fifth-century statesmen who had lived quite modestly.

## The Hellenistic Period

When Alexander died in 323 his generals carved up the territory he had conquered and then went to war with each other. In due course three major kingdoms were established in Egypt (the Ptolemies), in the Near East (the Seleucids), and in Macedonia (the Antigonids). Subsequently the Attalids of Pergamon took control of much of Asia Minor. Politically the once great Greek cities were now marginalized but Athens in particular was a cultural mecca for these new dynasties and benefited considerably from royal patronage. In the third century the Achaians and the Aitolians formed powerful confederacies and Epeiros enjoyed a period of success under the leadership of Pyrrhos. Then the Romans arrived and, after a series of victories, their conquest of Greece was completed in 146 BC.

The impact of Greek culture in the east is nicely epitomized by Ai Khanoum, a city in northern Afghanistan which was founded by the Seleucids in the late fourth century and destroyed in the mid-second century by nomadic tribesmen. Below the citadel, where the garrison was quartered, there is a typical Greek theater and gymnasium complex but the vast palace is more eclectic. The plan and the way that the reception rooms were laid out is modeled on Persian palaces, whereas the residential suite has many Greek features. The main temple, east of the palace, is Mesopotamian in style. The Seleucid capital was at Antioch on the Orontes river. Five broad avenues intersected by cross-streets formed a grid of 112- by 58-meter blocks which was strictly maintained as the city expanded across the plain. Alexandria, the Ptolemaic capital in Egypt, was one of the many cities which Alexander founded and named after himself. It was conceived on a truly grand scale and again makes use of a grid plan which measured 5 by 2 kilometers. The two main streets crossed in the center of the city and this was probably the location of the agora. The palace complex occupied an entire district and included the famous library. The Serapeion, the main sanctuary, was in the southwest of the city. Serapis, as worshiped in Alexandria, was a fusion of Greek and Egyptian gods designed to unite the two communities. Traces of his rather modest temple have been found but much of the ancient city has disappeared under modern Alexandria. However, recent excavations in the harbor have identified parts of the Pharos lighthouse, which was apparently over 120 meters high. Alexandria may have been modeled on Pella, the capital of Macedonia, where Alexander had been born. This was laid out on an elongated grid with blocks 47 meters wide and 110, 125, or 150 meters in length. The main street ran east–west through the middle of the enormous agora which occupied ten blocks. The palace was on the hill above the town but is aligned with the grid and clearly formed part of the configuration of the city.

The sites chosen for Antioch, Alexandria, and Pella were relatively flat and this facilitated their planned development. Pergamon, the Attalid capital, presented much more of a challenge because the city was built on a steep hill (figure 2.12). Consequently the streets could not be laid out in straight lines and a series of terraces had to be constructed on the summit. The result is a much more irregular but spectacularly successful plan. Pergamon was often at war and so the city was well fortified. The barracks for the garrison were on the acropolis, conveniently located beside the palace, a row of rather modest villas quite unlike the grandiose complexes favored by other Hellenistic rulers. Pergamon had the other great ancient library which was next to the sanctuary of Athena. The temple is not particularly large but was framed on three sides by stoas. Below the sanctuary is the theater which could seat 10,000 and provided the audience with a vertiginous view. A number of monuments at Pergamon celebrated military victories, in particular the altar of Zeus which was built by Eumenes II in the second century. The altar was set on a high colonnaded platform, decorated with a magnificent sculpted frieze which depicted the battle between the gods and the giants (figure 10.34). There was also an agora on the summit and another lower down by the gymnasium and the sanctuary of Demeter. One of the most impressive but least obvious features of Pergamon was the water supply which was brought by aqueduct from a source in

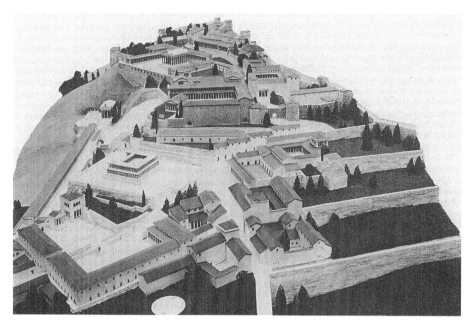

**Figure 2.12**   Reconstruction of Pergamon

the hills 45 kilometers away and then piped under pressure up to a reservoir on the citadel.

The Attalids made Pergamon a Hellenistic capital of culture. Their model was Athens which they and other Greek rulers reinvigorated in the second century. The most obvious change in Athens is in the Agora (figure 2.13). Attalos II built a stoa on the east side of the square which had rows of shops on each floor. The Middle and South Stoa complex was also commercial. The construction of the Metroon, which housed the state archives as well as the shrine of the Mother of the Gods, tidied up the west side of the Agora. Elsewhere in the city Eumenes II built an enormous stoa south of the Acropolis and work was resumed on the temple of Olympian Zeus that the Peisistratids had started, though this was not finished until the second century AD. The more formal layout of the Agora is reminiscent of Hellenistic cities in Turkey, for example Miletos. The agora at Assos is another good example of the way that stoas were used in this period (figure 2.14) but some sites were not planned so methodically. Delos was a sacred island, revered as the birthplace of Apollo and Artemis. In the second century it was made a free port and became a major commercial center, as well as the most important slave market in the Mediterranean. The population expanded rapidly as merchants and bankers settled on the island. Commercial facilities had to be fitted around the main sanctuary and the houses were crowded together on narrow streets. This period of prosperity ended abruptly in 88 BC when Delos was sacked.

**Figure 2.13**   Plan of the Athenian Agora in the Hellenistic period

Major political events do not always affect life in the countryside but a consistent pattern can be seen in much of mainland Greece. Most surveys have found that the number of rural sites remains the same at the start of the Hellenistic period but then drops sharply after the third century and it is not until the second or third century AD that the trend is reversed. Because of the threat from pirates and brigands, farmers may well have decided that it was safer to be based in town. Yet in Boiotia and the southern Argolid, for example, some major sites also disappear, so there was evidently depopulation and not just settlement nucleation. The situation in Messenia is different, since more rural sites have been found. No doubt it was independence from Sparta that provided the impetus for this expansion and the loss of Messenia had a similar impact in Laconia where site numbers also rose, though not immediately after the battle of Leuktra. Another exception is Methana where the Ptolemies established a naval base and the need to keep the garrison

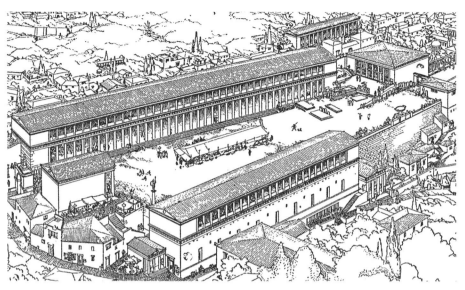

**Figure 2.14**   Reconstruction of the agora at Assos

supplied may have boosted the rural economy. Obviously conditions varied considerably and it is risky to generalize. Nevertheless, it is clear that old Greece suffered as a result of the reconfiguration of the political landscape. In the new Greek world the situation is rather different. Plainly the foundation of a city would have an impact on settlement and land use. What surveys have shown is that urbanization often led to an increase in the rural population and the level of agricultural productivity. This is the case at Ai Khanoum where the system of irrigation canals was extended so that the land could be more intensively exploited. However, the important point is that the agricultural regime that already existed was stimulated by the foundation of Ai Khanoum. The Greek settlers may have been colonists but they were not pioneers.

## Conclusions

Surveys have shown how the settlement pattern fluctuated over time. General trends can be identified, as well as differences between regions in any given period. Historical developments do have an impact, though this is not always the case. Some changes have an economic basis or reflect social decisions. The fact that surveys detect small sites which would otherwise be overlooked does mean that we get a good impression of the way that the countryside was exploited and of urban–rural interactions.

The contrast between the north and the south of Greece in the Neolithic period is significant and cannot be explained simply in terms of environmental factors. Similarly the expansion at the end of the period was not a result of population pressure. Communities made choices which may not appear rational but obviously fulfilled a purpose. By the Early Bronze Age settlement had spread across the landscape and there were many more farmsteads. We also see the development of site hierarchies. The growth in the size of certain key settlements is most obvious on Crete and the construction of the first palaces at the start of the Middle Bronze Age is the culmination of a process which is linked with the consolidation of political authority. In the Cyclades, settlement was more nucleated at this time, possibly because of the threat or conversely the economic opportunities presented by Crete. The Greek mainland also has relatively few sites but depopulation may be the explanation here. There is a recovery when the Mycenaean states were formed in the Late Bronze Age and then an even more dramatic downturn when they collapsed.

Many surveys have found no evidence of any activity in the Early Iron Age. Clearly there were fewer people and culturally they were impoverished. They become more visible once again in the eighth century and undoubtedly the population increased as well. A consequence of this was the rise of the polis, city states with well-defined territories. The pace of rural settlement in those territories differs but generally peaks in the fifth or fourth century. In some cases we can see how this correlates with historical events, yet just as often life in the countryside was shaped by other factors. Nevertheless, the political and economic decline experienced by so many mainland Greek communities in the Hellenistic period did result in a movement back into the towns.

This chapter has also focused on the process of urbanization. It is remarkable that villages of some size should have appeared so soon in the Neolithic period. Evidence of inequality has been noted at Sesklo and this is explored in more detail in the next chapter. Site hierarchies do not necessarily imply political control but there was possibly some form of central authority in the major Early Bronze Age settlements. With the Cretan Middle and Late Bronze Age sites we can speak of towns, exemplified by Knossos where different residential zones surrounded the palace. In the Cyclades there is a regular street system at Phylakopi, though the excavated section of Akrotiri was less carefully planned. It is still not entirely clear how Mycenaean towns were laid out. Because they occupy defensible sites, the houses were often grouped together on separate terraces. Early Iron Age settlements, such as Athens, may have consisted of similar clusters of houses, given the location of the cemeteries. Here we can sense the network of relationships which structured these communities and was reflected in the way that Athens grew as a city. The newly founded colonies developed a different model with a grid of streets which demarcated house plots and even divided up the countryside in some cases. Of course this was a practical way to distribute the available land but would have created an impression of equality as well. The colonial cities also pioneered the integration of civic, sacred, and residential space. This was more difficult in Athens where the creation of a proper Agora evidently caused considerable disruption. However, Piraeus was redeveloped in the fifth century by Hippodamos who extended and improved the use of grid plans. He provided a template for the imperial cities of the Hellenistic period.

# Bibliographical notes

This chapter uses the data from a number of survey reports, in particular Forsén and Forsén 2003 (Asea), Wells 1996 (Berbati), Cherry et al. 1991 (Kea), Cavanagh et al. 1996 and 2002 (Laconia), Renfrew and Wagstaff 1982 (Melos), McDonald and Rapp 1972, Davis et al. 1997 and Davis 1998 (Messenia), Mee and Forbes 1997 (Methana), Wright et al. 1990 (Nemea), Watrous et al. 2004 (Phaistos), and Jameson et al. 1994 (southern Argolid). For a more general critique of surveys see Alcock and Cherry 2004.

Runnels 2001 and Galanidou and Perlès 2003 discuss the Palaeolithic and Mesolithic periods. Perlès 2001 is excellent on early Neolithic Greece. Neolithic settlement in Thessaly is analyzed by Johnson and Perlès 2004, and Cavanagh 2004 reviews the evidence from southern Greece. See Andreou et al. 2001 for Sesklo and Whitelaw 2001a for the complexities of population estimates. Good summaries of Early Bronze Age Greece and Crete are provided by Rutter 2001, Watrous 2001, Pullen 2008, and Wilson 2008. Tzavella-Evjen 1985 reports on the excavations at Lithares, and Forsén 1992 examines the Early Bronze Age collapse. Watrous 2001, Rehak and Younger 2001, and Cunningham and Driessen 2004 give overviews of Protopalatial and Neopalatial Crete. Cherry 1986 looks at Crete from a peer-polity perspective and Warren 2004 analyzes territories. Whitelaw 2004a presents some of the results of the Knossos survey. See Barber 1987, Broodbank 2000, and Davis 2001 for the prehistoric Cyclades, and Doumas 1983 for Thera. Early Mycenaean Greece is discussed in Rutter 2001, Cherry and Davis 2001, and Wright 2008, Mycenaean palace sites in Shelmerdine 2001. French 2002 is a detailed account of Mycenae. Dickinson 2006 and Deger-Jalkotzy 2008 consider the causes of the Mycenaean collapse, and Nowicki 2000 the defensive sites on Crete.

For Early Iron Age Greece see Snodgrass 1971, Morris 2000, Lemos 2002, Dickinson 2006, and Morgan 2009. Coldstream 1977 and Morris 1987 and 2009 are good on the eighth century. Zagora is described in Cambitoglou et al. 1971 and 1988. The rise of the polis is reassessed by Morris 1991, Snodgrass 1991, and Whitley 2001. On colonization generally see Coldstream 1977, Boardman 1980, and Osborne 1996, also Ridgway 1992 for Pithekoussai and Vallet et al. 1983 for Megara Hyblaia. The archaeology of Archaic Greece is reviewed in Snodgrass 1980a, Osborne 1996, and Fisher and van Wees 1998. Whitley 2001 looks at Crete. Osborne 1989, Morris 1991, Morgan and Coulton 1997, Camp 2001, and Papadopoulos 2003 discuss Archaic Athens. For the way that cities were planned in the Classical and Hellenistic periods see Owens 1991, Tomlinson 1992, and Gates 2003. Alcock 1994 examines rural settlement. Chersonesos is described by Carter 2003, and Ai Khanoum by Sherwin-White and Kuhrt 1993.

# CHAPTER 3

# The Architecture of Power

## Introduction

Monumental architecture need not be an expression of power and it is not an inevitable consequence of the exercise of authority. Nevertheless, it can be one of the best sources of information about social organization. This chapter will examine a chronological range of examples to see what they tell us and the problems of interpretation that they present. The emphasis is on political power, although at times this cannot be separated from economic control or religious authority.

## Neolithic Dimini

At Middle Neolithic Sesklo in Thessaly some differences have been noted between the houses on the acropolis and those in the lower settlement. Yet none of the houses is significantly larger than the others. This is not the case in the Late Neolithic period when the acropolis was dominated by a single "megaron" structure. Another site in Thessaly with a dominant Late Neolithic megaron is Dimini, which was near the coast at that time but is now some distance from the sea (figure 3.1). The central part of the settlement is a low mound just under a hectare in extent. This was enclosed by a series of concentric circuit walls which were originally interpreted as defensive. However, there is no evidence that they were particularly high and they would not have deterred a determined attacker. It therefore seems more likely that these were boundary walls. Internal divisions have been noted on other sites in Thessaly and imply that communities were more divided. This impression is reinforced by the location of hearths. Whereas food had often been cooked in the open

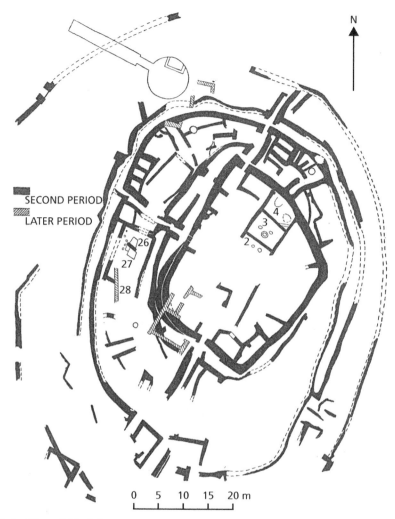

N

SECOND PERIOD
LATER PERIOD

**Figure 3.1** Plan of Dimini

in the Middle Neolithic period and presumably shared with neighbors, hearths were now located in courtyards or inside the house where meals could be prepared in greater privacy. If food was hoarded, it is possible that there was greater inequality and this may explain why the megaron at Dimini was constructed on top of the mound. Behind the porch were two spacious rooms. Stone was used for the lower courses of the walls and they were finished off in mudbrick. The roof was probably thatched. Architecturally the megaron is more impressive than the other houses but the finds from the central court area do not seem exceptional. The finest pottery, figurines, and jewelry were not concentrated here. Moreover, no obvious differences were noted in the animal bones, which indicate that the various households at Dimini must have exchanged livestock and were economically interdependent. Wealth may have varied but it is not an obvious mark of status, whereas the spatial

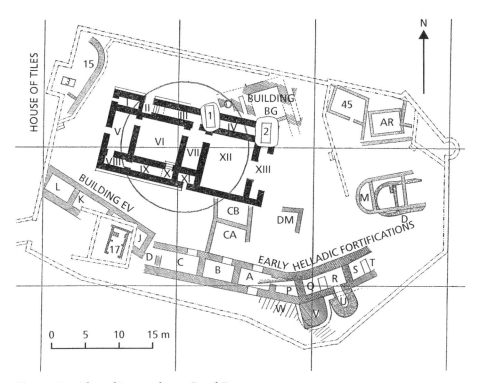

**Figure 3.2**    Plan of Lerna: phases C and D

configuration of the settlement clearly gives the megaron a privileged position. The
possibility that it served the community as a whole cannot be ruled out, though the
range of finds does not support this interpretation. A more plausible view is that
the megaron was occupied by a more highly ranked, though not necessarily wealth-
ier, household. If so, even in the Neolithic period there was some institutionalized
inequality.

## Early Bronze Age Lerna

Lerna is a coastal site in the Argolid which was first occupied in the Neolithic period
and expanded in the Early Bronze Age. Only the central part of the site has been
excavated and it is not clear how far the settlement extended. Fortifications were
constructed in EH II (figure 3.2). The well-preserved section on the south side of
the excavated area had been gradually extended and modified. There was an inner
and outer wall of stone topped by mudbrick. Partition walls provided a series of
rooms which could have been used for accommodation or storage. A semicircular
tower was built at the point where the direction of the wall changes, so that the
defenders would have a clearer view of any attackers. The fortifications are contemporary with a partially excavated structure known as Building BG, which was almost

12 meters wide and at least 17 meters in length. It had a deep porch and two main rooms with corridors on either side. The thickness of the walls suggests that there must have been an upper story. Stone and clay tiles covered the roof. Building BG was eventually demolished and the fortifications also went out of use around the time that the House of Tiles was constructed.

The House of Tiles is on a different alignment but otherwise has many of the same features as Building BG. It was just as large, 12 by 25 meters, with walls around 1 meter thick, built of mudbrick on stone foundations. The walls inside the house were covered in clay and then plastered. Staircases confirm the existence of an upper story. Over 8,000 tiles, mainly clay and some of stone, were needed for the roof. The main entrance was at the east end through a porch (XIII) which led into the largest room (XII). The next room (VII) could also be entered from the corridor that ran along the north side of the house. The shorter corridor on the south side opened off rooms V and VI. There was no access to rooms I and XI from the interior. The layout of the upper floor is conjectural but a good case can be made for balconies above the corridors and also rooms V and XIII. Benches outside the house were shaded from the sun by the roof. The relatively few finds from the House of Tiles do not provide much evidence about the activities that took place here. Food and drink had been prepared and consumed in the main rooms on the first (=ground) floor. There was some pottery stored in room XI, which could only be entered from outside. Also found here was a large deposit of stamped clay seals. They had been attached to wooden boxes, wicker baskets, and clay jars but it is not clear whether these containers were stored in room XI and had perished together with their contents.

Lerna is not the only site where EH II houses of this type have been excavated. The Weisses Haus at Kolonna on Aigina is remarkably similar and there are also corridor houses at Akovitika in Messenia and at Thebes. This distinctive layout must have functioned well, so what were these houses? One of their key features is the number of entrances. The House of Tiles has five, though two of these just provide access to rooms I and XI. The doors inside could be opened or closed to alter the configuration of the interior and also made it possible to control movement around the house. One suggestion is that the rooms on the upper floor were private and those on the first floor more public but in reality there may have been considerable flexibility in the way that rooms were utilized.

Because sealed goods were probably stored in room XI, it has been argued that the House of Tiles was an administrative center and foreshadowed the redistributive role of Minoan and Mycenaean palaces. However, bulk storage of foodstuffs in the house seems unlikely. The containers that had been sealed were evidently not very large and so their contents may have been special. Since it is thought that each of the 70 different seals must have belonged to a different individual, a record was apparently kept of who had made these contributions. This does sound like some form of taxation, though other possibilities include provisions for a communal feast and the pottery suggests that the House of Tiles could have been the venue for this type of activity. Nevertheless, the monumentality of the corridor houses sets them apart and supports the view that they were built for an elite who had some control over the community. This system did not last, however. After EH II there were no more corridor houses and the fate of the House of Tiles is instructive. When it burned down the ruins were covered by a circular tumulus and this was left intact for quite some time. Clearly the people of Lerna felt a certain respect for the House of Tiles which may have become a focus for cult.

## Neopalatial Knossos

Knossos is in a secluded valley 6 kilometers inland from the north coast of Crete. The first settlers arrived at the start of the Neolithic period, around 7000 BC, and occupied the Kephala hill, which would always be the center of the site. This was one of the earliest island settlements in the Aegean and there may not have been many other Neolithic villages on Crete. The site gradually grew in size and by the Late Neolithic period covered around 5 hectares. Because the hill had to be leveled off so that the palace could be constructed, the Early Minoan levels are badly disturbed. There was a large-scale reconfiguration of the settlement in EM II but it is unclear whether an embryonic palace formed part of this plan. The first palace is dated late MM IA or early MM IB. It was built at a time when Knossos had expanded at a phenomenal rate and would soon be a 100-hectare town. Sir Arthur Evans believed that the palace was originally laid out as separate blocks of rooms around the central court but this has been questioned. It seems more likely that the palace was always an integrated structure. Some reconstruction took place in MM II, though it is difficult to piece together a plan of this phase that does not rely on retrospection. At the end of MM II the palace was destroyed, possibly by an earthquake, and this prompted a major redesign. The new palace, built in MM III, was modified in LM IA and then damaged by an earthquake. The repairs may still have been under way when the Mycenaeans took control in LM II. Their tenure lasted until the final destruction in LM IIIA and does not seem to have involved any substantial alterations. What we see today at Knossos is a mixture of these architectural phases. Any discussion of the way that the palace functioned is almost inevitably based on the evidence from different periods but broad conclusions can be drawn and some important questions highlighted.

The palace at Knossos was not fortified and neither was the settlement. The site is a safe distance from the coast, though piracy does not seem to have been a particular concern in this period since there were towns by the sea which could easily have been attacked. This impression of a general sense of security may not be entirely accurate, but conditions must have been relatively peaceful. The palace is not physically separated off from the town. Instead the west court provides a point where they meet (figure 3.3). The three circular stone-lined pits here are usually interpreted as granaries and could have stored around 250 tons of cereals. They were later filled with debris from the first palace. The raised paths which cross the west court were probably intended for ceremonial processions because they link up with the theatral area. This has shallow steps on two sides where 500 spectators could

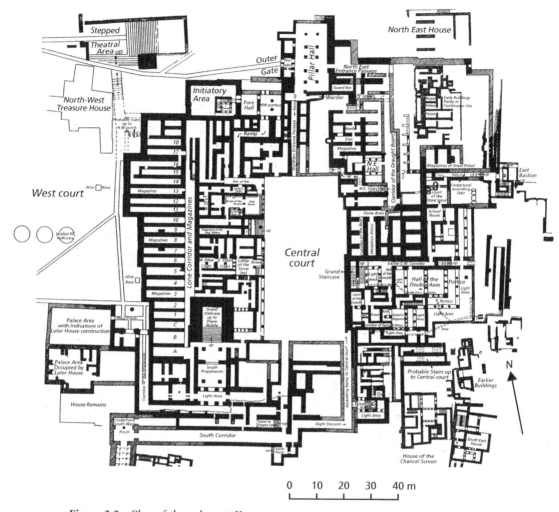

**Figure 3.3**   Plan of the palace at Knossos

stand and watch the events that were held there. The palace has a number of entrances but the way they were positioned suggests that access was carefully controlled. The narrow corridor that led from the west entrance would have disoriented any visitor who did not know the palace well, and this was evidently deliberate since a more direct route could have been provided. So the central court is more private than the west court.

A central court is the architectural sine qua non of a Minoan palace. It was laid out first and then the blocks of rooms were constructed around this nucleus. The builders therefore worked from the inside out and the exterior walls of the palace were in fact the back of each block, hence their irregularity. This meant that functional efficiency could be maximized, since the exterior walls did not restrict the space that was available. The central court was also the hub of a network of routes

**Figure 3.4**  The throne room of the palace at Knossos

which linked the different parts of the palace together. However, the court was primarily a ceremonial center and this is why it was so large, 54 by 28 meters. As many as 5,000 people could have assembled here but this was the stage rather than the auditorium. The spectators would have watched from the galleries around the court. We can only guess what they saw, possibly the dances, competitions, and feasts depicted in Minoan art which were clearly ritual events.

The rooms off the west side of the court underline this focus on ritual activity. A flight of steps leads down into an anteroom from which the throne room (figure 3.4) was entered. Evans found the gypsum throne still in situ, with stone benches on either side. Opposite the throne is a lustral basin, his term for a particular type of room which is at a slightly lower level and was partially screened off by a balustrade. What these rooms were used for is a mystery, perhaps quite literally given their seclusion. That it was some sort of ritual does seem likely and therefore whoever sat on the throne probably did so as a priest or priestess rather than as the ruler of Knossos. South of the throne room complex there is a flight of steps up to the second floor and then the facade of the tripartite shrine. In one of the rooms behind this a cache of votive objects, which included the famous faience snake goddesses (figure 10.6), had been sealed in a stone-lined repository under the floor. Two of the other rooms have massive pillars which do not appear to be structural. As double axes, a Minoan religious symbol, had been incised on the pillars, it is believed that these were cult rooms.

The west wing of the palace is divided in two by a corridor that linked a long row of storage magazines. Clay jars, known as pithoi, lined the walls of the magazines and some had stone cists in the floor as well to maximize their capacity. Agricultural produce was stored here, particularly olive oil which fueled the fire that destroyed the palace and left scorch marks on the stone. One positive outcome of the fire was that the clay documents on which the palace administration kept their records were baked and thereby preserved. Tablets were found near the magazines and whatever was stored there would have been carefully monitored.

The palace was a multistory structure and it is possible to work out how some of the rooms on the second floor would have looked. The way that the magazines are grouped together makes no obvious sense unless they were arranged like this in order to support the walls and internal columns of large rooms on the floor above. This is why some of the walls between the magazines are thicker than others and there are also buttresses. It is thought that the shallow recesses in the west facade of the palace, which are centered on each of the groups of magazines, mark the location of windows at second-floor level. So these rooms would have been well lit but not overlooked. How the rest of this floor was laid out is much more conjectural but we must bear in mind that the main reception rooms may have been here.

Because of the steep slope, the east wing had to be built on terraces cut into the hillside and consequently the best-preserved rooms are below the level of the central court. These lower floors opened off the grand staircase and included a suite of rooms which Evans identified as the domestic quarters of the royal family because there are two halls here. The Hall of the Double Axes is particularly splendid and could be divided into two by a row of wooden shutters, known as pier and door partitions. These were a characteristic feature of Minoan architecture, in houses as well as palaces. They allowed the configuration of a room to be altered for different purposes and improved the air flow in the summer but would be closed when it was cold and the room needed to be heated. The hall also had a light well at one end, essentially an open shaft which provided some additional light and air. The Minoans often used light wells where there were no exterior walls and therefore no windows but they also ensured greater privacy. No doubt this was one of the reasons for the pier and door partitions, which would have been important if ceremonies were held in these halls. Indeed it has been suggested that this was their primary function. Much of the northeast quarter of the palace consists of basement storerooms. The massive walls supported the upper floors. There is also some evidence for workshops, though this is not an obvious location for any industrial activity that involved the use of fire.

The point which comes across most clearly from this description of the palace is that it was multipurpose. The amount of storage space is remarkable. Of course there are reasons why the storerooms were on the first floor: they would have been more accessible here, weight was not a problem, and the thick walls kept the temperature cool. Nevertheless, it is difficult to believe that the foodstuffs stored here were solely for consumption within the palace. The magazines in the west wing had room for around 420 pithoi with an average capacity of 550 liters, a total of 231,000 liters. There must have been a surplus for the palace personnel, such as administrators, officials, and craftsmen. The palaces may also have provided support if a series of poor harvests caused a crisis. Indeed this insurance against the risks that farmers faced because of the low rainfall may be one of the reasons why the palace could institute some kind of taxation. The written documents underline how complex this system must have been. At first the Hieroglyphic script was used and then Linear A. Unfortunately neither of these scripts has been deciphered but most of the documents were evidently administrative. When the Mycenaeans took control of Knossos a new script was introduced and their records, written in Linear B, can be read. One set of tablets lists approximately 80,000 sheep which were kept for their wool. This was then issued to textile workers who manufactured different kinds of cloth and received rations from the palace in exchange. This mainly female workforce was based in different locations and the flocks of sheep were scattered across central Crete, so this was a sophisticated operation. We do not know whether the Mycenaeans had completely reorganized the palace economy but it seems more likely that they adapted the previous system and that Knossos had always been a major production center. Locally sourced or imported raw materials were turned into the high-value goods which the Minoans traded overseas.

Mycenaean Knossos was ruled by a king but the Minoans may have had a different type of government. In Egypt images of the pharaoh were ubiquitous but there is no comparable ruler iconography on Crete. Unlike a Mycenaean palace, Knossos was not built around a central throne room. The assumption that a royal family lived here has been questioned and doubts raised about whether this was a palace at all. Instead the role of Knossos as a communal ceremonial center has been stressed and it is true that there was an emphasis on ritual activity, especially in the courts. One interpretation of the palaces is that they were essentially cult complexes rather than political power bases but would the Minoans have known the difference? If religion was so fundamental, the palaces would have exercised considerable authority anyway. The complicated layout of Knossos and the range of activities that went on here does make much more sense as the legacy of a dominant elite.

## Mycenaean Pylos

Knossos was arguably the most powerful Minoan palace, whereas Pylos must have been overshadowed by Mycenae. However, Pylos is the best-preserved Mycenaean palace and has also produced the largest archive of Linear B documents. So this is the site where we can see how the mainland palace system operated. Mycenaean Pylos was at Epano Englianos, which is approximately 6 kilometers from the sea. Recent investigations have shown that a large artificial harbor was constructed just inland from the coast some time between 1400 and 1200 BC. There can be no doubt that the palace was responsible for this massive project, which also involved the creation of a lake to flush sediment out of the harbor basin. So Pylos did have a convenient port but the palace was safely located well away from the sea on a high ridge with views in every direction.

Pylos was already an important site in LH I–II. Three tholos tombs date from this period and the acropolis was apparently fortified. A section of the fortification wall has been uncovered east of the palace, though it is not clear whether this enclosed the whole of the hill. In LH III, when the walls of Mycenae and Tiryns were built, the rulers of Pylos left their palace unfortified. By then they had taken control of Messenia and may have felt safe from attack. Alternatively it is possible that they had decided to protect the town as well, because traces of what could be a fortification wall have been detected some distance away from the palace. Like so many other Mycenaean sites, Pylos was destroyed at the end of LH IIIB and the palace was never rebuilt.

The architectural development of Mycenaean palaces is unclear because what we have at Mycenae, Tiryns, and Pylos is just their LH IIIB layout. However, at the Menelaion in Laconia there is a LH II mansion which has a central megaron with rooms on either side, like the main unit at Pylos, so the Mycenaean palaces do have mainland Greek roots. The way that they were constructed, with stone and mud-brick walls set in a framework of wooden beams, is a Cretan technique and the use of frescoes is an even more obvious Minoan contribution. The Mycenaeans would have become familiar with the Cretan palace system when they ruled Knossos and it was probably in LH IIIA that the mainland states developed the need for their own high-level administrative centers. But the result was a very different type of palace.

At Pylos the palace occupies the western half of the acropolis and consists of four separate units (figure 3.5). The main unit was in the center and opened off a spacious stuccoed court. There was a grand entrance with columns on either side. Left of this were two rooms (7–8) where most of the Linear B tablets were found. Evidently administrative officials had their offices here and could check whatever went in and out of the palace. Through the entrance was an enclosed court from which the suites of rooms in the main unit could be accessed. It is possible that ceremonies were also held here, though not on the scale that is envisaged for the central court of a Minoan palace. The core of a Mycenaean palace was the megaron and the arrangement we see at Pylos is replicated at Mycenae and Tiryns: a wide porch with two columns, then a vestibule and finally the throne room (figure 3.6). The dominant feature of this room was an enormous circular hearth, 4 meters in diameter. Four columns supported a balcony on the floor above and also allowed the smoke from the hearth to escape through a terracotta chimney. There was no throne in situ but a rectangular depression in the floor on the right side of the room probably indicates where it had been positioned. The fresco on this wall depicted antithetic pairs of lions and griffins, a symbol of the authority that the ruler exercised. A banquet scene on one of the other walls may have been the culmination of a sacrificial procession which began in the vestibule (figure 10.9). This reinforces the impression that the throne room was a focus for ceremonial activities, some of which were religious rituals supervised by the ruler.

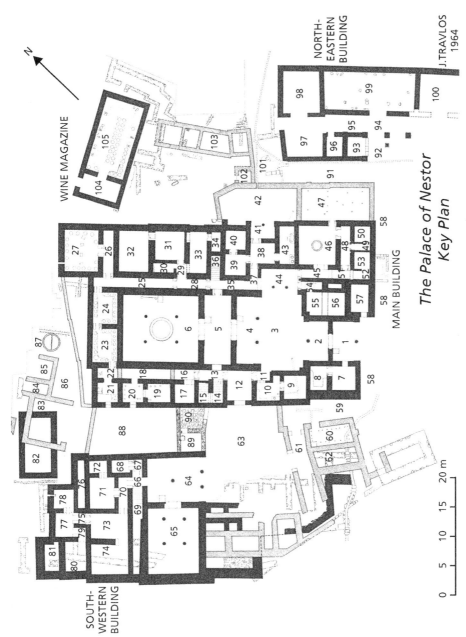

**Figure 3.5** Plan of the palace at Pylos

**Figure 3.6**    Reconstruction of the throne room of the palace at Pylos

Off the corridor on the west side of the throne room there is a row of magazines in which pottery was stored. Over 6,000 vessels were found here, particularly cups, and it is evident that the palace hosted feasts for hundreds or even thousands of guests. Behind the throne room were two more magazines with jars set in clay stands. Olive oil had been kept here, as well as in rooms 27 and 32. Linear B documents indicate that some of this was used to manufacture perfume. As these Mycenaean perfumed oils were widely exported, this must have been a lucrative industry for the palace. On the east side of the main unit were residential suites. The complex which consists of rooms 38–43 includes a bathroom (43) with the terracotta bathtub still in situ. The largest room in the second complex (46) has a circular hearth. There had apparently been private apartments on the upper floor in this part of the palace, as well as offices and storerooms. The southwestern unit is not as well preserved but does contain another large hall decorated with frescoes and more rooms in which pottery was stored. East of the main unit is a large magazine (104–105) with 35 jars set in stands, which had once been filled with wine. The northeastern unit has often been interpreted as a workshop but may have been an administrative and storage complex for military equipment. The idea that room 93 was a shrine now seems unlikely.

It is a great advantage that we have this combination of architectural, artefactual, and documentary evidence from Pylos. We would expect that the palace controlled a large territory and the Linear B tablets confirm this. The whole of Messenia had apparently been subjugated. There were two provinces, subdivided into districts which were administered by local officials. They presumably collected the taxes, in the form of staple goods and other commodities, which the palace levied. Some of these taxes were then used to support a sizable workforce. As well as the perfumed oil industry, textiles were manufactured and the palace supplied over 400 smiths with bronze. Pylos was ruled by a king whose title is the wanax. The lawagetas was also an important individual and the ruler had aristocratic companions, the hequetai. The way that the government was organized does not seem to have been unduly autocratic, especially if we bear in mind that the Linear B documents were just the palace records. While they may give the impression that the state monopolized economic activity, this was not in fact the case.

Nevertheless Pylos and the other Mycenaean palaces were obviously major administrative centers. In comparison with a Minoan palace like Knossos, there is not as much of an emphasis on storage space. This could reflect a difference in scale but the quantities of goods recorded in the Linear B documents from Pylos were substantial. Unless storerooms were located somewhere in the town, we must assume that it was information rather than the goods themselves that flowed through the palace. This would certainly have enhanced the position of the officials who managed the system. We do not know how closely they were supervised by the ruler, whose political functions are never described, but his symbolic role is absolutely clear. Because of the central location of the throne room, the palace was effectively built around the wanax. Is this a reflection of his divine status? He did have religious responsibilities but there is no evidence that he was worshiped as a god. In fact the main sanctuary was at a place called *pa-ki-ja-na* and not in the palace, so secular and religious authority were kept separate. However, the palace did function as a ceremonial and ritual center. In particular the enormous quantities of pottery indicate that feasts must have been held here and this suggestion is supported by large deposits of burnt bones from cattle and deer which had evidently been sacrificed and eaten. A religious festival would be the obvious occasion for this type of event to promote community solidarity. There may have been an element of competition as well, since festivals provided an ideal opportunity for conspicuous generosity and consequently self-promotion. This link with status would explain why the participants were apparently segregated. An elite group dined in the throne room. Another group used court 63 and hall 65, a more accessible location but still within the palace. The pottery stored in room 60 was possibly for a less privileged group of people who were served in the court in front of the main unit. The feasts may have been communal but social distinctions still needed to be maintained.

## Early Iron Age Lefkandi

Lefkandi is on the west coast of Euboia. The Early Helladic settlement on the Xeropolis headland expanded in the Middle Helladic period but was not a major Mycenaean center. In LH IIIC, after the destructions which affected many of the other sites in the region, the Xeropolis settlement was completely rebuilt and it is possible that there had been an influx of refugees. Despite a major fire, occupation continued until the end of LH IIIC and through the Submycenaean and Protogeometric periods as well. The Early Iron Age cemeteries were approximately 500 meters northwest of Xeropolis. The Skoubris cemetery has some of the earliest graves but Toumba is the site of the most remarkable discovery, the early tenth-century "Heroon" (figure 3.7a & b). This was first investigated in 1980 and then the owner of the plot bulldozed the central section of the structure. The east and west ends were subsequently excavated in 1981–3.

The "Heroon" faced east and was at least 47 meters in length and 10 meters wide. The west end had been destroyed but the curvature of the walls suggests an apse. The walls consisted of a massive stone socle, over one meter high, which provided a solid base for the upper courses of mudbrick. Rectangular wooden posts had been placed against the inner face of the walls and also down the center of the structure. More posts formed a sort of veranda around the sides and the apse. The roof had evidently been thatched with reeds or rushes and it is possible that there was a loft. The walls were plastered inside and a thin layer of clay covered the floor.

The main entrance was at the east end through a porch formed by an extension of the side walls. As the entrance is 4.80 meters wide, it may not have been closed by a door. In the southwest corner of the east room was a low platform. A circle of stones had been laid out in the southeast corner and the northwest corner was boxed off. It is not clear what these fixtures were used for. The central room was the largest, around 22 meters in length. There had originally been a door in the south wall but this was later blocked off. The two short walls in the northeast corner may have supported a wooden staircase. A clay box in the southeast corner contained wood ash and bone. Two shafts had been cut in the floor of the room. In the north shaft were the skeletons of four horses, two of which had iron bits in their mouths. The south shaft was deeper and had been lined with mudbrick, plastered in clay. The skeleton of a woman aged between 25 and 30 was laid out on the north side of the shaft. She had gilt coils on either side of her head, as well as a gold necklace and pendant around her neck. There were two gold discs and a lunate collar on her chest. She also wore gold rings and had a number of bronze and iron dress pins. An iron knife with an ivory pommel had been placed by her head. A bronze amphora, closed by a bronze bowl, on the other side of the shaft contained the cremated remains of a man, aged 30–45, wrapped in cloth. An iron sword, spear, and razor, as well as a whetstone, were on the floor next to the amphora. A corridor went from the central room into the apse. This was probably a store room, as there were pits in the floor for large jars. After a short period of

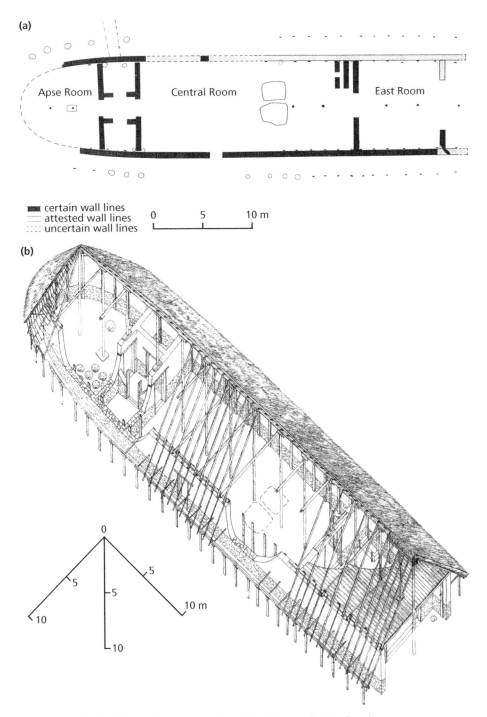

**(a)**

Apse Room    Central Room    East Room

certain wall lines
attested wall lines
uncertain wall lines

0          5          10 m

**(b)**

0
5
5
5
5
10 m
10
10

**Figure 3.7a & b**  Plan and reconstruction of the "Heroon" at Lefkandi

time, perhaps no more than 20 or 25 years, the "Heroon" was partially dismantled, covered with earth and made into an enormous tumulus 4 meters high. It is reckoned that this would have taken between 500 and 2,000 man days. A cemetery with some exceptionally rich tenth- and ninth-century graves was then established just east of the tumulus.

The "Heroon" is unique. It would be well over two centuries before structures of a similar size were built again and they were temples. In fact the "Heroon" does look rather like early Greek temples, though there can be no direct link. It is not out of the question that other monumental tenth- and ninth-century structures will be discovered in the future but, for the moment, the "Heroon" does not have any parallels. This makes interpretation more difficult, particularly because the exact sequence of events is uncertain. A crucial point is whether the "Heroon" was built before or after the burials. One possibility is that this was where the man and woman had lived and were buried when they died. Alternatively, the evidence for a fire on the floor of the central room may mark the location of the pyre on which the man was cremated. As this could not have been lit inside such a highly flammable structure, the "Heroon" would have been constructed as a tomb in the form of a house. How the woman died is another issue. One theory is that she committed suicide or was killed soon after the death of her husband. However, she could well have been buried later. The horses were certainly sacrificed. There is no evidence for any cult activity before the "Heroon" was dismantled or after the tumulus had been completed, so this was not strictly a hero shrine. Nevertheless, the way that the man was treated does anticipate the funerals of Homeric heroes. He must have been the ruler of Lefkandi, whether or not this was his palace as well as his tomb. The "Heroon" was a very visible symbol of his high status but did he also found a dynasty? It does seem likely that his descendants were buried in the Toumba cemetery. If so, membership of this elite group will have been hereditary, though none of his successors was obviously as powerful.

## Classical Athens

Archaic Greek cities may have built monumental temples but political authority is much less visible in their architecture. Perhaps this is because they were often governed by aristocratic families who showed off their wealth in other ways, with dedications in sanctuaries for example. The assumption that tyrants must have lived in palaces has also been questioned. There is no trace of a sixth-century palace for Polykrates on Samos. The suggestion that the Peisistratids based themselves on the Acropolis is equally unfounded. Building F, on the west side of the Agora, is a possible candidate for their palace. This was built between 550 and 525 and has rooms on two sides of a colonnaded court. It does seem to have been a private house but the link with the Peisistratids is speculative. If this was their palace, they had certainly not opted for a lavish lifestyle. In order to impress, tyrants promoted religious festivals, constructed temples, and improved civic amenities. It was their contribution to the community that they wished to stress, not their exceptional status as individuals.

In a democratic city there was less need for discretion. The power of the people could be more openly displayed and Athens provides the best example of the way that civic architecture evolved in the Classical period. Of course it is not the most typical Greek city but we know so much about Athens from documentary sources and the extensive excavations in the center.

After the reforms of Kleisthenes in 508 the most powerful body was the boule or council of 500, made up of 50 members from each of the 10 new tribes. The tribal contingents took it in turns to serve as prytaneis or presidents for one-tenth of the year. The prytaneis were on duty every day and some of them slept in the Agora overnight in case of an emergency. In the fifth century the boule was given greater administrative and judicial responsibilities but its primary function was to decide which items would be discussed by the ekklesia, the assembly of adult male citizens. The ekklesia had the final say on any course of action and important decisions required a quorum of at least 6,000 citizens. There were also elected officials, in particular the nine archons, whose powers were curtailed as the democracy grew stronger but who did retain a judicial and religious role. Most officials served for only one year, but the 10 generals could be re-elected and this was the office that Perikles held when he led Athens, from around 450 until he died in 429.

The Agora was the political center of Athens, although the ekklesia usually met on the hill of the Pnyx, west of the Acropolis (figure 2.9). It is not clear when the Agora square was first laid out. There was some construction activity in the sixth century under the Peisistratids but the boundary stones that were set up after the reforms of Kleisthenes suggest that a conscious decision had been taken to create a civic space. The development of the west side of the square had started when the Persians captured and sacked Athens in 480. Although they focused their attention on the Acropolis, the Agora suffered as well and not much was left intact by the time they retreated in 479. In the period of reconstruction that followed, Kimon was a prominent figure. His victory over the Persians at the battle of Eurymedon in 466 financed some of this work and he also landscaped the Agora.

Under Perikles few additions were made apart from the temple of Hephaistos. Funds must have been limited because of the cost of the Parthenon and the other projects that he initiated. Since Thucydides (2.65) described Athens at this time as "in theory a democracy but in reality government by the first citizen," Perikles may not have felt very enthusiastic about the political and administrative infrastructure of the city. At any rate there was a burst of activity in the last quarter of the fifth century, despite the financial burden of the war with Sparta which ended in 404 when Athens surrendered. Recovery from this disaster was slow and the priority in the early fourth century was the refortification of the city and the construction of border fortresses. No major changes took place in the Agora until the second century when wealthy foreign rulers remodeled the east and south sides of the square (figure 2.13).

Because of the close link between the administration and the judiciary, there were law-courts in the Agora. This was the commercial center of the city as well, with a daily market regulated by public officials. Numerous temples, shrines, and altars emphasize that no sharp distinction was made between the civic and the sacred. With so much activity concentrated here, the Agora was obviously the place where people would meet up and it must often have been packed.

The government operated from the west side of the square (figure 3.8). The council of 500 was provided with a purpose-built bouleuterion. The Old Bouleuterion may have been constructed soon after the council was set up by Kleisthenes. In the late fifth century it was replaced by the New Bouleuterion but remained in use as the public archive office. The documents kept here included laws, decrees, records of lawsuits, and financial accounts, under the protection of Rhea, the mother of the

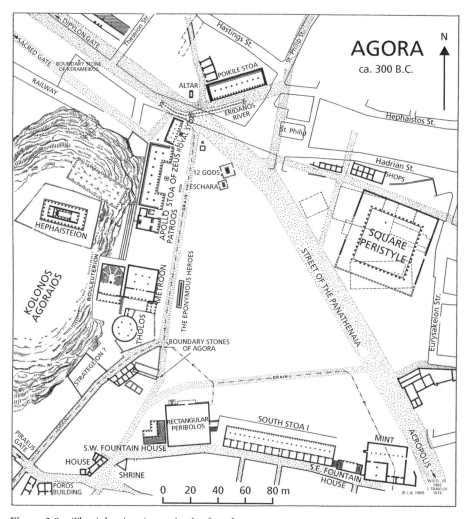

**Figure 3.8**    The Athenian Agora in the fourth century

gods. In the New Bouleuterion the members of the council presumably sat on wooden benches, though it is not certain how these were arranged. The circular Tholos is where the 50 prytaneis dined at public expense and those on duty slept overnight. Ambassadors from other cities, high officials, and priests were sometimes fed here as well. The structure just beyond the Tholos may have been the Strategeion, which was the headquarters of the 10 generals. In front of the Bouleuterion is the Monument of the Eponymous Heroes after whom the 10 tribes were named. The statues of the heroes stood on a high pedestal which was used for official notices, such as the legislative agenda for the ekklesia.

Stoas were particularly versatile. The late fifth-century Stoa of Zeus Eleutherios is of the type with wings on either side. It was dedicated to Zeus the liberator who had saved Greece from the Persian threat. In his invaluable description of the Agora, written in the second century AD, Pausanias (1.3) tells us that there was a statue of the god on the circular base in front of the stoa. He also mentions that the interior was decorated with pictures by the fourth-century painter Euphranor, which included personifications of Demos and Demokratia, the people and democracy. Those who died in battle could have their shields dedicated here and the stoa may have had an official function as the Thesmotheteion, where the six judicial archons deliberated. We know that Sokrates sometimes met his friends and pupils in the stoa as well.

The much simpler Royal Stoa was built for the archon basileus or king archon who had religious and legal duties (figure 3.9). The large stone in front of the stoa may be where magistrates swore an oath of allegiance before they took office. In the late fifth century a copy of the Athenian law code was inscribed on stone stelai, which were put on display in the wings on either side of the stoa. Not only were the laws made available for consultation but in a sense they were also enshrined here. A knowledge of the law would have been important because so many citizens served on juries, for which they were paid. The size of the juries varied but there were usually several hundred jurors and even larger panels were selected for some cases. It would therefore have been very difficult to bribe a jury, especially as the members

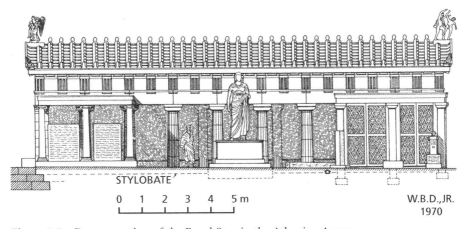

STYLOBATE

0  1  2  3  4  5 m

W.B.D.,JR.
1970

**Figure 3.9**  Reconstruction of the Royal Stoa in the Athenian Agora

were chosen at random just before the trial started. The Square Peristyle in the northeast corner of the agora was built in the late fourth century and may well have been a law-court because a number of the bronze ballots were found here which jurors used when they gave their verdict. Cases were also tried in the Stoa Poikile or Painted Stoa, named after the pictures of Athenian military victories by Polygnotos and Mikon, two of the most famous fifth-century painters. This was another multipurpose stoa and a favorite venue for philosophers, in particular Zeno who taught here so regularly that his followers became known as the Stoics. No doubt other law-courts were set up around the Agora on an ad hoc basis.

A similarly flexible approach must have been characteristic of much of the commercial activity because temporary stalls could be set up for the market traders and bankers who conducted their business in the Agora. The state made sure that customers were not cheated and sets of weights and measures were available in case of any sharp practice. The official inspectors of weights and measures, the metronomoi, were probably based in South Stoa I. The rooms in this stoa have off-center doors so that they could each accommodate seven couches on which the diners reclined as they ate. To be fed at public expense was one of the perks which state officials enjoyed and it seems likely that the boards of inspectors worked and dined in South Stoa I. The square structure in the southeast corner of the Agora may be the Mint. There was evidence of industrial activity here and the finds included dozens of bronze coin blanks.

With so many potential customers in the vicinity, it is understandable that craftsmen set up shop around the Agora and their importance can be gaged from the fact that Hephaistos and Athena, their patron deities, were worshiped jointly in the temple which overlooked the square. The Hephaisteion, which was started around 450 and finished off approximately 30 years later, is one of the best-preserved Greek temples. Other shrines and sanctuaries ensured that the gods were very much involved in the civic and commercial life of the city. The Street of the Panathenaia was named after the great festival held in honor of Athena, when there was a procession which crossed the Agora and then climbed the Acropolis. Athletic events formed part of the festival and this street was apparently used as a track for some of the races. Plays were also performed in the Agora in a temporary theater with wooden seats. In the fifth century this was replaced by the purpose-built Theater of Dionysos on the south slope of the Acropolis.

In the fifth and fourth centuries the citizen assembly occasionally met in the Theater of Dionysos but the Pnyx was their usual venue (figure 3.10). This was first laid out around 500 when the hillside was leveled off to create a semicircular auditorium where the members of the assembly could sit or stand. At the lower end of the slope was the rostrum for the speaker. At the end of the fifth century the Pnyx was remodeled and the direction of the slope was reversed. One explanation for this operation, which required a massive earth embankment, is that the Thirty Tyrants, who briefly ruled Athens at the end of the war with Sparta, wanted speakers to face the city rather than the sea, so that they would not be reminded of their maritime empire. However, when democracy was restored the Pnyx was not altered and the

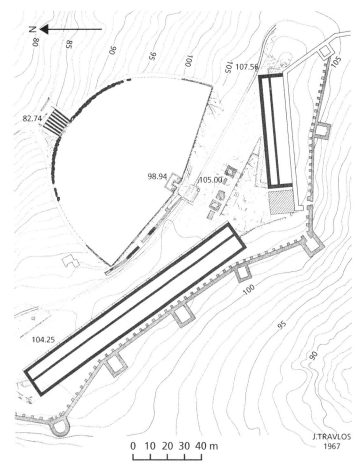

**Figure 3.10**   Plan of the third phase of the Pnyx in Athens

same arrangement was retained for the final construction phase. This was started around 330 and provided an even larger auditorium, which could have accommodated well over 10,000 people.

It is significant that this redevelopment of the Pnyx, which also involved the construction of two stoas, was never completed. The Theater of Dionysos had been rebuilt in stone around the same time and the assembly moved there in the third century. Athens had spent more on civic architecture than most other Greek cities, yet the level of expenditure on religion was always much higher. The Parthenon of course epitomizes this, and it is not just the size of the temples which is exceptional: they were also much better built. This is certainly true of the temple of Hephaistos in the Agora for example. Theaters and stadia were also an important component of some sanctuaries, and their development is a further indication of the way that religion was prioritized. Perikles knew very well that other Greek cities would be more impressed by the Acropolis than by the Agora.

# Hellenistic Macedonia

In the Hellenistic period monarchy became the prevalent form of government. Rulers had political, military, legislative, and judicial powers. They were supported by members of the royal family, counselors, court officials, military aides, a large staff, and servants. Given the size of this entourage, the palaces that they built must have been a practical necessity. They also became a conspicuous symbol of the absolute authority of the monarch. Although the palaces do vary quite considerably, they have a number of elements in common. An audience chamber was essential since this was where the king held court and conducted most of his official and ceremonial duties. The Macedonians were fond of banquets which sometimes took place in the audience chamber or in the open on special occasions when thousands of guests were invited. Most palaces also had a number of sumptuously decorated rooms for these banquets and symposia. Offices were needed for the administrative officials and barracks for the royal guard. There were private apartments for the royal family and members of the court and accommodation for guests, as well as storerooms, kitchens, and quarters for the service staff. Gardens and parks were a feature of many palaces, which were also major cultural centers with libraries and theaters.

Hellenistic palaces were architecturally eclectic. Alexander and his successors were familiar with Persian, Babylonian, and Egyptian palaces and imitated their vast scale, multiple courts, and gardens. This mixture of styles and royal extravagance resulted in some extraordinarily grand designs. At Alexandria the Ptolemies took over approximately a quarter of the city for their 200-hectare palace complex. Few traces of this remain but we do have descriptions which underline what an impact it made on visitors. Here we will focus on two of the palaces in Macedonia.

Vergina is now securely identified as Aigai, which was replaced as the capital of Macedonia by Pella around 400. Nevertheless, it remained the burial place of the Macedonian kings and three royal tombs have been excavated there (figure 9.18). The palace was built in the late fourth century and occupies a terrace on the slopes of the acropolis with a fine view over the Macedonian plain. It measures 105 by 89 meters and consists of a large peristyle court, which was probably laid out as a formal garden, with rooms on four sides (figure 3.11a & b). The main entrance was on the east side, through a monumental portico flanked by stoas. The room in the center of the east wing may have been the audience chamber. Next to this was the circular tholos which has a dedicatory inscription to Herakles, the heroic ancestor of the Macedonian kings. It could be a shrine or possibly the throne room. Most of the rooms around the court were used for banquets because they have off-center doors and raised platforms around the walls for the couches on which the diners reclined. There was space for at least 278 guests, whose status no doubt determined where they dined. The two rooms which opened off the porch in the center of the south wing were probably the most important. A terrace with a fine view over the city ran along the north side of the palace. Most of the residential accommodation

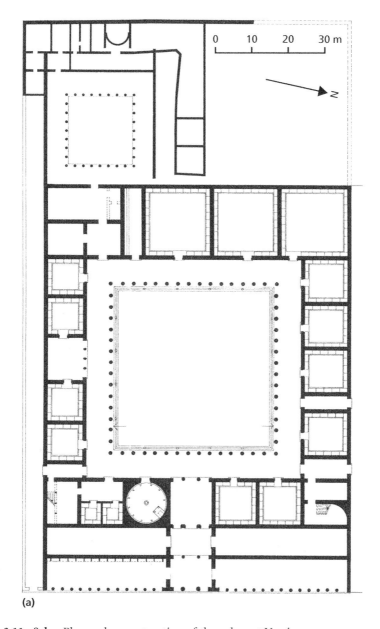

(a)

**Figure 3.11a & b**   Plan and reconstruction of the palace at Vergina

was presumably on the second floor. Another court was added at the west end of the palace, possibly as a service area which would have been very necessary given the emphasis on hospitality.

The palace at Pella was much larger, around 60,000 m², but lay in ruins by the first century AD and it is mainly the foundations that have been excavated. It was

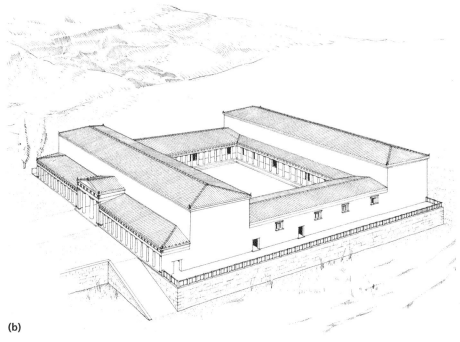

**(b)**

**Figure 3.11a & b**   (*Continued*)

probably built in the second half of the fourth century and then extended a century or so later. The palace is aligned with the grid that was laid out for the city and overlooks the agora. The main facade was on the south side and again consisted of an entrance portico flanked by stoas. Behind this were four courts of which court I was evidently the most important. There was an altar in the center of the court and, at the far end, one of the largest rooms in the palace which may have been an audience chamber. If statues of the Antigonid kings were displayed in the semicircular niches on either side of the court, as has been suggested, then this could be some sort of dynastic shrine as well. It is possible that court II was used for receptions and that courts IV and V were more private, since a bath complex with a pool and heated rooms were installed here. Alternatively court V may have been a palaistra. The western extension of the palace, courts III and VI, is not well preserved and had probably not been finished. Pella does at least give us an impression of the size of these Hellenistic palaces and their sumptuous decoration is echoed in some of the houses in the town.

## Conclusions

This chapter has obviously not considered every form of monumental architecture. Fortifications, temples, and tombs could also be used as symbols of power and there is considerable variation in the way that authority was visibly expressed. Does this correlate with the type of authority?

The spatial configuration and central location of the megaron at Dimini is symptomatic of the divisions within Late Neolithic society and has been interpreted as evidence of institutionalized inequality. Yet status does not seem to have been based on wealth. The House of Tiles at Lerna represents a new style of architecture, designed for functional flexibility. This does make it difficult to determine the reason why corridor houses were built and whose needs they served. It would certainly be a mistake to assume that they must be embryonic palaces and their layout suggests some sort of communal or possibly regional role. The nature of political authority does not become much clearer when we look at the Cretan palaces because the view that they were royal residences has been challenged. Nevertheless, they imply control of ceremonial, economic, and industrial activity, though not necessarily a monopoly of power which may have been contested. Fortunately we know more about political authority in Mycenaean Greece. The prominent location of the palace at Mycenae, surrounded by massive fortifications, emphasized the strength of the ruler. Yet the tablets from Pylos show that Mycenaean kings were not autocrats and underline the importance of their ceremonial role. Mycenaean society was competitive but the palace promoted social cohesion rather than division.

The Mycenaeans made the link between death and status explicit and set a precedent which Early Iron Age communities followed, most notably in the "Heroon" at Lefkandi. This was conceived as a house for the ruler, at least after he had died if not in life. Houses also provided the model for later Greek temples which used monumentality as a surrogate expression of power. Even tyrants avoided overt self-glorification and it is significant that the Agora in Athens was dominated by the temple of Hephaistos. Nevertheless, the political apparatus of democracy was well resourced and given prominence. The Athenians made the Agora a showcase for their civic identity and achievements in a way which few other Greek cities emulated. The absolute authority of Hellenistic monarchs is reflected in the grandeur of the palaces, though there were exceptions. The rulers of Pergamon lived quite modestly and used their wealth to create a great capital city. The medium may not always have been particularly subtle but monumental architecture could encode complex messages.

## Bibliographical notes

For the sites discussed in this chapter, see the following in particular. For Dimini: Theocharis 1973, Halstead 1992a, Papathanassopoulos 1996, Andreou et al. 2001, and Souvatzi 2008. For Lerna: Pullen 1986, Shaw 1987, Wiencke 2000, and Peperaki 2004. For Knossos: Cadogan 1976, Evely et al. 1994, Rehak and Younger 2001, Watrous 2001, Driessen et al. 2002, and Cadogan et al. 2004. For Pylos: Blegen and Rawson 1966, Palaima and Shelmerdine 1984, Dickinson 1994, Davis 1998,

Shelmerdine 2001, and Bendall 2004. For Lefkandi: Popham et al. 1993, Mazarakis Ainian 1997, Morris 2000, Lemos 2002, and Dickinson 2006. For Athens: Travlos 1980, Camp 1986 and 2001, Hansen and Fischer-Hansen 1994, and Whitley 2001. For Macedonia: Andronikos 1993, Siganidou and Lilimpaki-Akamati 1996, Nielsen 1999, and Hoepfner and Brands 1996.

# CHAPTER 4

# Residential Space

## Introduction

The houses that form the subject of this chapter were primarily residential but can incorporate other types of activity which do not strictly qualify as domestic. Houses are seldom functionally simple and they are also symbolically charged. They can embody notions about property rights, ownership, wealth and status, social organization, and personal identity. This aspect of houses, as well as their architectural development, will be examined here. The evidence for Greek houses is rather uneven. Given that they were easily the most common form of architecture, it is remarkable how few examples we have for some periods. One reason for this is that archaeologists have focused on the civic centers and sanctuaries in cities. The monumental is more attractive, though not necessarily more informative, than the mundane. Admittedly monumental architecture does tend to be better preserved. As many houses were designed to last for a couple of generations at most before they were demolished and rebuilt, the domestic architecture of earlier periods is absent from many cities. Ironically it is at Neolithic sites that we have some of the best stratified sequences of houses because tell settlements were made up of superimposed levels of architectural debris.

## The Neolithic Period

As we saw in chapter 2, the settlement pattern fluctuates over the course of the Neolithic period. It would be extraordinary if it had remained the same for several

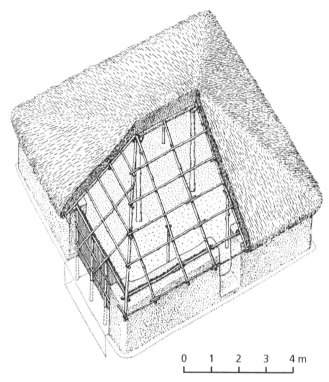

0   1   2   3   4 m

**Figure 4.1**   Reconstruction of an Early Neolithic house at Nea Nikomedeia

thousand years. Nevertheless, there is considerable stability, which is why tells built up as houses were constructed, renovated, and eventually replaced. The fact that houses were often rebuilt in exactly the same place on a tell suggests that individual households had property rights. However, there can also be discontinuity. At Sesklo in Thessaly the layout of the Middle Neolithic houses on the acropolis remains consistent, whereas in the lower settlement they regularly moved their location. So we should expect some variability at each site, as well as differences between sites.

The Early Neolithic houses at Nea Nikomedeia in southern Macedonia were square or rectangular. Their dimensions vary, but 6 by 8 meters is typical. If we allow 10m² of floor space for each individual, which is an average that is often used in population estimates, these houses would be the right size for single families. Some have internal partitions, and other features include platforms and hearths. There were hearths or ovens outside at least two of the houses. The walls consisted of a row of oak posts, set one meter or so apart in a foundation trench, which supported bundles of reeds or rushes. A thick layer of clay was then plastered over this framework (figure 4.1). A similar wattle-and-daub technique is found at other Early Neolithic sites, though mudbricks were also used, sometimes laid on stone foundations. The different methods of construction reflect what was locally available. There

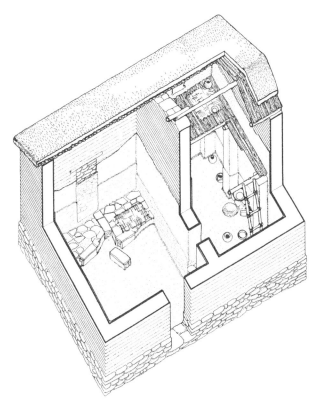

**Figure 4.2**   Reconstruction of a Middle Neolithic house at Sesklo

were evidently still woods around Nea Nikomedeia, and the reeds came from a nearby lake. It is assumed that the roofs were pitched and probably consisted of reeds on a framework of wooden rafters. The way that these houses were con-structed may sound rather primitive but suits the Greek climate. The thick walls provided excellent insulation, which meant that they could be kept warm in the winter and cool in the summer more easily than many modern houses.

At Sesklo the Middle Neolithic houses on the acropolis were some distance apart. They were much the same size as the houses at Nea Nikomedeia and had one or two rooms (figure 4.2). There were work areas with grindstones and querns where food could be prepared and then cooked in ovens or on open hearths. The walls were solidly built of stone and mudbrick. Terracotta models from Thessaly suggest that the houses had pitched roofs, possibly of wood covered in clay, with a hole for the chimney. Another type of house, found at Tsangli and Otzaki, had internal but-tresses. They may have supported the roof and also provided spaces which could be set aside for particular activities. In the Late Neolithic period a large megaron was constructed on the acropolis at Sesklo and also at Dimini (figure 3.1). Because of their location and size, it seems likely that these structures were built for a higher-status individual or family.

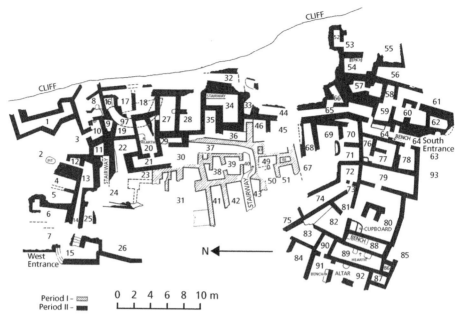

**Figure 4.3**  Plan of Myrtos

# The Early Bronze Age

Myrtos on the southern coast of Crete is one of the few settlement sites in Greece that has been completely excavated and fully published. Consequently it is a major source of information about the way that people lived in the Early Minoan period. The settlement was first occupied in EM IIA and this phase is represented by the architectural remains in the center of the site (figure 4.3). Myrtos then expanded in EM IIB and the second phase ended with the complete destruction of the settlement by fire. There has been some erosion, especially on the east side of the site where the cliff has been cut back by the sea. Nevertheless, it seems likely that most of the settlement has been excavated.

The site consists of approximately 90 rooms, corridors, and courts. Most of the walls had lower courses of stone and a mudbrick superstructure. They were finished off with a layer of lime plaster which was sometimes painted red. Wooden beams supported a flat roof made of reeds covered in coarse plaster. The construction techniques used at Myrtos were comparatively simple. On other EM II sites, such as Vasiliki in eastern Crete, the houses were two stories high and the walls were built around a framework of wooden timbers. Their layout is also more comprehensible, whereas Myrtos looks unplanned. This is partly because the site is not level and the terrain determined how some of the blocks of rooms were positioned. Careful study of the architecture has also shown that the settlement was constructed in successive stages and not as an integrated complex. The key is whether walls are bonded together or abut. If two walls were built at the same time they would be bonded for greater structural stability. Walls built at different times abut where they join. At Myrtos clusters of interconnected rooms can be identified in this way and it is thought that the EM IIB settlement started with the block of rooms numbered 27–28/34–35 and then grew from this. Eventually there may have been six or seven clusters. The rooms were fitted with benches, platforms, cupboards, and hearths. The inhabitants had also left many of their possessions behind. This combination of fixtures and finds gives us a good indication of the types of activity that went on in each room, for example where food was stored and meals were prepared, cooked, and eaten. Since each of the clusters had a similar range of facilities, they do seem to have been separate households. With an average of just under 50 m$^2$ of floor space available, we can assume that each cluster housed a single family. If there were six or seven families, the population of Myrtos would have been about 30. It is quite likely that the families were related, given the way that the settlement gradually expanded. Each household was basically self-sufficient, though they must obviously have cooperated. They also needed a wider network of support, not least because a group of this size could not have survived except by intermarriage with other communities.

At no other Early Bronze Age site can the houses be analyzed in such detail. In chapter 2 we looked at Lithares in Boiotia where around 20 EH II houses have been excavated on either side of a narrow street (figure 2.1). It is not always clear which rooms go together, because the doorways were above the level of the stone foundations and their location is consequently uncertain. Nevertheless, there seems to have been a range of house types. Some have one large room, which may open off a porch, others have three or four rooms in a row. Many of the houses had hearths and also stone platforms but the finds are not especially informative in terms of specific activities. The monumental corridor houses, of which the House of Tiles at Lerna (figure 3.2) is the best-known example, are also EH II and underline the variation in this period on the Greek mainland, as well as on Crete.

## Middle Bronze Age Greece

After the destruction of the House of Tiles, the architecture of the houses at Lerna changed. In EH III and in the Middle Helladic period the most common type of house is an apsidal-ended megaron, with a shallow porch, one or two main rooms, and a semicircular back wall (figure 4.4). This is one of the cultural innovations that have been linked with the arrival of a new population in Greece. However, further investigation has shown that there is greater continuity than was originally supposed and that apsidal-ended structures first appeared in EH II, not at the end of the period, so the transition was evidently more gradual.

Asine in the Argolid is a good example of a Middle Helladic settlement. Sixteen houses have been excavated, mainly on the Kastraki which was then a rocky island but is now a promontory. Although the site is naturally defensible, security does not seem to have been a major concern as there is no evidence of any fortifications. The population of Asine was probably between 300 and 500, most of whom lived in the lower town. Narrow lanes ran between the houses, some of which were quite sizable (figure 4.5). House B had at least 11 rooms and covered 110 m$^2$. The irregular shape

**Figure 4.4**   Middle Helladic house at Lerna

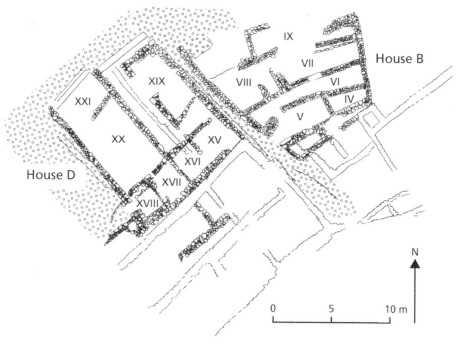

**Figure 4.5**   Plan of houses B and D at Asine

of this house may have been designed to make maximum use of the plot on which
it was built. House D, on the other side of the lane, is even larger at 200 m². The two
main rooms, XIX and XX, had separate entrances and another apartment formed
by rooms XIII and XIV was added later. It seems likely that two or more closely
related families lived here. There were storage facilities in some of the smaller rooms
and two ovens, one of which was in the paved court on the west side of the house.
Many graves were found in the lower town. Children had often been buried in and
around the houses, whereas most adult burials were in disused plots or open spaces.
The graves were sometimes grouped together, presumably for members of the same
family. This practice of intramural burial must have reinforced the bond between
the community and their homes, which suggests that property ownership and rights
of inheritance were clearly defined.

## Neopalatial Crete

The construction of the first Minoan palaces coincided with a rapid expansion in
the size of the towns at Knossos, Phaistos, and Mallia and also in the number of
sites on Crete. The monumentality of the palaces is echoed in Minoan domestic
architecture, particularly in the Neopalatial period when many "villas" were constructed. The use of this term has been questioned because it conjures up an image
of a grand country residence, which is inappropriate as most Minoan villas were in
towns. At a palace site, such as Knossos, they were the houses of an urban elite but
there were also villas in some of the smaller towns which had an important administrative role. It seems likely that the palaces controlled their territories through this
network of subsidiary centers.

Of the many houses that have been excavated at Knossos, the Little Palace is
undoubtedly the finest (figure 4.6). The quality of the architecture, exemplified by
the extensive use of gypsum, is reminiscent of the palace and we naturally wonder
who lived here. Was he or she a relative or rival of the ruler? The uncertainty about
the Minoan system of government makes any suggestion highly speculative but it
is significant that an elite lifestyle was not restricted to the palaces. The plan of the
Little Palace is typically Minoan in that it looks so irregular. This is partly because
a terrace had to be cut back into the steep slope. However, the main reason is the
agglutinative style of architecture which the Minoans favored, with blocks of rooms
designed as modular units. The suite of rooms on the east side of the Little Palace
looked out across Knossos and consisted of a hall divided by a row of pier and door
partitions, like the Hall of the Double Axes in the palace. South of this was a peristyle
hall and two rooms with columns supported by pillars on the floor below. There is
another pillar room in the southwest corner and also in the west wing is a bathroom
which later became a shrine.

The houses at Mallia were rather simpler. House Da is a good example and shows
quite clearly how the modular design system worked (figure 4.7a & b). On one side
of the porch (1) were two storerooms (12). Room 7 is a bathroom and there is a

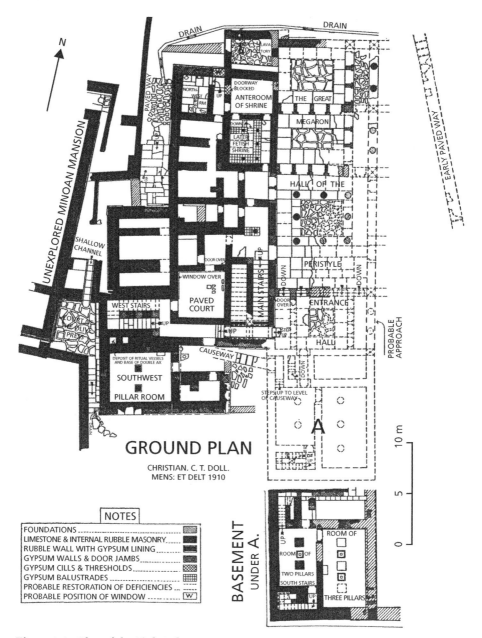

**Figure 4.6**   Plan of the Little Palace at Knossos

well-preserved lavatory in the corner of room 6. Room 3 is a hall, divided by the usual row of pier and door partitions, with a light well at one end. Rooms 8–10 may have been multipurpose. The flight of stairs (11) indicates that the house had an upper floor and this is restored with windows, (figure 4.7b) although balconies would be an alternative possibility.

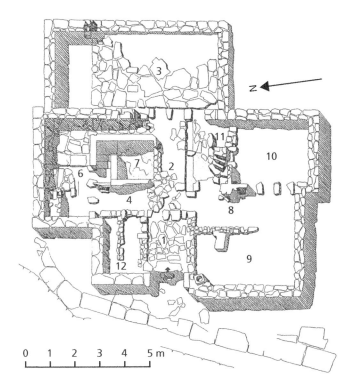

(a)

(b)

**Figure 4.7a & b**  Plan and reconstruction of House Da at Mallia

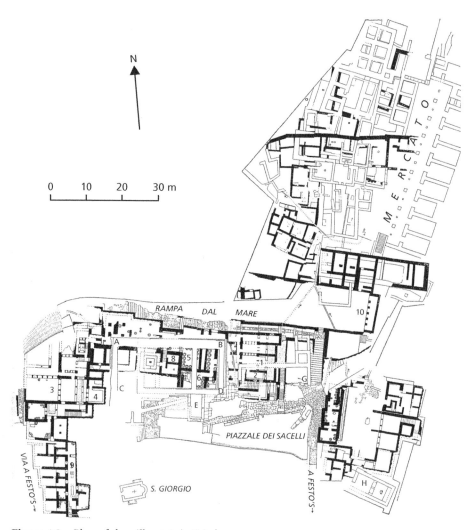

**Figure 4.8**   Plan of the villa at Ayia Triada

A short distance from Phaistos is the town of Ayia Triada where a magnificent villa was constructed in LM I (figure 4.8). This has three wings ranged around a court. The suites of rooms at either end of the north wing are particularly impressive because of the way that their configuration could be adapted by rows of pier and door partitions, while light wells supplied fresh air through a system of internal windows. The floors of these rooms were paved with gypsum and some of the walls were decorated with superb frescoes. In the center of this wing were storerooms and the east and west wings also had storage space. As there was an upper floor, the villa was originally even more extensive, and the palatial quality of the architecture is matched by the finds, which included stone vases, copper ingots, and a large archive of Linear A tablets. Because Ayia Triada and Phaistos are so close together, the two sites must have been linked, but how were they connected? The suggestion that the

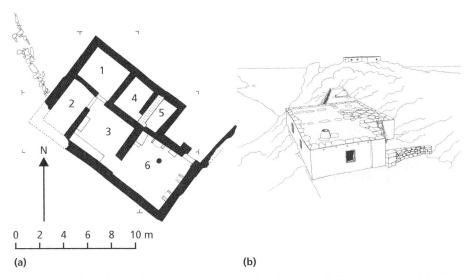

**Figure 4.9a & b**   Plan and reconstruction of the farmhouse at Chalinomouri near Mochlos

villa was the country residence of the rulers of Phaistos does not seem very likely, since they would surely have chosen a site in the mountains if they wanted to escape from the heat of the Mesara plain. An alternative theory is that the palace was not fully operational at this time and that Ayia Triada may have replaced Phaistos as the administrative center for southern Crete.

At the far end of the bay from the town of Mochlos, an isolated farm has been excavated and this is much more typical of the houses in which most Minoans lived (figure 4.9a & b). It was a single-story structure, built of stone and mudbrick, with a roof of schist slabs supported on wooden beams. The entrance led directly into the main room of the house (6) which had a stone platform and benches. Food was cooked and eaten here and also in room 3, where there is evidence of other types of work as well. Storage jars were kept in room 2, some of which had been buried beneath the floor, possibly to keep the contents cool or hidden. Room 1 is more secluded and this suggests that it was a bedroom. How rooms 4 and 5 were used is unclear, though they could only have been entered through a trapdoor in the roof. Behind the house was a yard with an oven or kiln and the household no doubt spent much of their time out here.

## The Cyclades

Cretan influence is very evident in the Cyclades at the start of the Late Bronze Age, though the houses in two of the main towns, Phylakopi on Melos and Ayia Irini on Kea, do not change significantly, even if some Minoan features were introduced. However, at Akrotiri on Thera the impact of Crete is much more obvious and the houses there are extraordinarily well preserved as a result of the volcanic eruption which buried the site in LC I.

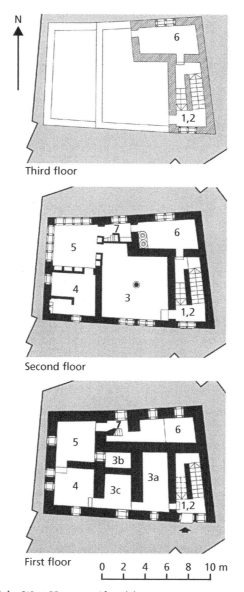

**Figure 4.10**  Plan of the West House at Akrotiri

The part of the town that has been excavated was near the harbor (figure 2.4). Some of the houses were detached and others were built close together in awkwardly shaped blocks which follow the line of the narrow streets and squares. Although the houses are similar in style and construction, they do vary in size and function. The West House could be considered fairly typical (figure 4.10). It is detached and has a slightly different orientation. Consequently it is not quite as hemmed in as some of the other houses. With eight first (= ground)-floor rooms, seven on the second

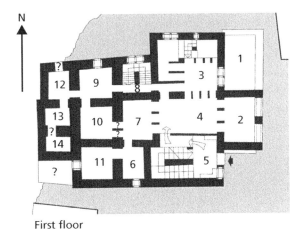

First floor

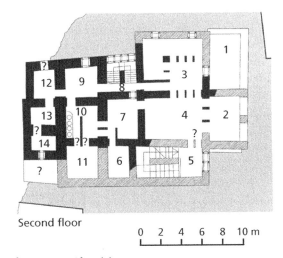

Second floor

0  2  4  6  8  10 m

**Figure 4.11** Plan of Xeste 3 at Akrotiri

floor, and one room on the roof, the West House was compact but spacious. The entrance opens directly off the street but a lobby gave some privacy. Because of the slope, some of the rooms on the first floor were almost basements, though windows ensured that they were reasonably well lit. There was a bench with three millstones in room 3 and pottery was stacked in rooms 5 and 6. A staircase leads from the lobby to the second floor. Room 3 upstairs was the largest in the house and a loom had evidently been set up there, but the decor is rather plain compared with rooms 4 and 5 where the walls were frescoed. With so many windows room 5 must have been wonderfully airy. Room 4 has an intact lavatory which was plumbed into the drain that ran outside.

Some houses may have had a more specialized role. Xeste 3 is almost twice the size of the West House and there were at least 35 rooms on three floors (figure 4.11).

The grand dimensions of the house were complemented by the fine ashlar masonry used for the outside walls. The main entrance is in the southeast corner and leads into room 4 which had Minoan-style pier and door partitions on three sides. The space that was available could therefore be adapted in various ways. Another Minoan feature is the lustral basin in room 3. The frescoes suggest that religious ceremonies were held here and possibly in the equivalent room on the floor above. Conceivably this was the sole function of Xeste 3, though the rooms on the west side of the house may have been residential.

The Cretan connection can clearly be seen in Xeste 3. The use of a wooden framework for the walls of most of the houses at Akrotiri is significant because there was not much good timber available locally, so this was an imported technology which had resource implications. However, the Therans may well have considered that the expense was justified because timber reinforcements made the walls more stable and they had just rebuilt their town after an earthquake. They did have plenty of stone which could be cut quite easily but ashlar walls were exceptional. Gypsum from Crete was also brought in for some floors. Pier and door partitions provided great flexibility and kept rooms cool in the summer. Nevertheless it seems likely that their presence in the houses at Akrotiri was symbolic and this is certainly true of the lustral basin in Xeste 3 where the iconography of the Minoan-style frescoes underlines the sanctity of this suite of rooms. Yet the result is not a transplanted Cretan town. Akrotiri retained a cultural individuality which was enhanced by these Minoan ingredients.

Because the houses are so well preserved and so much equipment was found in situ, we can visualize how the Therans lived. The first floors were principally for storage and heavy-duty activities. On the second floor was a large room which was probably multifunctional and this may have been where guests—anyone who was not a member of the household—were received. Off this room were the private apartments and also additional storerooms. But where did the Therans cook, eat, and sleep? Most of the houses do not have hearths or ovens, so they must have used portable stoves. No doubt rooms changed their function over the course of the day and it is probably a mistake to think that there was any rigid concept of what should happen where.

## Mycenaean Greece

In comparison with Crete and the Cyclades less is known about Mycenaean domestic architecture because relatively few houses have been excavated. This is particularly true of the early Mycenaean period, the sixteenth and fifteenth centuries, when the construction of monumental tombs was a major preoccupation. The mansion at the Menelaion near Sparta has many of the features found in the later palaces and proves that the elite lived as well as died in style at this time. But most early Mycenaean houses were completely rebuilt in the fourteenth and thirteenth centuries so their original design is rarely certain.

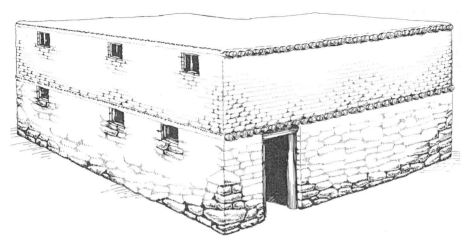

**Figure 4.12**    Reconstruction of Unit III-2 at Nichoria

Nichoria in the southwestern Peloponnese was an important Mycenaean center with a substantial LH II structure. This was replaced in LH IIIA1 by a megaron complex which may have been occupied by a high-status family. The palace at Pylos subsequently annexed Nichoria but there was still a town here in LH IIIB and it is one of the most extensively excavated Mycenaean settlements with an estimated population of around 700. Unlike Cretan and Cycladic towns the houses were not built in blocks but were detached and had room for courtyards, animal pens, and gardens. This loose arrangement was probably typical of most Mycenaean towns. Perhaps equally characteristic is the very variable layout of the houses, which partly reflects the way that rooms were added and other modifications were made over time. The result in most cases was a roughly square or rectangular, three- or four-room structure (figure 4.12). Some of the houses had an upper floor, others were single-story. The lower courses of the walls were built of stone, topped by mudbrick, and no doubt weather-proofed with plaster. It is thought that the roofs were flat and consisted of a layer of clay daub supported on wooden beams. There was also one apsidal house which probably had a pitched roof. This type of house was quite common in the Middle Helladic period and could indicate the continuation of an older tradition but is also found at Nichoria in the Early Iron Age. The juxtaposition of different styles shows how individual needs and preferences took precedence over any idea of conformity. Because the settlement was not destroyed and the inhabitants cleared their houses before they left, we have only limited evidence for the way that rooms were used, in the form of stone benches and storage for pithoi. However, it is suspected that most rooms were multifunctional.

A number of LH IIIB houses have been excavated at Mycenae. One group, known as the Panagia Houses, is near the Treasury of Atreus. In two cases the houses have a basic core of three first-floor rooms. There is a porch, the main room with a hearth, and a more private room behind this. Corridors provided access to

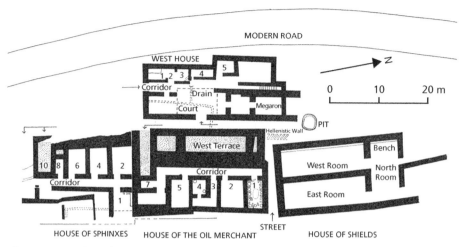

**Figure 4.13**  Plan of the Ivory Houses at Mycenae

additional rooms. The houses also have basements which must have been entered through trapdoors from the floor above. These basement rooms do not have windows and this suggests that they were primarily used as storage space for food because the thick walls ensured that the temperature remained relatively cool. Nearer the citadel are the rather grander Ivory Houses (figure 4.13). The same three-room core unit recurs here, for example in the West House. There were also store-rooms and a kitchen on the first floor. The staircase at the end of the corridor led up to the second floor. Olive oil was stored in pithoi in the basement rooms of the House of the Oil Merchant which evidently had a three-room unit on the first floor. The House of the Sphinxes also consists of basement rooms which were used as storage space. The House of the Shields seems to have had a more specialized function as a workshop and warehouse. The owners/occupiers of this group of houses were clearly high-status individuals who had close links with the palace authorities. As Linear B tablets were found here, they may well have been royal officials, though it is also possible that they were private individuals who acted on behalf of the palace. The houses at Mycenae have some structural similarities but just as many differences because of disparities in social status, as well as for practical reasons. Nevertheless, it is remarkable that the Mycenaeans did not develop a more distinctive style of domestic architecture, given that their palaces have such a consistent layout. No obvious common set of principles is reflected in the houses. Instead we see a combination of influences and traditions.

## The Early Iron Age

The evidence for Early Iron Age domestic architecture is limited. At the start of the period population levels were much lower and there were fewer settlements. On many sites the Early Iron Age houses have been completely destroyed as a result of later construction activity. This does make it difficult to observe how communities adapted as circumstances changed. One trend that has been noted is the occupation of easily defensible sites on Crete, a move which began in LM IIIC. Karphi is particularly precipitous but, despite the difficult terrain, the settlement was neatly planned (figure 2.7). The houses were solidly built of stone, which is just as well because it must have been bitterly cold in the winter. Much of the settlement is over 1,000 meters above sea level and very exposed. It is not a place where people would have lived out of choice, and in the late eleventh century they abandoned Karphi. There may have been 125 to 150 houses altogether, of which 25 to 30 have been excavated. The Great House has six rooms and is one of the largest but probably just consisted of room 9 originally. Later the porch (8) was added, as well as a storeroom (14) and three smaller rooms (11–13), two of which must have been entered through a trapdoor in the roof. In a block on the east side of the site were three-room (138–140), two-room (137 and 141), and one-room (136) houses, each with a hearth. Minoan houses do not usually have fixed hearths but a good source of heat was essential here. Equipment used in textile production was found in many of the houses because one advantage that Karphi did have was pasture for sheep and goats in the mountains around the settlement.

At Karphi Minoan architectural traditions were maintained and there is some continuity. The situation at Nichoria was very different and highlights the contrast between Crete and the Peloponnese at the end of the Late Bronze Age. The LH IIIB houses at Nichoria were abandoned for reasons that remain unclear. Eventually the settlement was reoccupied, probably in the eleventh century. The stone foundations of the Mycenaean houses were evidently still visible and may have been used to support flimsy shelters. In due course the village expanded and houses were built with wattle and daub or mudbrick walls and thatched roofs. Most of these houses had only one room and were very small, 4.00 by 3.75 meters in the case of Unit III-1. However, there was a much larger house, Unit IV-1, which measured 15.90 by 8.00 meters (figure 4.14). It had stone foundations and mudbrick walls. Wooden posts supported the steeply pitched roof. The architectural history of this house is not entirely clear but a fenced courtyard is restored in front of the porch. A circular stone platform was found in the main room and there were storage pits in the apsidal room at the back of the house. The size and central location of Unit IV-1 suggest that the most powerful person in the village lived here and that the house was a focal point for the community. If the circular stone platform was an altar, it is possible that this was where they worshiped.

Around 1000 BC Greek settlers occupied Old Smyrna on the west coast of Turkey. The site was a promontory which they protected with a massive fortification wall in the ninth century (figure 8.23). Their houses were not as ambitious and one of the best-preserved measures just 4.50 by 3.00 meters (figure 4.15a & b). It had rounded corners, was built of mudbrick, and is restored with a thatched roof. There were also blocks of houses. This same mixture of architectural styles is equally characteristic of the eighth-century houses at Smyrna.

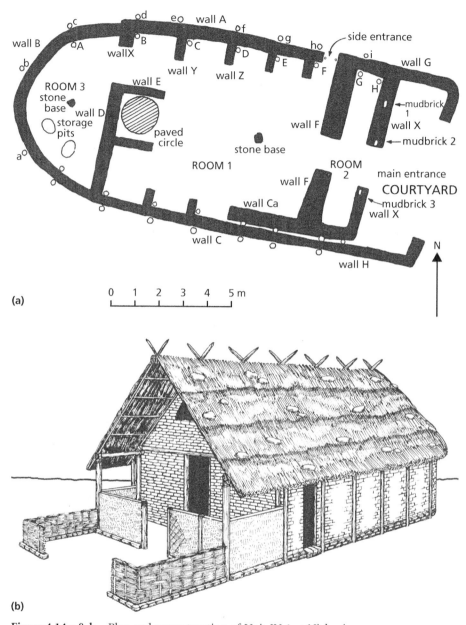

**(a)**

**(b)**

**Figure 4.14 a & b**   Plan and reconstruction of Unit IV-1 at Nichoria

Zagora on Andros is another fortified coastal site. The settlement was founded before the end of the tenth century but the population moved away around 700 BC, perhaps because by then they were less concerned about defense and wanted a better harbor with a good water supply. Plenty of stone was available, particularly schist, which splits into flat slabs. This was used for the walls, thresholds, and door frames,

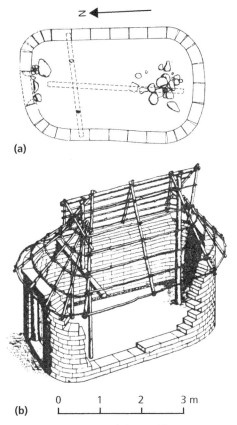

(a)

(b)

Figure 4.15a & b   Plan and restoration of the oval house at Smyrna

as well as the benches that were found in a number of the houses (figure 4.16). Some of the rooms were quite large and the roof beams would have been supported on wooden posts. The roofs were flat and consisted of a layer of thin schist slabs covered in clay. The blocks of houses must have been planned because the alignment of the walls is so consistent (figure 2.8). However, individual houses differ in size and the layout of the rooms also varies. The construction of the houses was evidently phased and many had been altered after they were built. For example H24/H25/H32 and H26/H27 were originally single rooms which were later partitioned. Because of the way that the houses were constructed, it is not always obvious which rooms belong together, and in any case this could be changed. There were originally three separate houses in the center of the settlement: H19/H21, H22/H23, and H28/H29. Then H22 and H28 were given side doors so that they could also be entered from H21, which was a courtyard. H19 was the main room in this complex, with a hearth and a stone bench in which storage vessels were fixed in place. Food was evidently kept and cooked in H19, some meals were eaten in H22, and H28 was a storeroom. Size and location suggest that someone in authority may have occupied this house,

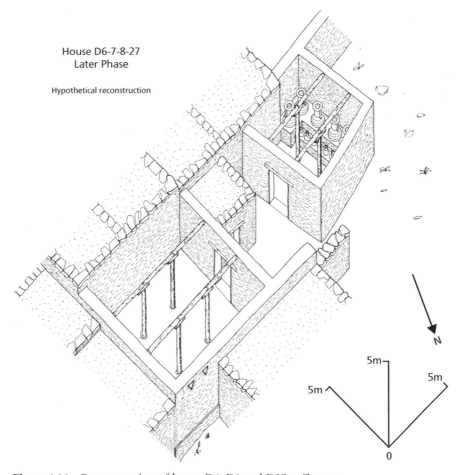

House D6-7-8-27
Later Phase

Hypothetical reconstruction

**Figure 4.16**   Reconstruction of house D6–D8 and D27 at Zagora

which is near the sanctuary. This outlasted the settlement and a temple, H30/H31, was built here in the ruins of the town in the sixth century.

## The Archaic and Classical Periods

In the Archaic period there were fewer apsidal and oval houses. One reason for this was the use of terracotta roof tiles instead of thatch. Rounded corners were fine for thatch but a rectangular ground plan provided better support for a tiled roof. Other structural improvements were also introduced. Stone foundations became more substantial and walls were strengthened with a timber framework, so that a second story could be added. Another trend, foreshadowed at Zagora in the eighth century, is an increase in the number of rooms in houses, which meant that some separation of household activities was possible. We also see a significant change in the layout

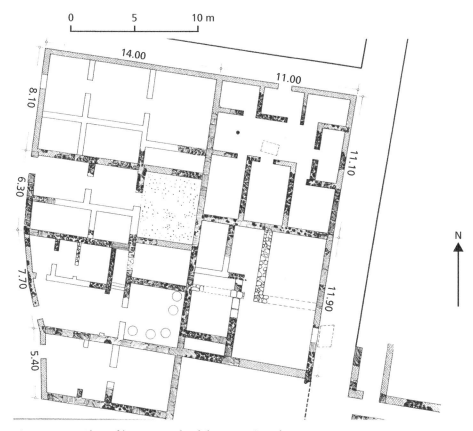

**Figure 4.17**  Plan of houses south of the Agora in Athens

of rooms. In an apsidal house the rooms were arranged axially. It was therefore
necessary to go through one room to enter the next. Now there was often a hall or
internal court and each room opened off this, which allowed a greater degree of
privacy. Since the court could be used for outdoor activities, members of the household would have had less contact with their neighbors. The idea that women should
be kept secluded, especially if male guests were present, may have prompted some
of these changes.

This new type of house can be seen in fifth-century Athens. A block of six houses
has been excavated south of the Agora (figure 4.17). The one which occupies the
northeast corner of the block had a porch which shielded the court from view. The
other rooms opened off the court and were not interconnected. The southwest house
is much smaller and the court was entered directly from the street. Although part
of the court was roofed, this would not have screened the main room. In the next
house the room opposite the entrance was full of storage jars. However, the rest of
the rooms could not be seen from the street. In a crowded city privacy was not
guaranteed. Not far away there were two houses which illustrate the way that the
irregular street system of Athens created awkwardly shaped plots (figure 4.18). One

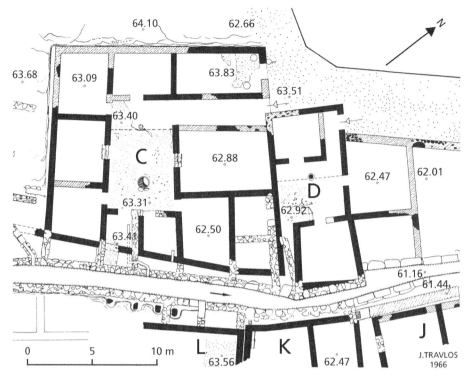

**Figure 4.18**   Plan of houses west of the Areopagos in Athens

of the rooms in House C opened onto the street and this may have been a shop. A long corridor led from the entrance into the court around which the other rooms were arranged. In the fourth century the two houses were joined together and D was used as a smithy. This sort of industrial activity must have been quite common in the houses near the Agora.

There were obviously fewer space constraints in the countryside. A large house was built near the Dema wall north of Athens in the late fifth century (figure 4.19a & b). Through the porch (VII) was a court (VIII) with a bathroom (IX) in one corner. The north side of the court was roofed over so that the main rooms would be protected from the glare of the sun but were still well lit and the occupants of the house could work outside whatever the weather. It is not entirely clear how each room was used but I may have been a dining room, II an annexe for III, the kitchen/ living room; IV has a hearth, V and VI were possibly work rooms. An upper floor seems likely and this is where the more private rooms would presumably have been. The Vari House in southern Attica is later in date, fourth or early third century, but has many similar features (figure 4.20a & b). The main entrance led directly into the court VIII. A portico of five columns shaded the rooms on the north side of the court. The house was occupied for some time, and various alterations were made to the rooms. The fitted pantry in the corner of I suggests that this was the kitchen.

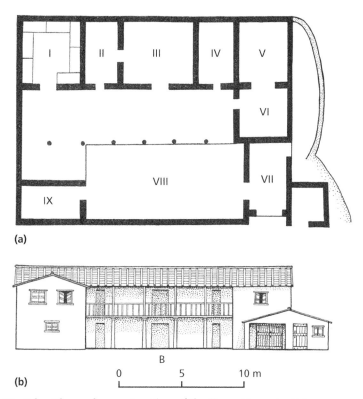

**Figure 4.19a & b** Plan and reconstruction of the Dema House in Attica

III, originally the largest room, was later subdivided, and a couch was fitted into IV so that three people could eat here. In VI and IX there was a long stone bench. Most of the interior walls are quite narrow and could not have taken the weight of an upper floor. However, room VII is much more sturdily built and it is thought that this was a two- or three-story tower. Isolated houses in the countryside were evidently at risk of attack.

A number of fourth-century houses have been excavated at Halieis in the Argolid (figure 4.21a & b). The first part of the house that anyone entered was the court (7-7), which was surrounded by a high wall and ensured some privacy. A well in the court provided the main water supply and household waste was composted in a large stone-lined pit. Inside the house there was often a general purpose room where meals were eaten (7-12). House 7 also had a more formal dining room (7-9) or andron with an anteroom (7-10) which opened directly off the court. 7-9 is identified as an andron because of the platform which runs around the room and the off-center door. The couches for the diners were set up on the platform and the position of the door ensured that all of the wall space could be utilized. The andron was often the best room in a Greek house and guests were entertained here. In particular it was where men met for symposia, in which the emphasis was on conviviality and the consumption of drink. On these occasions the andron, literally the

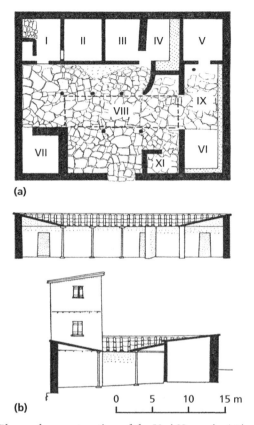

**Figure 4.20a & b**   Plan and reconstruction of the Vari House in Attica

room of the men, may have been a male preserve and care was taken to minimize contact between the guests and the women in the house. Visitors could go straight into the andron in House 7 and were kept away from the rest of the rooms. This does not mean that the andron was only ever used by men or that the male and female members of the household had separate quarters. The rigid gender divisions implied in some literary sources were certainly more flexible in practice. The houses at Halieis had kitchens: rooms 7-16 and 7-17 in the case of House 7. The fixed hearth that had been installed here is not a feature which is found in many of the other houses and most families must have cooked on portable braziers. Also on the first floor was a bathroom (7-11) and storerooms (possibly 7-14 and 7-15). The second-floor rooms could be reached by a staircase in the corner of the court. This was presumably where the bedrooms were situated, though no doubt these rooms had other uses in the daytime.

Olynthos on the Chalkidiki peninsula in Macedonia is a key site for the study of Greek houses. At first only the south hill was occupied but in 432/1 Olynthos was made the capital of a regional federation and many of the inhabitants of the other Greek cities in Chalkidiki moved there. Because of this influx a new suburb was laid

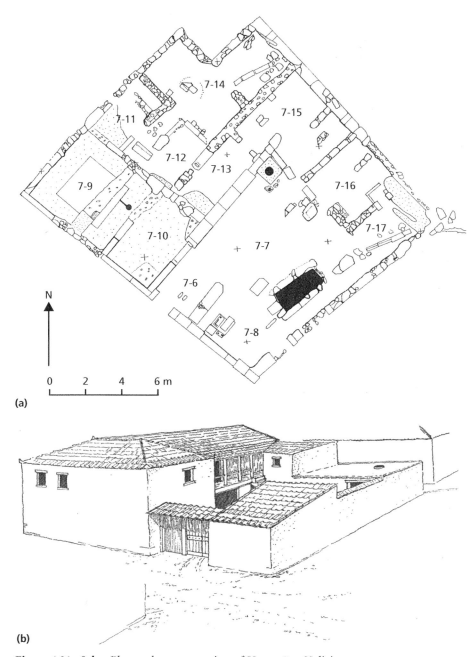

N

0   2   4   6 m

(a)

(b)

**Figure 4.21a & b** Plan and reconstruction of House 7 at Halieis

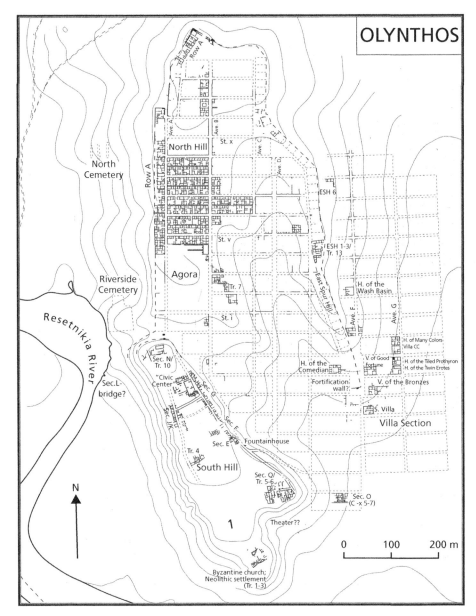

**Figure 4.22**    Plan of Olynthos

out on the north hill and on the plain east of the city. By the fourth century the federation was extremely powerful and this led to a clash with Philip II, the Macedonian ruler, who captured and destroyed Olynthos in 348. Most of the inhabitants were sold into slavery and the city never recovered from this disaster.

The irregular streets and houses on the south hill contrast with the precise Hippodamian grid plan and neatly built blocks of houses on the north hill (figure 4.22). An open space on the west side may have been the agora. Broad north–south

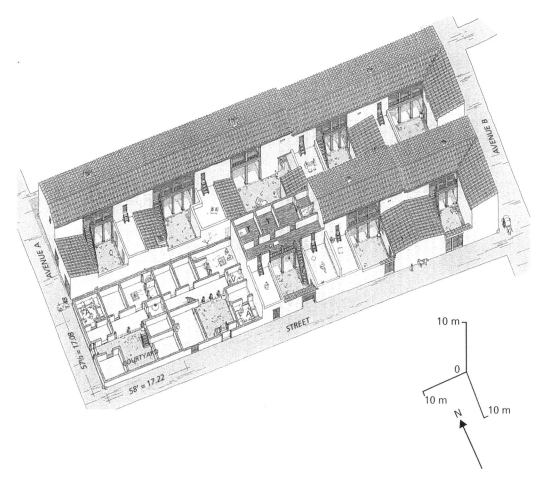

**Figure 4.23**   Reconstruction of a block of houses at Olynthos

avenues and east–west streets formed rectangular blocks, typically with two rows of five houses separated by a narrow back alley. The grid also extended onto the plain and many of the houses there were larger. The total extent of the city was around 50 hectares, of which approximately 5 hectares have been excavated and over 100 houses investigated.

The rows of houses in the blocks on the north hill must have been constructed at the same time because the outside walls were bonded together. Slight structural differences suggest that each house was built by a separate team of workmen, probably the owners assisted by relatives and friends. Because the roof over the houses in a row was continuous, some of the interior walls had to be aligned in order to support the main beams but the configuration of the rooms did not need to be the same (figure 4.23). It is therefore remarkable that the houses were so similar, though certainly not identical—there was no standard plan prescribed by the city

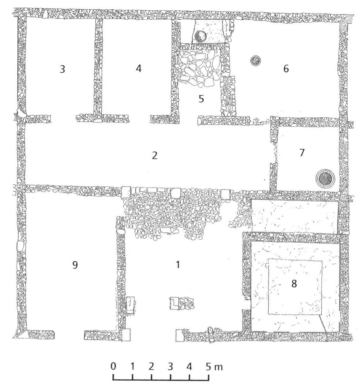

**Figure 4.24**   Plan of House A vii 4 at Olynthos

authorities. However, practical requirements, social constraints, tradition, and imitation did create a basic template.

A vii 4 is fairly typical of the houses on the north hill (figure 4.24). Through the double doors of the entrance there was a porch and this led into a cobbled court (1), for which a location on the south side of the house was always preferred. The court had been used for various different activities and a loom may have been set up here. On the north side of the court was a roofed portico (2). This well-lit room, known as the pastas, was also multipurpose. Pottery had been stored on shelves or in chests at the west end of the room and a set of weights and scales was also kept here. Most of the first-floor rooms opened directly off the court or the pastas. There were very few finds in the room in the northwest corner of the house (3) but another set of loomweights and more pottery came from the next room (4). A feature of many houses at Olynthos is the three-room kitchen complex. Food was prepared in the kitchen (6) and cooked in the flue (5), which had a layer of ash on the floor. The smoke from the flue went up a chimney. In the corner between the kitchen and the flue was the bathroom, though in this case the terracotta bathtub had been removed. The water would be heated over the fire in the flue which also kept the bathroom warm. By the kitchen was a storeroom with a pithos still in situ (7). On the east side of the court was the andron (8), separated from the rest of the house by an anteroom. These were the only rooms which had been painted, and in some houses the andron had a mosaic floor. The room opposite the andron (9) could be entered from the court or from the street and may have been a shop. Many households apparently ran small businesses. As there was a staircase in the court, A vii 4 was evidently one of the houses which had an upper floor.

The finds from the houses at Olynthos suggest that rooms were seldom used for just one purpose. The time of year will have been a factor because it can be very cold in the winter in Macedonia and the kitchen complex would be the best place to work then. Items associated with female activities were more common there but were also found in every other part of the house, so there does not seem to have been any restriction on where women could go, except perhaps for the andron when male guests were present.

Another type of Classical house is best represented at Priene, on the west coast of Turkey, where approximately 70 houses have been excavated. In a typical block there were eight houses, each of which has a court with rooms on either side (figure 4.25a & b). The court occupied the full width of the house and was shaded by the rooms on the south side of the row, which were used for storage and as workshops. The main apartments were entered through a porch, or prostas, with one or two columns. Off this was the andron which only had space for three couches—symposia at Priene must have been more private occasions. The largest room in the house, the oikos, was positioned behind the porch, like the cella in a temple. This arrangement also recalls the megaron-style houses of previous periods and may indicate a more conservative architectural tradition. The room off the oikos was secluded and quite dark. It could have been a bedroom, though there were also rooms well away from visitors on the second floor.

## The Later Fourth Century and the Hellenistic Period

The Athenian politician Demosthenes (*Aristokrates* 207) claimed that fifth-century statesmen, like Perikles, lived quite simply whereas his fourth-century contemporaries demanded more luxurious houses. Although there was an element of rhetorical exaggeration in this statement, it is certainly true that some fourth-century houses were much larger and more sumptuously decorated. Houses had now become a medium for the rich and powerful to display their wealth and status in a way that we have not seen before. This new trend for extravagance is typified by some of the houses at Eretria on Euboia.

In the center of the House of the Mosaics was a peristyle court. The columns supported a roof around the sides of the court and shaded the rooms from the sun (figure 4.26). Room 9 was an andron with space for seven couches, entered through an anteroom (8). Both of these rooms had pebble mosaic floors. Room 7 was also an andron with 11 couches and room 5 was probably a three-couch andron. Room 4 was evidently some sort of reception room. There was a well in one corner of

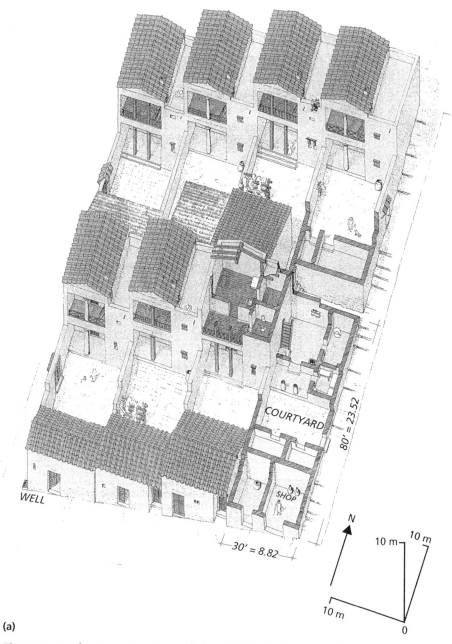

WELL

COURTYARD

SHOP

$80' = 23.52$

$30' = 8.82$

N

10 m

10 m

10 m

0

(a)

**Figure 4.25a & b**    Reconstruction and plan of a block of houses at Priene

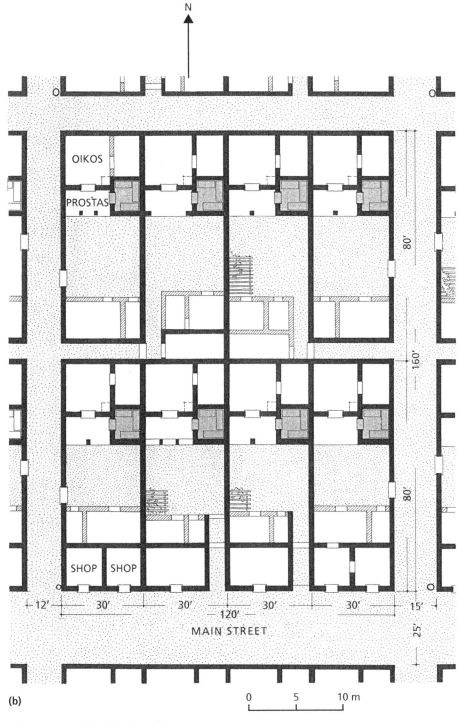

**Figure 4.25a & b**   (*Continued*)

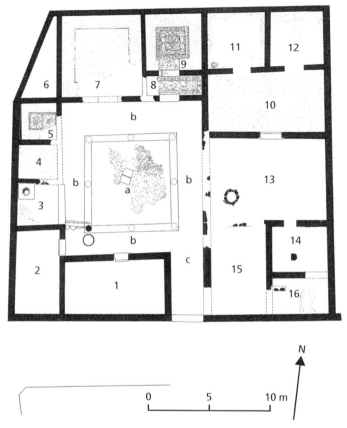

**Figure 4.26**  Plan of the House of the Mosaics at Eretria

room 3 and 1 was a storeroom. A door in the wall on the east side of the court led into 13. This was a second court and also had a well. As room 14 is identified as a kitchen and 16 as a bathroom, these must have been the private apartments. The rooms in this part of the house were not as well decorated but did have pebble floors and stuccoed walls.

House II on the west side of the city was even larger, over 1000 m², and had many of the same features (figure 4.27a & b). There was a spacious peristyle court with a well and a water channel. The suite of rooms on the north side of the court replicates the arrangement in the House of the Mosaics. Room f was a seven-couch andron with an anteroom (g); 11 couches could be fitted into room e and probably three more in m. The second court (1) was more private and the rooms which opened off this again included a kitchen (a), a bathroom (a1), and three bedrooms (b–d). We see a greater emphasis on the entertainment of guests in these houses at Eretria. This was a way for the rich to expand their social network and enhance their position. As houses became more public, the additional court and the rooms that opened off it ensured a proper level of privacy for female members of the family when guests were present.

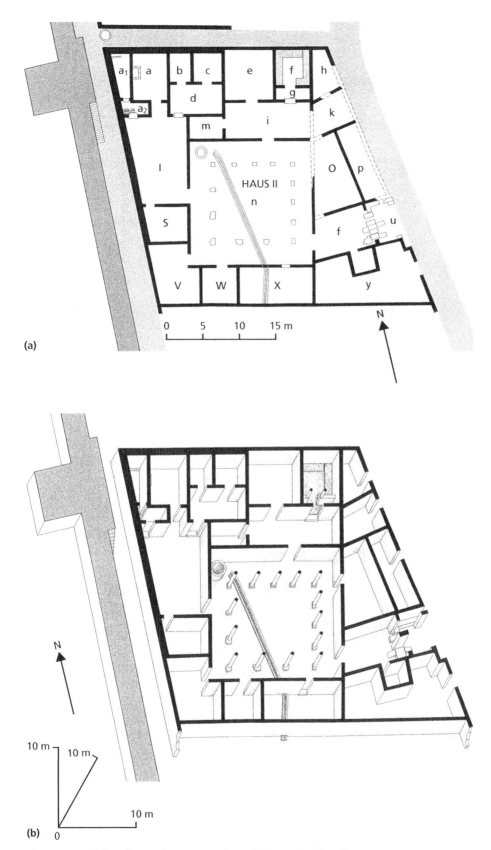

**Figure 4.27a & b** Plan and reconstruction of House II at Eretria

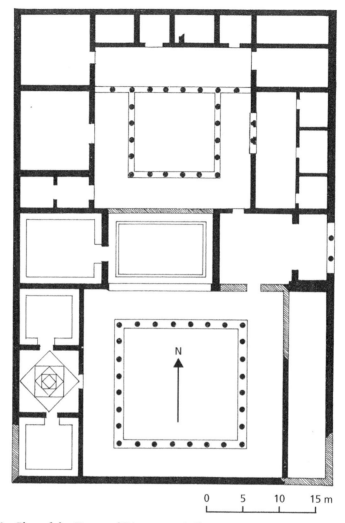

**Figure 4.28**   Plan of the House of Dionysos at Pella

Some of the late fourth-century houses at Pella in Macedonia were positively palatial. The House of Dionysos was over 3000 m$^2$ and occupied most of a city block (figure 4.28). Again it is of the type with two courts but they are more formally laid out. The rooms around the north court are quite small and it seems likely that these were the private apartments. There was evidently an upper story above the rooms at the north end of the court. The main entrance was on the east side of the house and brought visitors into the reception rooms around the south court. The androns here had superb pebble mosaic floors and each was entered through a large ante-room. Other grand houses at Pella have similarly impressive facilities for the banquets which the Macedonians enjoyed so much. The influence of the palaces and of the royal lifestyle is obvious—these houses were conspicuously glitzy.

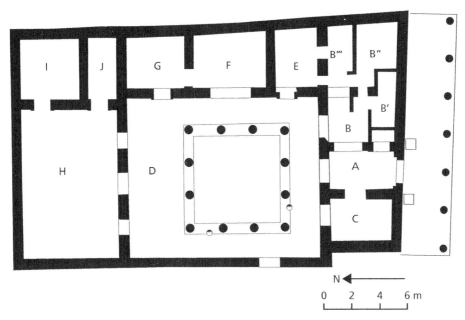

**Figure 4.29**  Plan of the House of the Dolphins on Delos

The island of Delos was made a tax-free port in 166 BC and became a major
commercial center. It was a base for the slave trade, as well as the export of wine
and oil. The population was remarkably cosmopolitan, with merchants and bankers
from Italy, Greece, and the East. As the settlement grew in size, the district around
the theater developed rather chaotically, though north of the sacred lake the residential blocks were laid out more carefully. Houses of different sizes, shops, and
business premises were built side by side. The houses, of which over 100 have been
excavated, do not have a set plan. There is often a court in the center and service
rooms at the front of the house with the main rooms at the back. However, many
were altered so that visitors, who will have included clients and customers, could
appreciate the wealth and taste of the owner. Houses were enlarged, entrance and
reception rooms were added, courts were given peristyle porticoes. Some rooms
were sumptuously decorated with mosaic floors, frescoed walls, and marble statues.
The House of the Dolphins is particularly impressive (figure 4.29). Altars had been
placed on either side of the entrance and the symbol of the Phoenician lunar
goddess Tanit was on the mosaic floor in the vestibule (A). The peristyle court had
Doric columns and the eponymous dolphin mosaic in the center. Three doors led
into the main room of the house (H), which was flanked by side rooms (I and J).
Additional reception rooms opened off the court (F and G). The service rooms at
the front of the house included a lavatory (B′) and a kitchen (B″). The architecture
of the houses on Delos is essentially Greek but some Italian influence can be seen.
With such an emphasis on display, there may also have been less of a concern for
privacy here.

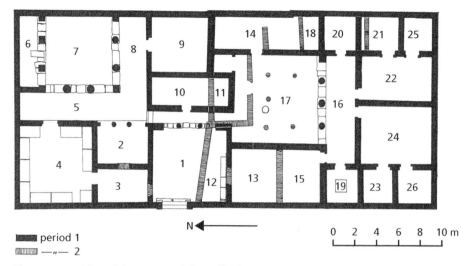

**Figure 4.30**  Plan of the House of the Official at Morgantina

Across the Greek world, houses at the top end of the size range have much more in common in the Hellenistic period. The houses in southern Italy and Sicily had previously been quite different in style, but from the late fourth century there is a gradual assimilation of mainland Greek traits. This culminates in the appearance of houses which have two courts, at sites such as Megara Hyblaia and Morgantina, in the third century. These houses were more ostentatious and fit in with the general trend for the rich to use their homes as a medium for self-promotion. The House of the Official at Morgantina (figure 4.30) also suggests that the social conventions implicit in houses of this type in Greece were accepted in Sicily. The reception rooms were grouped together in the southern half of the house and kept quite separate from the domestic apartments around the north court.

## Conclusions

Houses tell us much about the way that people structured their lives. Sometimes we see common design elements which suggest that certain modes of behavior were widely shared. Yet there is always flexibility, and the function of rooms could vary. Houses represented stability but were constantly modified. They reflect the composition and also the character of the household.

The construction methods introduced in the Neolithic period proved remarkably resilient because the available raw materials were used so effectively. Traditions soon developed, especially on tell sites where houses were often rebuilt again and again, which must have reinforced the sense of continuity. In some cases space was partitioned off or demarcated for particular activities. How households were organized and interacted is particularly clear at Myrtos. This is a different, almost organic style of architecture, made possible by the limited extent of the settlement. Many sites on Crete were already built up, none more so than Knossos, where the construction of the palace complex in MM I would have been extremely disruptive. The formal arrangement of the reception rooms in the palaces is replicated in some of the Minoan villas and houses which were evidently not just designed as private residences but had a more public role as well. This may have caused tensions and would explain why circulation was so carefully controlled. The modular system of blocks of rooms had practical advantages and also allowed a separation of social and household activities.

Cretan influence is obvious at Akrotiri in the way that the houses were built and in features such as the use of pier and door partitions. The frescoes strengthen the impression of a transplanted lifestyle, but much of the architecture of the town was still Cycladic. The houses in mainland Greece were much less impressive. The typical Middle Bronze Age megaron has just one or two main rooms, though there were more substantial houses at some sites, such as Asine. The surprise is that the quality of the architecture does not improve more markedly in the Mycenaean period. Even at Mycenae the houses were not particularly grand compared with those on Crete. Nichoria demonstrates the variety of house styles that coexisted. The Mycenaeans do not seem to have conceived of their houses in terms of a structured set of principles.

The contrast between Crete and Greece continued in the Early Iron Age. Minoan traditions were maintained at Karphi, despite the difficulties presented by such a precipitous site. On the mainland most of the houses were very small and not well constructed, though some were extended as status distinctions became more pronounced. The process can be followed at Zagora as the blocks of houses laid out when the site was first occupied were gradually modified. We also see a greater division of space within the houses. This increase in the number of rooms is a key feature of Archaic and Classical houses. As the rooms could not be arranged axially, one behind the other, a common point of access was required. Usually this was an internal court which brought the outside inside the house and ensured privacy. So interaction between households was fundamentally affected by these changes, as well as movement around the house. No doubt women were believed to need protection but the implication is also that households must have operated more independently. The subtle variations in the way that houses were laid out in the blocks at Olynthos expresses this independence, though an element of socially constrained conformity is evident. There may have been an emphasis on privacy, yet parts of the house were on display, in particular the andron which was often expensively decorated. The trend in the Hellenistic period is for houses to be opened up and become much more opulent. Certainly for the rich they were now the most conspicuous measure of success.

## Bibliographical notes

Neolithic domestic architecture is discussed by Andreou et al. 2001, Perlès 2001, and Souvatzi 2008. See Pyke and Yiouni 1996 for Nea Nikomedeia, Warren 1972 and Whitelaw 1983 and 2007 for Myrtos, Tzavella-Evjen 1985 for Lithares, Nordquist 1987 for Asine, and Forsén 1992 on the changes at the start of the Middle Bronze Age in mainland Greece. The Cretan evidence is reviewed in Cadogan 1976, Graham 1987, Myers et al. 1992, Hägg 1997, and Rehak and Younger 2001. The farm at Mochlos is decribed in Soles 2003. For the Cyclades in general see Barber 1987 and Davis 2001, and for Akrotiri Doumas 1983 and Palyvou 2005. Darcque 2005 is a comprehensive study of Mycenaean domestic architecture; McDonald and Wilkie 1992 cover Nichoria, Mylonas Shear 1987 and Tournavitou 1995 the houses at Mycenae. The Early Iron Age evidence is discussed in depth in Mazarakis Ainian 1997 and also in Coldstream 1977, Lemos 2002, and Dickinson 2006. See Nowicki 2000 for Crete, McDonald et al. 1983 for Nichoria, and Cambitoglou et al. 1971 and 1988 for Zagora. Nevett 1999 is excellent on Archaic, Classical, and Hellenistic domestic architecture; Hoepfner and Schwandner 1994 and Ault and Nevett 2005 should also be consulted. See Ault 2005 for Halieis; Robinson and Graham 1938 and Cahill 2002 for Olynthos; Ducrey et al. 1993 and Reber 1998 and 2007 for Eretria; Siganidou and Lilimpaki-Akamati 1996 for Pella; Bruneau and Ducat 2005, Tang 2005, and Trümper 2007 for Delos.

# CHAPTER 5

# The Countryside

## Introduction

The Greeks depended on the countryside but it was not easy to live off the land. Greece is mountainous and only around 20 percent of the country is relatively flat. Even though hill slopes can be cultivated and mountain sides grazed, good agricultural land is limited. The Mediterranean climate is also a challenge, because rainfall is low and fluctuates from year to year. It is higher in the north and west of Greece, yet even over quite short distances there may be significant variations. The mountains are wetter and supply most of the water in the rivers but these generally run dry in the summer. Although the climate was evidently cooler and moister at the start of the Neolithic, it had become more arid by the Bronze Age and conditions have remained much the same since then.

Farmers in the past and indeed more recently have led a precarious existence, so how did they cope with the threat of starvation? The response has traditionally been diversification. It makes sense to grow a range of crops and exploit whatever other resources may be available. Scattered plots of land can provide a mosaic of micro-environments which further reduces the risk of crop failure. In traditional agriculture there are no rules about what should be grown where and farmers often plant different crops side by side. Nevertheless the best land tends to be used for cereals, in particular wheat and barley, and pulses. Terraced hill slopes are a characteristic feature of the Greek landscape (figure 5.1). They level out the slope, conserve water, and control erosion. Cereals, vines, olives, and other tree crops are all found on these terraces. Land which cannot be cultivated and has typical Mediterranean maquis or phrygana vegetation is grazed by sheep and goats. Pigs forage in the woods and forests are a source of timber and fuel. Every ecological niche is utilized.

Of course we cannot simply transpose recent agricultural practices back into the past, not least because the landscape has changed. There has certainly been

*Greek Archaeology: A Thematic Approach*   By Christopher Mee
© 2011 Christopher Mee

**Figure 5.1**   Terraces on Methana

deforestation, if not on the scale that was once envisaged. Erosion and alluviation have transformed the coastline in places. Wetlands have been drained and the sea level has risen considerably since the Mesolithic period. Still it is instructive to see how Greek farmers have planned for the bad years that they know they will face. One obvious strategy is the production of a surplus which can be stored and used in the event of a shortage in the future. After a particularly good harvest, some of the surplus may be fed to livestock, sold, or exchanged. Loans to needy neighbors, in the expectation that the favor will be returned or repaid, are a form of indirect storage. In this chapter we will look at the ways in which the countryside was exploited in the past and the social consequences.

## The First Farmers

The introduction of agriculture in the Neolithic period was a momentous development. The sequence of events can best be followed at Franchthi in the Argolid. The Mesolithic inhabitants of the cave hunted red deer and wild boar, fished for tuna, and gathered a range of plants which included wild oats, barley, and lentils. In the earliest Neolithic levels most of the animal bones come from sheep and goats. There were also pigs and in due course cattle. The seeds indicate that emmer, einkorn, and barley were cultivated. In addition, new types of chipped stone tools, made from obsidian, flint, or chert, were used to harvest cereals. The evidence from Franchthi suggests that the transition from a hunter-gatherer lifestyle may have been a gradual process. The plants and animals that make up the Neolithic agricultural "package" did not all appear simultaneously but over a period of several centuries. A key question is whether they were domesticated in Greece or introduced from elsewhere. Cereals and pulses did form part of the diet at Mesolithic Franchthi. However, most of the plants that were grown by Neolithic farmers came from the Near East. Similarly, although a case could be made for the domestication of wild boar and cattle, the first sheep and goats were not native species.

That agriculture spread from the Near East does seem likely. One possibility is that farmers moved west from Anatolia through Thrace and Macedonia or across the Aegean. Alternatively the Mesolithic inhabitants of Greece could have acquired the technology. This theory has been questioned because the number of known Mesolithic sites suggests that the population was very low. However, if coastal locations were favored, which does seem to have been the case, the postglacial rise in sea level would have destroyed many sites. So the size of the indigenous population has probably been underestimated. Nevertheless some people evidently did move, since Crete was colonized at the start of the Neolithic period by settlers who must have arrived with their livestock and supplies of seed.

Clearly the introduction of agriculture was a complex phenomenon and cannot easily be explained. It is possible that environmental changes had reduced the resources that were available to Mesolithic foragers and consequently they became farmers. Yet this can hardly have been the motivation for the first settlers on Crete. They were already farmers, there was surely no lack of suitable land wherever they had came from, so why would they have undertaken such a risky venture? It is significant that the origin of these settlers has not been determined. Culturally they have no obvious affinities with groups in Anatolia, which is considered their most likely point of departure, or Greece. Instead they rapidly created their own identity and this highlights the social dimension. The spread of agriculture involved choices. It was not an inevitable process driven by purely economic considerations. This may explain why the major outcome is a new social construct, the village communities of Neolithic Greece.

These communities relied almost exclusively on agriculture for their subsistence needs. Wild animal bones, mainly red deer and hare, account for only 5 percent or so of the faunal assemblage on most Neolithic sites. Nor is there much evidence that wild plants were systematically collected, but here we must bear in mind the issue of preservation and also the recovery techniques used. It is easier to identify plants which have been cooked or processed for storage rather than eaten raw. Although figs and other fruits did form part of the diet, cereals and pulses were the staples. This apparent reluctance to exploit wild food resources is understandable, given the extra effort that was involved. Nevertheless the emphasis on cultivated plants and domesticated animals has been seen as symbolic. Certainly those parts of the countryside which had been tamed and those which were still wild would have been perceived very differently.

The most common cereals in the Neolithic period were einkorn and emmer. Barley, which can tolerate drier conditions, is also found on most sites. The main pulse crops were lentils, peas, and bitter vetch. It is difficult to calculate the relative importance of cereals and pulses because of the factors that influence their identification archaeologically. Charred plant remains would not only have been unfit for consumption but also tend to be more resilient. Some cereals, such as emmer, were parched in order to remove the husk and therefore were more likely to be accidentally charred than pulses which were boiled. So the high proportion of cereals in most seed samples could reflect a taphonomic bias, in other words their higher survival rate. Probably most Neolithic farmers grew a range of cereals and pulses. Diversification provided a measure of security, since some species are more drought-resistant, and this would ensure a reasonable crop even in a year when the rainfall was low. Crop rotation would also have maintained soil fertility because pulses restore the nitrogen which cereal cultivation depletes.

It seems likely that land was used intensively with a high input of labor to maximize yields. Farmers may have been able to produce as much as 1000 kg of cereals and pulses per hectare, sufficient to feed five people for a year. So even if allowance is made for some fallow and the fact that it was essential to aim for more than the minimum requirement, the 300 hectares of land within a 1-kilometer radius of a settlement would easily have been enough for a typical Neolithic village. Farmers would not have had far to travel to their fields, which was obviously an advantage, but it does emphasize how isolated communities could potentially have become.

Of course there was another component in the agricultural system, namely livestock, and it is easy to imagine that animals grazed well away from the village. Traditional transhumant shepherds can spend the whole of the summer in the mountains and only return for the winter months. The movement of flocks and herds would therefore bring communities into contact and perhaps make the wild countryside seem less dangerous. However, it is significant that sheep were more common than goats, pigs, or cattle on most Neolithic sites, as they could be grazed on cleared land which their manure would fertilize or on fields sown for fodder. So this preference for sheep suggests that animals were generally kept near the village.

Sheep in particular store fat well and could be fed any surplus food that was left over after a successful year, then killed off if necessary. The age at which they were slaughtered implies that they were reared for their meat, rather than milk or wool. Nevertheless a sheep would have produced far more meat than a household could easily have consumed and there is no evidence that carcasses were processed so that some could be stored. When pigs or cattle were killed even more meat would have been available. So it is assumed that this would be the occasion for a suprahousehold feast which brought the community together. Indeed the opportunity may have been taken to invite people from other settlements and thereby establish or reinforce social ties which could be vital in times of need.

## The Secondary Products Revolution and Mediterranean Polyculture Revisited

In southern Greece there is an expansion into more marginal environments in the Late and Final Neolithic period. We now find sites on poorer soils and where the rainfall is lower. Given the risks that this move entailed, the obvious explanation is population growth and consequently a need for more agricultural land. Yet the number of known settlements does not suggest that resources had become seriously overstretched.

Many of these new sites were in locations which provided good access to pasture, as well as some arable land. Caves were also occupied at this time and may have been used by shepherds. So there seems to have been more of an emphasis on livestock. Study of the animal bones indicates greater diversity with an increase in the number of goats, pigs, and cattle, though sheep still feature prominently. Local environmental factors evidently influenced the composition of the herds. Sheep and particularly goats are the dominant species at cave sites because they could graze on scrubby vegetation. Cattle and pigs are more common on lowland sites where better pasture was available and they could forage in woodland.

Does this diversity indicate specialization? Many of the Final Neolithic sites in marginal locations were small and short-lived. Was this because they were occupied by groups of pastoralists on a temporary basis, possibly transhumant shepherds who grazed their herds in the lowlands in the winter and then moved them up into the mountains for the summer? It is difficult to determine whether a settlement was permanent or seasonal but the fact that some of the animals were killed when they were still young implies that the sites were occupied in the late winter or early spring. Moreover, in most cases there was arable land nearby. So it seems likely that these groups relied more heavily but not exclusively on livestock. Presumably they exchanged some of what they produced with farmers in the lowlands. They were probably not dependent on these transactions, though the consequence could have been a measure of interdependency. Animals were in some respects a luxury because cereals and pulses would have provided basic subsistence needs more efficiently and reliably. The possession of livestock may therefore have signified wealth and in fact there does seem to have been greater inequality in the Late Neolithic period. The provision of meat for communal feasts would have conferred status and consequently created a demand for animals. Perhaps this encouraged a more systematic exploitation of the resources that the countryside offered.

It has been suggested that animals were now kept for their "secondary products" and not just as a source of meat. Milk could be converted into a range of dairy products and wool made into textiles. If this was the primary role of livestock we would expect a change in the composition of the herds and the age at which animals were slaughtered. In fact most sheep and goats were still killed between 6 months and 4 years of age, presumably for their meat. Nevertheless, there is some evidence for dairy products. Large jars with holes around the rim may have been used to make cheese and the wider range of storage vessels could indicate that new types of food needed to be preserved. A further possibility is that cattle were worked as draft animals. Traction-induced stress marks on some of the bones from Knossos could have resulted from the use of cattle to pull plows. However, it was some time before animal power was systematically utilized. For most of the Neolithic period fields were apparently tilled by hand. The reason was probably the cost which the upkeep of draft animals would have entailed.

The plant remains from later Neolithic sites do not indicate any major changes in the cereals that were cultivated. The most common types of wheat were still emmer and einkorn. Bread wheat is sometimes found but grows best in soils with a higher moisture content than is typical for much of southern Greece. These dry conditions favored barley and the more productive six-row variety now replaces two-row barley. There is some evidence that a wider range of pulses was being grown with chickpeas and horse beans, as well as lentils, peas, and bitter vetch.

The suggestion that the move into more marginal environments was made possible by the domestication of the olive and the vine has been questioned. Wild varieties of both of these species are found in Greece and it is not always easy to differentiate wild and domesticated olive stones and grape pips, especially if the sample is small. So the occasional appearance of olives and grapes on Neolithic sites is not conclusive. Even in the Late Bronze Age, when the palaces stored large quantities of oil and wine, there is not a marked increase in the number of olive stones and grape pips. Evidently the way that the fruit was processed did not generally result in archaeologically detectable residues, so we cannot be sure when the olive and the vine were fully domesticated. It was probably a gradual process and may have been one of a number of adaptations that opened up the Greek countryside.

The initial expansion in the Final Neolithic period was followed by a gradual spread of settlement across the landscape in the Early Bronze Age. This involved the clearance of woodland and cultivation on hill slopes, activities which could have increased the risk of erosion. Indeed it has been argued that one consequence was catastrophic erosion which ultimately forced many sites to be abandoned. However, while it is true that some major erosion episodes can be dated to the Early Bronze Age, this was not a widespread phenomenon. Moreover it is uncertain how the type of agriculture that was practiced at this time could have triggered massive erosion. Extreme weather events or earthquakes are a much more likely cause. Similarly the theory that the abandonment of sites was followed by hill-slope degradation ignores the rate at which the natural vegetation regenerates and consequently inhibits soil loss. Agriculture undoubtedly had an impact on the Greek landscape but not on the scale that has sometimes been suggested.

## Royal Estates

When the first Minoan palaces were built at Knossos and Phaistos in MM I, the provision of storage facilities for agricultural produce was clearly a priority. Those who were resident in or worked for the palace were presumably the main beneficiaries. Supplies may also have been needed for feasts and festivals. Nevertheless, it seems likely that there was a surplus which was held in reserve so that support could be offered in a crisis. A guarantee of protection from starvation would have made taxation and consequently some loss of self-sufficiency more acceptable, even if the palaces obviously gained the most from this redistributive economic system.

One question which arises is whether the palaces simply received a proportion of what was produced or took a more interventionist role. Redistribution does create opportunities for greater agricultural specialization, theoretically at least, because the center can regulate exchange between communities. This would allow a strategy which aimed at the optimal use of resources rather than risk reduction. To examine how the palaces operated we need to look at documentary sources as well as the archaeological evidence and this means the Linear B texts, since Minoan Hieroglyphic and Linear A have not been deciphered. Linear B is of course the script which the Mycenaeans used for their administrative records and we cannot assume that they practiced agriculture in exactly the same way as the Minoans. However, much of our information does come from Knossos when the palace was apparently under Mycenaean control.

A set of documents from Pylos lists the tax assessment for each of the districts in one of the two provinces in terms of a range of commodities which includes olive oil, flax, spices, honey, and hides. It is always the same commodities which are listed in the same proportions, so this does not suggest that specialization was encouraged. Moreover, local officials collected these taxes, so the palace was not directly involved. Cereal production was much more closely monitored. Most of the records deal with wheat rather than barley and mainly one species, though it is uncertain whether this was bread wheat or emmer. A tablet from Knossos gives a figure of approximately 775 tons for the wheat harvest at Dawo, which was in the Mesara plain in the south of Crete. Cereal cultivation on this scale would not have been a realistic proposition unless fields could be plowed and Knossos did own teams of oxen. Nevertheless the palace would have needed a large workforce for the harvest. Some of the labor may have been provided by local communities which made land available in exchange for a share of the crop. The palace contributed the oxen, a considerable investment given the amount of fodder they consumed, but no doubt the return more than justified the outlay.

The Linear B texts seldom mention pulses which are well represented in the archaeobotanical record and would have been an important component of the diet. The implication is that the palaces did not control all agricultural production. Nevertheless, the demand that they created must have had a profound impact on the rural economy. The pithoi in the west magazines at Knossos could hold around 230,000 liters and many contained olive oil. There was also a large quantity of olive oil stored at Pylos, where it was used as a base for perfume, and the palace required 40 to 60 tons of flax each year for the production of linen textiles.

The textile industry at Knossos is particularly well documented. The wool from which the cloth was made came from 590 flocks of sheep. The texts record the composition of these flocks which consisted primarily of castrated male sheep. This indicates that they were kept for their wool rather than the meat. The flocks were scattered across central Crete and the total number of sheep was around 82,000. If the sheep were culled at 5 or 6 years of age, some 15,000 additional animals would have been needed annually but the palace does not seem to have had sufficient replacement stock to maintain the flocks. It is therefore likely that the shepherds made up the shortfall from their own flocks. We can only guess how many privately owned sheep there were but this was clearly a major economic activity.

The palaces were also supplied with animals for feasts and sacrifices. A fresco from Pylos depicts a religious procession with a bull as the central motif (figure 10.8). The animal bones from the palace include parts of the carcasses of cattle and deer which had been sacrificed and eaten. The Linear B texts do mention deer but a much wider range of wild animals is attested in the samples of animal bones from Minoan and Mycenaean sites. Boars, bears, wolves, lions, and lynxes were hunted and we have frescoes which indicate that this was a high-status activity. Perhaps there was also a perception that a successful hunt tamed the power of the wilderness and brought more of the countryside under control.

The impact that the Mycenaeans made on the landscape can best be seen in Boiotia. In the Classical period the Kopais basin was a shallow seasonal lake, famous for fish and eels. It was not until the twentieth century that the lake was finally drained but there is a much earlier system of canals and dikes for which a Mycenaean date seems most likely. This would have channeled the water which fed the lake into natural swallow holes at the eastern end of the basin. It is estimated that one of the main canals was around 50 meters wide and must have been over 20 kilometers in length, so this was an extraordinarily ambitious project. That it was also successful is evident because the Mycenaeans built an immense fortress at Gla, which had been an island in the middle of the lake. The fact that roads run across the basin from the fortress shows that the lake had been partially, if not completely drained. The palace at Orchomenos may have overseen this project and the construction of Gla, where the storerooms could hold approximately 2,000 tons of cereals. The canals and dikes no doubt fell into disrepair soon after the fortress was destroyed around 1200 BC and Kopais then became a lake again.

## Early Iron Age Pastoralists?

It has been argued that one consequence of the destruction of the Mycenaean palaces and the economic system they maintained was a different agricultural regime with a greater emphasis on pastoralism. The fact that we cannot detect any signs of life in the countryside in the Early Iron Age has been cited in support of this theory. Pastoralists are more mobile and may only have occupied sites for a relatively short time before they moved on. What they left behind would be minimal and not very obvious archaeologically. It has also been noted that the dedication of animal figurines in the sanctuary at Olympia peaks in the tenth century and then falls. The animal bones from Early Iron Age Nichoria in Messenia indicate an increase in the proportion of cattle, though the initial assumption that these were bred primarily for their meat has been revised because of the age at which they were killed. However, we cannot tell from the bones whether the absolute number of animals at Nichoria had risen because the process of deposition is context-specific. In other words people do not always dispose of carcasses in exactly the same way and so we can only guess how many live animals there were at any time. This is one of the reasons why the Linear B texts are so useful.

On Crete there was a move into the mountains in the twelfth and eleventh centuries. Defensibility was obviously a factor, but it has also been pointed out that upland pastures would have been more accessible from these remote sites. The use of seasonal summer settlements at high elevations was a common practice on Crete until quite recently. In the fall the shepherds came down from the mountains with their flocks which grazed on the stubble left in the fields after the harvest. Was a similar type of transhumance instituted in the twelfth century and does this indicate more of a reliance on pastoralism? It has been pointed out that many of the Early Iron Age settlements on Crete were substantial and must have been occupied permanently, not seasonally. Moreover, there were no equivalent sites down in the plains and therefore no market for the milk, cheese, and wool that the shepherds produced. Crucially, many of the sites in the mountains were so close together that they could not have subsisted on pastoralism alone, because this would have required more land than they had available and in any case was a risky strategy. It seems likely that crops and livestock each made a contribution.

Most of those who support the pastoralist hypothesis do not envisage a complete cessation of cereal cultivation but more of a shift in favor of livestock. One explanation for this may have been the power vacuum which followed the collapse of the palaces. It is possible that cattle in particular had become a symbol of elite status in a society which apparently used feasts as an opportunity for extravagant displays of hospitality. Those who owned cattle could also cultivate more land and rent out teams of plow oxen. So, although the circumstances were very different, we do see some parallels with the end of the Neolithic period, when livestock may also have had a more prominent role.

## Down on the Farm?

Many of the remote sites on Crete were abandoned in the tenth century in favor of more nucleated settlements where there was room for expansion and access to better-quality agricultural land. In the Archaic period rural sites appear which would have brought more of the countryside within reach and in some cases may have served as a seasonal or permanent base for farmers. It is not only on Crete that we have evidence of a more intensively exploited landscape. Most Greek surveys have observed an increase in rural activity but the pattern does vary. For example in some regions, such as Boiotia and the southern Argolid, we see a steady growth with a peak in the fourth century. However, in Laconia the number of rural sites drops after the mid-fifth century. Messenia was under Spartan control until the fourth century and it is only then that settlement in the countryside starts. Obviously the particular historical circumstances must be taken into account.

Surveys have revealed an artefact-rich landscape. In many fields there is a continuous scatter of sherds and pieces of tile, much of which is broadly Classical or

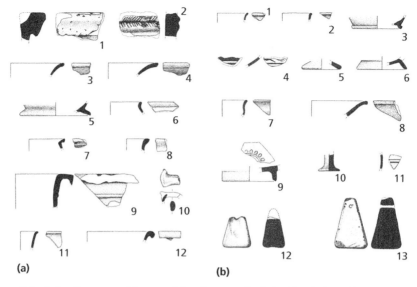

**Figure 5.2a & b**   Pottery and loomweights from an Archaic-Classical rural site in Laconia

Roman in date. Sometimes the scatter is very thin and may fade out completely or become an obvious concentration, which is treated as a site. It is not always easy for survey archaeologists to define what constitutes a site but in Greece at least the artefact density does tend to be significantly higher than the background scatter. On Methana the mean density on-site was just under nine artefacts per square meter, as against an average of 0.1 off-site.

What can be deduced about life in the countryside from the survey data? Many of these rural sites have been identified as farmsteads. Typically they are quite small, around 0.5 hectares or less in size, with plenty of roof tile and pottery. Stone tools and other types of equipment may also be found. Architecture is sometimes visible but this does not prove that there was occupation. The pottery is a better indication of this. A site which has a high proportion of storage vessels may simply have been a storehouse. However, the presence of fine-ware bowls and cups suggests that people did live there (figure 5.2a & b). Terracotta loomweights imply that women must have spent some time at the site but we cannot tell whether residence was seasonal or permanent. Study of recent land use in Greece has shown that families may live on their farms for only part of the year and commute from their village when the work is less intensive.

A survey around the ancient deme of Atene in southeastern Attica recorded a number of Classical farmsteads with well-preserved architectural features (figure 5.3a & b). Some of the houses were quite substantial and many had towers. There were enclosures where animals could have been penned. The circular structures resemble alonia on which modern Greek farmers traditionally threshed cereals. Olives may have been a valuable crop and this could explain why the fields around the farmsteads were extensively terraced. Because graves have been found in the

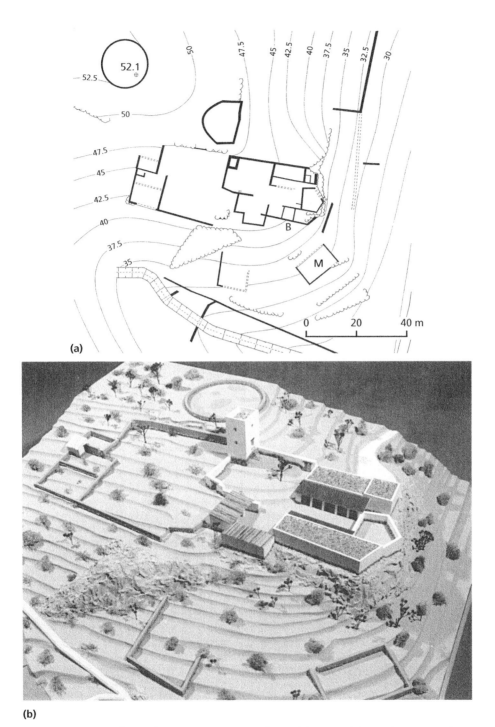

**(a)**

**(b)**

**Figure 5.3a & b**   Plan and reconstruction of a Classical farmstead in southeastern Attica

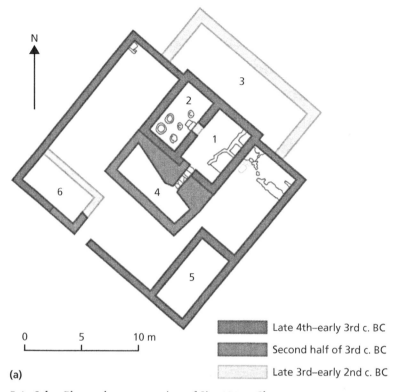

N

0        5        10 m

Late 4th–early 3rd c. BC

Second half of 3rd c. BC

Late 3rd–early 2nd c. BC

(a)

**Figure 5.4a & b**   Plan and reconstruction of Site 151 at Chersonesos

vicinity of the houses, it has been argued that they must have been occupied throughout the year.

A few rural sites in Greece have been excavated, notably the Vari House which is also in southeastern Attica (figure 4.20). Like the houses at Atene this had a tower. From literary sources we know that these provided secure storage for agricultural produce and occasionally protection for the household. Raids would have been a problem, especially near the coast. There was also a large slave workforce in the silver mines at Lavrion which may have posed a threat. The enclosures in front of the Vari House suggest that the owners kept livestock but few of the finds were obviously agricultural except for some cylindrical vessels which were scored inside. These have been identified as beehives and high-quality honey is still produced in this part of Attica.

At Chersonesos, a Greek colony in the Crimea, the peninsula which formed the agricultural chora of the city was divided into over 400 plots in the middle of the fourth century (figure 2.10a & b). There were farmhouses on around a third of the plots, often with towers as an integral feature. In the case of Site 151 the tower was built first and then the enclosure wall (figure 5.4a & b). The other rooms were added in the third century. In one of the first(= ground)-floor rooms of the tower

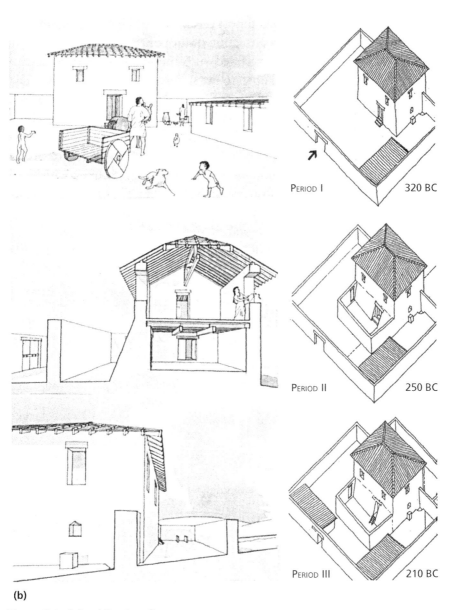

PERIOD I                    320 BC

PERIOD II                   250 BC

PERIOD III                  210 BC

**(b)**

**Figure 5.4a & b**   (*Continued*)

were vats in which grapes were evidently fermented. The wine was then stored in
large jars which were embedded in the floor of the adjacent room. The family
presumably lived on the floor above. Vineyard walls are visible on many of the plots
and underline the importance of viticulture at Chersonesos. It does seem likely
that most of the farmhouses were occupied but, even in the case of the excavated
sites, we cannot tell whether the rural population was permanently based in the

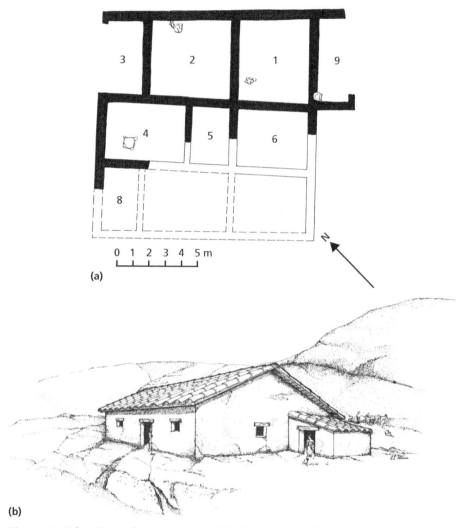

**Figure 5.5a & b**   Plan and reconstruction of the Fattoria Fabrizio farmhouse at Metapontion

countryside. Some of the plots without a farmhouse must have been cultivated by farmers who commuted from the city.

It was in the late sixth century that gridded plots of land were set out at Metapontion in southern Italy and the number of rural sites then increased rapidly. However, perhaps because of a rise in the water table, much of the chora was abandoned in the middle of the fifth century. It is not clear whether any systematic attempt was made to drain the fields but farmhouses reappear in the countryside in the fourth century. Fattoria Fabrizio is a relatively small example (figure 5.5a & b). It was a single-story structure, built of mudbrick on a stone foundation, with a tiled roof and nine or 10 rooms, of which numbers 1 and 2 had been used for

**Figure 5.6**   Olive press from Olynthos

storage. Meals were prepared in room 9, which had a mortar fixed in one corner, and cooked on a hearth in room 4. Unlike a typical mainland Greek house of this period, Fattoria Fabrizio does not have a courtyard and so the pattern of circulation would have involved more movement between rooms. The location of the cemeteries at Metapontion is of interest. They were placed just outside the city, along the main roads and also in the countryside. Some of the graves were located near the division lines between plots, which implies that people lived, as well as worked, in the chora.

There is evidence of agricultural activity in Classical Greek cities as well. A number of the houses at Olynthos had facilities for the production of oil, wine, or flour. There was an olive crusher (figure 5.6) in the courtyard of House A6, as well as seven millstones and five saddle querns on which cereals were ground. The fact that the owners had invested in so much costly equipment suggests that they helped out other households, no doubt in exchange for a share of the proceeds.

Press installations were found in at least five of the houses at Halieis in the Argolid. In room 6-29, which opens off the courtyard in House D, there was a plaster platform with a marble press bed in situ (figure 5.7). A basin had been sunk into the platform in front of the press and a large jar to one side. A stone block in the doorway between rooms 6-27 and 6-29 was probably the weight for the wooden

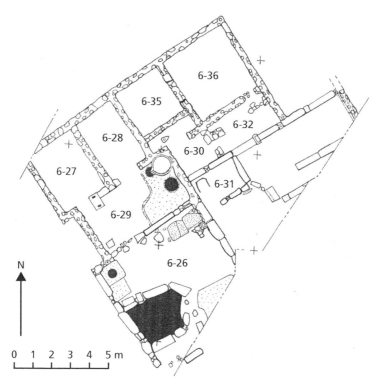

**Figure 5.7**  Plan of House D at Halieis

press beam. It seems likely that these presses were used to extract the oil from crushed olives. Most had apparently been installed in the houses in the fourth century and would have facilitated an increase in olive oil production, possibly to meet local demand or for export. There was also press equipment on a number of the Classical-Hellenistic rural sites in the southern Argolid.

Several of the houses at Halieis have large stone-lined pits in their courtyards. Over 1,500 sherds and 1,000 fragments of roof tile were found in the pit in House D. Some of the tiles may have fallen off the roof of House E, which overlooks the courtyard of House D, but most of the pottery had been dumped in the pit along with other organic and inorganic items of household refuse. This was not just a convenient way to keep the house clean and tidy. The refuse was composted and would then have been used as fertilizer, which takes us back into the countryside and the off-site artefacts that surveys have recorded. It does seem likely that there were pieces of pottery and tile in the manure that was spread on the fields but it is questionable whether this would have been transported very far from the farm-house. Some of the low-density artefact scatters must have been generated by other types of agricultural activity. The countryside was clearly a busy place in the Classical-Hellenistic period.

Ancient Greek writers seldom describe life in the country but occasionally they do provide some hints. At the start of the *Dyskolos*, a fourth-century comedy by Menander, Pan sets the scene for the audience: "this farm on my right is the home of Knemon." The farmhouse is quite isolated but, despite his desire for solitude, Knemon does have neighbors. He evidently occupies the type of rural site that surveys have recorded and this, as far as we can tell, is his only home. There must have been many farmers like Knemon, self-sufficient but not particularly prosperous. Menander tells us that he owned the farm and that it was worth two talents. The size of the property is not specified but 3.6–5.4 hectares is reckoned to be typical for family farms in Classical Greece. This is not particularly large, and the land must have been farmed quite intensively if many of these smallholders were to survive. Some did not, and this is no doubt one of the reasons why estates generally became larger over time. Around Halieis in the southern Argolid, the average size of fourth-century properties was over 13 hectares. The figure suggested for Spartan estates is 18 hectares because the labor force consisted of the helots who were serfs. It is possible that they worked as sharecroppers for a proportion of the produce from the estate.

The rich were the great landowners. For example, it has been estimated that in the fourth century 7.5 percent of the Athenian population controlled 30 percent of the cultivable land. Inscriptions record individuals with a number of properties, not all of which were in Attica. Obviously most of the work on these estates must have been undertaken by tenants or slaves. The rich also needed crops which could be sold, because of public and private financial commitments. So they would probably have specialized and invested in labor-intensive projects, such as the construction of terraces, and expensive items of equipment in order to maximize yields.

Clearly the rich owned land in different places but was this also true of the less wealthy? Some have argued that it would make no sense for a farmer like Knemon to live in the countryside unless his property was consolidated in one block of land; otherwise it would be simpler to commute from the nearest town. However, in most parts of Greece there was a system of partible inheritance, whereby every son received an equal share of the property. So this and the transfer of land as part of a dowry inevitably resulted in scattered plots, which did reduce the risk of crop failure. Land could also be leased, and the inscriptions which set out the conditions often mention structures such as towers, storehouses, cattle byres, and sheepfolds. In some cases the lessee is required to live on the property, but the wealthy men who leased estates from the sanctuary of Apollo on Delos would certainly not have taken up residence there.

From this combination of archaeological evidence, literary sources, and inscriptions we can deduce that there were many different types of structure in the Greek countryside in the Classical-Hellenistic period. They included farmhouses which were occupied by the owners, tenants, serfs, or slaves. Obviously the practice was not the same everywhere. The size of the rural population varied and changed over time. However, the consistent feature is the scale of activity which underlines the fundamental role of agriculture in the economy.

## Works and Days

The literary sources also describe how agriculture was practiced in ancient Greece. Homer draws on the countryside for similes in the *Iliad* and *Odyssey*. Hesiod's *Works and Days*, composed around 700 BC, advises on the time of year when each agricultural task should be prioritized, though it is not a comprehensive manual. In the philosophical conversation between Sokrates and Ischomachos, which Xenophon sets out in the *Oeconomicus*, the importance of agriculture is outlined from the perspective of a gentleman farmer. The *Historia Plantarum* and *De Causis Plantarum*, written by Theophrastos in the late fourth or early third century, are botanical treatises with useful information on cultivated plants. Agricultural activities are occasionally depicted on Archaic and Classical pottery as well.

Ancient authors are not very specific about the types of cereal that were grown but do mention two types of wheat and barley. Hesiod recommends that cereals should be sown in November, after the fields have been plowed for a third time. The implication is that the land had been left fallow for a year, the two-field system which maintained soil fertility. The fields were first plowed in the spring, again in the summer, and finally in the fall. This broke up the topsoil, which was then more moisture-retentive, and kept weeds down. The plow was an ard which cuts through the surface but does not turn the soil. The ard described by Hesiod and illustrated on an Attic black-figure cup (figure 5.8) consisted of a curved piece of wood to which a pair of oxen or mules were yoked. This was attached to a pointed sole plate tipped with a bronze or iron plowshare. A wooden bar was used to guide the plow. When Hephaistos decorated the shield he had made for Achilles

> he depicted a large field of soft, rich fallow, which was being ploughed for the third time. A number of ploughmen were driving their teams across it to and fro. When they reached the ridge at the end of the field and had to wheel, a man would come up and hand them a cup of mellow wine. Then they turned back down the furrows and toiled along through the deep fallow soil to reach the other end. The field, though it was made of gold, grew black behind them, as a field does when it is being ploughed. The artist had achieved a miracle. (*Iliad* 18.541–9; translation Rieu)

On the cup a man works the plowed soil with a tool which looks like a pickax but may be a broad-bladed hoe. Another man with a basket sows the seed. The cup gives the impression that all of these activities took place at the same time, whereas in

**Figure 5.8**   Plowmen on a black-figure cup (Paris, Louvre)

**Figure 5.9**   Satyrs pick and tread grapes on a black-figure amphora (Würzburg, Martin von Wagner Museum)

fact they would have been spread out. Once a field was planted with cereals it had to be weeded every so often until the harvest in May or June. Metal sickles were used to cut the stalks. The sheaves were then taken to be threshed. Evidently they were trampled by draft animals to free the kernels and the heaps of straw were winnowed so that the chaff blew away.

The pulses mentioned by ancient authors include beans, peas, lentils, chickpeas, and vetch. They were sown in the fall or spring and often cultivated intensively. Theophrastos is aware that pulses can improve soil fertility but it is unclear whether the Greeks practiced a three-field system of crop rotation, with cereals followed by pulses and then fallow.

It seems that vines were generally grown from cuttings. Once established they had to be pruned each year, usually in the winter. The shoots and leaves were thinned out in the spring and the soil in the vineyard was regularly weeded and turned over to increase the amount of moisture that reached the roots. The grapes were picked in September and collected in large wickerwork baskets. They were either dried and made into raisins or the juice was extracted and then fermented. Appropriately, the vintage is often depicted on the pottery in which wine was stored, mixed, and served (figure 5.9). The workforce regularly consists of satyrs, the unreconstructed companions of Dionysos, the god of wine. The grapes are placed on a raised wooden board, either in a basket or a sack, and trodden. The juice runs off the board into a container. A large vat is sometimes used instead of a wooden board and stone press beds have also been found. The must was fermented in pithoi and then transferred to amphorae for storage. In Athens the new wine was first tasted at the Anthesteria festival in late February. The wines from Rhodes, Kos, Chios,

**Figure 5.10**    The olive harvest on a black-figure amphora (London, British Museum)

Lesbos, and Thasos were particularly renowned in antiquity and viticulture was clearly a major enterprise on these islands.

Cuttings were used to propagate olives, and shoots could also be grafted onto wild stock. The trees mature slowly, though Hesiod exaggerates when he claims that a man who planted an olive grove would not live to eat the fruit. Theophrastos reckons that olives usually lived for 200 years, so they were a good long-term investment. He states that the trees need to be pruned but not how often. He also recommends that the soil between the trees should be hoed. However, in more recent times cereals have often been grown around olives and there is some evidence for this practice in antiquity. Olives only produce a good crop every other year. The fruit is generally picked between November and January. On a black-figure amphora three men beat the branches of a tree with sticks, while a fourth man picks up the olives from the ground and puts them in a basket (figure 5.10).

In order to extract the oil the olives had to be crushed and pressed. At first a cylindrical stone roller was probably used to crush the fruit. In the fourth century a more efficient device known as a trapetum was introduced. This consisted of a circular stone basin, around which one or two millstones could be turned on a wooden pivot (figure 5.6). An olive press is shown on an Attic black-figure skyphos (figure 5.11). One end of the horizontal beam was fixed to a wall and massive boulder weights were attached to the other end. One of the two men hangs from the beam to increase the pressure on the sacks of crushed olives behind him. A mixture of oil and water runs into the vessel on the floor. Most of the components of this type of level press were made of wood and are therefore difficult to identify archaeologically. We do find cut blocks of stone which were used as weights, though some may come from Roman screw presses. Finally the liquid had to be left in a vat or tank until the oil rose to the surface and could be skimmed off or the water drained away.

**Figure 5.11**    Olive press on a black-figure skyphos (Boston, Fine Arts Museum)

## Conclusions

Life is never easy for farmers and in Greece they certainly had good reason to complain. Much of the land was poor and unproductive; drought was always a possibility and consequently the risk of a food shortage. Yet agriculture drove the ancient
economy and strategies were devised which sustained growth rather than just survival. This is obvious when we see how densely settled Thessaly became in the
Neolithic period. It is not easy to calculate the number of Mesolithic foragers but
over the course of a few centuries population levels soared. The explanation is not
a mass movement of farmers from Anatolia, as was once suspected, because the
agricultural package was adopted gradually. Instead we should envisage a combination of immigration and indigenous adaptation. Much of the population growth
was internally generated. The symbolic component of an agricultural economy was
also important and is reflected in the minimal dietary contribution of wild plants
and animals. The reliance on agriculture was a choice, not a necessity. The social
implications of the Neolithic "revolution" were profound because we now find
sizable communities with a high level of daily interaction, though in some parts of
Greece they must have been quite isolated. Mechanisms were therefore required to
create social networks, and commensality was one of the ways in which friendships
could be made and maintained. Possibly there was an increased demand for meat
at feasts and consequently more of an emphasis on livestock at the end of the
Neolithic period. Herd size could also have become an indication of wealth and
status. Consequently the move into more marginal areas at this time would not be
a sign of desperation but a conscious strategy. Although most farmers still opted
for a mix of arable and livestock agriculture, greater specialization would have
increased the need for exchange.

    This is where the palaces come in—or do they? The storage facilities at Knossos
suggest a system of redistribution which could provide support when necessary in
return for taxes. However, it is clear that the palaces did not own most of the land.
What they were able to do was to maximize returns through mechanization in the

form of plow teams and a more organized labor force. Similarly the textile industry was based on the wool from sheep which the palaces did not necessarily supply and contributions of flax. Without the involvement of the palace at Orchomenos, the drainage of lake Kopais could surely not have been undertaken.

The destruction of the Mycenaean palaces clearly provoked a crisis but did this result in a new agricultural regime? In fact there was considerable continuity and, if pastoralism did increase, it was again because the ownership of cattle denoted high status in a society which still used feasts as an occasion for self-promotion. In the Archaic and Classical periods the level of activity in the countryside intensified. Whether or not the rural farmsteads were permanently occupied—and no doubt this varied—they did provide a convenient base for farmers much nearer their fields. They were also a visible symbol of ownership, and the way that cities such as Chersonesos and Metapontion carved up their territories is similarly proprietorial. Over time the level of specialization increased, with a focus on the production of wine and oil. The rich could afford the investment that was needed and the risks involved. Poor farmers could only complain.

## Bibliographical notes

There is a detailed description of the ecology of Mediterranean Europe with superb pictures of the Greek countryside in Grove and Rackham 2001. Horden and Purcell 2000 provide a thematic overview of the links between the landscape and history of the Mediterranean. Halstead 1996 and Perlès 2001 discuss the introduction of agriculture. See Renfrew 1973 and Halstead 2006 for agricultural practices in the Neolithic, and Hansen 1988, Cavanagh 1999, Halstead 2000, and Isaakidou 2006 for the developments at the end of the period. Halstead 1992b, 1998–99, and 2001 draws on documentary sources and the archaeological record to reconstruct the economic role of the Minoan and Mycenaean palaces. The draining of Kopais is discussed by Hope Simpson and Hagel 2006. For the arguments in favor of the Early Iron Age pastoralism hypothesis see Snodgrass 1987, and Dickinson 2006 for the case against this. Wallace 2003 analyzes the situation on Crete. The interpretation of rural sites on the basis of survey data is examined by Cavanagh et al. 2005. See Lohmann 1992 for Atene, Jones et al. 1973 for the Vari House, Carter 2006 for Chersonesos and Metapontion, Cahill 2002 and 2005 for Olynthos, and Ault 2005 for Halieis. Alcock et al. 1994 is a comprehensive treatment of manure. The evidence from written sources and inscriptions is discussed by Osborne 1987, Jameson 1992, and Roy 1996. On Greek agriculture generally see Isager and Skydsgaard 1992. The role of the olive in the ancient economy is examined in detail by Foxhall 2007.

# CHAPTER 6

# Technology and Production

## Pottery

Anyone involved in an archaeological field survey in Greece soon realizes that there is an extraordinary amount of pottery scattered across the countryside. On town sites the sherd density can reach very high levels and what we see on the surface is just the tip of the iceberg. Obviously pottery must have been widely used in the past but the main reason why we find so much is that it is both fragile and durable. The vessels themselves broke easily, were seldom mended, and would usually be discarded. However, sherds are more robust and can survive for thousands of years even in the topsoil. In addition pottery has been manufactured since the start of the Neolithic period and so it is consistently the most common artefact type found on sites. Consequently archaeologists take a peculiarly close interest in broken crockery. It is on the basis of the associated pottery that many sites are dated. How it was made can tell us about technology and production methods. Because pottery was often traded, we need to know where it came from to investigate exchange networks. How it was used is another key consideration.

## Neolithic pottery

As pottery first appeared in Greece just after the introduction of agriculture and these developments were presumably linked, we would expect that it was used to store, cook, and serve the types of food which were now available. However, most Early Neolithic vessels were quite small and would not have been suitable for bulk storage. Nor is there any indication that they had been exposed to direct heat. It

*Greek Archaeology: A Thematic Approach*   By Christopher Mee
© 2011 Christopher Mee

**Figure 6.1**    Middle Neolithic cooking vessel from Kouphovouno

seems that pottery was just made for the consumption of food and drink, possibly on special occasions because production was very limited at first. Clearly it would have taken some time for the potential of pottery to be recognized, given the challenges that this new technology presented. For example cooking vessels should conduct heat efficiently and withstand high temperature variations. Only after considerable experimentation would a suitable shape and clay composition have been discovered.

By the Middle Neolithic period some vessels had evidently been designed for use over a fire (figure 6.1) but they only make up a relatively small proportion of the pottery. The emphasis is on finely crafted and often vividly decorated cups, bowls, and jars (figure 6.2a–b). It was intended that these vessels should be displayed and their high quality suggests that food may have been shared at communal meals. As well as close links within communities, there must also have been contact between sites because the same shapes and style of decoration are found across entire regions, for instance in Thessaly and in the Peloponnese.

Middle Neolithic potters were technically accomplished. They knew which clay sources would give them the properties they required. The preparation of the clay was thorough and they could alter the paste with the addition of a temper, such as sand or calcite, if greater strength was needed. The wheel was not yet in use, so they built up their vessels from coils or slabs of clay which were carefully joined together. Then excess clay was removed and the walls were thinned down. The smaller vessels can be remarkably delicate and well formed. Some of the shapes are quite complex and would have been difficult to model. There were several ways in

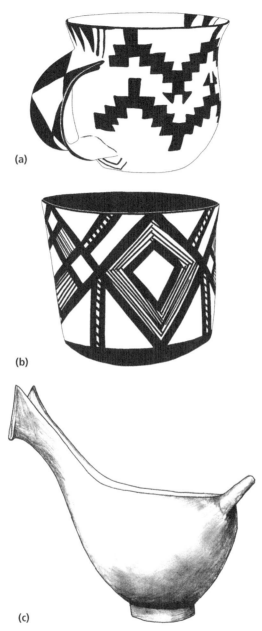

**Figure 6.2a–c** Middle Neolithic cup from Tzani (Volos Museum), bowl from Asea (Tegea Museum), and EH II sauceboat from Lerna (Argos Museum). Not to scale

which the surface was treated. It could be coated with a slip which is essentially a liquid layer of clay. A stone or bone tool was often used to burnish the surface which was then less porous and had a glossy finish. Painted decoration is also very common in this period. The paints were usually fine solutions prepared from iron-rich clays. When the pottery was fired the paint would turn red if oxygen was present in the kiln. If oxygen was excluded from the kiln, the paint would be black. The bowl from Asea (figure 6.2b) must have been fired in several stages and at a temperature high enough to vitrify the paint. This ensured that the paint would remain black in the final oxidation phase which produced the light surface color. The ability to control the way that the pottery was fired is extraordinary because there is no evidence that proper kilns were used. It seems more likely that bonfires were built for this purpose.

The fact that the potters were so skillful does raise the possibility that they were specialists. Discussion about the way that pottery production was organized has mainly been based on studies of modern traditional potters. The simplest level is household production in which the potters, who are usually women, make pottery for their own use. Household industries involve some specialization in that the potters, still mostly women who work from home, supply other households in exchange for payment. In a workshop industry men make up more of the labor force. They do not necessarily manufacture pottery full-time but this does provide a significant proportion of their income. Since it is unlikely that there were work-shop industries in the Middle Neolithic period, women may well have taken respon-sibility for pottery production. Whether each household was involved or only some families, a lengthy apprenticeship would have been required, given the high quality of the pottery.

Compared with the uniformity of Middle Neolithic pottery, we see much more diversity in the Late Neolithic period. The different decorative styles may reflect a greater emphasis on individuality. Although communal feasts still took place, it seems that food was not shared so often and that households were more independ-ent. At the same time pottery became more utilitarian, since there is an increase in the number of coarse-ware vessels which now include large storage jars. Even the fine pottery looks more robust but is still well made. However, in the Peloponnese at least, this high standard was not maintained in the Final Neolithic period. Most of the pottery is very coarse, poorly fired, and easily broken. This is a good example of what has been termed the evolution of simplicity, an illustration of the fact that technology does not always advance over time. Much less effort was invested in the production of pottery, possibly because it did not have the same symbolic impor-tance, and consequently the level of skill declined.

## Early Bronze Age Pottery

In the Early Bronze Age the quality of the pottery is better and households had a wide range of vessels in which they could store, cook, and serve their food. Decoration is generally simple, a solid wash of paint rather than the complex designs which were so common in the Neolithic period. Pottery was obviously not expected to

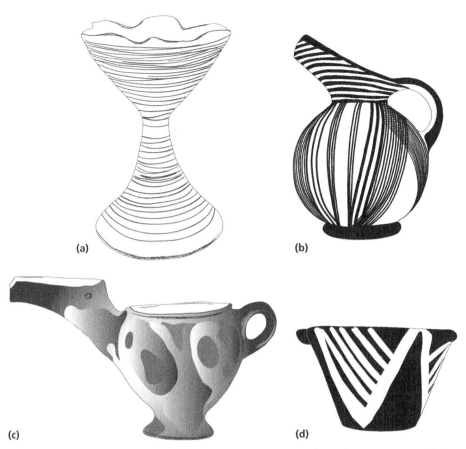

(a)

(b)

(c)

(d)

**Figure 6.3a–d** EM I chalice from Pyrgos (Herakleion Museum), jug from Ayios Onouphrios (Herakleion Museum), EM II teapot from Vasiliki (New York, Metropolitan Museum of Art), and EM III bowl from Vasiliki (Penn Museum). Not to scale

communicate as much information, yet it does indicate widely shared cultural conventions. Certain vessel types appear on sites across Greece, in particular sauce-boats (figure 6.2c). Because of their idiosyncratic shape, it seems likely that they had a specific function and this may have involved the consumption of an alcoholic drink. There is now greater standardization in the size and shape of vessels which could indicate production by specialists rather than by every household. Clay analysis has shown that pottery was exchanged between sites in the Argolid and again this is consistent with specialization.

On Crete there is more variation in the surface treatment of the pottery. Typical of EM I are Pyrgos ware and Ayios Onouphrios ware (figure 6.3a & b). The pattern-burnished decoration of Pyrgos ware is reminiscent of wood grain and the shape of some Ayios Onouphrios jugs could have been inspired by gourds. Vasiliki ware appears in EM II and has a mottled surface (figure 6.3c). It is not entirely clear how this effect was produced but a careful control over the way that the vessels were fired was evidently crucial. A new shape is the teapot which could be considered the

Minoan equivalent of the sauceboat and may similarly have been designed for a special brew, probably more potent than tea. EM III sees the introduction of pottery with decoration in white paint on a dark slip (figure 6.3d) and in due course this becomes the classic Middle Minoan pottery style.

The question of specialization has been raised, not least because one of the rooms at Myrtos contained eight circular clay disks which were almost certainly used to make pottery. Although these were not wheels of the type described below, they could have been turned as the potter formed the vessel. The room in which the disks were found was not a workshop but this does hint at a more specialized system of production. Examination of the pottery from Myrtos has shown that around 50 percent was locally made. The rest had a quite different fabric composition and must have come from at least 20 kilometers away. This included large vessels such as pithoi, so quite bulky goods moved between sites. Analysis of samples from Knossos has underlined the scale of this Early Minoan pottery trade. We would expect a site the size of Knossos to have been self-sufficient but much of the high-quality pottery was imported from the south of Crete. Some of the ordinary domestic pottery also came from other sources. It would therefore appear that certain production centers concentrated on specific types of pottery which were distributed across the island. So there was clearly specialization and the pottery must have been valued, possibly because it was used for ceremonies or other formal occasions.

## Minoan and Mycenaean pottery

What impact did the palaces have on the way that Minoan pottery production was organized? There were already specialist potters in the Early Minoan period but were they now under elite control? Had they become attached specialists? If so, we would expect technical improvements, which could explain the introduction of the wheel. Most of the evidence for the use of the wheel has come from examination of marks inside vessels which show whether they were turned when they were formed. A few EM III and MM IA wheel-made vessels have been identified and the number increases in the Protopalatial period. However, only small vessels were thrown on the wheel in MM IB and even in MM II most of the larger shapes were still hand-made. The device that Minoan potters used apparently consisted of a wheel head which was attached to an axle that revolved in a stone socket (figure 6.4). The enlarged rim suggests that it was turned manually, possibly by an assistant so that the potter had both hands free.

The finest MM I–II pottery is Kamares ware which is black-slipped and has polychrome decoration in white, red, and yellow paint (figure 6.5a). Some of the vessels have very thin walls and the execution of the motifs, which often cover most of the surface, is equally skillful. The obvious conclusion is that Kamares ware must have been produced in palace workshops, yet once again it has been shown that the pottery from Knossos was imported, mainly from the south of Crete. Quite possibly the centers that had supplied Knossos in the Early Minoan period were still active.

**Figure 6.4**   Reconstruction of potter's wheel

Whether they were independent of Phaistos is less clear. Nevertheless the assumption that the palaces monopolized pottery production is certainly unfounded.

A temperature of 850–1000°C would have been needed to achieve the metallic sheen of the best Kamares ware. This is just about possible in a bonfire but does suggest that potters now had proper kilns. However, most of the Minoan kilns which have been excavated are dated LM I–III. Nor is it always certain that they were for pottery rather than metals, glass, or lime, which are also worked at high temperatures. So we can only guess when pottery kilns were first used. The known examples are of two main types. The simplest is usually circular or oval, with a chamber around 2 meters in diameter. The fire burned in the lower part of the kiln and, if necessary, more fuel could be added through a stoke hole. The heat rose through a grate on which the pottery was placed, drawn up by a vent in the domed roof. The other type of kiln has a larger rectangular chamber, below which there were parallel channels. Because the fire chamber was not directly under the grate, the heat was more evenly circulated. Kilns gave potters much better control, which would have reduced the risk of a misfire, and were also more fuel efficient.

Given this level of technical expertise, it is curious that MM III–LM I pottery is often rather carelessly made. One explanation for this is that there may have been

(a)

(b)

(c)

(d)

**Figure 6.5a–d** MM II jug from Phaistos (Herakleion Museum), LM IA bowl from Knossos (Herakleion Museum), LM IB flask from Palaikastro (Herakleion Museum), and Cycladic jug from Phylakopi (Athens, National Archaeological Museum). Not to scale

more metal vessels in use. Many Minoan pottery shapes do look as though they were copied from metalwork and the shiny finish supports this idea. However, very few metal vessels have been found on Crete, no doubt because they were melted down. It is therefore difficult to say whether they were more common in the Neopalatial period. Alternatively the deterioration in the quality of the pottery could be due to mass production. The quantity of plain conical cups in particular suggests that they were used once or twice and then thrown away. Potters would consequently have prioritized speed rather than finesse. Nevertheless, they did make excellent pottery as well. In MM III–LM I a new style of decoration was introduced with glossy dark paint on a light slipped surface (figure 6.5b). Some of the pottery is superb, especially the LM IB Marine Style (figure 6.5c) which is widely distributed across Crete but may have been produced in a few workshops, perhaps centered on Knossos.

Marine Style pottery is found in the Cyclades where Minoan influence is very obvious in LC I. At sites such as Akrotiri on Thera and Phylakopi on Melos local pottery styles do exist (figure 6.5d) but Minoan shapes and motifs were also imitated. What can we infer from this about contacts between Crete and the Cyclades? The imported Minoan pottery on the islands presumably demonstrates some form of trade, though the ships which moved the goods were not necessarily Cretan. The fact that Minoan pottery was copied only tells us that it was appreciated; perhaps it had a certain cachet because it was foreign. But what are we to make of the Minoan domestic pottery which appears in the Cyclades and many other sites around the Aegean? Does this indicate the presence of Cretans? Pottery alone cannot answer these questions and we need to take account of the whole range of available evidence. However, sometimes there is only the pottery, which can easily be overinterpreted. The Cyclades provide a nice cautionary tale. The Marine Style sherds from Phylakopi on Melos and Ayia Irini on Kea should reflect a link with Crete and more specifically Knossos. Yet clay analysis has shown that most of the sherds are from Attica, so Mycenaean Greece must have become a supplier of high-quality LM IB-style pottery. It is not out of the question that Cretan potters had set up workshops in mainland Greece but what this does underline is just how complex the reality can be.

The Mycenaeans also developed a taste for Minoan pottery. They used the same decorative technique with paint fired a lustrous black or red on a light-colored surface. Many Minoan shapes and motifs were borrowed, but by LH IIB a distinctive Mycenaean style can be seen, epitomized by the Ephyrean goblet which has a single motif on either side (figure 6.6a). Ephyrean goblets also appear on Crete at Knossos in LM II, when the Mycenaeans may have taken control of the palace. Perhaps a Mycenaean did drink from one of these goblets but they should be seen as another instance of the stylistic cross-currents which created such a rich fusion of cultural traditions at this time.

LH IIIA–B pottery is technically proficient but does not score highly for artistic merit. A standard set of shapes was produced and the decoration generally consists of stylized motifs. For example, the octopus is now rendered very schematically (figure 6.6b), though this type of symmetrical composition does suit the shape well.

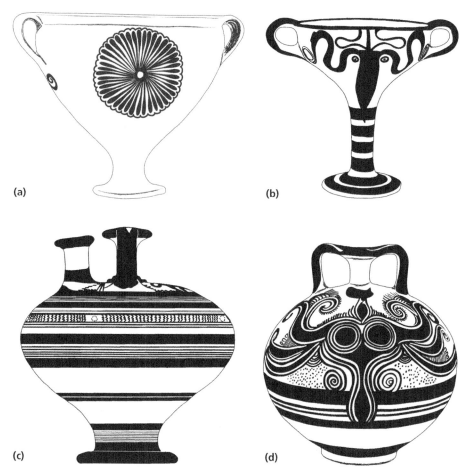

(a)

(b)

(c)

(d)

**Figure 6.6a–d**  LH IIB goblet from Mycenae (Nafplion Museum), LH IIIB1 kylix from Ialysos (Rhodes Museum), LH IIIB1 stirrup jar (National Museums Liverpool), and LH IIIC octopus stirrup jar from Ialysos (Rhodes Museum). Not to scale

The pottery is remarkably similar wherever it comes from, a reflection of the influence exerted particularly by workshops in the Argolid whose style was widely copied. Often, as in the case of stirrup jars filled with perfumed oil (figure 6.6c), it was the contents rather than the container that customers wanted. Nevertheless, there was also a market for the pottery which extended well beyond the Aegean. In this respect the stylistic uniformity is a problem because it can be difficult to say with any certainty where the Mycenaean pottery found in Cyprus, for instance, was actually made. A series of projects have therefore used clay analysis to resolve this issue, often with unexpected results. It has been shown that much of the LH IIIA2–B pottery on Cyprus was imported from the Argolid and may have been produced specifically for this market. Kraters with chariot scenes were very popular, more so than in the Argolid. A few have also been found on Rhodes where many ships no doubt stopped on the journey between mainland Greece and Cyprus. The Mycenaean pottery from Rhodes also includes certain distinctive shapes which were believed to have been made there, yet it turns out that the Argolid was again the main supplier. So consumer demand had created a highly specialized pottery industry. A significant point is that pottery from Tiryns is marked in a way which suggests that some of the merchants may have come from Cyprus.

How involved were the Mycenaean palaces? Pottery is seldom mentioned in the Linear B documents, though a royal potter is listed on a tablet from Pylos. Moreover the palaces did have economic interests which required a supply of pottery, such as the perfumed oil industry. When Pylos was destroyed over 8,000 vessels were stored in the palace for the feasts which the ruler hosted. Most of this pottery was undecorated and may only have been used once. So the palace was undoubtedly a major consumer. Differences in the fabrics and other technical details suggest that several producers supplied the pottery. However, it seems unlikely that they worked exclusively for the palace. There is certainly no evidence that pottery manufacture in Messenia was centrally controlled. So the destruction of the palaces would not necessarily have had a major impact on the pottery industry which still flourished in LH IIIC. Distinctive regional styles evolved (figure 6.6d) and not only in the Aegean. Mycenaean pottery was also made in Cyprus and Italy. Ultimately the decrease in demand resulted in a loss of quality. A type of hand-made pottery which appears in LH IIIC has been interpreted as an indication of renewed household production but this is questionable.

## Early Iron Age pottery

There were still specialist potters when the Protogeometric style was introduced in the middle of the eleventh century. Although most of the shapes and decorative motifs were not new, Protogeometric pottery does look different (figure 6.7a). One innovation is the use of a pivoted multiple brush to paint symmetrical circles and semicircles. The glossy black finish also suggests improvements in the way that the pottery was fired. Test sherds have been found which were evidently removed from the kiln at intervals so that the color could be checked (see below). The pottery is better shaped as well but there is no obvious technical explanation for this, such as a faster wheel. These developments are particularly clear in Athens, where most of the pottery comes from graves and includes the impressive amphorae which were used as cremation urns. At other sites in central Greece, such as Lefkandi, a related Protogeometric style evolved (figure 6.7b). Elsewhere the pottery can be quite idiosyncratic, though the multiple brush is often a common denominator. The eleventh and tenth centuries were a period of relative isolation but these technical and stylistic interchanges do imply some contact. At the same time it would seem that in certain respects pottery had become a mark of identity once again.

Around the start of the ninth century the Geometric style evolved in Athens. The range of shapes is similar but, instead of circles and semicircles, rectilinear motifs

**Figure 6.7a–d** Late Protogeometric amphora from Athens (Athens, Kerameikos Museum), Late Protogeometric skyphos from Rheneia, Early Geometric I amphora from Athens (Athens, Agora Museum), and Early Geometric II amphora from Athens (Athens, Kerameikos Museum). Not to scale

were now preferred. At first the decoration consisted of narrow bands, and glossy black paint covered most of the surface (figure 6.7c). However, over time the geometric patterns multiplied and can look very like embroidered or woven textiles, from which motifs may have been copied (figure 6.7d). Sometimes the pottery of this period symbolized high status, for example the cremation urn and model granary in the grave of a rich Athenian woman. The use of kraters and amphorae as grave markers is another indication of this.

Over the course of the ninth century Athens influenced the pottery style of other regions, presumably as a result of the increase in trade, though some movement of potters is always a possibility. The trend for figure scenes in eighthcentury Athens (figures 9.13 & 14) was also widely imitated. This type of composition offered more scope for individuality. In the Argolid the iconography reflects elite activities with representations of horses, dance processions, and warfare. It therefore seems likely that this new form of decoration was exploited as an expression of social status. Study of the Early Iron Age pottery from sites in the Argolid has shown that they formulated a common style but there is some variation. The links between the sites are not always dependent on their relative proximity and hint at political alliances, particularly in the eighth century when Argos threatened their independence.

## Archaic, Classical, and Hellenistic pottery

Most of the Geometric figure scenes seem more generic than specific. The funerals depicted on Athenian grave markers are not personalized, even though they commemorated a particular individual. However, we can occasionally identify myths. In the seventh century narrative compositions become more common and painted inscriptions sometimes indicate who the characters are and therefore which story this is. Scenes from the Trojan War imply that the *Iliad*, *Odyssey*, and other epic poems were one source of inspiration but many of the monsters and fantastic creatures came from the Near East. These oriental motifs were apparently copied from imported metalwork, ivories, and possibly textiles. Near Eastern influence is most obvious in the pottery made at Corinth in the late eighth and seventh centuries. An exotic style of decoration may have been considered appropriate for the small flasks in which perfumed oil was exported. Because of the demand for Corinthian products, especially in Italy, pottery was manufactured on a scale which we have not seen previously. Some is exquisite, such as the Macmillan aryballos, which is just 7 cm high (figure 6.8), but as output increased the compositions became more stereotyped with endless animal friezes. Details on the animals and fill motifs were incised so that the clay shows through the paint, a technique adapted from engraved metalwork which was taken up in Athens in the late seventh century.

Athenian pottery had not been as commercially successful as Corinthian and the fact that the animal friezes were copied, as well as the black-figure technique, does suggest a more market-oriented approach. It seems that craftsmen were encouraged to come and settle in Athens in the early sixth century. They may have included

**Figure 6.8**   Macmillan aryballos (London, British Museum)

potters from Corinth and even from outside Greece. We know the names of some sixth-century potters because they "signed" their work. Lydos, the Lydian, was presumably from western Asia Minor. It is quite likely that many of these foreign craftsmen were or had been slaves. In the sixth century the quality of the best Athenian pottery was exceptionally high and there is great skill in the way that the black-figure technique was used (figure 6.9). Athens gradually overtook Corinth as the major production center. Around 530 a new technique was invented. Red-figure is in certain respects the reverse of black-figure in that the background was painted black so that the figures were highlighted in the red-colored clay (figure 6.10). Details could not be incised and were therefore painted, which did allow more subtle effects. Both techniques were in use for a time but red-figure became the dominant style in the fifth century. Trade intensified particularly with southern Italy, where some Athenian potters eventually set up workshops.

Myth scenes were very common on black-figure and red-figure pottery. Daily life is also depicted, though rather selectively and with an aristocratic bias. A favorite theme is the symposion, which is entirely appropriate because much of the pottery was used for these male parties. The wine was brought in amphorae, water in hydriai (figure 6.11). The Greeks did not drink their wine neat, so it was diluted with water in a krater and then served in oinochoai. The cups came in a range of shapes and sizes. Many imitate metalwork, the splendid silver and gold vessels which aristocrats owned. Only a small proportion of the pottery produced in Athens in the sixth and fifth centuries was figure-decorated. Much of the fine ware was simply painted black but has a metallic lustre.

**Figure 6.9**    Athenian black-figure hydria (National Museums Liverpool, World Museum)

**Figure 6.10**    Athenian red-figure lekythos (National Museums Liverpool, World Museum)

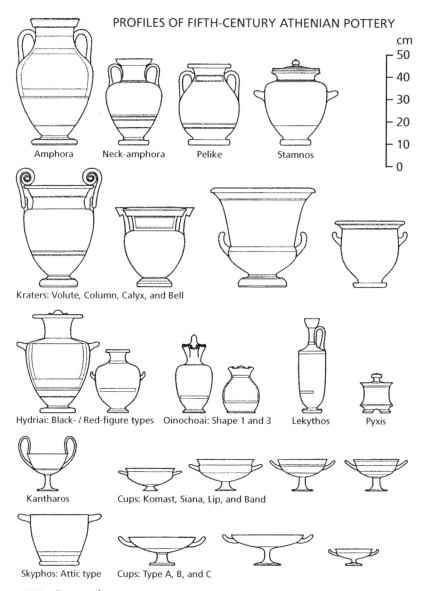

PROFILES OF FIFTH-CENTURY ATHENIAN POTTERY

cm
— 50
— 40
— 30
— 20
— 10
— 0

Amphora    Neck-amphora    Pelike    Stamnos

Kraters: Volute, Column, Calyx, and Bell

Hydriai: Black- / Red-figure types    Oinochoai: Shape 1 and 3    Lekythos    Pyxis

Kantharos    Cups: Komast, Siana, Lip, and Band

Skyphos: Attic type    Cups: Type A, B, and C

**Figure 6.11**    Pottery shapes

In the fourth century Athenian red-figure pottery is often rather ornate, with details picked out in white and yellow or gilded. Although some is still excellent, there is generally a decline in quality, and the red-figure technique went out of use by the end of the century. The market in southern Italy and Sicily was now dominated by local workshops which favored even more grandiose compositions, frequently inspired by the theater. Decoration becomes simpler in the Hellenistic period. The West Slope style, which originated in Athens and was widely copied, has vine tendrils and ivy wreaths painted in white and yellow on the glossy black surface. The influence of metalwork is evident in some of the complex shapes and also in the relief decoration on mold-made bowls known as Megarian bowls, though there were many centers of production. The design was stamped on the inside of a clay mold, which was fired and fixed on a wheel. The bowl was thrown inside the mold, left to dry, and could then be removed and painted. Megarian bowls were usually fired dark brown or black but later Hellenistic pottery often has a shiny red finish. This was subsequently combined with relief decoration in the Arretine wares of the Roman period.

## Pottery production at Athens and Corinth

Most of the workshops in Athens were concentrated in the Kerameikos, the district "of the potters," on the northwest side of the city (figure 2.9). At first the potters were based in the Agora but, perhaps in the late sixth century, they moved out to the area around the cemetery where their kilns were presumably less of a nuisance and a hazard. At Corinth potters worked on the western edge of the city near sources of clay and fuel. They also had access to farmland there, which may have been an additional incentive, but potters often operate in marginal locations because of their relatively low social status.

   Although kilns have been excavated and also production debris, such as wasters and test pieces, the layout of the workshops is unclear. Fortunately a black-figure hydria does give us a glimpse inside one of these establishments (figure 6.12). The man with the staff is obviously in charge. On the left workers finish off large amphorae which are then carried across to the kiln. This is being stoked up or raked out. The bearded head just above the stoke hole is presumably a god who will oversee this critical stage in the production process. The workshop depicted on a red-figure hydria has Athena herself in attendance with two winged Nikes who crown the staff as they paint kraters and hydriai. Of course we cannot take these scenes literally but they do suggest that a typical workshop may have had five or six employees. One of the workers on the red-figure hydria is a woman, no doubt a member of the family which ran the establishment. It is clear from the signatures of Athenian

**Figure 6.12**   Pottery workshop on an Athenian black-figure hydria (Munich, Glyptothek und Museum antiker Kleinkunst)

**Figure 6.13**   Clay quarry on a Corinthian pinax (Staatliche Museen zu Berlin)

potters that sons often followed their fathers in this trade, as we would expect in
view of the lengthy apprenticeship. One estimate is that the workforce in Athens
numbered around 500 in the fifth century BC, though there would have been seasonal fluctuations.

Corinthian potters evidently fetched their own clay (figure 6.13), whereas in
Athens the main sources were some distance from the city and the workshops may
have relied on suppliers. The clay had to be purified and would often have been left
for several months before it was used. The wheels depicted on a black-figure cup
(figure 6.14a & b) are set quite low and the potter sits on a stool or stands when
extra pressure is needed. An assistant rotates the wheel which was not turned
mechanically. Once thrown, the pottery would be left to dry and then the bases and
handles were attached. The next stage was the decoration. The paint was a very fine
clay solution with a deflocculant agent, possibly potash, added so that the particles
would remain in suspension. Experiments have shown that the painters used a range
of brushes. After the paint had dried, details could be incised with an engraver or
picked out in other colours such as white and purple.

The batch of pottery was now ready for the kiln. Excavated examples suggest that
these were quite simple and consisted of an arched tunnel through which the fuel
was pushed into the fire chamber (figure 6.15). The heat from this rose through the
pierced floor on which the pottery was carefully stacked. The domed roof was made
of clay and would have been dismantled after the pottery had fired. There was a
vent in the roof, clearly indicated on votive plaques from Corinth (figure 6.16a &
b), and a door in the side. This was probably a spy-hole so that the potter could
monitor the condition of the pottery. The hooked rods held by the potters on the
plaques may have been used to retrieve test pieces through the spy-hole or the vent.

**Figure 6.14a & b**  Potters on an Athenian black-figure cup (Badisches Landesmuseum Karlsruhe)

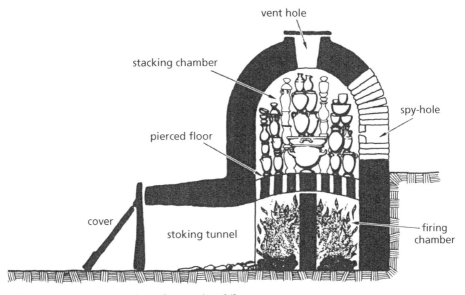

**Figure 6.15**  Reconstruction of an ancient kiln

(a)

(b)

**Figure 6.16a** & b   Kilns on Corinthian pinakes (Paris, Louvre and Staatliche Museen zu Berlin)

To achieve the contrast between the red color of the clay and the black paint of Athenian pottery, three stages were necessary. First the temperature in the kiln was raised to around 800 degrees and the vent was then opened. The oxygen turned the clay a pale pink and the paint red. Wet leaves or green wood were added and the kiln was sealed for the second stage. The temperature increased to around 950 degrees and, with no oxygen in the chamber, the clay became greyish-black and the paint sintered black. Consequently, unlike the clay, the paint did not turn red again when the vent was reopened. It would be a day or so before the kiln cooled down and could be dismantled.

Some of the pottery was doubtless sold in the local market and customers must also have bought directly from the workshop. This would be the case if a batch of pottery was ordered, for example the amphorae which were filled with olive oil and given as prizes in the Panathenaic games at Athens. Pots were occasionally marked on the underside of the base before or after they had been fired. These abbreviated inscriptions sometimes list the type, quantity, and cost of the pottery which made up a batch. Most of the inscriptions are on pottery which was exported. The pottery from Corinth was apparently shipped by Corinthians but in Athens there were merchants from other Greek cities as well as Athenians involved. This is evident from the letter forms of the inscriptions. The Etruscans were good customers and the Athenian potter Nikosthenes targeted this market. He produced black-figure versions of Etruscan amphorae, a nice blend of the exotic and the familiar. The trademarks do give some prices, though it is not always clear whether this was what the merchant had paid for the pottery or what he charged. The prices quoted range from half an obol for a skyphos to eighteen obols for a hydria at a time when a skilled worker earned six obols a day. So pottery was not expensive but must have been profitable, which is why so much was exported.

## Metallurgy

The start of the Bronze Age in the late fourth millennium should signify a techno-logical revolution, the replacement of stone tools by metal artefacts. Predictably, it is not quite so simple. As we will see, there was some metalwork in circulation in the Neolithic period. Moreover the production of chipped and ground stone tools actually increased in the Early Bronze Age, which is in any case a misnomer since most of the metalwork was made of copper. This was a "revolution" which took around 2,000 years.

### The Neolithic and Early Bronze Age

The earliest metalwork in the Aegean comes from Late Neolithic sites and consists of small trinkets—beads, awls, and bracelets—mainly of copper. By the Final Neolithic period the range of artefact types had expanded and included axes, chisels, and daggers. Silver and gold were used for beads and pendants. Parallels have been noted with metalwork in the Balkans, where copper metallurgy began much earlier, in the late sixth millennium, and which may have been the source of some of the finds. The amount of metalwork does not increase significantly in EB I—quite the opposite in fact—but this does not necessarily reflect a hiatus in production. With metals we are very dependent on deliberate deposition. If an artefact broke and could not be repaired, the metal was usually recycled. So what we typically find is metalwork that was taken out of circulation and buried with the dead. However, this was not a common practice in EB I, possibly because there was less of an emphasis on wealth and status. The situation changes in EB II. Metalwork and metallurgical activity become more visible in the archaeological record.

Argentiferous lead ores were mined at Lavrion in Attica and Ayios Sostis on the island of Siphnos in the Cyclades. Silver was then separated from the lead by cupellation, which is described below. The copper ore deposits that were exploited in the Early Bronze Age seem to have been mainly surface outcrops. When the ore weathers and oxidizes it forms the blue and green copper minerals, azurite and malachite, which prospectors would have easily recognized. Deposits in the Cyclades were certainly worked and sometimes the ore was smelted nearby. At other sites copper ore had apparently been brought from several different sources to be processed. The locations chosen were often, though not always, away from settlements. An exposed promontory, such as Chrysokamino on the northeast coast of Crete, was ideal because the wind provided a natural draft for the furnaces. Enormous amounts of slag have been found at some sites, around 5,000 tons at Skouries on the island of Kythnos. The furnaces were clay cylinders, 40–50 cm in diameter, which were placed on top of a shallow depression and the filled with the charge (figure 6.17). This consisted of crushed ore, fuel, and a flux, for example silica if the ore was iron-rich. The holes in the side of the cylinder provided some of the oxygen that was needed. Blowpipes and bellows fitted with clay nozzles / tuyères were also used. Once the temperature reached around 1250–1300°C the ore was reduced to metal and the flux combined with the gangue or non-metallic component of the ore to form slag, which settled at the bottom of the furnace. Under the slag the heavier copper formed an ingot. When the furnace had cooled down, the clay cylinder was broken open so that the ingot could be removed. The slag was crushed and any residual copper extracted. There may have been around 20 furnaces at Skouries which implies quite a large workforce and an impressive display of pyrotechnics if they were fired up at the same time.

The next stage involved another change of location. Evidence for the manufacture of tools and weapons has been found in the Early Minoan settlement at Poros-Katsambas on the north coast of Crete. There are clay crucibles in which the copper was remelted, molds for daggers, tuyères, and fragments of slag. We will never know whether it was the same individuals who mined, smelted, and worked the copper into artefacts or alternatively whether each stage in the process was the responsibility of a different group. Whatever the level of specialization, early metallurgy in the Aegean was coordinated in a way that would most obviously have benefited the metalsmiths.

Analysis has shown that artefacts were sometimes made from an alloy of copper and arsenic. This may have been produced accidentally because copper ores can contain mineralized arsenic. Yet in many cases the amount of arsenic present is such that the alloy was certainly intentional. At Chrysokamino arsenic was added when the ore was smelted, whereas at Poros-Katsambas molten copper was enriched. The alloy has a number of advantages, particularly an increase in hardness. It also melts at a lower temperature and is therefore easier to cast. The silvery surface of copper-arsenic artefacts would have been an additional attraction. However, when heated, arsenic is volatile and highly toxic. This could be why tin bronze became the preferred alloy and it is slightly harder as well. A major disadvantage is the availability of tin, since there is none in the Aegean.

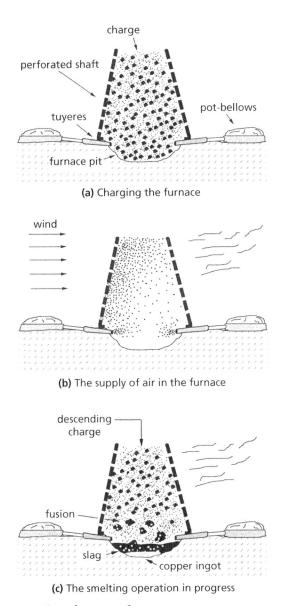

**(a)** Charging the furnace

**(b)** The supply of air in the furnace

**(c)** The smelting operation in progress

**Figure 6.17**   Reconstruction of a copper furnace

## Second-millennium metalwork

Metals were more in demand across the Mediterranean in the second millennium. This led to the commoditization of silver in particular. In the Near East the value of raw materials was often expressed in terms of silver in the form of bars and ingots of a standard weight. The copper ingots that were transported by ship around the eastern and central Mediterranean resemble oxhides and generally weigh around

30 kg. This distinctive shape may have made the ingots easier to load but implies that there was a recognized exchange rate for copper as well.

In the context of this well-developed Mediterranean metals trade, the rich silver deposits around Lavrion in Attica would have been a very valuable resource. Silver ores were certainly mined and processed at Thorikos but it seems doubtful whether this site had any sort of monopoly over production. Lavrion has been identified by lead isotope analysis as one of the main sources of copper as well. All copper and silver ores, ingots, and artefacts contain some lead. Because the isotopic composition of the lead in ore deposits varies, this technique can indicate where the copper or silver came from, though it would be more accurate to say that a likely source is established by a process of elimination. Reservations have been expressed about lead isotope analysis. Nevertheless, it would appear that Lavrion produced most of the copper for the Aegean bronze industry and only around 20 percent was imported from the massive Cypriot ore deposits.

There were Cypriot copper ingots on board two ships, presumably bound for the Aegean, which sank off the southern coast of Turkey (see chapter 7). The cargo included tin as well. Possible sources for this include southwestern Turkey, Afghanistan, and central Asia which were linked with the Near East by trade networks. Tin is also found in Italy, Spain, France, Britain, and central Europe. Egypt provided Near Eastern states with gold and some may have reached the Aegean this way. Gold was mined in Greece in the Classical period but it is unclear whether these deposits, on Siphnos, Thasos, and in Thrace, were known earlier.

Given the economic importance of metals and consequently their significance as a symbol of high status, Minoan and Mycenaean elites would have wanted to exercise some control over the supply chain. It is questionable whether the palaces were involved in maritime trade but they did take a direct role in the production process. Linear B texts from Pylos record between 300 and 400 smiths who received specified quantities of bronze from the palace. The smiths were organized in groups of 20 or so and based at various locations, possibly near sources of fuel. The amount of bronze they were given was small, which suggests that they did not work exclusively for the palace. Nevertheless, the size of the workforce does give us an idea of the scale of the bronze industry.

Most bronze tools and weapons were cast. The optimum alloy consists of 10 percent tin and 90 percent copper. A higher proportion of tin increases the hardness but the bronze is more brittle and cannot be worked as easily. The crucibles were made of heat-resistant clay, and stone was also used. They were usually placed on a bed of charcoal and sometimes fuel was heaped over the top of the crucible as well. A temperature in excess of 1100°C was needed to melt pure copper, around 1000°C for 10 percent tin bronze. Once the crucible was removed from the heat the cast had to be poured quickly because the metal soon solidified. Simple tools and weapons were cast in a one-piece mold. For a more complicated object, such as a socketed double ax (figure 6.18), a two-piece mold was required. The molten metal had to be poured into the mold steadily to ensure that trapped gases escaped which would otherwise cause defects. When the metal had cooled, the

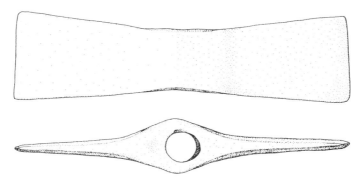

**Figure 6.18**    Double ax (National Museums Liverpool, World Museum)

rough surface was cleaned and polished. Edges were cold-hammered, which hardens the bronze.

Minoan and Mycenaean bronzesmiths produced some spectacular weapons. In the shaft graves at Mycenae there were swords with narrow blades 90 cm in length (figure 8.1b). The hilt was attached to a short tang and this must have been a point of weakness because a new type of sword was introduced with a flanged hilt which was cast as part of the blade. These swords sometimes have elaborately decorated gold hilts and pommels. Although they could still have been used, the emphasis on display is obvious. Later Mycenaean swords have projections from the shoulder which protected the hand and are generally shorter. Technically the most impressive weapons are the inlaid daggers from the shaft graves (figure 8.7). On either side of the cast bronze blade is a sheet of oxidized silver with inset gold and silver figures. Details are picked out in niello, a bluish-black compound of copper and silver sulphides.

For bronze figurines a different type of mold was used. The figure was modeled in wax or resin and coated with a layer of clay which was heated. The wax/resin melted and was poured out through the base. The mold could then be filled with molten metal. This technique is known as cire perdue or lost wax. Vessels were made out of sheet metal. For a simple hemispherical bowl, a copper or bronze disk was carefully hammered over an anvil, thinned out, and formed into shape. In the case of larger vessels, sheets were riveted together (figure 6.19). Attachments, such as handles, were usually cast separately and riveted in place. The same techniques were used for bronze armor (figure 8.8).

Gold and silver vessels were worked in much the same way as those of copper and bronze but many have additional decoration. This was often embossed or repoussé. The sheet was placed on a soft surface, such as wax or pitch, and the design was modeled from the back with hammers and punches, then finished off on the front. Two gold cups from Vapheio in Laconia show the level of detail which was possible with this technique (figure 6.20). Some of the jewelry is equally skillful. The remarkable bee pendant from Mallia illustrates the technique of granulation, tiny beads of gold which were soldered in place (figure 6.21).

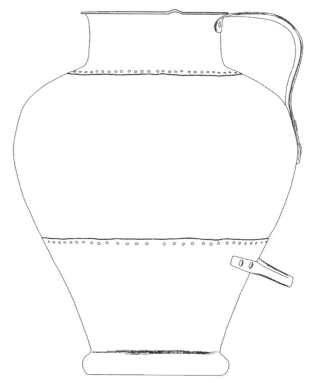

**Figure 6.19** Bronze hydria from shaft grave IV at Mycenae (Athens, National Archaeological Museum)

**Figure 6.20** Gold cup from Vapheio (Athens, National Archaeological Museum)

**Figure 6.21**   Gold bee pendant from Mallia (Herakleion Museum)

## The age of iron

Many of these skills were lost in the Aegean after the Mycenaean palaces were destroyed. However, there was a major technological development: the introduction of iron metallurgy. Iron, some of which may have been meteoric, had occasionally been used for items of jewelry in the Bronze Age. It seems likely that iron was also obtained as an accidental by-product of copper metallurgy. On Cyprus iron-rich copper ores were smelted and iron oxides sometimes added as a flux. Both of these processes would have produced small quantities of spongy but workable iron. This could be considered the first stage in the development of iron metallurgy. Next, some weapons and tools were made of iron and finally, at the start of the Iron Age, bronze was replaced as the most common utilitarian metal.

The transition from bronze to iron would not have been straightforward because there are major differences in the way that the two metals were worked. Iron ores were smelted in a similar type of furnace with charcoal as a fuel and blowpipes or bellows used to increase the temperature. However, 1300–1400°C was the maximum that could be achieved in these furnaces and the point at which iron melts is 1540°C. Consequently, although the ores were reduced to a spongy mass, the iron did not become liquid and form an ingot. Much of the spongy mass consisted of slag which had to be extracted. Because of the high temperature needed to melt iron, it could not be cast. This only became possible with the introduction of blast furnaces much later. The smelted iron bloom was therefore heated until it was malleable and hammered into shape. Unlike bronze, which was cast and sharpened when the metal was cold, iron is hardened by carburization—the carbon content is raised so that it is converted into steel. This was probably discovered by chance because the iron was heated in a charcoal fire. Ancient smiths may not have understood why this made the iron harder but they soon learned how to reproduce the effect. There was one more technique that they needed to master. Once the iron has been carburized, it can be significantly strengthened if it is quenched in cold water and then tempered, that is reheated to a lower temperature and cooled again. Greek smiths certainly knew how to quench and temper iron by the time the *Odyssey* was composed, probably in the eighth century BC . When Odysseus and his companions blind the Cyclops with a red-hot wooden stake, his eye sizzles just like a "great axe or adze which a smith dips in cold water as he tempers it, for through this the iron is strengthened" (*Odyssey* 9.391–93). A bronze ax or adze treated in this way would become brittle instead.

It was in the Near East and Cyprus in the twelfth century that the production of iron first took off. Iron knives with bronze riveted bone or ivory hilts were particularly popular, and examples, possibly imported from Cyprus, have been found in the Aegean. The start of the Early Iron Age in Greece is dated around the middle of the eleventh century, though it is questionable whether the technology was well established at that point. However, by the tenth century iron was used for swords, daggers, spears, arrows, axes, chisels, pins, and fibulae. As most of these items come from graves and tools were only occasionally buried with the dead, the range would no doubt be even greater if we had more evidence from settlement sites. The adoption of iron was therefore a relatively rapid process compared with the very gradual introduction of copper and bronze. So what was the attraction of iron? In certain respects it is technically superior in that an iron sword, for example, is lighter than one made of bronze and could be resharpened more easily but the blade would not necessarily be harder unless the smith was experienced. In this respect skilled bronzeworkers may have had the edge, quite literally, at first. A major advantage of iron must have been availability. Greece has more iron ore than copper deposits and no tin. Indeed it has been argued that the production of iron spread so quickly because the supply of copper and tin was disrupted in the eleventh and tenth centuries. This would explain why items such as pins were laboriously forged from iron rather than cast in bronze which was much simpler. Once trade resumed, the use of bronze increased again. It does seem likely that there was a shortage of bronze for a time, though sources evidently still existed. Bronzes from Lefkandi and Nichoria have a high tin content, over 15 percent in some cases. The intention may have been to produce a silvery surface but, whatever the reason, it shows that tin was available. However, the tin content in Early Iron Age bronzes is very variable, which suggests that metals were recycled and must have been difficult to obtain. Iron would also have appealed because, initially at least, it was novel and exotic. We know from Near Eastern texts how highly iron was valued and this may have been the case in Greece as well. Indeed, it is possible that iron symbolized a new era and a conscious rejection of the recent past.

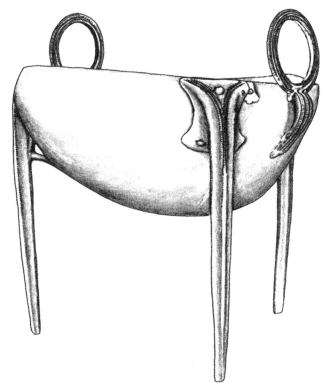

**Figure 6.22**    Bronze tripod cauldron from Olympia (Olympia Museum)

As production increased, the value of iron would presumably have fallen and function became a more decisive factor. Iron was still preferred for swords but pins and fibulae were made of bronze. The reason why bronze was also used for spearheads could be technical, since a hollow socket was easier to cast than forge. Nevertheless, it is significant that so many bronzes were dedicated in sanctuaries in the eighth century: weapons, jewelry, figurines and massive tripod cauldrons (figure 6.22). Bronze evidently had a certain cachet, possibly because of the link with the heroic past celebrated in the Homeric epics. Ironically, analysis of some of these dedications has shown that the bronze is often of poor quality with high levels of lead and iron but perhaps this did not matter since they were simply made for display. What the sanctuary dedications also demonstrate is the level of demand for metal which provided much of the impetus for overseas trade.

## The silver mines at Lavrion

The best evidence for the way that precious metals were exploited comes from Lavrion in Attica. Production of silver started here in the Bronze Age and had certainly resumed by the sixth century. Early in the fifth century the "third contact," a deeper but much richer ore deposit, was discovered. The Athenians used this windfall to build a fleet of triremes and thereby made their city a major naval power. So it is clear that the state had some control over the proceeds of the mines but individuals also benefited. The Athenian general Nikias had 1000 slaves for hire at an obol per man per day. Many of the slaves who worked in the mines escaped when the Spartans set up a military base in Attica in 413 BC and the industry collapsed. The next boom period was in the fourth century. Inscriptions set up in the Agora in Athens by officials known as poletai recorded the leases which individuals had taken out. The state apparently owned the mines but they were operated by private contractors, some of whom made enormous profits. It was claimed that Epikrates of Pallene and his associates received 300 talents in three years from one concession. In the Hellenistic period there was a decrease in activity, exacerbated by a slave revolt, and by the second century AD Lavrion was simply the place "where the Athenians once had silver mines" (Pausanias, 1.1).

Geologically Lavrion consists of superimposed layers of limestone and schist which have been folded and eroded. At the junction or contact zone between the layers, veins of lead, zinc, and iron ore were deposited by hydrothermal action. It was the lead ore which contained silver. Erosion had exposed some deposits and these were the first to be worked. Short tunnels were cut through the rock when a vein ran below the surface. However, the "third contact" lay at a much deeper level and was reached by vertical shafts, some of which descended 100 meters or more. Once the vein had been located, side galleries were opened up. They were never more than one meter high and the miners had to lie on their backs or sides. The tools they used were simple—iron hammers, chisels, picks, and shovels—so progress was slow, just a few centimeters each shift. For light they relied on torches or oil lamps which must have made the atmosphere in the cramped galleries even more intolerable. Ventilation was a major problem and sometimes shafts were sunk in pairs so that one could provide an air supply but miners still suffocated. No wonder most of the workforce were slaves and that they frequently ran away.

When the ore had been lifted to the surface, it was processed in a workshop a short distance from the mine. First it was crushed and ground in a mill (figure 6.23). Then the ore was washed in order to separate out the lead. The ore washeries are one of the most distinctive features of Lavrion and clearly represented a considerable investment on the part of their owners. They usually consisted of a rectangular stand tank from which water could be released at high pressure through funnel-shaped holes into wooden troughs. These contained the crushed ore which was stirred so that the heavier particles of lead sank and remained in the trough. The dross was swept into a channel and ran around the plastered platform on which the concentrated ore was dried. Sedimentation basins ensured that the lighter particles were removed and the water was then recycled. Massive circular cisterns were constructed in order to collect rainwater and can be seen in the vicinity of most of the workshops.

MINING

mica-schist

contact ores

shaft

galleries

1

limestone

3 grinder

MECHANICAL
TREATMENT

crushing stone

2

crushed to grains
of < 1mm

WASHERIES - CONCENTRATING

settling tank

cistern

4

drying of concentrated ore

concentrated ore

**Figure 6.23**   Reconstruction of the methods used to mine, crush, and wash lead ores at Lavrion

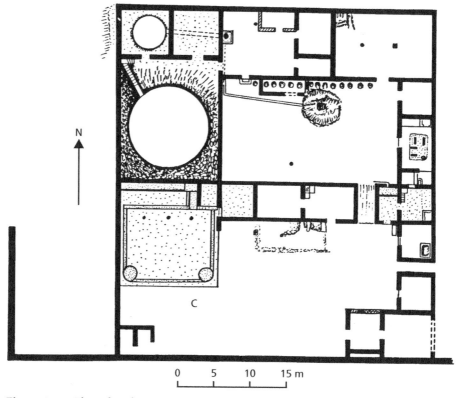

**Figure 6.24**   Plan of washery C at Agrileza

A good example of a workshop complex has been excavated at Agrileza. Workshop C is late fourth century and the washery is one of the largest in Lavrion (figure 6.24). Note the three column bases which supported a roof over the stand tank and the square platform. This would have kept the sun off the workers and also reduced evaporation—water was a precious commodity in this dry region. The water for the washery came from a cement-lined cistern, 11.20 meters in diameter, which could be entered by a flight of steps and cleaned out periodically. East of the washery is a court with rooms on three sides built of stone and mudbrick. Ore may have been stored in the room by the washery and there were workrooms, as well as a possible bathroom. A ramp leads up to a second court. One of the rooms on the east side of this has four stone blocks embedded in the concrete floor, presumably for a work surface, and a bloomery hearth. Two more workshops have been excavated at Agrileza and just beyond the complex is a tower which may have been part of a farmhouse. Although this is not prime agricultural land, the miners created a demand for food and perhaps a need for security as well. Even in the main town at Thorikos some of the houses have towers and the presence of workshops and washeries gives a sense of the level of industrial activity here in the fourth century (figure 6.25). Unfortunately, after this boom, Thorikos went bust.

**Figure 6.25** Washery at Thorikos

The furnaces in which the lead ore was smelted have proved more elusive. They may have been sited away from the mines and workshops because they gave off noxious fumes, although the health and safety of the workforce were clearly not a major concern. A source of fuel may have been more important, since Lavrion was soon deforested. Two furnace complexes have been excavated on the coast and one up in the hills. The furnaces were built of stone and lined with clay. They were bottle-shaped with an internal diameter of around one meter at the base and may have been three or four meters high (figure 6.26). Layers of charcoal and ore were loaded into the furnace and then they were fired. Bellows raised the temperature until the metal melted and ran out through tap holes. Once the metal had cooled and solidified, the silver could be separated from the lead. It was reheated in a cupellation furnace to around 1000°C in a strong current of air, supplied by bellows, which caused the lead to oxidize and form litharge. The litharge was absorbed into the fabric of the cupellation hearth or scraped off the surface with iron rods which had been dipped in cold water. The silver still contained some lead and would continue to be refined until it was almost pure.

The Athenians minted coins from the silver produced at Lavrion. Silver had been used as a measure of value and a means of exchange in the Near East as early as the third millennium but it was not until the sixth century that the first coins were struck by the Lydians whose capital was at Sardis in western Asia Minor. The Lydian coins were made of electrum, a natural alloy of gold and silver. The Greeks preferred silver, and many cities had started to issue coins by the end of the sixth century. The

**Figure 6.26** Reconstruction of the furnaces used to roast lead ores at Lavrion and the cupellation process

(a)                                                                              (b)

**Figure 6.27a & b**   Athenian tetradrachm of around 450 BC (University of Liverpool, Garstang Museum of Archaeology)

incentive was partly political because coins were a powerful symbol of civic identity. The growth of a market economy was also greatly facilitated by the spread of coinage. In fifth-century Athens state payment for military service, jurors, attendance at the assembly, and even the theater further boosted the use of coins. The Athenian coins had a helmeted head of Athena on the obverse and an owl with the name of the city abbreviated as ΑΘΕ on the reverse (figure 6.27a & b). These "owls" became the dominant currency in the eastern Mediterranean and were widely copied. Athens was of course a powerful city, politically and economically, but the purity of the silver must also have been a factor. When Alexander issued coins he used the Athenian weight standard. Although his currency had the widest circulation in the Hellenistic period, the Athenians continued to mint silver coins until the first century.

## Conclusions

This review of developments in the production of pottery and metallurgy has shown how the process of innovation varies. The potential of pottery was not immediately recognized at the start of the Neolithic period. At first it was just used to serve but not store or cook food. There could be technical reasons for this, because larger vessels would not be as easy to make, and conservatism must also have been a factor. Tradition dictated how food should be prepared and eaten. The low level of production may therefore reflect the low demand for pottery. The introduction of metallurgy was even more protracted. Obviously metals were less readily available than clay for pottery and the technology was more complex. Yet the response to potential was once again belated. The superiority of a new type of artefact was not always immediately apparent or accepted. A technical innovation, such as the use of the wheel, took time to master but was quicker and consequently more efficient. Nevertheless, some pottery was still made by hand because this was the tradition. Given the generally slow pace of change, it is remarkable that iron metallurgy was established so quickly, especially as different skills were required. Iron tools and weapons were not necessarily better, so a shortage of bronze may well have speeded up the process. In this case the novelty of iron was also an attraction at a time when values had become more fluid.

There has been considerable speculation about the way that production was organized. The high quality of Neolithic pottery could indicate specialization, though it is quite possible that most households were involved. The level of exchange in the Early Bronze Age, particularly on Crete, is consistent with workshop production. Considerable expertise was also required to mine and smelt metal ores. This may have been a seasonal occupation but certainly qualifies as specialized. The technical developments in the second millennium suggest some control of the workforce. Pylos did provide smiths with bronze, yet it seems unlikely that they all worked full-time for the palace. Knossos and Pylos also obtained much of their pottery from independent suppliers. In Athens the pottery workshops were of course privately owned and here we can gage the scale of production. Significantly, the state did not invest directly in the silver mines at Lavrion but leased out concessions. A point which has repeatedly been stressed is the way that pottery and metals moved around and their role in trade will be examined in more detail in the next chapter.

## Bibliographical notes

### Pottery

For pottery production generally see Rice 1987. Neolithic pottery is well illustrated in Papathanassopoulos 1996. Mee 2007 focuses on the role of pottery in the Neolithic Peloponnese. Betancourt 1985 is a good account of Minoan pottery. The organization of pottery production on Crete is discussed in a number of the papers in Laffineur and Betancourt 1997 and also by Day and Wilson 1998. Knappett 1999 and Evely 2000 examine the technical developments. On the Minoan pottery from the Cyclades see Mountjoy and Ponting 2000. Mycenaean pottery is described in Mountjoy 1986 and 1993. Jones 1986 discusses analytical projects, Whitelaw 2001b pottery production at Pylos. The Protogeometric and Geometric pottery styles are described in Snodgrass 1971, Coldstream 1968 and 1997, Lemos 2002, and Dickinson 2006. Morgan and Whitelaw 1991 analyze the Early Iron Age pottery of the Argolid. Rasmussen 1991 gives a concise account of Corinthian pottery. Sparkes 1991 is excellent on every aspect of Greek pottery but does not consider the iconography in detail. The bibliography on this is vast, but Boardman 1975, 1989, and 1991,

Osborne 1998a, and Robertson 1992 can be recommended. The relationship of pottery and metal vessels is examined by Vickers and Gill 1994. Athenian and Corinthian pottery production is discussed by Noble 1988, Arafat and Morgan 1989, Hemelrijk 1991, Sparkes 1991, and Papadopoulos 2003. See Johnston 1991 for trade marks.

## Metallurgy

Tylecote 1987 and Craddock 1995 are excellent introductions. The papers in Day and Doonan 2007 provide a comprehensive overview of Early Bronze Age metallurgy in the Aegean. See Kassianidou and Knapp 2005 for the wider Mediterranean and Pare 2000 for the European context. Stos-Gale and Gale 2003 discuss the results of lead isotope analyses. Evely 2000 describes the techniques used for each type of artefact. On the introduction of iron metallurgy see Snodgrass 1980b and 1989, Sherratt 1994, and Waldbaum 1999. Wheeler and Maddin 1980 give a good description of the technology. The bronze shortage hypothesis is discussed *inter alia* by Snodgrass 1971, Morris 2000, and Kayafa 2006. For Early Iron Age metalwork see Lemos 2002 and Dickinson 2006.

Conophagos 1980 is the best general account of the silver mines and workshop installations at Lavrion. Healey 1978 and Rihll 2001 are also useful. Jones 1984–5 describes the washeries at Agrileza, and Mussche 1974 summarizes the evidence from Thorikos. Kraay 1976, Carradice 1995, and Howgego 1995 are good introductions to Greek coins.

# CHAPTER 7

# Trade and Colonization

## Introduction

This chapter focuses on the movement of goods and people overseas. Although the Greeks were generally self-sufficient, key raw materials did need to be imported. Moreover, because of the mountainous terrain, a journey by sea was often the best option. The long coastline provided plenty of sheltered harbors and the number of islands in the Aegean archipelago meant that land was rarely out of sight, which simplified navigation. Sailors in the Mediterranean did not have to contend with tides but the weather was a concern. June to mid-September was the best time to set sail. The skies were usually clear, the winds moderate, and the sea calm. Mid-March to the end of May and mid-September to mid-November were riskier. Storms and high winds made the winter months dangerous, though short journeys could still be undertaken on good days.

In summer the winds in the Aegean often blow from the northwest or northeast, so that it is possible to sail in a southerly direction but more difficult to head back. In the spring there is a greater likelihood of a wind from the southeast or southwest and consequently better conditions for a voyage northwards. Ships bound for the eastern Mediterranean sailed south from Crete and followed the African coast as far as the Nile Delta. They then turned north and made their way up the Levantine coast to Cyprus. The return leg was along the dangerous southern coast of Turkey and across the Aegean via Rhodes. A long-distance voyage like this took weeks or months and the crews of these ships must have been experienced sailors. Most of the vessels which traveled around the Aegean made much shorter journeys, often rather opportunistically. This type of trade, known as cabotage, is difficult to iden-tify archaeologically because the goods do not necessarily move directly between

*Greek Archaeology: A Thematic Approach*   By Christopher Mee
© 2011 Christopher Mee

producer and consumer. Moreover, many of the items involved may leave no trace. This is true for example of foodstuffs and livestock, any human cargo, whether passengers or slaves, and products made of organic materials, such as textiles. Even in the case of more durable items, it may not be clear where they were made and how they reached the place where they were eventually found.

The transport of goods presupposes some movement of people but settlement overseas is a different proposition and raises a number of questions. It is not always obvious where the settlers came from, since new cultural traditions can evolve quickly in a different environment. Indeed, cultural affiliations may have no connection at all with ethnicity. Why people moved is often equally uncertain, even when we have texts which supposedly explain their motivation, as in the case of the Greek colonization of Italy and Sicily in the eighth and seventh centuries. These are some of the issues which will be examined in this chapter.

## Neolithic

Obsidian from the island of Melos has been found in the Upper Palaeolithic levels at Franchthi in the Argolid, dated around 10,000 BC. Although the sea level was lower at this time because of the ice sheets which covered much of northern Europe, a voyage of almost 100 kilometers would still have been required, more if a less direct route was taken via Seriphos and Siphnos, as seems likely. In the Mesolithic period the quantity of obsidian at Franchthi increases and there are bones from large fish the size of tuna. So the coastal location of the site was clearly exploited. We can only guess what type of boat the Mesolithic inhabitants of Franchthi had. One possibility is that they tied bundles of reeds together to make a raft which they paddled. Neolithic log boats have been excavated in Italy and may have been used in Greece as well.

Evidence of settlement on the islands is elusive. The Cyclops cave on Yioura in the northern Aegean is one of the few Mesolithic island sites. At the start of the Neolithic period there was an influx of settlers at Knossos on Crete who presumably transported their livestock—cattle, pigs, sheep, and goats—on rafts. The size of Crete must have been one of the main attractions for these intrepid colonists because it was not until the Late Final Neolithic period that most of the other islands were first occupied.

The late settlement of Melos is a surprise because obsidian accounts for a high proportion of the chipped stone tools on Neolithic sites in Greece. As the island was apparently uninhabited before the Final Neolithic period, the obsidian must have been procured directly from the quarries on the northeast coast. It seems unlikely that every Neolithic village made expeditions to Melos, a journey of several hundred kilometers from Thessaly for example. There were probably only a few groups of individuals who had the necessary expertise. Once they returned with the obsidian it could have passed from village to village through a system of "down-the-line" exchange. However, if this was the case, we would expect a high concentration of obsidian on coastal sites and a gradual decrease inland. The fact that just as much obsidian reached villages which were some distance from the sea suggests that it was supplied by itinerant traders, perhaps the seafarers who had made the voyage to Melos. Alternatively, given the consistently fine quality of the blades, specialist knappers may have traveled around and produced whatever each village needed. That obsidian was traded is certain, and blades of honey-coloured flint were also imported, possibly from the Adriatic.

Other types of flint, chert, and stone for axes were more readily available and circulated over shorter distances. Pottery was also exchanged, but this represents a different form of trade. As pottery was made in every village and perhaps by most families, the motivation must have been more social than commercial, to build and maintain relationships. Even in the Neolithic period trade was a complex phenomenon.

## Early Bronze Age

In the Early Bronze Age more Aegean islands were colonized and the number of settlements increased. In southern Greece there is a similar expansion into rather marginal environments with poorer-quality soils and low rainfall. This may have been made possible by a greater reliance on livestock, and the islands would certainly have provided plenty of rough pasture for sheep and goats. Yet life must have been very precarious for these communities which typically consisted of just a few households. They would have needed support networks and regular contact with their neighbors on other islands.

Initially the pattern of movement in the Cyclades was small scale but by EB II there were more extensive trade networks. The way that metals were mined, processed, and traded was certainly a factor in this. The islands were now much more closely interconnected and Cycladic influence is evident on coastal sites in Crete and mainland Greece. Voyages across the Aegean were made easier by improvements in boat construction. Incised on the bottom of a number of terracotta "frying pans," the actual function of which is a complete mystery, are representations of boats (figure 7.1). Four lead models, supposedly from the Cyclades, are rather similar (figure 7.2), though doubts have been expressed about their authenticity. Most of the "frying pans" came from the cemetery at Chalandriani on Syros, so they should be genuine. The boats on the "frying pans" are rendered rather schematically and this makes interpretation a problem. It is usually assumed that the high end, topped by a fish emblem, is the stern. The prow is also raised, though not at such a steep angle, and has a short projection. The diagonal lines above and below the hull presumably represent paddles or oars. Although they do not give us an accurate indication of the size of the crew, the implication is that these boats were quite large. They may have been 15–20 meters in length and this would allow for a crew of perhaps 25. The zigzag lines on some of the boats may signify that they were plank-built. Alternatively the rather narrow hull could indicate that this was a log boat with plank extensions at either end.

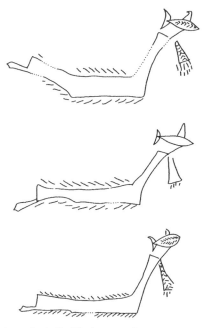

**Figure 7.1**    Boats incised on Cycladic "frying pans"

**Figure 7.2**    Lead boat model (National Museums Liverpool, World Museum)

How far a boat like this traveled in a day would obviously depend on the weather. The sides look quite low and not well adapted for rough seas. Nevertheless a journey of 40–50 kilometers was probably possible if conditions were reasonable, twice as far as a smaller boat could have managed. Different opinions have been expressed about the amount of cargo that these vessels carried. One view is that they were built for raiders rather than traders and this was certainly a culture in which weapons feature prominently but, given the investment involved in their construction, they probably had a range of uses. They may also have been a luxury which only a few communities could afford, because of the cost and the size of the crew. There were not many settlements with 25 adult males available, though the members of the crew need not all have come from the same place.

Some of the largest Cycladic settlements, such as Chalandriani on Syros, Grotta on Naxos, and Ayia Irini on Kea, were particularly well located for trade, often at the point where sea lanes intersected. Mochlos on the north coast of Crete is another example of a community which evidently benefited from the development of

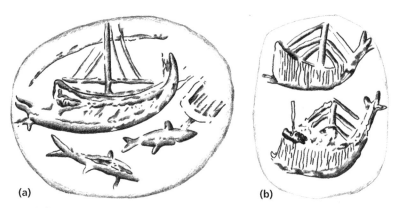

(a)                                          (b)

**Figure 7.3a & b**     Representations of ships with sails on Minoan sealstones

maritime exchange networks. The rich tombs in the cemetery (figure 9.4) underline just how wealthy certain families had become. Significantly the tombs face the open sea rather than the hinterland of Mochlos which is rugged and not particularly productive. It was through trade that the imported goods and raw materials in the cemetery were acquired and it was through gateway communities like Mochlos that they reached the rest of Crete. The more exotic imports, Egyptian stone vessels and scarabs, Near Eastern cylinder seals and ivory, may have arrived by a circuitous route, perhaps via Anatolia, as a result of down-the-line exchange. However, developments at the end of the third millennium made direct contact between Crete and the eastern Mediterranean possible. A terracotta boat model from Mochlos has pivots on each side which imply that it was propelled by oars rather than paddles. More importantly there are ships on Minoan sealstones with a central mast supported by stays fore and aft (figure 7.3a & b). No sail is shown on the earliest examples but one of the ships does have a lowered yard. The diagonal lines above this must be halyards which were used to raise the yard and the rectangular sail. Because of the small scale of the representations, the size of the ships is unclear but the deep curved hulls suggest that they were designed for the open sea.

The first ships with sails which appeared in the Aegean may have come from Egypt or the Near East. The obvious advantages of this new technology no doubt inspired local experimentation, though it would have taken some time to master the skills needed to build and maneuver these ships. Their impact must have been profound. The Aegean and indeed the Mediterranean effectively became much smaller because a journey of 100–150 kilometers could now be covered in one day. Overseas connections were certainly a factor in the developments on Crete, though it was sites with the best agricultural resources, notably Knossos, Phaistos, and Mallia, rather than maritime communities like Mochlos which ultimately became the most powerful centers. In the Cyclades new nucleated settlements were founded, often near the best harbor on an island. The change in the scale of communication networks was surely one of the reasons for this move.

## The Thalassocracy of Minos

Minos, according to tradition, was the first person to organise a navy. He controlled the greater part of what is now called the Hellenic Sea and ruled over the Cyclades, in most of which he founded the first colonies, installing his sons as governors, after having driven out the Carians. And it is reasonable to suppose that he did his best to suppress piracy in order to secure his own revenues. (Thucydides, 1.4)

Is there any truth in this account, written by Thucydides in the fifth century, of Crete as a prehistoric sea power under the leadership of Minos, the legendary ruler of Knossos? How should we interpret the evidence of contact between Crete and the Aegean islands?

At Kastri on Kythera settlers apparently arrived from Crete as early as EM II. This conclusion is based on the presence of locally made pottery which is Minoan in style and technique. It is quite different from the pottery previously produced on Kythera, which continued in use elsewhere on the island for a time. The connection with Crete was maintained in the Protopalatial period when a peak sanctuary was constructed at Ayios Georgios, which overlooks Kastri. The settlement expanded in the Neopalatial period and intensive survey has identified over 100 rural sites which were probably farmsteads. The increase in the population could have been internally generated, though it is possible that there were new settlers as well. The main reason why Kythera flourished in the Neopalatial period was undoubtedly because the island linked Crete and the southern Peloponnese. Kastri was integrated in this network of trade routes and does seem to have been an independent community, not simply an outpost of Crete.

The situation in the Cyclades underlines the different ways that interaction with Crete could develop. At Phylakopi on Melos there is Minoan pottery in the Middle Bronze Age levels, most of which was imported, though MM III shapes and motifs were copied. An earthquake apparently destroyed the site at the start of the Late Bronze Age. Subsequently a "mansion" was built which may have been an administrative center since a tablet written in the Cretan Linear A script was found nearby. Minoan influence is also evident in the frescoes and particularly the LC I pottery. Yet Phylakopi does not experience the major cultural transformation we would expect if Cretans had become the dominant element in the population. The fact that the settlement was still more or less the same size and is the only site on Melos also argues against any large-scale influx of settlers. The Linear A tablet could indicate political control, though the introduction of Minoan administrative practices seems just as likely, since Phylakopi clearly had close economic ties with Crete. One consequence of this was elite emulation of the Minoan way of life which has been described as the "Versailles effect" after the impact of the French court on eighteenth-century Europe. Crete similarly offered a model for islanders with aspirations.

Ayia Irini on Kea is like Phylakopi in many respects. Minoan influence gradually increases but pottery was imported from the nearby mainland as well as from Crete.

**Figure 7.4**   Reconstruction of the ship fresco from the West House at Akrotiri

If any settlers had come, they kept a low profile. Again the most plausible explanation is a process of acculturation, an assimilation of Minoan cultural traits. Akrotiri on Thera is different and not only because the site is so well preserved. The architecture of the houses (figures 4.10 & 4.11) is much more reminiscent of Crete, because of the way they were built, with a timber framework and ashlar masonry, as well as features like pier and door partitions and lustral basins. This hints at a shared ideology and therefore a greater level of contact. Moreover, a number of farmsteads have been identified on Thera, which is not the case on Melos or Kea, whereas this type of site is found on Crete and of course Kythera. Nevertheless, Akrotiri was not a Minoan town, though it is quite possible that there were some resident Cretans, especially since this was one of the closest islands, just over 100 kilometers away.

The extent of Minoan influence did not just depend on the distance from Crete. Kea is one of the northernmost islands in the Cyclades but well placed for access to the mineral deposits of southern Attica. Ships headed for the Argolid would usually have stopped over on Melos. These islands facilitated trade and therefore the supply of key raw materials. So were they simply convenient ports or did they offer Crete more, ships and sailors for example? A remarkable fresco from the West House at Akrotiri depicts a fleet of 11 vessels which has embarked on a short journey between two towns. Spectators watch the procession from the roofs of the houses and the shore. The vessels vary in size but are similar in design. The bow is slender and elaborately decorated in the case of the larger ships (figure 7.4). On the stern there is a cabin, perhaps for the captain. The helmsman stands in front of this and steers the ship with an oar, while passengers sit in the structure amidships. One of the ships is under sail and two more have masts. Most are propelled by paddlers who have to lean over the side, rather awkwardly, so that they can reach the water. It has been suggested that the ships were only paddled on special occasions and this does look like a ceremonial procession. They were quite sizable vessels, possibly 20–30 meters in length, which could have been used to transport goods, passengers, or troops.

East of Crete is the island of Karpathos where the settlement at Pigadia has imported and locally made Minoan pottery. The MM III–LM IA chamber tombs

nearby suggest that there may have been Cretans here and at other site:
island. Beyond Karpathos is Rhodes, the largest of the group of islands in tl
eastern Aegean known as the Dodecanese. Excavations at Trianda in the nortn ∪.
Rhodes have uncovered part of a settlement which may eventually have extended
over 17 hectares. Cretan influence is evident in the architecture of the houses, some
of which have pier and door partitions and were decorated with frescoes. The LB I
pottery is mainly Minoan in style, as well as the figurines and loomweights. This is
Minoanization on a scale which could indicate colonization, especially if Trianda
was founded in this period. However, parts of the settlement were occupied in the
Middle Bronze Age and the pottery from these levels is local with only a few imports
from Crete. So it is possible that the original population of Trianda essentially took
on a Minoan identity over time. Given the size of the settlement there may also have
been some resident Cretans, for whom the attraction of Rhodes would undoubtedly
have been the trade routes that intersect here.

The Seraglio site on Kos was also extensive, if not as large as Trianda. A Cretan
connection is implicit in the architecture and pottery but it is unclear how this
should be interpreted. At Iasos, which was formerly an offshore island, some of the
Minoan-style pottery apparently came from Kos. There were LM IA imports from
Crete as well but not all from the same region. The pottery made at Iasos is mostly
Anatolian, though Minoan vessel types were also manufactured in a way which
suggests that the potters may have been Cretan, possibly settlers. Study of the
pottery from Iasos has shown how careful analysis can tease out the web of contacts
that these sites maintained.

Miletos was a coastal site at the mouth of the Maeander river but is now some
distance inland as a result of alluviation. Links with Crete started early in the second
millennium when MM I–II Kamares pottery was imported. Minoan-style pottery
was also produced at Miletos and one of the kilns has been found. This has parallel
channels below the chamber like some kilns on Crete. Although most of the pottery
is still Anatolian, the presence of Minoan coarse ware vessels and loomweights may
possibly indicate settlers. In MM III–LM I Cretan influence is very evident, though
less so in the architecture of the houses which do not have features such as pier and
door partitions. However, there were frescoes, possibly with religious scenes, and a
sanctuary has been excavated in which cult was practiced in a way that seems typically Cretan. Around 95 percent of the pottery is now Minoan, and Linear A inscriptions were incised on a number of sherds. It does seem likely that Cretans settled at
Miletos but they probably joined quite a diverse community. Trade must always have
been, if not the raison d'être, then certainly a core activity for a site that was so well
located. The Maeander valley is one of the main routes inland from the west coast
of Turkey and Miletos had fine harbors as well. A port of trade here, where goods
were exchanged, could potentially have given Cretans access to Anatolian metals.

Crete did have close ties with sites in the southern Aegean in the Neopalatial
period and trade was undoubtedly a major motivation for this. There may have
been some settlement, though not on a scale which suggests a policy of colonization.
It is difficult to determine whether Cretans exercised any sort of political control,

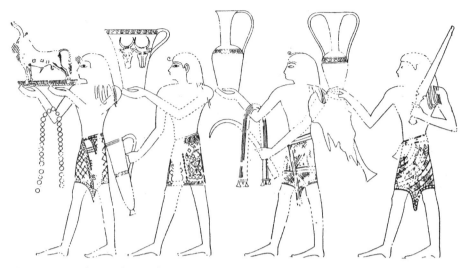

**Figure 7.5**    Keftiu in the tomb of Menkheperrasonb at Thebes, Egypt

though their economic and cultural impact was significant. A thalassocracy of the type envisaged by Thucydides does seem implausible, not least because of the questionable proposition that Knossos ruled Crete. The evidence is more easily explicable as the result of many separate initiatives by groups and individuals in which the islanders were actively involved and not simply passive recipients.

The nature and extent of Cretan links with the Near East and Egypt are less clear. The inspiration for a number of innovations in the Protopalatial period may have come from the east, such as the ashlar facades of the palaces, certain administrative practices, and artistic motifs and techniques. Obvious imports are not very common but the Cretans may have been more interested in raw materials. Metals were no doubt a high priority, and this could explain the Minoan pottery from sites on Cyprus, which was potentially a source of copper. Although the exchange value of the pottery would have been limited, it does indicate that trade between Crete and Cyprus gradually increased. By LM I a reasonable amount of pottery moved in both directions, yet lead isotope analysis of ingots from Crete does not suggest that much Cypriot copper was imported.

The Near Eastern port cities were important commercial centers, particularly Ugarit. A text from the palace at Mari on the Euphrates records a consignment of tin for the chief merchant of the Kaptarians in Ugarit. As Kaptara is believed to be Crete, he was presumably a Cretan. A text from Ugarit mentions that one of their merchants was expected from Crete with a cargo of grain, beer, and oil, goods which would be archaeologically undetectable. We do not know whether this was a journey he made regularly but the texts imply that trade between the Aegean and the Near East was well established by the middle of the second millennium.

The tombs of Eighteenth Dynasty officials at Thebes in Egypt are sometimes decorated with processions of foreigners, who have brought tribute for the pharaoh. These foreigners include "men of Keftiu" (figure 7.5), who must be Cretans, given the way they are dressed and some of their gifts, particularly the metal vessels and animal rhyta. They also have weapons, jewelry, textiles, and copper ingots. The artists who painted these scenes were not concerned with absolute accuracy and the items shown with different groups of foreigners may have become confused. There is an element of propaganda as well because, in the case of the Keftiu, this is not tribute brought by people from a subject state. Nevertheless, what we can infer is that envoys came from Crete with gifts, possibly to secure an alliance or trade concessions. It is also likely that Cretan craftsmen worked in Egypt because of the Minoan-style frescoes, some of which depict bull leapers, from the site of Tell el-Dab'a in the Nile Delta.

The role of the Cretan palaces in overseas trade has variously been assessed as minimal, moderate, or major. It is clear that they had a vested interest as both consumers and producers. The type of ceremonial gift exchange which was the convention in Egypt certainly required the presence of envoys, and negotiations with Near Eastern states may also have been undertaken by palace officials. However, as the texts from Ugarit show, there was plenty of scope for entrepreneurial trade. Merchants kept the ships at sea and the fact that they were sometimes given ambassadorial duties is an indication of their importance. They must have enjoyed a measure of independence, if only because their activities could not easily be controlled. No doubt they had a close relationship with the palaces but supplied other markets as well. Perhaps the palaces were more directly concerned with the circulation of goods and raw materials within their territories.

## Mycenaeans Overseas?

After the eruption of Thera in LM IA, the Cretans could not use the harbor at Akrotiri and trade must have been disrupted for a time. Subsequently the Mycenaeans became more actively involved. Clay analysis has shown that much of the Minoan-style pottery at Ayia Irini and Phylakopi was actually imported from Attica, and this may be the case at other sites in the Aegean as well. The mainland had been relatively isolated in the Middle Bronze Age but the rich burials at Mycenae and other sites reflect increased contact with Crete and the Cyclades. Trade could be the main source of this wealth. One theory is that a high-value commodity, such as horses, was exchanged for the high-quality products which early Mycenaean leaders acquired to enhance their status. Greece also supplied metals, in particular copper and silver from Lavrion, and more distant sources may have been exploited. There is LH I–II pottery from coastal sites in Macedonia, which has gold and silver ore deposits, and the Mycenaeans apparently went west as well as north. LH I–II pottery has been found at a number of sites in Italy and Sicily but is concentrated on Lipari, one of the Aeolian islands, and Vivara in the bay of Naples. It is not immediately apparent what the islands offered. Obsidian from Lipari was widely used in the central Mediterranean but not in the Aegean where Melos was the principal source. The most likely explanation is that the islands provided access to local exchange

networks, through which the Mycenaeans could obtain metals and other raw materials. Many more sites in Italy, Sicily, and Sardinia have LH III pottery, so Mycenaean
links with the west continued and expanded.

Although it is questionable whether Mycenaeans caused the LM IB destructions
on Crete, they may well have taken control of Knossos because the Linear B script
was used by the palace officials who must therefore have spoken Greek. A Mycenaean
presence at Phylakopi on Melos is also suspected. A mainland-style megaron was
built here in LH IIIA1, possibly as an administrative center. Although the architecture of the town does not otherwise change significantly, the pottery at Phylakopi
and on the other Cycladic islands is mainly Mycenaean in LH IIIA–B. The close ties
between Mycenaean Greece and the Cyclades may have led to settlement on a
limited scale, though systematic colonization seems unlikely. Perhaps Phylakopi did
come under Mycenaean political control but nowhere else is there evidence which
necessarily indicates direct rule. The potential of the islands to facilitate trade will
have been their great attraction for mainland states.

A similar cultural transformation can be seen in the eastern Aegean where cemeteries of chamber tombs have been found on many of the islands, particularly
Rhodes and Kos. The tombs look like those in mainland Greece and the dead were
buried in the same way with Mycenaean grave goods. The obvious conclusion is
that there was an influx of Mycenaean settlers, especially as the number of tombs
steadily increases over the course of the LH IIIA period. However, this could indicate
that the islanders themselves had started to use chamber tombs. If so, they must
have been aware that in some respects they had redefined their identity. The fact
that culture can be such a fluid medium does make it difficult to trace population
movements. Moreover, because so few settlements have been excavated in the
eastern Aegean, we are dependent on the evidence from the cemeteries, which is a
serious limitation. Nevertheless, it is clear that the Mycenaeans had a major impact
on these islands, and trade was undoubtedly the reason for this. Rhodes would have
been a port of call for any ships which had come from or were headed for Cyprus.
Indeed the site of Trianda-Ialysos may have been a port of trade where cargoes were
offloaded and exchanged. Mycenaean pottery was certainly exported from the
Argolid via Rhodes.

There is a chamber tomb cemetery at Müskebi on the west coast of Turkey opposite Kos, and the grave goods suggest that Mycenaeans had settled here. Chamber
tombs have also been excavated near Miletos where most of the pottery is Mycenaean
in LH III but the architecture has Anatolian as well as Aegean affinities. This is
especially true of the Hittite-style fortifications which were built after the settlement
was destroyed by fire in LH IIIA2. Further up the coast, the cemetery at Panaztepe
has a range of different tomb types, a mixture of inhumations and cremations,
Anatolian and Mycenaean pottery, bronzes and jewelry. Culturally, and no doubt
ethnically, these were very diverse communities.

Very few Mycenaean finds have been reported from sites away from the west coast
of Turkey, so it would appear that trade between the Mycenaeans and Hittites was
minimal, although they did come into contact. One of the states mentioned in texts

from the Hittite capital at Boğazköy is Ahhiyawa, which can be translated as Achaia. Since Homer refers to the Greeks as Achaians, Ahhiyawa should be a Mycenaean state. The earliest of the texts reports that the Hittite king had to protect one of his vassals from an Ahhiyawan warlord. In 1320 BC the Hittites sacked the city of Millawanda which had formed an alliance with Arzawa and Ahhiyawa. Subsequently they attacked and captured Apasa, the capital of Arzawa. It has now been confirmed that Apasa is Ephesos and this supports the identification of Millawanda as Miletos, which was destroyed around this time. In a letter written in the mid-thirteenth century the king of Ahhiyawa is addressed as "My Brother, the Great King, my equal." However, soon after this the ruler of Amurru is told that he should "let no ship of Ahhiyawa go to (the Assyrians)" with whom the Hittites were at war. Since the Hittites used economic sanctions against their enemies, this may have been a trade embargo. It is not clear where exactly Ahhiyawa was located but the Mycenaeans controlled some territory in Anatolia and, as a result, they occasionally clashed with the Hittites.

Mycenaean activity in the northern Aegean is less evident except at Troy where there is some LH II pottery and even more in LH IIIA. Mycenaean shapes were also copied in the local grey and tan fabrics. The recent excavations have shown that the settlement extended well beyond the citadel and covered around 200,000 m$^2$ at this time. Troy was a major center and trade must have been a factor. Ships that were headed for the Black Sea would often have had to wait for a favorable wind before they could pass through the Dardanelles. Troy may have supplied the crews of these ships and marketed their goods. There was obviously the potential for a port of trade here.

By LH III Cyprus supplied approximately 20 percent of the copper in the Aegean. The amount of Mycenaean pottery exported to Cyprus also increased significantly. On settlement sites, such as Hala Sultan Teke and Kalavasos-Ayios Dimitrios, it typically constitutes less than 2 percent of the pottery but, in ritual contexts, and especially in tombs, the proportion is often much higher. The dead were given stirrup jars and flasks, which presumably contained perfumed oil, and in the richer tombs, there were also cups, bowls, and kraters. Clay analysis has shown that most of this pottery was imported from the Argolid and had evidently been made specifically for the Cypriot market. The marks incised on pottery from Tiryns suggest that some of the merchants who accompanied the shipments were Cypriot.

They faced a hazardous journey which ended disastrously for the ship which sank at Uluburun, off the rocky southern coast of Turkey, around 1300 BC. Most of the cargo consisted of raw materials, in particular almost 500 copper ingots which weighed approximately 10 tons. There was tin and terebinth resin, which may have been burned as incense, glass ingots, blackwood and cedar logs, ostrich eggshells, and elephant and hippopotamus tusks. Manufactured items included pithoi full of Cypriot pottery, copper and bronze vessels, gold and silver jewelry, and an ivory trumpet. Weapons, tools, weights, almonds, olives, fruits, and spices have also been recovered from the wreck. It seems likely that this valuable cargo was a royal shipment but from where and to whom? The mixture of finds—Egyptian, Nubian,

Assyrian, Babylonian, Cypriot, Mycenaean, Italian, and Balkan—makes it difficult to identify the home port of the ship. However, the general consensus is that it was a Near Eastern vessel and may have sailed from Ugarit via Cyprus. It is believed that Mycenaean merchants or officials were on board, so the ship may have been headed for mainland Greece.

The Uluburun wreck provides us with a snapshot of Late Bronze Age trade in action. Moreover, because organic remains often survive better under water than on land, we have a clearer idea what was traded. In this respect Near Eastern and Egyptian texts are also invaluable. Goods recorded in the archives at Ugarit include grain, wine, oil, honey, salt, resin, timber, ivory, linen, and textiles, which were exported to Egypt, Mesopotamia, Cyprus, Anatolia, and the Aegean. Trade often took the form of lavish gift exchanges between rulers. In one consignment sent to the king of Babylon by the Egyptian pharaoh there were objects of gold, silver, copper, and bronze, jewelry, mirrors, thrones, perfume, cloth, stone vessels, and ebony boxes, all weighed and numbered so that their value could be calculated.

It seems that Mycenaean rulers were involved in these exchanges but perhaps rather peripherally. A Hittite text mentions a gift from the king of Ahhiyawa, and faience plaques at Mycenae may have been sent by the pharaoh Amenhotep III. Nevertheless, the level of direct contact with Egypt and the Near East has been questioned. There is Mycenaean pottery from around 30 sites in Egypt, in settlements, temples, and tombs. Most of the pottery, 1,500–1,600 sherds, comes from just one site, Tell el-Amarna. This was the city built by the pharaoh Akhenaten, c. 1353–1337 BC, as the capital of Egypt and abandoned soon after his death. Mycenaean pottery has also been found at 90 sites in the Near East. However, it is possible that cargoes that had arrived from the Aegean were offloaded in Cypriot ports, divided up, and then shipped on. If so, any Mycenaean merchants who had sailed as far as Cyprus would not necessarily have traveled further east. Similarly, the Mycenaean pottery in Egypt could have been transported by Near Eastern intermediaries.

One reason why the role of the Mycenaeans in these trade networks has been played down is the silence of the Linear B texts on this subject. However, they do reveal that the supply of key raw materials, such as bronze, was carefully controlled. The palace at Pylos was the center of a perfumed oil industry and may also have manufactured textiles for export. Even if merchants were independent, they would surely have needed official authorization. The artificial harbor constructed on the coast below the palace is an indication of the level of state investment in port facilities and perhaps of a dependence on trade which ultimately proved unsustainable.

## Into the Iron Age

Trade may already have been disrupted in the thirteenth century, which would explain why much of the LH IIIB pottery found in Cyprus, the Near East, Macedonia, and Italy was locally made. The fact that defensible sites were occupied in the

**Figure 7.6**  Galley on a krater from Pyrgos Livanaton

Cyclades is symptomatic of the insecurity that was felt throughout the eastern Mediterranean, particularly in the early twelfth century when Egypt was attacked by the Sea Peoples. The groups that made up this coalition have not been conclusively identified from the Egyptian records but it seems quite likely that Mycenaeans were involved and they certainly used similar ships. A LH IIIC krater from Pyrgos Livanaton depicts one of these galleys (figure 7.6). Although there is a mast, the oars indicated by the diagonal lines below the hull provided most of the power. With a crew of 40 or 50, they would have been fast vessels which the helmsman could quickly maneuver. While the presence of the two warriors could be a precaution against attack, these ships were obviously well equipped for warfare and piracy. In an unsettled period, they would undoubtedly have had an impact on the dynamics of trade. Smaller-scale networks now connected communities across the Aegean.

By the eleventh century the situation had clearly deteriorated and much of Greece was left isolated. As we saw in the previous chapter, one reason why iron replaced bronze as the most common utilitarian metal may have been because the supply of copper and tin was disrupted. However, the introduction of iron metallurgy does presuppose a continued link with Cyprus and the Near East. Despite the upheavals in the eastern Mediterranean, Cypriots still traded as far west as Sardinia and they were soon joined by the Phoenicians, whose main concern was the acquisition of metals. Initially they operated out of their ports in the Levant, such as Byblos, Tyre, and Sidon, but by the late ninth century they had established an outpost at Kition on Cyprus and subsequently settled in Sardinia, Sicily, southern Spain, and North Africa, most notably at Carthage. At Kommos on Crete a temple with Near Eastern features was built around 900 BC, perhaps for the crews of ships which were headed the central and western Mediterranean. Knossos may have been another port call.

One settlement in Greece that remained in contact with the eastern Mediterranean in the eleventh and tenth centuries was Lefkandi on Euboia. An antique Cypriot bronze amphora was used as a cremation urn for the man who was buried in the "Heroon" and the graves in the Toumba cemetery contained an impressive array of Near Eastern and Egyptian bronze vessels and faience jewelry. These exotica were evidently prized, possibly because they were obtained as gifts and therefore had an added cachet. If trade had become more entrepreneurial, which does seem likely, partnerships would have been vital. Phoenician merchants may have struck up relationships with particular individuals at Lefkandi who had access to raw materials. The wide distribution of Euboian Protogeometric pottery suggests that Lefkandi had a network of connections across the northern Aegean, through which goods could be channeled. There is also Euboian pottery in the Near East, especially at Tyre.

More Greek pottery was exported to the eastern Mediterranean in the late ninth and eighth centuries, mainly from Euboia. It is concentrated in northern Syria, particularly at Al Mina where around 1,500 Geometric sherds have been found. This has led to speculation that Greek merchants settled there in the eighth century. As Al Mina was the main port for the kingdom of Unqi in the Amuq plain, it is unlikely to have been under Greek control. The Assyrians were the great political power in the region and the tribute sent from Unqi included metals and other imported goods. The rulers of Unqi needed to regulate trade and the port at Al Mina would have facilitated this. The architecture of the settlement is typically Syrian. Only the pottery provides any evidence for a Greek presence but consists of fine ware vessels in a restricted range of shapes which could have been destined for other sites in Syria or the Near East. Nevertheless, a case can be made for a special relationship with Al Mina, in which the Euboians were actively involved.

## Magna Graecia

Euboians also had a major role in the expansion of Greek trade with the central Mediterranean. There is early eighth-century Euboian pottery from Sardinia, where the Phoenicians already had commercial contacts, and from sites on the west side of Italy. Some of this pottery may have been made by resident Greek potters, possibly based at Veii in southern Etruria. Veii could have supplied metals from Etruscan sources further north, an attractive proposition for the Euboians, whose technical expertise was clearly appreciated, and a mutually beneficial relationship was negotiated.

Conditions must have favored these overseas ventures because in the mid-eighth century the Euboians founded a settlement at Pithekoussai on the island of Ischia in the bay of Naples. The site they chose had an acropolis, Monte Vico, with steep cliffs which could easily be defended, and bays on either side. There was iron ore and slag, as well as bronze and lead in workshops on the Mezzavia ridge, just inland from the acropolis. More metallurgical debris—bellows, crucibles, slag, and iron ore from the island of Elba—had been dumped on the eastern slopes of Monte Vico. In the Valle di San Montano, between the acropolis and the ridge, was the cemetery. Over 1,300 graves have been excavated, mainly of the eighth and seventh centuries. It is estimated that they represent only 5 percent of the total, which implies that the population of the settlement must have been around 5,000–10,000. Some adults had been cremated, then the burnt bones and grave goods were removed from the pyre and covered by a circular stone tumulus. There were also adult inhumations in pit graves, generally with fewer grave goods. Children were usually buried in pit graves, or jars in the case of infants. The tumuli were often clustered together with child inhumations, presumably in family plots. As well as the main settlement at Pithekoussai, smaller sites have been identified elsewhere on the island which could be farms.

Strabo (5.4.9) states that there were Euboians from Chalkis and Eretria at Pithekoussai. This does seem likely from the way that the settlers buried the dead and the Euboian-style pottery. However, much of the pottery from the cemetery is Corinthian, some of which was locally made. Perfume bottles were imported from Rhodes and a cup with one of the earliest inscriptions in the Greek alphabet which reads: "Nestor had a fine cup but anyone who drinks from this will soon be struck with desire for fair-crowned Aphrodite." Curiously, this came from the grave of a boy who was aged about 10 when he died, a token of the misspent youth he never enjoyed. Oriental trinkets were found as well: Near Eastern seals and Egyptian scarabs. Pithekoussai was certainly not an isolated community and may have been quite mixed. It is possible that Corinthians were also based here. A Semitic inscription on an amphora used for the burial of an infant could indicate resident Phoenicians. The suggestion that some of the settlers married Italian women is more speculative, though not implausible.

Strabo cites the fertility of the soil as one of the reasons for the prosperity of Pithekoussai. This seems odd because there is not much high-quality land on Ischia. The volcanic soil is excellent for viticulture, however, and the wine could have been exported. Strabo also mentions goldwork and, even though the jewelry from the cemetery is not particularly impressive, there were definitely metalworkers at Pithekoussai whose market may have been the Italian and Etruscan communities which had access to raw materials. Goods moved around these local exchange networks and over longer distances but not without risk. On a krater from Pithekoussai is a shipwreck scene (figure 7.7). The vessel has capsized and the sailors are in the water, at the mercy of some very large and not particularly friendly fish.

Euboians also settled at Kyme on the Italian coast opposite Ischia around 740 BC As well as an acropolis and a harbor, there was good agricultural land nearby. The settlement flourished, and at the end of the eighth century a warrior was buried in the cemetery with an extraordinarily eclectic array of iron weapons, bronze cauldrons, silver vessels, and electrum jewelry. This is very reminiscent of the warrior grave by the West Gate at Eretria but also of princely Italian and Etruscan tombs.

**Figure 7.7**   Shipwreck on a krater from Pithekoussai

The success of Kyme did have repercussions for Pithekoussai, possibly exacerbated by the earthquakes and eruptions which Strabo describes, and commercial activity declined sharply after 700 BC.

The ships headed for Pithekoussai must have sailed up the coast of Sicily and through the straits of Messina. There was contact with local communities in the early eighth century, though not on the scale we would expect given that the Greeks' were about to settle in eastern Sicily and southern Italy. A number of ancient authors wrote about the colonization of this new world which became known as Magna Graecia, effectively greater Greece. Thucydides (6.3–5) in particular specifies when the colonies were founded and where the settlers came from. However, his account is only as reliable as the sources he used. Events which had taken place 300 years previously will often have been reshaped retrospectively. The archaeological evidence can also be ambiguous. Has the earliest pottery been found on these sites? Does this necessarily imply settlement rather than trade? Do the finds really indicate who the settlers were? Nevertheless, it is clearly an advantage that we have both literary texts and archaeological evidence. Judiciously combined, they should give us an insight into the process of colonization.

Thucydides says that the first Greek colony in Sicily was founded at Naxos by Euboians from Chalkis in 734 BC. Presumably some settlers came from the island of Naxos in the Cyclades and perhaps from other cities as well. They chose a site on a promontory which did not control much territory inland but was well placed near the southern end of the straits of Messina. There had been a local Sicel settlement and we do not know whether this was removed or absorbed. Naxos provided a springboard for two more Euboian colonies at Leontini and Catana which were founded in 728 BC. Leontini was not on the coast but could easily be reached from the sea. The colonists included Megarians as well as Euboians and they evidently lived alongside the Sicels for a time. Between Leontini and Catana was the rich plain of the river Symaithos and their location was undoubtedly decided with this in mind, though Catana also had an excellent harbor.

Syracuse would become the most important city in Sicily. The Corinthians arrived here, possibly in 733 BC, and occupied Ortygia, the island on the east side of the great harbor. It is said that they drove out the Sicels, whose settlement was destroyed. In the earliest graves in the Fusco cemetery, many of the dead were buried in stone sarcophagi, which was the practice at Corinth, but there were also pit graves and some cremations. The colonization of Syracuse does seem to have been a carefully planned enterprise, which was apparently led by a Corinthian aristocrat, and the city soon expanded across the narrow channel which separated Ortygia from the mainland. The Megarians were not so well organized and it was only after several attempts that they founded a colony at Megara Hyblaia, between Syracuse and Leontini. The name of the city honors Hyblon, the Sicel king who gave them the land. No doubt he hoped that this alliance would provide some protection against the Greek advance, but his capital at Pantalica, just 20 kilometers inland from Syracuse, was destroyed around 700 BC. A grid of streets was laid out for the houses at Megara Hyblaia, with a central space which became the agora in the seventh century.

Zankle, on the straits of Messina, was named after the sickle-shaped promontory which encloses the harbor. Thucydides claims that the first Greek settlers were pirates from Kyme, though no doubt they traded as well. In due course more colonists arrived from Kyme and Chalkis. With the foundation of Rhegion on the Italian coast opposite Zankle, control of the straits was secured. There were other eighth-century colonies in southern Italy. Sybaris was an Achaian settlement, chosen because of the fertile plain which eventually made the city so wealthy that "sybaritic" came to epitomize a lavish lifestyle. Croton was not quite so well endowed but did have a better harbor. However, this does not compare with the superb double harbor at Taras, the only Spartan colony. Given their lack of interest in trade, the Spartans were not obvious colonizers but the explanation for this venture seems to have been a political crisis at home.

In the seventh century the Greeks pushed further west in Sicily. Gela was founded in 688 BC, though Rhodians from Lindos may already have established a base there. They were eventually joined by Cretans and possibly some Peloponnesians. Much of the early pottery from Gela is Corinthian, which is true of every Greek colony, but some is from East Greece and Crete as well. The Sicilian cities were responsible for the next phase of colonization. Syracuse expanded inland and also founded Kamarina on the south coast. Most of the southeast corner of the island thereby became Syracusan territory. Megara Hyblaia set up a colony in the far west at Selinous. The opportunity to trade with the Phoenicians, who were based at Motya, and the local Elymians may have been one of the main attractions of this remote site. Selinous certainly prospered and was one of the richest Sicilian cities in the sixth century. Zankle founded Mylai and then Himera on the north coast. This would have facilitated trade with the Aeolian islands and Sardinia. Himera also had good agricultural land. In Italy more colonies were established on the south coast, at Metapontion, Siris, and Lokroi, as well as further north at Poseidonia. This created an overland route which avoided the hazardous voyage through the straits of Messina.

Even a brief account of the Greek colonization of Sicily and Italy highlights the fact that this was a complex process and the motivation for those involved must obviously have varied. Nevertheless, some general causes have been suggested, in particular overpopulation and consequently the need for more land. It is certainly true that the eighth century was a period of expansion in Greece but there is no evidence that agricultural resources were overstretched. However, land ownership may have been a source of tension, and conflict is often cited in the written sources as the reason why a colony was founded. Some colonists were no doubt forced to leave home, yet a move overseas also represented a great opportunity because more land was available and new markets which could be exploited. The Greeks described these settlements as apoikiai, a home from home. Apoikia is a more neutral term than colony, which implies state involvement. Sometimes cities did have a major role but individuals provided much of the impetus for the colonization movement. Politically and culturally the colonies soon asserted their independence. As we have seen, some Syracusans were initially buried in stone sarcophagi, a tradition which presumably came from Corinth, though the dead were laid out in an extended rather than a contracted position and in due course other grave types were preferred. At Megara Hyblaia there were inhumations and cremations in amphorae, which was not the custom at Megara. The Rhodians and Cretans cremated their dead but not the settlers at Gela. In fact the Greek cities in Sicily were more influenced by each other. The use of stone sarcophagi at Megara Hyblaia and Gela in the seventh century can be attributed to their connections with Syracuse.

It was inevitable that the colonies would forge their own identity because they were quite disparate communities. They also interacted with their Sicilian and Italian neighbors. Relations must have been decidedly strained at first, as the Greeks seized more and more territory. Nevertheless, they did receive some assistance from native rulers, notably Hyblon. There may also have been a significant native element in the population of many colonies, not least because some of the settlers married local women. Over time close economic ties formed between the Greeks and their neighbors. The Greek cities supplied manufactured goods, wine, and olive oil in return for commodities such as textiles, timber, produce, and slaves. This trade inevitably had a major impact on the local communities. A cultural transformation can be seen which has been described as Hellenization but is better defined as hybrid. The natives did not become Greek, they assimilated elements of Greek culture, and their influence on the colonists should not be overlooked.

## France and Spain

Seventh-century Greek pottery has been found at sites on the south coast of France and could be evidence of direct contact or may have been brought by Etruscan traders. Around 600 BC Phokaians settled at Massalia (modern Marseilles). Although their home city was on the west coast of Turkey, the Phokaians were more actively involved in the western Mediterranean than any of the other Greeks, and their reputation as intrepid seafarers is fully justified. It seems that a local ruler gave them the land and one of the settlers apparently married his daughter. A major attraction of Massalia was the excellent harbor which is reasonably near the mouth of the river

**Figure 7.8** Vix krater

Rhône and the routes inland. The settlement was not particularly large at first but grew in size after the middle of the sixth century. The imported pottery is mainly East Greek—presumably shipped from Phokaia or one of the other Ionian cities—Corinthian, and Etruscan. Later there is Athenian pottery as well and local production of transport amphorae for wine. The Massaliots traded along the coast and also inland. Bronze vessels had moved up the Rhône into France and Germany in the seventh century. Once the colony was established, this route became more accessible. The rulers of the hillforts in central France developed a taste for wine which they were sent in Massaliot amphorae, accompanied by kraters, jugs, and cups. The most spectacular of these finds comes from the grave of a princess at Vix near Châtillon-sur-Seine, not far from Paris. This is an enormous bronze krater, 1.64 meters high, with a procession of warriors and chariots around the neck (figure 7.8). It had been transported in pieces and then reassembled. Greek imports also reached southern Germany in the sixth century.

Soon after they settled at Massalia, the Phokaians founded Emporion (modern Ampurias) on the northeast coast of Spain. Emporion is a term often used for commercial colonies, which does seem to have been the rationale in this case. Initially the settlement was on a small island but moved to a site on the coast, surrounded by marshes, in the middle of the sixth century. Emporion was an excellent base from which the Phokaians could expand their trade links with Spain, although they did face competition from the Phoenicians. Greek pottery is found as far west as Huelva on the Atlantic coast where metals, in particular silver, were available.

## The Black Sea

In the Early Iron Age Greeks migrated across the Aegean. The sites where they settled on the west coast of Turkey and the islands offshore would become the cities of East Greece. Colonies were also founded in the northern Aegean on the Chalkidiki peninsula, notably at Torone. Later, in the early seventh century, Thasos was colonized. The mineral wealth of the island was no doubt the main incentive for the Parians who led this move and subsequently took control of the Thracian coast opposite. By the middle of the seventh century there were Greek cities in the Propontis. The Milesians secured the port of Abydos on the Hellespont and then occupied Kyzikos. One of the Megarian colonies was Byzantion, later known as Constantinople. The first Greek settlements around the Black Sea, at Sinope, Amisos, Trapezos, Berezan, Histria, and Apollonia, were probably founded in the late seventh century and Miletos was responsible for this initiative. The incentive was the range of resources that the Black Sea could offer, which included metals, timber, and fish. Another reason why the Milesians were so active is that they were under pressure from the Lydians who seized much of their territory. Consequently they set up more colonies in the sixth century and looked for sites which had good agricultural land, such as Olbia. Eventually the Black Sea cities would supply much of the grain needed especially by Athens (see below).

## The Eastern Mediterranean and Egypt

At Al Mina the proportion of Greek pottery increased in the seventh century but there is less from Euboia. Corinthian pottery, which may have been brought by merchants from Aigina, is more common, and also East Greek. The source of the East Greek pottery is not always certain. However, it was probably shipped from Miletos or Samos. The Aiginetans, Milesians, and Samians traded with Egypt as well and formed part of the Greek community at Naukratis in Egypt. Greek mercenaries fought for the pharaoh Psamtik I (664–610 BC). They also joined the expedition which Psamtik II (595–589 BC) sent against the Nubians and took the opportunity to scratch their names on the colossal statues at Abu Simbel. As a reward for their assistance, the Greeks were given land and allowed to settle in Egypt. By the end of the seventh century they were established at Naukratis in the western Delta, near Sais, the royal capital. Herodotos (2.178–9) describes some of the privileges that Naukratis was granted by the pharaoh Ahmose (570–526 BC). Goods which arrived in Egypt from Greece had to go through the port, which was under the jurisdiction of locally appointed Greek officials. Merchants from Aigina, Chios, Halikarnassos, Klazomenai, Knidos, Lesbos, Miletos, Phaselis, Phokaia, Rhodes, Samos, and Teos were based there, temporarily or permanently. Herodotos mentions their temples, some of which have been excavated. Like most of the merchants, much of the pottery is from East Greece. Athenian, Corinthian, and Laconian pottery was also imported. The Greeks traded silver, wine, and oil for linen and papyrus. Certainly later, though not necessarily in the sixth century, Egypt supplied grain as well. More immediate was the impact which Egypt had on the development of Greek art and architecture. This can be seen in the style of Archaic Greek statues, particularly the kouroi (figure 9.15), and the construction of massive stone temples.

## Ships and Cargoes

Representations of ships appear on pottery in the eighth century. Some of the vessels are open galleys, others have a raised deck. In one case two rows of oarsmen are shown (figure 7.9). This could indicate a double bank of oars, though the crew may be seated side by side. The sharp projection on the prow is almost certainly a ram and there can be no doubt that these were warships. Nevertheless, they did have room for some cargo, and galleys were used as merchant ships later because of their speed and reliability. Generally they were broader in the beam and had larger sails than the war galleys. By the sixth century some ships relied on wind power. These vessels were more capacious but not especially fast or maneuverable. On a sixth-century cup, a merchant ship of this type is overhauled by a sleek pirate galley (figure 7.10).

Wrecks which have part of the hull preserved provide evidence for the way that these vessels were constructed. The planks were fitted together first and then the frame was added. In the case of a late sixth-century cargo ship excavated in the harbor at Marseilles, the planks were mainly fastened by mortise and tenon joints but were sewn at the ends of the hull and the frame was attached with iron nails. For the Kyrenia ship, which sank off the north coast of Cyprus around 300 BC, only mortise and tenon joints were used. The hull was built of Aleppo pine and had been sheathed in lead below the waterline. With an overall length of 13.6 meters and a

**Figure 7.9**  Galley on a bowl from Thebes, Greece (London, British Museum)

**Figure 7.10**   Merchant ship and pirate galley on an Athenian black-figure cup (London, British Museum)

**Figure 7.11**   Reconstruction of the Kyrenia ship

beam of 4.4 meters, this was not a large vessel. The cargo capacity would have been approximately 25 tons. A full-scale replica of the ship has been constructed (figure 7.11) and sailed from Piraeus to Paphos on Cyprus, a distance of 600 nautical miles, in three weeks. Over 400 amphorae were found with the Kyrenia wreck and 10,000 almonds which had apparently been stowed in sacks. There were plates, bowls, cups, and spoons in sets of four and this was presumably the size of the crew. Their stock of food included olives, nuts, lentils, garlic, grapes, and figs. Iron spearheads embedded in the hull suggest that this was another merchant ship which was captured by pirates and quite possibly scuttled.

Amphorae mark the location of many wreck sites. They were widely used to transport liquids by sea, particularly wine, olive oil, and fish sauce. A fourth-century shipment of 3,000 wine amphorae is recorded which would have weighed over 100 tons. The shape can indicate where an amphora was made. In the Kyrenia wreck there were 343 Rhodian amphorae and others from Kos and Samos, which may tell us where the ship had been. One advantage of amphorae is their durability. Even after centuries on the seabed they are still easily recognizable. Pottery provides much of our evidence for trade because it survives well and the source of imports can be established visually or analytically. This does not necessarily prove direct contact between the place of manufacture and the final destination. Nevertheless, we do get a good impression of the way that trade networks developed over time. Much of the Greek pottery which was exported contained products such as perfumed oil. It no doubt helped if this came in an attractively decorated Corinthian aryballos. There was also a market for high-quality pottery *per se*, which the Athenians effectively monopolized in the late sixth and fifth century. The marks incised on some of the batches indicate that East Greek as well as Athenian agents dispatched the pottery. An impressive amount reached Italy and was buried in Etruscan tombs. Yet it seems unlikely that pottery would have made up most of the cargo of ships headed west. Pottery was relatively inexpensive, especially compared with metal vessels which sometimes traveled great distances, like the bronze krater found at Vix. Metals were certainly shipped in bulk and have frequently been identified as the major incentive for trade.

The marble for many of the Archaic kouros and kore statues came from the islands of Naxos and Paros and must have been moved by sea. The statues were roughed out in the quarry by the sculptor, which reduced the size of the block substantially, but they could still weigh a ton or more. In the sanctuary of Apollo on Delos a 20-ton kouros stood on a 30-ton base. Marble was always in demand and transport by ship was often the only option. However, it would not have been easy to maneuver the blocks on board, even if the quarry was by the sea. Marble is very durable, unlike so many of the other goods that ships carried, such as the timber from which they were made. It is thought that there may have been textiles in the Kyrenia wreck but this is just a guess based on the fact that part of the cargo had evidently disintegrated. The amphorae do give us an idea how much wine and oil was shipped. Regional specialities such as cheese, sauces, olives, nuts, fruits, and spices would also have been a profitable sideline.

In the fourth century some Greek cities, particularly Athens, imported substantial amounts of grain. Attempts have been made to calculate how reliant the Athenians were on these imports, based on the size of the population, how much grain would have been consumed, how much could have been produced locally, and therefore the potential shortfall. Many of the figures used in these calculations are estimates, and factors such as variations in the annual grain production further complicate the equation. A speech by Demosthenes implies that the Athenians imported over 30,000 tons of grain each year. This may be an exaggeration but does provide an indication of the scale of the trade, which would have required a fleet of around 270 ships. As the population of Athens was higher in the fifth century, the need for imported grain would presumably have been greater then and even in the sixth century there was apparently a demand for high-quality wheat. Given their dependence on grain imports, it is significant that the Athenians did not build a commercial fleet as well as a navy. Instead they relied on independent merchants who were closely monitored. It is evident from the written sources that some of these emporoi were Athenian citizens, some were from other Greek cities, and some were foreigners. Most of the shipowners, the naukleroi, also traded. The emporoi and the naukleroi usually took out loans to cover the cost of the cargo. The lenders who made these loans were repaid when the cargo was sold and also took a substantial cut of the profits. In return they effectively underwrote the loan which would be canceled if the ship sank. Once again this emphasizes the risks that overseas trade entailed and no doubt the rewards, though not many of the known fourth-century emporoi and naukleroi could be described as wealthy.

## Conclusions

Overseas trade took many forms which often converged. Sometimes no exchange was involved, as in the case of the obsidian which was procured directly from Melos in the Neolithic period and then traded. The distribution of obsidian away from the coast suggests that this was not down-the-line but directional trade. At the same time there were reciprocal exchanges which moved goods over shorter distances, essentially as gifts. The colonization of the islands created trade networks which were extended as ship construction improved, particularly with the use of sails. Goods were channeled through gateway communities, such as Mochlos, and ports of trade developed at Trianda, Miletos, and Troy in the eastern Aegean. When the Mycenaeans and Euboians first operated in the central Mediterranean, they relied on intermediaries to supply the metals they wanted. A permanent base obviously facilitated overseas trade ventures. This may have been why Cretans settled at Kastri on Kythera. Trade with Italy was certainly boosted when the Euboians founded Pithekoussai and the Phokaian colonies in France and Spain were equally successful. Naukratis gave the Greek an opportunity to develop closer commercial ties with Egypt.

Trade at Naukratis was regulated and states often imposed restrictions on the merchants they dealt with. We can see this in fourth-century Athens, and the Mycenaean palaces may have followed a similar policy. They carefully monitored the circulation of goods within their territories but we have no evidence that they were directly involved in overseas trade. Nevertheless they must have had some control over the merchants who used their ports. It is also possible that merchants acted on behalf of the palaces in an ambassadorial capacity, since so much trade was conducted as gift exchange. Of course there was always scope for individual enterprise, certainly in the case of settlement overseas. The Minoan and Mycenaean states did not send out colonies. It is questionable whether Pithekoussai was officially sanctioned. Greek cities did have a role in the colonization movement but their level of engagement often appears marginal. The cultural identity of these communities was multifaceted, made up of imported and indigenous components, with any concept of ethnicity subordinated. Trade and colonization can best be described as interaction at a distance.

## Bibliographical notes

Casson 1995, Wachsmann 1998, and McGrail 2001 are excellent on sea conditions, trade routes, and the early boat types found in the Mediterranean. Neolithic trade is discussed from a Mediterranean perspective by Robb and Farr 2005 and with an Aegean focus by Perlès 2001. See Broodbank 2000 for a perceptive analysis of the Early Bronze Age in the Cyclades and Whitelaw 2004b on the role of Mochlos. Broodbank 2004 looks at the concept of Minoanization especially in the context of Kythera. Wiener 1990 and Davis 2008 examine the links between Crete and the Aegean islands. Many of the papers in Gale 1991, Cline and Harris-Cline 1998, Laffineur and Greco 2005, and MacDonald et al. 2009 deal with aspects of Minoan and Mycenaean trade in the Aegean and the eastern Mediterranean. Cline 1994, van Wijngaarden 2002, Vanschoonwinkel 2006, and Mee 2008 review the Mycenaean evidence. Trade between Greece and the Near East in the Early Iron Age is covered by Whitley 2001, Luke 2003, Lemos 2005, and Dickinson 2006. For Greek settlement in Italy and Sicily see Coldstream 1977, Boardman 1980, Ridgway 1992, D'Agostino 2006, Domínguez 2006a, and Greco 2006. Snodgrass 1987 questions the foundation dates of the Sicilian colonies, Osborne 1998b considers the question of state involvement, Shepherd 1995 and 2005 analyzes the evidence from Sicilian cemeteries, and Antonaccio 2005 examines the concept of hybridity. Trade with France and Spain is discussed by Shefton 1994, Domínguez 2006b, and Morel 2006, the colonization of the Black Sea by Boardman 1980 and Tsetskhladze 1994. For Naukratis see Möller 2000. There is a detailed catalogue of Mediterranean shipwrecks in Parker 1992. Johnston 1991, Arafat and Morgan 1994, and Gill 1994 offer different interpretations of the trade in pottery. Snodgrass 2006a looks at the movement of heavy freight and Foxhall 1998 reflects on the role of semi-luxury goods. Whitby 1998 and Oliver 2007 review the parameters of the Athenian grain trade which is also discussed by Reed 2003 from the perspective of the traders.

# CHAPTER 8

# Warfare

## Introduction

Wars fought by the armies of cities or states can be differentiated from other types of conflict, such as raids. Indeed it has been argued that true warfare did not exist until there were state-level societies. This has led to an assumption that more egalitarian societies were comparatively peaceful. Violent incidents may have occurred but such societies did not engage in large-scale warfare. The problem with this perception of a peaceful past is the nature of the available evidence. We know about wars from written sources which do not take us back earlier than the first states. The archaeological evidence is more equivocal. Some injuries on skeletons were inflicted deliberately. Weapons can be identified and also fortifications. Nevertheless, it is difficult to judge just how prevalent conflict was in a given society. In Mesolithic Europe mass burials suggest violent clashes between communities. By the Neolithic period weaponry had evolved and some settlements were protected by ditches, banks, and palisades. Do we see similar developments in Greece?

Warfare is often a consequence of competition for resources. In the Early Neolithic period the Thessalian plain was densely settled with sites just over 2.5 kilometers apart. There was definitely the potential for conflict yet no obvious concern for defense can be detected. Cooperation rather than confrontation was surely the basis on which these communities coexisted. The situation may have changed in the Late Neolithic period. At Dimini in eastern Thessaly circuit walls enclosed the central part of the tell (figure 3.1). They seem defensive but were not particularly high and could easily have been scaled. An alternative hypothesis is that the walls demarcate divisions within the settlement. As such they would reflect a desire for greater privacy and control of resources. Here we can see an incipient awareness of wealth

*Greek Archaeology: A Thematic Approach*   By Christopher Mee
© 2011 Christopher Mee

and status, the cause of so much conflict. These developments therefore anticipate the more prominent role that warfare takes in the Early Bronze Age.

## The Early Bronze Age Aegean

The introduction of metallurgy boosted arms production. Weapons account for a high proportion of the metalwork of this period, approximately 80 percent in the case of Crete. The fact that most of the metalwork comes from tombs may give us a rather distorted impression of the range of artefacts in use because weapons were undoubtedly more prestigious than tools and were therefore more likely to be buried. Still, it is significant that this new technology was closely linked with the evolution of weaponry and especially daggers (figure 8.1a).These have a triangular blade, 10–20 cm in length, often with a midrib for rigidity. The hilt, of wood or bone, was attached by rivets but many of the daggers had snapped at this point because of the stress exerted here when they were used. Occasionally there is decoration on the blade and some daggers were even made of silver, which highlights the immediate appeal of weapons as status symbols. Not so many spears have been found, and their size suggests that they were also designed for close combat.

A number of marble figurines from the Cyclades apparently represent warriors or hunters who wear what may be a strap for their weapons diagonally across one shoulder. Combat and hunt scenes were roughly worked on a series of stone plaques from the site of Korfi t-Aroniou on Naxos. They are difficult to interpret but on one there is a man who holds a bow, a horned animal, and a ship. Possibly this is a raid, a feature of life in the Cyclades at this time. The longboats (figures 7.1 & 7.2) had a crew of 25 and could cover 40–50 kilometers in a day. Although they may have carried cargo, it seems likely that these ships were also used for sudden raids. This would explain why some of the settlements on the islands were in easily defensible locations. Kastri on Syros is high above the sea and any attackers would have been clearly visible well before they climbed the steep slope up to the site. When they reached the top of the hill, they were faced by a double line of fortifications (figure 8.2). An overlap in the outer wall formed a narrow entrance which was presumably closed by a gate. The inner wall was protected by a series of semicircular towers so that attackers would be exposed to cross fire from the defenders. Several other Early Bronze Age sites in the Cyclades were fortified and also coastal settlements in mainland Greece. At Lerna in the Argolid the section of the fortifications excavated on the south side of the tell consists of two parallel walls, just over 2 meters apart (figure 3.2). A tower, originally semicircular but later rectangular, was placed at the point where the wall changed direction. It seems that the fortifications were in a state of disrepair by the time Lerna was destroyed at the end of EH II.

## Pax Minoica

Despite their enthusiasm for weapons, Early Bronze Age Cretans do not appear to have been particularly concerned about security and they did not feel the need for

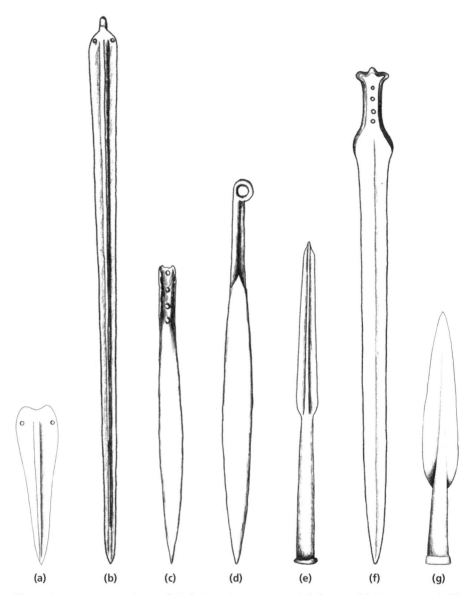

(a)        (b)        (c)        (d)        (e)        (f)        (g)

**Figure 8.1a–g**   Bronze Age and Early Iron Age weapons: (a) dagger; (b) Type A sword; (c) knife; (d) Schlachtmesser; (e) spearhead; (f) Type II sword; (g) spearhead. Not to scale

fortifications. Conditions may have deteriorated at the end of the period because some sites were fortified in MM IA. Ayia Photia on the north coast of Crete was enclosed by a wall with four irregularly spaced towers. At Mallia stretches of a substantial wall have been found which was apparently constructed in EM III–MM I and could have been defensive. However, the palace would surely have been built further inland and in a more elevated location if a serious threat existed in the Protopalatial period. The palaces at Knossos and Phaistos were not quite as acces-

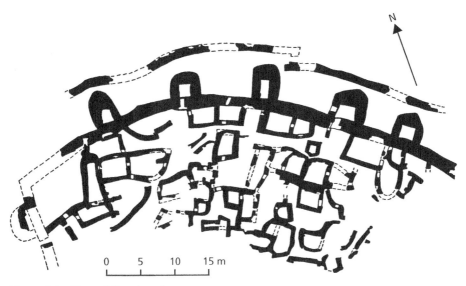

**Figure 8.2**   Plan of Kastri on Syros

sible but no provision was made for defense. Indeed the impression given by most Minoan towns is that they had no real fear of attack. Yet it is difficult to believe that Crete was so peaceful. Guard houses protected some of the roads in the east of the island. There were developments in weaponry, notably swords with blades as much as a meter in length. Men are shown with daggers very visibly displayed on a belt around their waists (figure 8.3).

Cretan aggression has been cited as a possible explanation for the construction of fortifications on Middle Bronze Age sites in the Cyclades. At Ayia Irini a wall with a semicircular tower was built on the north side of the settlement. Later the fortifications were extended and strengthened. Large blocks of limestone were used and rectangular towers were positioned at key points. Phylakopi has an equally massive wall, some sections of which should be Middle Bronze Age or early Late Bronze Age (figure 2.5). At both of these sites the defenses did not face the sea but were designed to counter a land attack. This is also true of the fortifications at Kolonna on Aigina which were built in EH III and then remodeled at least five times by the end of the Middle Helladic period. Initially the towers were semicircular, as is so often the case. Theoretically they provide a more open field of fire than rectangular towers but, military considerations aside, there must have been a perception that this is how fortifications should look. After a destruction, although still in EH III, the defenses were expanded. The original wall became an outwork. Inside this a new wall was added, 5 meters thick in places and 3.40 meters high, built of closely packed stones (figure 8.4). The towers were now rectangular and flanked the gates, which were set back so that attackers would be forced into a narrow corridor where they could easily be picked off. Subsequently the towers were enlarged and the entrances were made progressively more complex. These additions resulted in an extremely

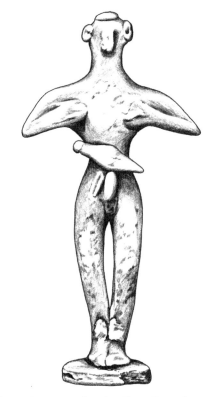

**Figure 8.3**  Middle Minoan terracotta figurine from Petsophas

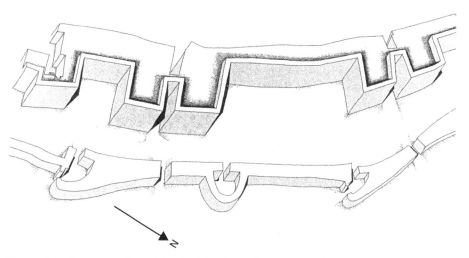

**Figure 8.4**  Reconstruction of the fortifications of Kolonna Stadt VI

impressive system of fortifications and quite possibly they were as much a show of strength as a defensive necessity, given the limited capacity of spears and arrows to penetrate 8 meters of solid masonry.

Because it seems likely that they used their ships for raids, the Middle Bronze Age Aeginetans may have incurred reprisal attacks. On a barrel jar from Kolonna there are ships crewed by round-headed sailors who reappear on another jar armed with spears. Their respect for military prowess is highlighted by the man in his twenties who was buried directly in front of the fortification wall, near the main gate of the settlement, with a sword, a spear, a dagger, two knives, six arrowheads, and a boar's tusk helmet, as well as a razor and a gold diadem (figure 8.5). He was clearly an individual of high status who had perhaps performed some exceptionally heroic act, which is why his grave was placed in such a conspicuous position.

## Well-greaved Achaeans

Weapons feature prominently in Early Mycenaean graves, and warfare was presumably a more common occurrence as elites competed to take control. The warrior in shaft grave II at Mycenae with his sword, massive spear, and dagger is typical, though rather modestly equipped in comparison with some of his peers. One of the men in shaft grave V had at least 15 swords and daggers. There were five swords and four spears buried with the man in the tholos tomb at Dendra in the Argolid and 10 swords and daggers beside one of the men in the tholos tomb at Routsi in Messenia. We do not know where the Mycenaeans believed they went when they died but, as it seems unlikely they would have required quite so many weapons, this is simply ostentation.

Swords were undoubtedly the most prestigious weapons. The Mycenaeans acquired Type A swords from the Minoans (figure 8.1b). The blade is long and narrow with a high midrib. A short tang and rivets held the hilt in place but not very securely. Type B has a similar, though slightly broader, blade and a flanged extension which forms the hilt. It must have been felt that some additional protection was needed for the hands and so in Type C the shoulders were lengthened and swept back, whereas Type D swords have a cruciform guard. When the swords are shown in use on gold rings from the shaft graves, they are thrust at an opponent (figure 8.6). Experimentation has demonstrated that they could easily penetrate flesh and linen or leather but not bronze armor. The high midrib limited the effectiveness of cut strokes, though a nasty wound would have been inflicted if the blade was drawn across the flesh.

Most daggers were shorter versions of the swords, with blades less than 30 cm in length. Some have inlaid decoration and were works of consummate craftsmanship (figure 8.7). Knives may also have been made as weapons. One type has a flanged hilt, a straight back, and a slightly curved blade (figure 8.1c). The even larger Schlachtmesser, or battle knife, is 50–70 cm in length (figure 8.1d). The hilt is folded round and ends in a loop so that the knife could be attached to a strap. As there is

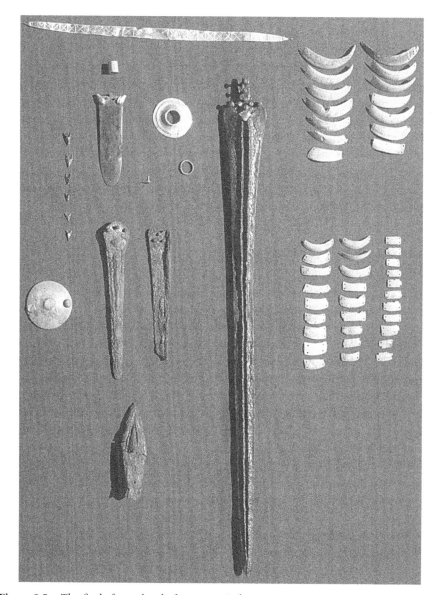

**Figure 8.5**  The finds from the shaft grave at Kolonna

no midrib, these knives would have caused deep cuts. The most common type of spearhead has a tubular socket for the wooden shaft (figure 8.1e). Warriors are often shown with a spear, which must have been standard equipment. Bows were certainly used to hunt and quite possibly fight.

In most scenes of warfare the armor is minimal, though this may reflect an element of heroic bravado. Boar's tusk helmets were permitted, no doubt because they signified prowess as a hunter. They apparently consisted of a conical leather cap to which the pieces of tusk were attached (figure 8.8). It is not clear how effec-

**Figure 8.6**  Gold ring from shaft grave IV at Mycenae with combat scene, the "Battle in the Glen" (Athens, National Archaeological Museum)

**Figure 8.7**  Lion Hunt dagger from shaft grave IV at Mycenae (Athens, National Archaeological Museum)

tive they would have been. Less courageous warriors and hunters protected themselves with large shields, which were either rectangular or shaped like a figure of eight. The decoration suggests that they were made of oxhide, stretched over a wooden framework (figure 8.7). Bronze armor did exist, in particular the remarkable cuirass from a LH IIIA1 chamber tomb at Dendra (figure 8.8). This has a front and back shell which were laced together. A collar and shoulder guards protected the neck, three hoops covered the lower torso and thighs. There was also a boar's tusk helmet with bronze cheek pieces and a pair of greaves. The cuirass is not especially heavy but would have restricted mobility. This and the expense may be the reason why warriors did not regularly equip themselves with bronze armor. Only a

**Figure 8.8**    Bronze cuirass from a chamber tomb at Dendra

few other pieces have been found and it seems likely that leather or linen was used instead.

Chariots appear on several of the stone stelai which were set up above the shaft graves at Mycenae, as well as on gold rings and sealstones. We do not know whether any chariots were buried in Early Mycenaean graves because they would have completely disintegrated. However, there were pairs of horses in a tumulus at Dendra in the Argolid and a tholos tomb at Marathon in Attica. Ownership of a chariot must have been a mark of high status and we can assume that their role was often ceremonial. They are rarely depicted in military contexts, though the man on one of the grave stelai is about to draw his sword and perhaps attack the person in front of the chariot. On a gold ring from Mycenae two men in a chariot pursue a stag (figure 8.9). One drives while the other takes aim with his bow. These scenes imply that chariots could have served as a mobile platform for combat. However, their main purpose may have been to transport heavily armed warriors to and from the battlefield where they would dismount to fight. They would also have been useful if messages needed to be sent quickly. Given the terrain in Greece, it is unlikely that massed chariot charges were ever a feature of Mycenaean warfare.

**Figure 8.9**    Gold ring with chariot scene from shaft grave IV at Mycenae (Athens, National Archaeological Museum)

A silver rhyton from one of the shaft graves provides us with a more complex, though very incomplete, battle scene (figure 8.10). On the largest piece of the rhyton men armed with bows and slings stand in front of a walled coastal town. Women on the battlements raise their arms in distress. It is evident that the town is under attack from the sea, a classic raid of the type that must have been a frequent occurrence in the Aegean. A similar scene is depicted on the miniature fresco from the West House at Akrotiri on Thera. A file of 10 to 12 warriors marches towards a town (figure 8.11). They are armed with long spears, wear boar's tusk helmets, and carry shields. The ships on the left appear to have been damaged, and bodies float in the sea. This is the aftermath of a battle and the fact that the people in the town do not seem very anxious suggests that the warriors are their men or reinforcements who have just repelled an enemy raid. There has been much debate about the location of this military action and the identity of the warriors who could be Mycenaeans or Cretans but may well be Therans. The flotilla of ships discussed in chapter 7 was also part of the fresco. The presence of helmets, shields, and spears on some of the ships links the two scenes (figure 7.4—note the boar's tusk helmet on top of the stern cabin). This was a narrative composition, perhaps an account of a real event or some legendary expedition.

## Well-built Mycenae

Whoever the warriors on the Thera fresco may have been, it is widely believed that there was Mycenaean military activity in the Cyclades and that Mycenaeans had some role in the destructions on Crete in LM IB. The Minoan palaces were evidently

**Figure 8.10**  Silver Siege Rhyton from shaft grave IV at Mycenae (Athens, National Archaeological Museum)

weakened by the eruption of Thera and this gave the Mycenaeans an opportunity to intervene. That they could have assembled a sufficiently large force for an invasion is doubtful, however, because politically Greece was so divided at this time. Quite possibly there was conflict on Crete in which some Mycenaeans were involved. Eventually they took control of Knossos, since Greek became the language in which the palace officials wrote their documents.

Trade links with the eastern Aegean developed in LH IIIA and Mycenaeans may have settled on some of the islands. This could have been a peaceful process, yet we know that they deployed troops in the region. Around 1400 BC the Hittite king Arnuwanda I came to the assistance of his vassal Maduwatta who had been attacked by Attarisiya, a man of Ahhiya. The identification of Ahhiya/Ahhiyawa as a Mycenaean state now seems certain and Attarisiya had at least 100 chariots, so he was evidently a powerful warlord. The Hittites forced him to retreat but he later raided Cyprus. Fragments of a painted papyrus found at Tell el-Amarna in Egypt depict a battle scene with a group of warriors who wear distinctive yellow helmets divided into panels. These could be boar's tusk helmets and so the warriors may be Mycenaeans, possibly mercenaries who fought in the Egyptian army.

**Figure 8.11**    Battle fresco in the West House at Akrotiri

It is unclear whether the Mycenaean palaces initiated military ventures overseas, though they did have the capability. The Linear B tablets from Pylos indicate centralized control of personnel and equipment. Men were conscripted from each district for service in the army or with the fleet. The 600–700 rowers mentioned could have provided crews for around 15 ships. The officers who commanded these detachments were appointed by the palace. Items of equipment were ordered, inspected, and repaired if necessary. The list includes spears, swords, javelins, armor, and helmets. A number of tablets deal with chariots, which were apparently serviced in a palace workshop. There is no indication how many chariots Pylos had available but at Knossos the estimate is 175–250. The military situation reflected in the tablets could of course be exceptional, since they were baked and consequently preserved by the fires which destroyed the palaces. The threat of an invasion would explain why Pylos had recruited 800 coastguards.

The construction of fortifications was one of the most obvious defensive measures taken by Mycenaean palaces. Mycenae does not seem to have been fortified before LH IIIA when the first circuit was built. This followed the edge of the limestone outcrop which forms the summit of the acropolis. The distinctive masonry

**Figure 8.12**   Cyclopean fortifications at Tiryns

style is known as Cyclopean (figure 8.12). The outer and inner face of the wall consist of large, unworked or roughly finished blocks of limestone with smaller stones fitted in the gaps. The core was a fill of earth and rubble. These fortifications were massive: 5–6 meters thick on average and over 8 meters high. In LH IIIB the circuit was extended south and west so that Grave Circle A was now within the citadel (figure 8.13). The main entrance, the famous Lion Gate, was protected by a bastion constructed in ashlar masonry. There was also a postern gate on the north side of the citadel. The fortifications of Mycenae were certainly impressive, a powerful statement of military superiority. However, they did leave much of the settlement undefended and it is questionable whether, in the event of an attack, there would have been sufficient space on the citadel for those who lived outside the walls.

Tiryns was also fortified, first the upper part of the citadel where the palace was situated in LH IIIA. Then the circuit was extended around the whole of the acropolis in LH IIIB (figure 8.14). The walls were constructed entirely in the Cyclopean technique. Their maximum height is still almost 8 meters and must have been over 10 meters originally (figure 8.12). The entrance system was complex, with a succession of gates and courts in which any attackers would have come under heavy fire from defenders on the ramparts. An enormous bastion on the west side of the citadel was built around a flight of steps which led down to the postern gate. There were other

NE ext.

26a

26

28

258.6

27

24

265.6

30 255.0

NG

23

S.E.T.

EC.

PALACE

278.0

17

19

18 272.5

254.4

20 21

266.6

14

260.6

32

254.4

31

N

33

240.7

LG

241.4

4

A

240.3

242.9

246.7

CC

PT

234.9

249.6

**Figure 8.13**   Plan of Mycenae

N

0   10   20   30   40   50 m

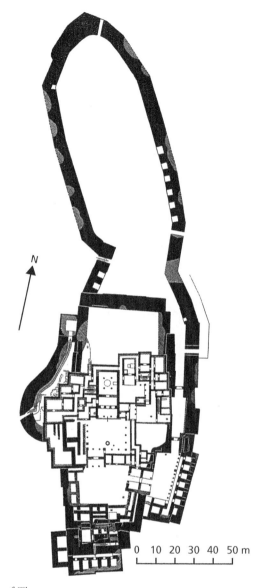

**Figure 8.14**   Plan of Tiryns

fortified sites in the Argolid, particularly Midea where a LH IIIB date for the construction of the circuit wall seems likely. Perhaps this network of citadels was established so that the Argive plain could be protected from attack.

Stretches of a fortification wall built in the Cyclopean style can be seen on the
Acropolis in Athens. The length of the circuit would have been approximately 700
meters, compared with 900 meters in the case of Mycenae and 725 meters at Tiryns.
The citadel at Gla in Boiotia is much larger. This limestone outcrop in the Kopais
basin was encircled by a wall 2800 meters in length. Although not as high as the

fortifications at Mycenae and Tiryns, the wall is 5.50 meters wide on average. Unusually there are four gates, one on each side, linked with roads which ran across the basin. Only part of this enormous fortress was occupied. Recent excavations have shown that cereals were stored in the central enclosure and the L-shaped structure on the north side of the citadel is interpreted as a base for the officials who governed Gla. The construction of the fortifications at the end of LH IIIA2 was evidently undertaken in conjunction with the drainage of the Kopais basin. This operation may have been supervised by the ruler of Orchomenos and provided high-quality agricultural land which clearly needed protection. As well as the citadel at Gla, a system of forts around Kopais was built to deter attacks. The Thebans may have been a threat, since they would not have regarded an expansionist Orchomenos with much enthusiasm. Thebes was a major Mycenaean palatial center and it has now been confirmed that the fortifications around the Kadmeion would have enclosed the whole of the town. Only a few short stretches of this wall have been excavated and it does not seem to have been particularly wide, perhaps 3 meters or so.

Geophysical survey at Pylos has detected a possible fortification wall on an alignment which would have taken in most of the lower town as well as the acropolis. We do not yet know when this was built, but LH IIIB is a period marked by a greater concern for security. A major weakness of many Mycenaean citadels was that they had no water supply. At Mycenae, Tiryns, and Athens subterranean cisterns were constructed in LH IIIB2, so that there would be water available even if the citadel was blockaded. In the Cyclades defensible sites such as Koukounaries on Paros and Ayios Andreas on Siphnos were occupied, while Phylakopi on Melos was refortified. Martial imagery was prominent in the fresco decoration of the palaces in LH IIIB, notably at Mycenae where battle scenes were painted on the walls of the throne room. On a fresco from Pylos, warriors equipped with boar's tusk helmets and greaves fight a group dressed in animal skins (figure 8.15). The warriors should be Mycenaeans but the identity of their opponents is a mystery. Clearly the Mycenaeans will win the battle, though they have suffered casualties. The reality for Pylos was rather different because the palace was destroyed at the end of LH IIIB and never rebuilt, which does suggest that this was a hostile act and not an accident. The destruction of Mycenae and Tiryns around the same time may also have been a consequence of the disruption which affected so much of the eastern Mediterranean.

## Warfare in Transition

Conditions may have improved at the start of LH IIIC but there was further instability which resulted in the abandonment of many settlements over the course of the twelfth and eleventh centuries. The move away from the coast to more remote sites on Crete is indicative of the sense of insecurity that communities must have felt. Although maritime trade did continue, the art of this period suggests that journeys by sea became more hazardous. Galleys powered by oars are depicted on

**Figure 8.15**   Battle fresco from Pylos

kraters from Pyrgos Livanaton (figure 7.6). The warriors on board are ready to
throw their spears at another vessel, so this is a naval battle. No doubt these galleys
were also used for sudden raids. The Warrior Vase from Mycenae vividly evokes
these unsettled times (figure 8.16a & b). On one side six warriors march off. They
are saluted by a woman whose gesture recalls the mourners on the terracotta larnakes from Tanagra (figure 9.10), so it is possible that they will not return. The five
warriors on the other side of the krater may be the enemy they will face. Each of
the warriors is armed with a single spear. They wear horned or spiky helmets and
carry semicircular shields. They are protected by body armor, possibly made of
leather, and greaves.

   New weapons were introduced in LH IIIC, in particular the Type II sword, which
could be used for a cut or thrust stroke (figure 8.1f), and a shorter type of spearhead.
Weapons now appear in tombs, more often than had been the case in LH IIIA2–B.
There is a concentration of these warrior burials in Achaia, though they do occur
across Greece and in the islands as well. The standard equipment of a warrior in
this period consisted of a sword and one or two spears. Daggers, knives, helmets,
greaves, and shields are also found. With the breakdown of the political system,
competition for power intensified and military prowess, real or claimed, evidently
became a mark of high social status again. The warriors were members of new elite
groups which set out to strengthen their position as Greece entered the Iron Age.

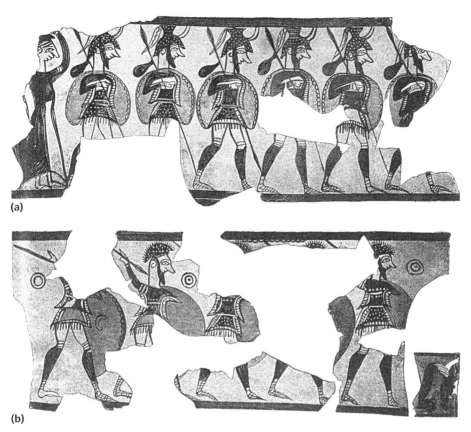

(a)

(b)

**Figure 8.16a & b**   The Warrior Vase from Mycenae (Athens, National Archaeological Museum)

One of the attractions of iron, initially at least, must have been the status value of this new metal. Once the complex production process had been mastered, iron weapons were also technically superior in certain respects. Yet it is remarkable that bronze went out of favor so quickly. By the tenth century most weapons were made of iron. There were Type II swords and daggers. The spearheads have a leaf-shaped blade with a midrib and a socket for the shaft (figure 8.1g). A shorter and narrower type could potentially have been thrown as a javelin as well as used for close combat. Few iron arrowheads have been found, though one was embedded in the shoulder of a man buried in the Kerameikos cemetery in Athens, which does suggest that bows had a role in warfare. Because there are no more depictions of warriors until the eighth century, we do not know how they protected themselves in this period. A bronze helmet from an eleventh-century grave in Tiryns is unique. Bronze disks may have reinforced the center of shields, though this is not certain.

The tradition of warrior burials continued and weapons clearly denoted high status. This is most obvious in the case of the man in the "Heroon" at Lefkandi. Weapons appear in a number of other tenth-century graves at Lefkandi and Athens.

In the tombs in the North Cemetery at Knossos several generations of the same elite families maintained this practice. Perhaps the best ninth-century example is the cremation grave in the Agora in Athens with a sword, two spearheads, and a pair of horse-bits which may show that this man had owned a chariot (figure 9.11).

## Hoplite Warfare

A bronze helmet and corslet were found in an eighth-century grave in Argos, though any weapons must have been removed (figure 9.12). The corslet is of a central European type, whereas the helmet looks Assyrian. This mixture of influences suggests that production of bronze armor was a recent development in Greece. Moreover, the helmet would not have been very effective since it is top-heavy and left most of the face unprotected. The man who commissioned this armor evidently intended to make an impression. Warriors also reappear on pottery, often as combatants in land or sea battles (figure 9.13). How accurately these scenes reflect eighth-century warfare has been questioned. Because the figures were painted as silhouettes, the emphasis on duels is inevitable but this may not have been the way that battles were fought. There is also an element of heroization and it is possible that the Homeric epics were a source of inspiration. The curious shields with the sides cut away could be a rather hazy recollection of the figure-of-eight type which the Mycenaeans had used.

By the end of the eighth century warriors are shown with circular shields, which became a standard item of equipment for hoplite infantry. The hoplite shield was a meter in diameter and made of wood, sometimes plated with bronze. Inside there was an armband and a strap handle so that the shield could be held more securely. The body armor of a hoplite consisted of a bronze corslet of the type worn by the Argos warrior but his impractical helmet was soon superseded. The Corinthian helmet was introduced around 700 BC and completely covered the head (figure 8.17). In the din and dust of a battle, it must have been difficult to hear or see very much. Bronze greaves protected the legs and a cautious hoplite could add arm and thigh guards as well. A full set of armor was expensive, 75–100 drachmas in the Classical period when one drachma was the average daily wage. Moreover, the weight of this equipment and the shield was around 25–30 kg, which obviously restricted mobility. Consequently various modifications appear in due course: lighter types of helmet were preferred and a linen corslet with shoulder guards and flaps below the waist. The main hoplite weapon was a spear, two or more meters in length, which had a bronze or iron blade and a butt spike. There was also a short sword in case the spear broke.

A hoplite battle is depicted on the Chigi Vase, a Corinthian olpe of around 640 BC (figure 8.18). The front ranks have their spears raised and are about to clash. The hoplites in the second row are led by a piper who keeps them in step. The significance of this scene is that it seems to show a phalanx formation. Certainly by the fifth century Greek armies lined up for battle in a phalanx which was generally eight

**Figure 8.17**   Corinthian helmet (Great North Museum)

**Figure 8.18**   Hoplite battle on the Chigi Vase (Rome, Museo Nazionale di Villa Giulia)

**Figure 8.19**    Peltast on an Athenian black-figure cup (Copenhagen, National Museum)

rows deep. One theory is that this originated in the eighth century and led to the development of a standard set of equipment. Alternatively it has been suggested that the introduction of the new items of equipment revolutionized tactics. But quite possibly this was a gradual process and the battle on the Chigi Vase may well represent a transitional stage. It is undoubtedly the case that as Greek citizen armies grew in size there would have been a need for greater discipline and hence a more orderly formation than had been traditional when warfare was a predominantly aristocratic activity.

The broken terrain of Greece was not ideal for an infantry formation which relied on cohesion and would be vulnerable if the ranks of hoplites could not keep in line. Ideally the phalanx would advance at a steady pace but it was not uncommon for the troops to break into a run once the enemy was close. Only the front two or three ranks could actually fight but those behind would have moved forward to replace their injured or exhausted comrades. At times battles must have been like a scrum as the two sides pushed and jostled. Eventually, unless there was a complete stalemate, one phalanx was forced back. This was the moment when the battle could become a rout. If the defeated side turned and ran, they would suffer heavy casualties, but an orderly retreat was not an easy maneuver for a phalanx. Fortunately the victors did not necessarily keep up the pursuit once they had control of the battlefield.

There were also light-armed troops, mainly those citizens who could not afford hoplite equipment. Peltasts, named after their crescent-shaped wicker shields (figure 8.19), were generally armed with two javelins and a short sword. They were particularly effective on rough ground where their mobility gave them a distinct advantage over the hoplites. Peltasts were used for hit-and-run attacks, ambushes, and reconnaissance missions. Archery was a Cretan speciality, and Scythian mercenaries

**Figure 8.20**   Scythian archer on an Athenian red-figure plate (London, British Museum)

appear on Athenian pottery in the late sixth century, equipped with composite bows made of wood, horn, bone, and sinew which had a range of around 150 meters (figure 8.20). Trained slingers could fire their lead bullets even further, around 200 meters. The Thessalians were renowned for their cavalry but in the sixth century most Greeks who could afford a horse rode into battle and then dismounted to fight. By the fifth century some cities, such as Athens, had developed cavalry units to protect their infantry, launch raids, and attack isolated enemy hoplites. Javelins were the main weapon used by cavalrymen who sometimes wore armor, though this must have slowed down their horses which were only the size of ponies.

## Naval Warfare

Some of the galleys depicted on eighth-century pottery have a projection in front of the prow which may be a ram, and the scene is often a naval battle. These pentekonters with a crew of 50 were still the most common type of warship in the sixth century but were gradually superseded by more powerful vessels. One of the galleys apparently has two banks of oars, though this could be an overhead view of oarsmen seated side by side (figure 7.9). Triremes added a third level and this became the standard configuration for warships (figure 8.21). It is not certain when or where the trireme originated. The Phoenicians may have tried out this three-level system first in the early seventh century but it evidently took some time to perfect. By the end of the sixth century the Ionian Greek cities had trireme fleets, possibly supplied

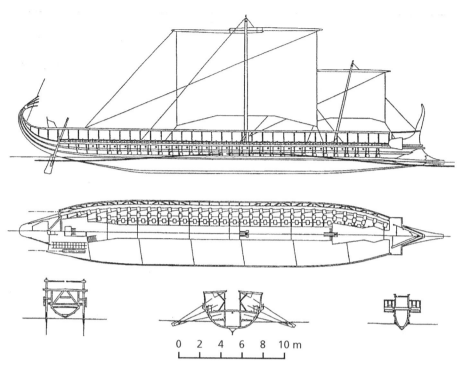

**Figure 8.21**   Plans for the reconstruction of the trireme *Olympias*

by the Persians who had taken control of western Turkey and wanted to build up their navy. The Persian threat eventually spurred on the mainland Greek cities, particularly the Athenians who used the proceeds from the discovery of a rich vein of silver in the Lavrion mines to construct 200 triremes. At the battle of Salamis in 480 BC a Greek fleet of 380 triremes defeated a Persian force of perhaps 1,000 ships. The trireme now dominated naval warfare.

There is some uncertainty about key details of the way that triremes were built because no wrecks have been found. This does seem curious, given that we know the exact location of many naval battles. However, triremes were quite buoyant and the victorious fleet usually towed away damaged vessels. Consequently we have to rely on written sources, art, and architectural evidence. The debate about the finer points of the design culminated in the construction of a full-scale replica trireme, the *Olympias*, in 1985–7 (figure 8.22). This was built plank first and then the frame was added, in line with the techniques used for cargo vessels such as the Kyrenia ship. The size of the *Olympias* was established on the basis of the shipsheds in the port of Piraeus. Measurement of the slipways suggested that the maximum length of a trireme was 37 meters and the width 6 meters. After the sea trials of the *Olympias* a revised estimate of just under 40 meters has been proposed. The number of oarsmen is known to have been 170 and they were arranged on three levels with those lowest down seated closest to the center line of the ship. Triremes also had

**Figure 8.22**   The *Olympias* at sea

two masts for a main sail amidships and a smaller foresail. With the wind behind, the *Olympias* could easily sail at 7 knots. Under oar an average speed of 5.8 knots was achieved for one hour, 7 knots for a nautical mile, and 8.9 knots for a short burst. An ancient trireme may have been even faster because an average speed of 7–8 knots has been estimated for some voyages.

A major advantage of triremes was obviously their mobility. They were quick and could be used to launch surprise attacks. However, there was not much room even for essential supplies. Consequently the crew disembarked for meals and overnight, so it was difficult to keep up a naval blockade. Triremes were also expensive to build and maintain. In the fifth century the Athenians had a fleet of around 300. Those at sea each needed a crew of 200: a helmsman, a boatswain, a purser, a bow officer, a shipwright, a piper, 10 sailors, 10 hoplites and four archers, as well as 170 oarsmen. Piraeus was developed as a fortified naval base with an arsenal and shipsheds around three of the harbors in which the triremes were kept when they were not in use.

Before a battle triremes were stripped down so that they could accelerate faster. They were equipped with a heavy bronze ram and one tactic was to break through the enemy line, then turn and attack from the side or astern. Once a ship had been rammed, the trireme pulled away and was ready for another engagement. Alternatively the hoplites would attempt to board and seize control of the other vessel. For a raid triremes carried additional hoplites and were sometimes adapted as cavalry transports. In the Hellenistic period larger warships were constructed. The higher deck of these vessels provided a platform from which missiles could be thrown or fired and some were equipped with towers for this purpose. They were much heavier and sturdier than triremes, though not as fast.

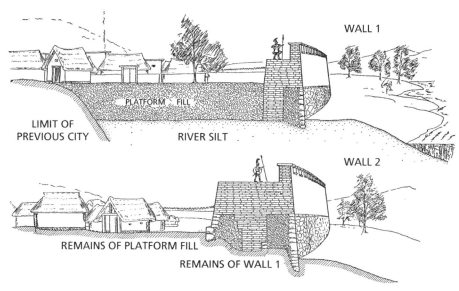

**Figure 8.23**   The fortifications of Old Smyrna

## Fortifications

Possibly because piracy was such a threat, many eighth-century settlements in the Cyclades were in easily defensible locations and some were fortified. Zagora on Andros was protected by a massive wall across the headland which has steep cliffs on three sides. The fortifications at Old Smyrna on the west coast of Turkey were even more impressive (figure 8.23). They were built in the mid ninth century and then enlarged in the eighth century. The walls were 9.50 meters wide and faced with large blocks of stone, backed by a rubble and mudbrick core. Smyrna was eventually destroyed by the Lydians around 600 BC. In the sixth century the Ionian Greek cities were confronted with the expansion of the Persian empire. This may have prompted the construction of a much more extensive fortification system at Miletos. However, the Persians were experts at siege warfare and few cities held out when attacked. Better defenses were needed and the late sixth century fortifications at Buruncuk, which may be the site of ancient Larisa, incorporated regularly spaced towers (figure 8.24). Many of the cities on the Greek mainland did not have circuits. The Acropolis in Athens was still protected by the Mycenaean wall but it is uncertain whether the rest of the city was fortified in any way. Most of the Athenians left before the Persians arrived in 480 BC which suggests that they were not prepared for a siege. Part of Corinth was walled in the sixth century but perhaps not the whole of the city. The Greeks who settled in Italy and Sicily were obviously concerned about security because they often chose promontory sites. Nevertheless, with the possible exception of Akragas, Leontini, and Megara Hyblaia, the colonies were not fortified.

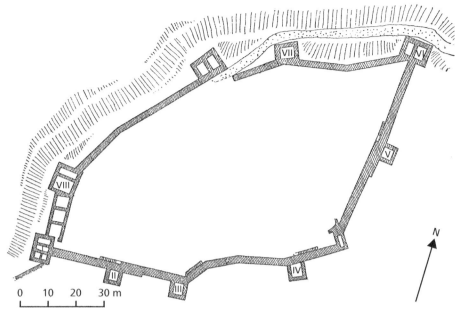

**Figure 8.24** Plan of the fortifications at Buruncuk

The Persian invasion revealed how vulnerable the Greeks were. The response was a more defensive mentality and the construction of fortifications which now enclosed the whole of the city. This was not an entirely new concept. Thasos and Eretria had sixth-century circuits which were over 4 kilometers in length and ran down from the acropolis to the sea. Both cities were captured by the Persians, so fortifications did not guarantee safety. However, a major incentive was the fear of an attack by other Greeks who were not as skilled in the techniques of siege warfare and had fewer men than the Persians. When the Athenians decided to fortify their city in 479 BC the Spartans objected and would have intervened if they had not been duped by Themistokles. The work had to be finished as quickly as possible and Thucydides (1.93) remarks that: "even today you can see it was done in a hurry. The foundations are made of different sorts of stone which sometimes were not shaped to fit. There are many slabs taken from tombs and fragments of sculpture mixed in. For the city boundaries were extended on all sides, and so in their haste they used whatever came to hand." Thucydides also tells us that Themistokles persuaded the Athenians to complete the walls of Piraeus, which had been started before the Persian invasion (figure 2.11). Because Athens now had such a powerful navy, this ensured that supplies could be brought in by sea. Once the long walls had been constructed, the city was secure against a blockade.

The massive circuit, over 30 kilometers in length, would not have been easy to defend, especially if trireme crews were away on duty. So why did the Spartans simply raid the countryside and not attack Athens when they invaded Attica each

summer at the start of the Peloponnesian War? Obviously they hoped that the
Athenians would come out and fight but this would have been suicidal because
the Spartan army was much stronger. The Athenians must have been confident
that the Spartans would not risk a direct assault and the prospect of heavy casualties.
There were some developments in siege warfare in the fifth century. The Athenians
apparently used a battering ram when they besieged Samos in 440 BC and the
Thebans invented a type of flame thrower. Earth ramps and mines are also mentioned but a blockade was the most common tactic. Sometimes a city surrendered
after a brief siege, usually through treachery, though it took the Athenians almost
three years to capture Thasos. The determination of the defenders was quite understandable because sieges often ended with a massacre of the men and the enslave-
ment of the women and children.

The Spartans eventually established a permanent base in Attica, at Dekeleia, and
this disrupted Athenian food supplies. Nevertheless, it was only after the destruction
of their fleet that they surrendered in 404 BC. The fortifications of Athens and
Piraeus were demolished but by 390 they had been rebuilt. In the fourth century
Greek cities invested heavily in the construction of very impressive defenses.
Undoubtedly they felt the need for greater security because this was a period of
political instability and siege warfare had also become more sophisticated. Yet the
sheer size of the fortifications and the quality of the masonry suggest a symbolic
dimension as well.

Walls now followed natural lines of defense along ridges and ravines, which
resulted in some enormous circuits. The fortifications of Syracuse stretched for 27
kilometers after they were extended around the plateau west of the city by Dionysios
I. Messene was founded in 369 BC and provided with a 9-kilometer circuit which is
one of the best examples of fourth-century military architecture (figure 8.25). The
ashlar masonry, squared blocks of limestone, roughly finished and laid in regular
courses, is typical of this period. The Athenians constructed a system of border forts
so that an invasion of Attica could at least be impeded if not blocked. Their tactics
in the Peloponnesian War had been effective, since they avoided a battle with the
Spartans, but the devastation of the countryside had major economic and psychological repercussions. The forts—at Rhamnous, Phyle, Eleutherai, and Eleusis—
guarded the main passes (figure 8.26). If an enemy force approached, the intention
was that the garrison would hold out until reinforcements arrived. Towers are one
of the most common security measures found in the Greek countryside and on the
islands. They were built beside roads, to protect agricultural land, and as lookout
stations on the coast. In Attica and on Thasos there were towers near the mines,
presumably because of the threat posed by the slave workers. The number of farmhouses with towers, for example in Attica and the Crimea (figures 4.20 and 5.3 &
4), suggests that life in the countryside could be dangerous as well as difficult.
Nevertheless, the height of some of the towers seems excessive if they were purely
defensive. Given their visibility, an element of ostentation must also be suspected.

Over the course of the fourth century there were changes in the way that fortifications were constructed in response to developments in siege warfare. In 379 BC

**Figure 8.25** The fortifications of Messene

**Figure 8.26** The border fort at Eleutherai

**Figure 8.27**   Fortifications at Aigosthena

Dionysios I of Syracuse used mobile towers and catapults when he captured the Carthaginian city of Motya. The towers were apparently six stories high and equipped with gangplanks so that the attackers could reach the battlements. The catapults seem to have been mechanized bows which were still hand-held, but gradually they became larger and more powerful. In due course they were able to fire iron-tipped bolts around 400 meters and stone balls which weighed as much as 40 kg. The siege towers grew in size as well. For the siege of Rhodes in 304 BC, Demetrios Poliorketes commissioned a tower over 40 meters high.

To counteract these new devices, defenses had to be improved. The Athenians built a ditch 11 meters wide to keep siege engines away from the city wall. Towers were strengthened so that the defenders could use catapults against attackers. At Aigosthena, a late fourth-century fort on the Corinthian gulf, one of the towers remained more or less intact until an earthquake in 1981 (figure 8.27 was taken before the earthquake). It is 9 meters square and was originally 18 meters high. The base is solid up to the level of the battlements. The two floors above this have slits either for archers or for catapults which fired bolts. The windows on the top floor indicate that larger catapults were installed here.

## The Rise of Macedon

In 359 BC Philip II instigated a major reform of the Macedonian army. The soldiers in the phalanx were equipped with sarissas, long spears with a 5- to 7-meter wooden shaft, an iron tip, and butt spike. They weighed 6–8 kg and needed both hands. A circular shield was held by an arm band and a neck strap. The soldiers also wore a helmet and greaves. The obvious advantage of the sarissa was that more of the men in a Macedonian phalanx could engage the enemy, though the vision and movement of those who were not in the front row must have been rather restricted. Considerable coordination was required and Philip trained his army rigorously. The phalanx was supported by light infantry and specialized units such as Cretan archers. The cavalry had a major role, especially under Alexander. For his Persian expedition he took 5,100 cavalry and 32,000 infantry. Horsemen were armed with spears and often a sword as well. Their armor usually consisted of a helmet and cuirass. They went into battle in a wedge formation. Philip and Alexander also had the men and resources to exploit the innovations in siege warfare. When he attacked Perinthos in 340 BC, Philip used a combination of artillery, rams, massive towers. and mines. Tyre presented Alexander with one of his most serious challenges because the city was on an island just off the Phoenician coast and heavily fortified. His attempts to build a mole out from the mainland were constantly thwarted by the defenders and eventually he breached the walls with rams mounted on ships.

## Conclusions

After Alexander captured Tyre all the men of military age were crucified and approximately 30,000 women and children were sold into slavery. This harsh treatment was not unusual and reinforces the impression that war had become more brutal, the culmination of a process which started with the introduction of the hoplite phalanx. The advent of citizen armies decisively raised the stakes. As the scale of warfare increased, the potential gains became greater and also the casualty levels, especially when cities were besieged. Do we see a similar escalation in earlier state-level societies? Did they also practice "true warfare"? Apparently not in the case of Crete which seems to have been relatively peaceful, though it is difficult to believe that the Minoans were unable to protect themselves against an attack. The Mycenaean palaces did conscript and equip military personnel. This could have been a defensive measure but does imply a capacity for aggression which was no doubt exploited. Inter-state warfare may well have been a factor in the collapse of the Mycenaean political system. Subsequently we see an emphasis on warrior status in many Early Iron Age graves, just as there had been at the start of the Late Bronze Age. At a time of renewed competition for power, military prowess had an added cachet and this would have favored the type of heroic combat later described by Homer.

The link between weapons and status was established as soon as metals became available and possibly even earlier. Daggers were worn prominently, though it is questionable whether they were the most effective weapons for close combat and spears may have been widely used. The first swords came from Crete and then new types were developed as part of the arms industry which supplied Early Mycenaean warriors. Weapons were subsequently modified, iron eventually replacing bronze, but no major changes in equipment were introduced until the first hoplites appeared. Indeed the Dendra warrior would not have looked entirely out of place on a Classical battlefield. Mechanization did have an impact, quite literally in the case of triremes which were conceived as a sort of seaborne missile. The use of the torsion principle made it possible for catapults to fire heavy projectiles, so that cities under siege could be bombarded. The response was the construction of better defenses which were clearly needed. Yet there was always a tendency to build fortifications as a deterrent rather than simply as a barrier. This can be seen in the size of the walls at Kolonna and Mycenaean citadels. Fortifications were also a declaration of independence, notably at Messene, and a conspicuous symbol of success.

## Bibliographical notes

Papers in Carman and Harding 1999 review aspects of ancient warfare in the context of prehistoric Europe. See Branigan 1999 for Early Bronze Age weaponry, Barber 1987 for fortifications in the Cyclades, and Wiencke 2000 for Lerna. Chryssoulaki 1999 comments on the system of guard houses which protected Minoan roads. Walter and Felten 1981 is the definitive account of the fortifications at Kolonna on Aigina, and the warrior grave there is discussed by Kilian-Dirlmeier 1997. Cavanagh and Mee 1998 lists Early Mycenaean warrior burials. Dickinson 1977 and 1994 describes the typological development of Mycenaean weapons and Hiller 1999 analyzes the scenes of warfare and combat in art. Molloy 2008 investigates the way that swords were used, and Crouwel 1981 is a detailed study of chariots. Deger-Jalkotzy 1999 and Palaima 1999 consider the military references in the Linear B texts. See Iakovidis 1983, Loader 1998, and Hope Simpson and Hagel 2006 for Mycenaean fortifications. Deger-Jalkotzy 2006 discusses the LH IIIC warrior tombs. Snodgrass 1964, Lemos 2002, and Dickinson 2006 describe the weapons in use in the Early Iron Age. Snodgrass 1971 and Coldstream 1977 review the eighth-century evidence. For the development of hoplite equipment, the phalanx formation, and warfare in the Archaic and Classical period, see Ducrey 1986, Anderson 1993, Hanson 1993, Whitley 2001, van Wees 2004, Connolly 2006, Snodgrass 2006b, Hunt 2007, and Wheeler 2007. Naval warfare and the role of the trireme are discussed in Casson 1995, Morrison et al. 2000, McGrail 2001, and Strauss 2007. Winter 1971, Lawrence 1979, and Adam 1982 are the most detailed accounts of Greek fortifications. Ober 1985 is good on the system of Athenian border forts, Kern 1999 on ancient siege warfare, and Rihll 2007 on catapults. Sekunda 2007 is a concise survey of the evidence for the Macedonian army.

# CHAPTER 9

# Death and Burial

## Introduction

The dead can tell us a great deal, which is just as well because it is often the case that most of our evidence comes from cemeteries. They certainly do not speak to us directly, however. Funerals are highly ritualized events with a complex agenda. The person who has died is obviously the focus of attention and their future needs will be a primary concern. The opportunity may be taken to emphasize their position in society and commemorate their achievements. But, as has often been pointed out, the dead do not bury themselves and the funeral is an equally important occasion for the relatives of the deceased. They have to come to terms with their loss and begin a process of adjustment. There may be issues of inheritance and succession which make this a particularly tense moment, with potentially wider repercussions if someone in authority has died.

Study of the skeletal remains from a cemetery can provide information about the life expectancy, health, and diet of the group that was buried there. It may also be possible to determine the composition of the group from the age and gender of the skeletons and to identify any differences in the post-mortem treatment of adults and children, for example. Beliefs about the afterlife are often an important aspect of the funeral ceremony but it can be very difficult to understand the thought processes that the rituals represent. The link with religion may be just as uncertain unless some form of literary evidence is available. Art is another useful source, and archaeologists have drawn on anthropology as a way to explore perceptions about death. Obviously no direct analogy can be made with the societies that anthropologists have examined but their observations show how questions about social organization and status can be approached through the study of the dead.

*Greek Archaeology: A Thematic Approach*    By Christopher Mee
© 2011 Christopher Mee

## Neolithic Greece

In the Mesolithic period several adults and infants were buried near the entrance of the Franchthi cave in the Argolid. Two of the adults, a male and a female, had apparently been cremated. So funeral practices were already well developed before the start of the Neolithic period. As the population increased with the growth of settlements, we would expect more graves. However, the number of excavated Neolithic burials can be counted in the hundreds, whereas tens of thousands of people lived and died in Greece between 7000 and 3000 BC. Obviously we will never find everyone, but the Neolithic dead do seem unusually elusive.

Intramural burial within settlements was not common, especially for adults. Most of the cases that have been recorded were infants or young children. The situation is different in caves that were occupied at this time, such as Franchthi and Alepotrypa in Laconia. The remains of adults and children have been found at both of these sites, but few of the skeletons were articulated. Although some may have been disturbed, it is clear that secondary burial was a regular practice. If an individual had been buried, their remains would be exhumed and reinterred or placed in an ossuary. At Alepotrypa two ossuaries have been excavated and each contained a mass of bones. Particular attention had been paid to the skulls which were sometimes surrounded by a circle of stones. The darkness of the cave would undoubtedly have heightened the psychological impact of these rituals.

Secondary burials have occasionally been reported in settlements. There were 11 skulls under one of the houses at Prodromos in Thessaly. However, most of the dead must have been buried elsewhere. An Early Neolithic cemetery was discovered a short distance from Souphli, another Thessalian site. The dead had been cremated on pyres and included adults and juveniles. Once the body had burned the remains were removed from the pyre while still hot and buried in a pit. Some of the pottery with the burials was scorched and had obviously been placed on the pyre. Cremation is a more elaborate rite which requires a considerable amount of fuel, so it is significant that no distinction seems to have been made as regards the age or gender of the deceased. Neolithic cremations have been found at a number of other sites but inhumation was probably the most common practice. So where were most of the dead buried? Excavators could easily miss a cemetery which was some distance from a settlement, yet it is remarkable that there have not been more accidental discoveries, particularly in Thessaly which has hundreds of Neolithic sites. The explanation may be that most graves were quite shallow and have consequently been destroyed or disturbed.

This makes it sound as though death was treated rather casually, perhaps because it was such a common occurrence at a time when life expectancy was so short. Children were especially susceptible, and most will have died before they reached adulthood. Neolithic society has also been perceived as relatively egalitarian, which meant that families did not use the funeral as an opportunity to stress status distinctions and in any case they could not afford a lavish ceremony. Yet some communities did have complex ritual practices which they observed in the case of children as well as adults and which may well reflect a more widely held set of beliefs. Moreover, there is evidence of inequality in the Late Neolithic period, if not earlier. Neolithic funerals were probably not as simple as they seem.

## Early Bronze Age Greece

In the Final Neolithic cemetery at Kephala on Kea the graves were built of stone. As a result the dead had a much more visible presence, and this new trend was soon taken up elsewhere in the Cyclades. Early Bronze Age cemeteries have been exca-vated on most of the islands. Generally they consist of 15–20 graves, though some are much larger, in particular Chalandriani on Syros with more than 600. The typical grave is a cist, a rectangular or trapezoidal stone-lined pit covered by slabs. Because the graves were usually less than a meter in length, the dead were buried in a contracted position with their legs bent up. It is possible that this was symbolic and not just a practical necessity. Quite often graves were used again, presumably for another family member. The remains of previous burials would then be moved aside to make room, though the skull was usually left undisturbed. In some cists an extra floor was added so that the upper chamber could be used for burials and the lower chamber as an ossuary.

In many graves there were no goods, though we must bear in mind that perish-able items may have been left with the dead. No doubt they were dressed or wore a shroud and could have been given items of food which have not survived. Pottery is the most common type of grave good that we do find, particularly bowls, cups, and jugs which suggests that the dead needed provisions for the afterlife. If the obsidian blades were razors, they were also expected to look respectable. Wealth is sometimes emphasized with metal or marble vessels, weapons, jewelry, and figu-rines. These were not necessarily the favorite possessions of the individual con-cerned and may never have been used before. Once buried they were taken out of circulation, as a reminder of the status that the deceased had enjoyed in life and which was expected to continue even after death. This display of wealth was no doubt intended to promote the position of the family as well. The marble figurines are particularly impressive (figure 10.2a & b) and their artistic appeal is unfortu-nately the reason why so many Early Cycladic graves have been looted. They under-line the religious dimension of the rituals that were performed at the funeral, and the discovery of stone platforms in some cemeteries is an indication that ceremonies may have been held at other times as well.

In Greece most of the Early Bronze Age cemeteries are concentrated in the eastern mainland, in the Argolid, Corinthia, Attica, Boiotia, and on Euboia. The cemetery of built graves at Tsepi in Attica was laid out in rows. Each grave was carefully marked off by a border of stones (figure 9.1a & b). The sides of the grave were lined with rubble or slabs, a row of slabs formed the roof, and there was a narrow entrance at one end. The graves were used repeatedly. The latest burial had generally been

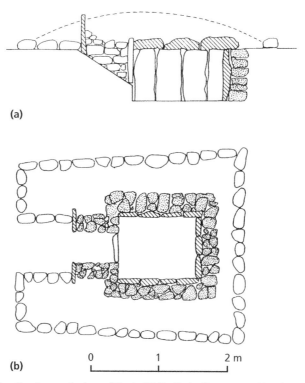

**Figure 9.1a & b**   Section and plan of Early Helladic built grave at Tsepi

left just inside the entrance and a mass of bones was stacked at the back of the chamber, though more care was taken with the skulls which were sometimes lined up on one side. This is reminiscent of the way that earlier burials were treated in the islands, and much of the pottery, though locally made, is Cycladic in style.

In a number of cemeteries there were chamber tombs. At Manika on Euboia the entrance was a vertical shaft and the subterranean chamber, which could be rectangular, trapezoidal, or circular, opened off this (figure 9.2a & b). The chamber was carefully blocked off by slabs or stones. The dead had usually been buried in a contracted position, despite the fact that the chambers were often over two meters in diameter. So the size of the tomb did not necessarily dictate how the body would be laid out. Earlier burials were pushed to one side and in some cases the bones had apparently been removed and put in an ossuary. The quantity and quality of the finds does vary, presumably because of differences in status. A connection with the Cyclades is also evident and the presence of marble figurines suggests that these shared tastes reflect similar beliefs.

On Lefkas in western Greece the dead were cremated and the grave goods were also placed on the pyre. Once this had burned down the remains and some of the grave goods were collected together and put in a pithos, which was sealed with a slab. A circular stone platform was then built around the pithos and this also covered

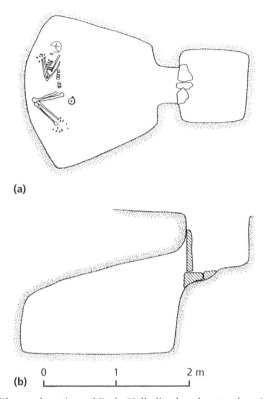

(a)

(b)    0          1          2 m

**Figure 9.2a & b**    Plan and section of Early Helladic chamber tomb at Manika

the pyre. The platform was in turn covered by a mound of earth and stones which formed a tumulus. In many of the tumuli additional graves were inserted in the stone platform later. This is the start of a vogue for circular tombs in western Greece which continues in the Middle Bronze Age, though elsewhere on the mainland there is more of a break.

Different traditions also developed on Crete. In the north and east of the island the dead were often buried in caves or rock shelters, a practice which started in the Neolithic period. Because of later disturbance, it is not at all clear what sort of funeral ceremony was held, though the caves were evidently not just used as ossuaries. The tombs in the south of Crete were circular stone tholoi. The first tholoi were con-structed in EM I and this was still the most common tomb type in the Protopalatial period. Around 90 tholoi have been discovered in cemeteries of one, two, or three tombs. At sites where there is more than one tomb their use overlaps. They were built a short distance from the settlement, often within 100 meters or so. The dead were near, but the tombs were oriented so that the entrance faced away from the settle-ment. Consequently they could not see their homes and would be less inclined to return. The fact that the tomb entrances were carefully blocked underlines this desire to keep the dead in their place. Nevertheless, because of the size and solid construc-tion of the tombs they were a very visible and permanent presence. Many of the tombs remained in use for centuries and would have been a powerful symbol of the entitlement that a community could claim to land and other key resources.

A tholos has a circular wall made up of a rubble core faced with larger blocks of stone, which can be over 2 meters thick in the case of the largest tombs with a diameter of 10 meters or more (figure 9.3). There has been considerable speculation about the type of roof. Because the walls lean in and masses of fallen stone have sometimes been found in the chamber, the obvious solution is a stone vault. However, it seems unlikely that the walls could have supported the weight of a stone roof in the largest tombs. A timber framework may have been used, and a mudbrick roof is another possibility. The entrance is almost always on the east side of the tomb, so sunrise may have had a special significance. A number of tholoi have annexes in front of the entrance which had been added later.

Because of the length of time that the tholoi were in use and the fact that most have been looted, it is not easy to reconstruct the funeral rites. The dead were apparently laid out on the floor of the tomb with personal possessions which could include weapons, tools, jewelry, sealstones, and pottery. Cups suggest that a toast was drunk by the mourners either inside the tomb or in one of the annexes. Few skeletons have been found in situ and it is evident that, once the body had decomposed, the bones were moved aside. It seems that the tombs were periodically cleaned out and purified. The bones would then be transferred to one of the annexes which were used as ossuaries. When the remains of earlier burials were removed, there was no doubt a ceremony to mark this final stage in the journey. The tombs may well have been a focus for cult activity at other times as well, which implies that the dead were venerated if not worshiped. As far as we can tell, most adults were buried in these tombs, though not necessarily all children. Some tombs were probably reserved for particular groups of families, which would explain why settlements had two or three tholoi, but differences in status were not emphasized.

As well as the caves and rock shelters, there were stone-built tombs in the north and east of Crete. These were rectangular structures with one or more compartments. In some respects they resemble houses but it is questionable whether they were conceived as a home from home for the dead. The cemetery on the island of Mochlos was positioned so that the tombs would be visible from the sea as ships approached but they could not be seen from the settlement. Approximately 30 tombs have been excavated, built up against the rock face in such a way that they seem like part of the landscape (figure 9.4). A path winds up through the cemetery to the most elaborate tombs, I/II/III and IV/V/VI. Although the tombs have been disturbed, they were evidently used for primary burials. In due course the bones were moved to another compartment where the skulls were carefully stacked together. Much of the jewelry that was buried in the tombs is of gold or silver and there were also many superb stone vessels. The finest objects were not found exclusively in the largest tombs, though they were concentrated in I/II/III and IV/V/VI. Status must have been a more contentious issue at Mochlos and this was clearly the case at Mallia where one of the tombs is enormous. Known as the Chrysolakkos or gold pit from the spectacular finds, most of which were looted, the tomb measures

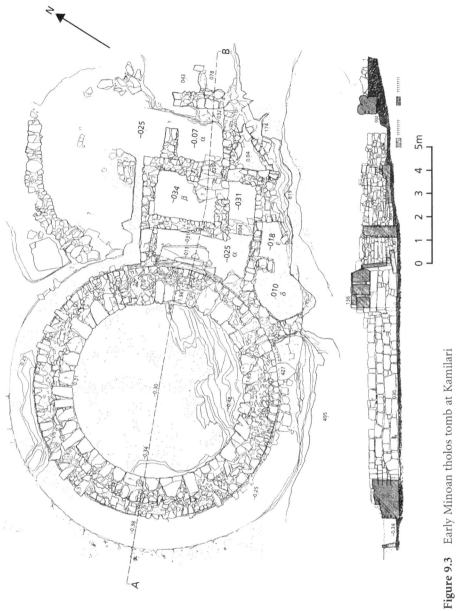

**Figure 9.3**  Early Minoan tholos tomb at Kamilari

**Figure 9.4**   Reconstruction of tomb I/II/III on Mochlos

approximately 40 by 30 meters and the interior was divided up into rows of burial compartments. It was built at the start of the Protopalatial period, at around the same time as the palace at Mallia, and was surely reserved for the elite.

The burial record is not always an accurate barometer of social change but the political upheavals on Crete did have an impact. The cemetery at Archanes in the north of the island is unusual in that there were tholoi and rectangular built tombs. This fusion of two distinct architectural styles integrated different traditions and continued in the Middle Minoan period when the cemetery expanded in size. Tomb B, a two-story structure with a tholos enclosed on three sides by annexes, is particularly impressive. Many of the dead were buried in clay jars or terracotta coffins known as larnakes. It is unclear whether this was an indication of higher status or was bound up with a greater emphasis on individuality which is evident from the choice of personal items in these tombs. The sealstones especially were a mark of identity. It is significant that the level of activity at Archanes increased in MM IA, just before the first palaces were constructed, a time when the competition for power must have intensified.

## Middle Bronze Age Greece

In Greece the situation was very different. Many of the Early Helladic cemeteries went out of use, and burial in simple pit or cist graves became the rule. The most

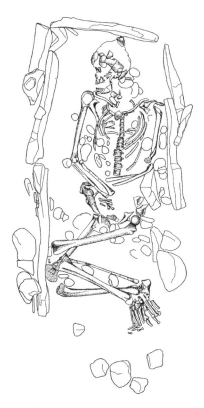

**Figure 9.5**   Cist grave at Kouphovouno

impressive Middle Helladic tombs were tumuli, which can be as much as 25 meters in diameter. However, even though there is sometimes a central grave, which does suggest a recognition of higher status, the finds are generally rather modest, especially in comparison with the Early Helladic tumuli on Lefkas. In the pit and cist graves this impression of austerity is even more apparent. Less than 30 percent of the 200 Middle Helladic burials at Lerna had any recognizable grave goods, and this figure is fairly typical. Some settlements did have cemeteries with clusters of graves in which members of the same family had presumably been buried. Intramural burial was also very common, though the graves were often in a part of the settlement that had been abandoned or was not occupied at the time. It was usually children who were buried under houses.

As an example of a Middle Helladic cemetery let us look at Kouphovouno in Laconia, where 16 graves have been excavated. Some were pits, often edged with stones which had supported a roof made of perishable materials. There were also cists constructed of upright slabs (figure 9.5). The dead had usually been buried on their sides in a contracted position and only a few had grave goods. The remains of 27 individuals have been identified, adults and children, males and females (table 9.1).

**Table 9.1**   The age and sex of the burials in the cemetery at Kouphovouno

| Age group | Number of individuals | Male | Female | Indeterminate sex |
|---|---|---|---|---|
| Infants (0–1 yrs) | 5 | | | 5 |
| Young children (2–5 yrs) | 3 | | | 3 |
| Older children (6-12 yrs) | 1 | | | 1 |
| Adolescents (13–19 yrs) | 5 | 3 | 1 | 1 |
| Young adults (20–34 yrs) | 3 | 3 | | |
| Middle adults (35–49 yrs) | 4 | 3 | 1 | |
| Old adults (50+yrs) | 2 | | 2 | |
| Adults (20+yrs) | 4 | 1 | | 3 |
| Total | 27 | 10 | 4 | 13 |

The greatest likelihood of death was in infancy/early childhood and late adolescence/young adulthood. The mortality rate between birth and 5 years was very high in these communities. At Lerna the figure is almost 50 percent, so parents could expect that half their children would have died before age 5. The reason for this was nutritional deficiency combined with childhood diseases. The second phase of increased mortality in late adolescence/young adulthood is usually due to the risks of childbirth but women of this age are under-represented at Kouphovouno and they may have been buried in another part of the cemetery. A number of the males in this group had suffered serious injuries; one had somehow been cut in two. In some graves there were the remains of adults and infants. The natural assumption is that a mother and child had been buried together but in one case the adult was male.

The people of Kouphovouno were not very healthy. Study of the skeletons has shown that, as children, they were malnourished and had suffered from various diseases, in particular rickets, scurvy, measles, and smallpox. Hard work had caused degenerative changes in the adult skeletons of both sexes. Arthritis and osteoporosis were also common. Stable isotope analysis of the carbon and nitrogen in bone samples from Kouphovouno indicates a diet which mainly consisted of plant foods, such as wheat, barley, and fruits. Some animal protein was consumed, either as meat or dairy products, but not in significant quantities.

For many Middle Helladic communities life must have been fairly grim and it is difficult to escape the conclusion that this was a period when most people were desperately poor. However, there were exceptions. Kolonna on Aigina was a fortified settlement which had built up a network of trade contacts and was consequently quite prosperous. Just in front of the main gate in the fortifications a man was buried with an array of weapons and a gold diadem (figure 8.5). He was clearly an exceptional individual who was commemorated as a warrior, perhaps because of his military prowess. He also set a precedent for the spectacularly rich burials in the shaft graves at Mycenae.

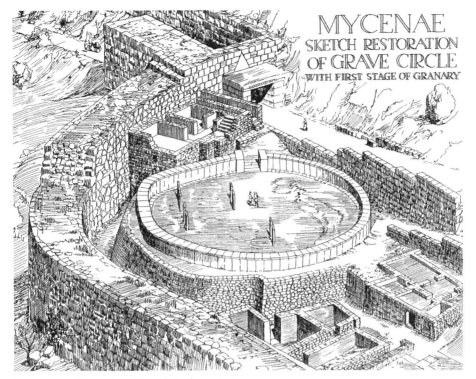

**Figure 9.6** Reconstruction of Circle A at Mycenae

## Mycenaean Greece

Although the two shaft grave circles were in use before the end of the Middle Helladic period, they do mark the start of a new era. Circle A is prominently positioned just inside the Lion Gate but this arrangement dates from LH IIIB when the fortifications were extended (figure 9.6). At the same time the grave circle was carefully restored and the original enclosure wall was replaced. This was done three centuries or so after the final burial had taken place and indicates a reverence for the dead. Quite possibly they were venerated as the founders of the royal dynasty, whatever their relationship with the later rulers of Mycenae may in fact have been. There were six shaft graves in Circle A, the largest of which measured 4.50 by 6.40 meters and was 4.00 meters deep. The graves consisted of a rectangular shaft cut through the earth and rock with a ledge at the lower end to support the roof. Nineteen people had been buried in the graves: eight men, nine women, and two children. The men had an extraordinary array of weapons, an arsenal of finely crafted swords, daggers, spears, and knives. They are depicted as heroic warriors and hunters on some of the gold rings from the graves. Men and women were covered in jewelry, in particular gold disks which were sewn on their clothes or shrouds. Some of the men wore gold funeral masks. The dead were also provided with gold

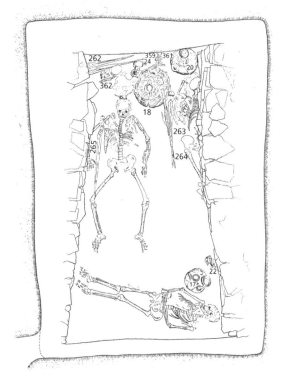

**Figure 9.7**   Plan of grave Gamma in Circle B at Mycenae

and silver cups and goblets, presumably so that they could dine in style with their friends in the underworld.

Grave Circle B was only a short distance from the citadel but had evidently been forgotten by LH IIIB. The 14 shaft graves were generally not as large as those in Circle A, and 11 cist and pit graves were also found. It was not possible to determine the age and gender of all the burials but adults outnumber children 24:8 and there were three times as many men as women. The maximum number of burials was four in grave Gamma: three men and a woman (figure 9.7). One of the men had been buried first and then the woman. Their skeletons were subsequently moved aside for the burial of the man in the center. Finally another man was laid across one end of the grave. He had suffered a head wound and part of his skull had been surgically removed in the hope that this would relieve the pain. After each burial the roof was replaced and sealed with clay. The shaft was then filled with earth and the grave was marked by a low mound and sometimes a carved gravestone. The range of grave goods in Circle B is impressive, but many of the dead only had pottery. The Circle A burials were generally much richer. However, it is important to note that, although the two circles did coexist for a time, Circle B was in use first. So it could be argued that what we see is an escalation in conspicuous consumption. The reason for this extravagance was a desire for prestige and consequently status.

This was evidently a period of political instability and funerals were an occasion when the transfer of power and rights of succession could be legitimized. Those buried in the grave circles were clearly an elite who had set themselves apart. Yet there must also have been divisions within this group, which would explain why Circle A was established.

The shaft graves were essentially enlarged pit graves and could be viewed as another example of the ostentation which is such a feature of this period. However, their size also facilitated a move to collective burial and this is equally true of tholos and chamber tombs. These new types of tomb were designed to be reopened periodically for the burial of individuals who were no doubt related in some way. Generations of their ancestors may already have been buried in the tomb and so this practice places a much greater emphasis on hereditary status. Tholos tombs originated in Messenia at the end of the Middle Helladic period. The narrow dromos leads to the entrance of the tomb. The circular burial chamber has a corbeled stone vault. Unlike Minoan tholoi, the Mycenaean tombs were cut into the bedrock so that the vault was buttressed and they were covered by an earth mound. Soon tholos tombs appeared in the Argolid and Laconia as well as Messenia. In LH II seven were constructed at Mycenae where they replaced the shaft graves as the high-status option. It seems quite likely that some tholoi were royal tombs, though they were probably not just reserved for rulers. Most had been robbed but a few were still intact or there were pits in the floor of the chamber which had not been opened. This was the case at Dendra in the Argolid and Vapheio in Laconia for example. The character and quality of the finds underlines how important the funeral had become for these image-conscious individuals, who were much less concerned about where they lived.

Chamber tombs have a similar layout but were rock-cut rather than stone-built (figure 9.8a & b). Some have circular chambers like tholos tombs or are rectangular. Often the chamber is an irregular shape. At Prosymna in the Argolid the size of the chamber ranges from 5 to 30 m². The Minoans also had rock-cut chamber tombs which the Mycenaeans may have seen and adapted. This distinctive mainland style of tomb is then found at Knossos in LM II–IIIA when it is believed that the palace was under Mycenaean control. The warriors who were buried in these tombs have quite naturally been identified as Mycenaeans but this assumption has been questioned. It is equally possible that they were Minoans whose way of life had been influenced by the warrior ethos which was so prevalent in Greece at this time. There may be a more subtle explanation for changes in the burial record than an alteration in the ethnic makeup of a community.

LHIII is often regarded as a period of greater uniformity and it is true that there is less experimentation. However, regional differences can be seen. For example, Messenia has few chamber tomb cemeteries, unlike Boiotia where tholos tombs were a rarity. Variation is also evident at a more local level, possibly because communities wished to maintain their traditions and consequently an independent identity as the Mycenaean palaces grew more powerful and influential. Some rulers may well have imposed restrictions. Mycenae and Tiryns were the only sites in the Argolid

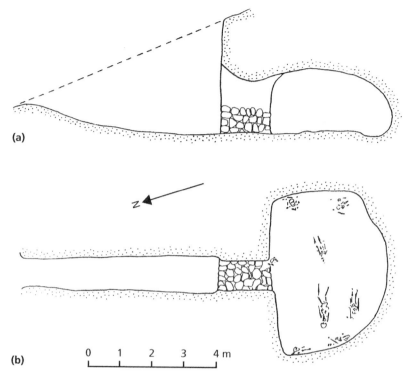

(a)

(b)

0    1    2    3    4 m

**Figure 9.8a & b**   Section and plan of chamber tomb 525 at Mycenae

where tholos tombs were constructed in LH IIIA–B. Moreover, the tombs at Mycenae were the magnificent Treasury of Atreus and the Tomb of Clytemnaestra. It would have taken around 20,000 man days to build the Treasury of Atreus (figure 9.9). The tomb is approached down a dromos 36 meters in length, which is lined with ashlar masonry. The facade was decorated with green and red marble columns. Above the entrance, which was sealed by double doors sheathed in bronze, there is a lintel block which weighs approximately 120 tons. The chamber is 14.50 meteres in diameter and 13.20 meters high with 33 smoothly finished courses of masonry. The ruler who built this tomb was no doubt buried in the side chamber.

   Chamber tombs were much more common in LH III and must have been used by a wider cross-section of society. It does seem likely that they were family tombs but, at those sites where the skeletal remains have been properly studied, children were clearly under-represented. Moreover they had often been buried in a niche in front of the entrance, rather than in the chamber, or were given separate tombs. The fact that children were treated differently does not imply a lack of concern or respect. Parents would have grieved when a child died but, with the mortality rate at around 50 percent for those under age 10, this was a frequent occurrence. To cope psychologically with their loss, they may have not have viewed children as fully fledged members of society who needed to be ritually reunited with the ancestors.

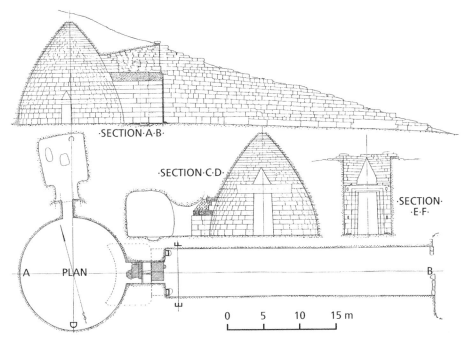

·SECTION·A·B·

·SECTION·C·D·

·SECTION·
·E·F·

A        PLAN                                                                                    B

0      5      10      15 m

**Figure 9.9**    Plan and section of the Treasury of Atreus

Of course some children were buried alongside adults and it is evident that the conventions which governed behavior were very flexible. Curiously, men also out-number women in Mycenaean tombs. Although it is true that female skeletons are not as robust and would therefore be more likely to have disintegrated, this does not fully account for the discrepancy. There does seem to have been a gender bias, which may be linked with the dependent status of most women, as wives and daughters, in Mycenaean society.

We can reconstruct the ceremonies at the graveside from the hundreds of exca-vated chamber tombs but the first part of the funeral took place away from the cemetery, probably in or outside the home of the person who had died. Terracotta larnakes from Tanagra in Boiotia depict processions of women who raise their hands to their heads in a gesture which clearly expresses their grief (figure 9.10). The way they are dressed suggests that they led the mourners when the corpse was laid out and the community came to pay their respects. Other women with shaved heads and lacerated faces were presumably close relatives. In one highly emotional scene they lower the body of a child into a larnax. Men occasionally appear on the larnakes but do not seem to have been as closely involved, perhaps because there were taboos which restricted how they should act.

The journey to the cemetery began a process of separation which took the dead physically and symbolically away from family and friends. Once the body had been brought into the tomb it was laid out, normally in an extended position, on the floor or a bench. Terracotta larnakes and wooden coffins were occasionally used.

**Figure 9.10**    Larnax from Tanagra (Thebes Museum)

The pottery provided often includes jars of perfumed oil, a tradition which would continue for centuries. The oil was a luxury and also signified purity. Vessels with food and drink may be the residue of a funeral feast, though it was evidently expected that the dead would need supplies for the afterlife. They were given jewelry and no doubt wore their finest clothes as well. The emphasis on weaponry is less obvious, perhaps because it was now believed that bronze should be kept in circulation. Terracotta female figurines (figure 10.13), found with children, probably offered protection. The entrance was then carefully blocked with stone, a toast was drunk, and the cups were shattered against the wall. Finally, the dromos was backfilled with earth. When the next funeral took place, the dromos and the entrance would be unblocked and the process repeated. However, the time would come when there was no more room in the chamber. At this point earlier burials were moved to one side or the bones were collected together and placed in a pit. This practice is often seen as rather cavalier and a contrast has been drawn between the care taken when the dead were first buried and their later treatment. However, tombs have been excavated in which none of the skeletons was undisturbed. It seems likely that the chamber had been reopened for a ceremony which involved some rearrangement of the last burial. Ceremonies of this type were probably a regular occurrence and marked the final stage in the journey that the dead had undertaken. Like many societies, the Mycenaeans evidently believed in a liminal phase between life and death. This ended when the body had decomposed and the spirit was freed. Ceremonies ensured that the dead were placated and would not cause trouble. They also gave the bereaved time to adjust to their loss.

After the destruction of the palaces at the end of the LH IIIB period, no more grand tholos tombs were built and fewer chamber tombs. Sometimes tombs which had gone out of use were cleared and reused, presumably by a different group. There were some new chamber tombs, notably at Perati in Attica, but they were small and not as well constructed. This is not a sign of poverty, however, because some of the Perati tombs were quite rich. Nevertheless many of the tombs only have one or two skeletons, which suggests a change of beliefs. It was no longer the custom that generations of the same family would be buried together and this anticipates the move to individual burial in the Early Iron Age. The funeral ceremony may also have been curtailed, which could explain the introduction of cremation. The first Mycenaean cremations were in the cemetery at Müskebi in western Anatolia and the rite may have spread from there. The puzzle is that, at Perati for example, we find cremations and inhumations in the same tomb. So it seems unlikely that those who were cremated came from a different ethnic group. Changes such as the move to individual burial and the adoption of cremation were once used as evidence of population movements in the twelfth and eleventh centuries. What they actually reflect is the sense of insecurity which had undermined confidence in the social order and the traditions that underpinned this.

## Early Iron Age Greece

The upheavals at the end of the Late Bronze Age resulted in a remarkably diverse set of practices. The Kerameikos was one of the main cemeteries in Athens. The Submycenaean burials here were mainly inhumations in pit and cist graves. In the Protogeometric period cremation became the predominant rite. The dead were cremated on a pyre and the incinerated bones were collected up and put in an amphora. This was buried in a pit which had been cut down at one end. The remains of the pyre were also placed in the pit, together with any grave goods. The pit was then filled with earth and covered by a stone slab. Most of the burials in the Kerameikos were adults, though elsewhere in Athens, for example in the Agora, there were children as well. In the Argolid, at Argos and Asine, individual burial in cist and pit graves was also the rule but cremation was not particularly common. Lefkandi on Euboia had at least six separate Early Iron Age cemeteries with cremations and inhumations. Most of the cremation pyres had been built over large pits. In the fill of the pit there was often pottery and personal items which had evidently been burned on the pyre with the body. The inhumations were in cist or shaft graves. The most spectacular burials at Lefkandi were on the Toumba hill, in the "Heroon" which is described in chapter 3. The man who was buried here must have been the ruler of Lefkandi and his tomb became the focal point of an exceptionally rich cemetery. The trend for individual burial was not taken up everywhere. In Thessaly there were small tholos tombs, as well as cist grave cemeteries, and chamber tombs were used on Crete, for example at Knossos.

What this brief survey shows is that each region was different and many communities also had a mixture of practices. It is difficult to see a pattern but these were not random choices. No conventions had been established about the way that particular aspects of the social persona should be expressed when someone died. The move to individual burial does suggest less of an emphasis on kinship, though the graves in some cemeteries were apparently clustered together in family plots. It is also significant that many of the chamber tombs at Knossos went out of use after just one or two generations. The major changes may have been linked with beliefs about the importance of ancestry and descent. If continuity was not such a concern, we would expect more flexibility. This may explain why cremation was taken up so selectively. Even in the most enthusiastic communities there were still some inhumations and not necessarily of a specific group, such as children. Cremation was a more complex and costly procedure. Fuel was needed for the pyre which had to burn for several hours. It could therefore have denoted high status but was surely symbolic as well. The use of fire has been linked with beliefs about purification and sacrifice. Social pressures may also have been a factor. This is certainly true of Great Britain where cremation was illegal in the early nineteenth century but is now the predominant rite. Athens adopted cremation in the eleventh century and then reverted to inhumation in the eighth century, a change which is discussed below and seems to have been politically motivated. The choice of rite was clearly dependent on many different considerations.

Naturally there is also considerable variation in the grave goods. In Athens gender distinctions were emphasized. It is no surprise that weapons were buried with men but women were now given most of the jewelry, whereas in the Mycenaean period this was not the case. Certain types of pottery also seem to have been particularly associated with men or women. Few of the Protogeometric graves in Athens could be described as rich. The lack of gold and silver jewelry, for instance, could be construed as evidence of isolation and impoverishment. However, it is possible that differences in status were not sharply defined and therefore stressed. This is also true of the Argolid but certainly not Lefkandi. Although the burials in the "Heroon" were clearly exceptional, they do mark the start of a trend, particularly in the Toumba cemetery, for greater extravagance. Items imported from the Near East and Egypt were especially prized. There were children as well as adults buried in these rich graves, an indication perhaps of the status they would have enjoyed had they lived.

The taste for orientalia continued in the ninth century at Lefkandi and there is gold jewelry in a high proportion of the graves. Status is given more prominence in Athens as well. In an early ninth-century grave near the Agora the cremated remains of a man in his thirties were found in an amphora which had been sealed with a stone (figure 9.11). An iron sword had been bent around the neck of the amphora and symbolically killed. This is quite a common practice and may have deterred grave robbers, since the valuable sword could not be used again. This well-armed

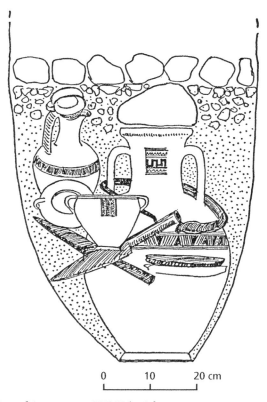

0          10          20 cm

**Figure 9.11**   Section of Agora grave XXVII in Athens

warrior also had two spearheads, a javelin point, two knives, and an ax, as well as a whetstone so that he could keep his weapons sharp. A pair of horse bits showed that he had owned a chariot, which was presumably a mark of his high status. A jug and three cups had been provided in case he needed a drink. There were other ninth-century warrior burials in Athens and wealth is generally much more visible.

Weapons also appear in the richest chamber tombs in the North Cemetery at Knossos. This is consistently the case in every phase of their use which can cover two centuries or more. The implication is that this was a class distinction rather than a reflection of the military prowess of these individuals. The warrior ethos was still prevalent in the eighth century. A grave in Argos contained a bronze suit of armor which consisted of a helmet, corslet, and greaves (figure 9.12). Unfortunately the grave had been disturbed and no weapons were found. However, there were a pair of iron fire-dogs and 12 spits, so that this aristocrat could roast meat for his friends, just like a Homeric hero. Fire-dogs and spits were an accessory of the elite at Knossos as well. The cemeteries at Lefkandi went out of use in the late ninth century, around the time that Eretria was founded. At the end of the eighth century a warrior was buried in the West Gate cemetery there. His cremated remains had been wrapped in a cloth and placed in a bronze urn. This was enclosed by stone

**Figure 9.12**   Armor from grave 45 in Argos

slabs and covered by a layer of mudbricks. In the grave were five swords and six spearheads. Six more cremations followed and then, early in the seventh century, a triangular stone platform was built over the graves and a hero cult was instituted. Although the circumstances are different, there is clearly an echo of the "Heroon" at Lefkandi in this.

In Athens the eighth century was a time of change. Inhumation became the dominant rite, though cremation was still practiced. It was also more common for children to be buried in the same cemeteries as adults, sometimes in adjacent graves and presumably in family groups. The grave goods are generally more modest with less gold jewelry. The richest burials were in fact in the countryside, for example two women, possibly priestesses of Demeter, who were buried at Eleusis. However, attention-seekers could now invest in grave markers which were a much more conspicuous memento mori. In the ninth century kraters with pierced bases for libations had been placed over some male graves. This tradition continued in the eighth century, alongside the introduction of equally enormous amphorae as grave markers for women of high status. These vessels were elaborately decorated, often with funerary scenes (figures 9.13 & 9.14). Typically the dead man or woman is shown laid out on a bier and covered with a checked shroud which is cut away so that we

**Figure 9.13**   Krater from Athens with funeral scenes (Athens, National Archaeological Museum)

can see how tall they were. Male and female mourners sit and stand around the bier, their hands clasped to their heads. Often there is a procession of chariots which no doubt accompanied the funeral cortège, though perhaps their presence is also a reminder of the games held in honor of a dead hero, most famously Patroklos at Troy. Battles are depicted on some of the kraters and may commemorate an action in which the dead man fought but once again the theme is heroization.

Another feature of eighth-century Athens is a sharp rise in the number of burials, of adults and children. Athens had grown in size and more sites in Attica were now occupied, which does suggest a higher population. Nevertheless it has been argued that there was also an increase in the proportion of the population who were buried in a way that is archaeologically visible. Burial in a cemetery had been a privilege but was now made more accessible. Stated thus the implication is that the elite had

**Figure 9.14**  Amphora from Athens with funeral scenes (Athens, National Archaeological Museum)

imposed restrictions, and an element of competition is certainly evident in the ninth century. Yet the inclusion of more children in eighth-century cemeteries is an indication of a more fundamental change which promoted family ties over the achievements of the individual, a concept with a greater appeal across the social spectrum. Consequently the dead were generally given a higher profile. The elite could still mark themselves out, but death was more of a leveler.

## The Archaic Period

The "citizen cemetery" with modest tombs and grave goods is a feature of many Greek cities in the seventh century, such as Argos and Corinth. However Athens rejected this new civic ideology in favor of more exclusive practices. After a short interlude in which inhumation had predominated, cremation was once again in favor but with a difference. The dead were now cremated on a pyre in the grave. Primary cremation was a much simpler process in that the ashes did not have to be transferred from the pyre. However, the grave did need to be made much larger with adequate ventilation so that the fuel would combust. Once the pyre had burned down, the grave was filled with earth and marked by a circular mound. This change seems to have been an attempt by Athenian aristocrats to reassert their ancestral privileges in a way that harked back to an earlier era yet also set new standards. What is known of Athens in the seventh century suggests that this was a period of political instability, and the dead were evidently drawn into this ideological battle.

In sixth-century Athens there was a greater emphasis on the visual impact of graves. Weapons and jewelry were rarely buried with the dead but pottery was still provided, sometimes sealed in a pit or ditch with burnt animal bones. The earth mounds which covered graves grew in size. One in the Kerameikos was over 30 meters in diameter and 6 meters high. Stone grave markers now appear. Some consist of a narrow slab or stele set in a rectangular base and crowned by a sphinx, the guardian of the dead. Often there is a figure in profile on the stele, usually male, typically an athlete or a warrior. It is not a portrait as such but was presumably intended to represent the deceased whose name was inscribed on the base. Life-size marble statues were also used as grave markers (figure 9.15). They depict young men and women, kouroi and korai. The inscription on the base of a kouros from Anavysos in Attica reads: "Stand and mourn at the marker of dead Kroisos whom one day wild Ares slew as he fought in the front rank." A kore from Merenda is identified as: "The marker of Phrasikleia. I shall ever be called maiden, a title which the gods allotted me instead of marriage." So this kouros and kore stood for Kroisos and Phrasikleia, as a poignant reminder that they had died before their time.

These sculpted grave markers were obviously expensive and could only have been afforded by wealthy aristocrats who evidently used funerals as an opportunity for a show of strength. Consequently legislation was passed which imposed restrictions. Cicero (*De Legibus* 2.26.64) records: "On account of the size of the tombs which we see in the Kerameikos, it was decreed that no-one should make a tomb which required the labour of more than ten men over three days, and that no tomb should be decorated with plaster or have the so-called herms [presumably kouros and kore statues] set on it." It is not clear when this law was introduced but there was certainly a change in the late sixth century when grave monuments became much simpler. This coincided with an increase in the number of inhumations and child graves, which suggests that the democratic reforms of Kleisthenes did alter practices.

## The Classical Period

Texts supplement what we can deduce from archaeology about the way that Classical funerals were conducted. When a person died the women of the family bathed and anointed the body with perfumed oil. It was then wrapped in a white shroud

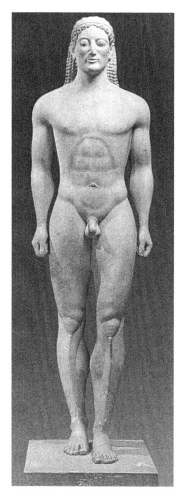

**Figure 9.15**    Grave marker of Kroisos (Athens, National Archaeological Museum)

and laid on a bier. A pillow was placed under the head which was often crowned with a wreath. The prothesis was held on the day after death. Friends and family came to pay their respects and sing dirges in which they lamented their loss. On the third day the corpse was taken to the cemetery on a hearse or by pall-bearers. Most adults were buried outside the city boundaries. Tombs often lined the main roads so that they would be seen and the epitaph may ask passers-by to remember the person who had died. In Athens the procession to the graveside, the ekphora, apparently took place before sunrise. This seems to have been a legal requirement and was intended to limit the attention that the cortège would attract.

In most Greek cities inhumation was more common than cremation in the Classical period. This is especially true for children who were often buried in jars. Adult inhumation graves were usually pits or cists. Large roof tiles were used for the floor and sides of some graves. Primary and secondary cremation continue as

(a)                                          (b)

**Figure 9.16a & b**   White-ground lekythos (Athens, National Archaeological Museum

well; there was no conformity. Once the corpse, or the urn that contained the ashes in the case of a cremation, had been lowered into the grave, libations were poured. An Athenian law prohibited the sacrifice of an ox at the graveside. This could never have been a regular occurrence but fits in with the trend for greater restraint which is reflected in the low value of most of the grave goods in this period. The mourners then returned to the house for a funeral feast, the perideipnon. A ceremony known as the enata was held nine days after death and this was followed by the triakostia after 30 days, which may have ended the prescribed period of mourning. The members of the family had still not completely fulfilled their obligations however, because annual commemorative rites formed part of the festival of the Genesia in Athens. This was one of the occasions when family and friends would visit the tomb, a scene which is often depicted on Athenian white-ground lekythoi in the fifth century (figure 9.16a & b). The lekythoi, which contained perfumed oil, were a favorite gift, as well as flowers, and ribbons were tied around the gravestone. Failure

**Figure 9.17**   Classical grave stele (Athens, National Archaeological Museum)

to perform the appropriate rituals each year could lead to an heir being disinherited, and it is clear that the dead were thought to be present when their tomb was visited. On another white-ground lekythos two youths stand on either side of a grave stele, apparently unaware of the seated youth who is presumably their dead friend, there in spirit. For the Greeks death was a gradual and protracted process of withdrawal from this world.

Unlike most Greek cities the Athenians did not bury their war dead on the battlefield but brought the remains home. After a public funeral they were buried together in a state grave on which the names of those who had died were inscribed. Someone then spoke on their behalf, and the historian Thucydides (2.35–46) gives us his version of the speech made by Perikles in the winter of 431/0 BC after the first year of the Peloponnesian War. Perikles takes the opportunity to set out his vision of Athens as a community of equals which the collective commemoration of these military heroes exemplified. But the democratization of the dead was being challenged by the end of the fifth century when elite families started to build peribolos tombs. The impressive facades of these tombs were often constructed of ashlar masonry, and grave markers appear once again, positioned so that they would be visible from the street. On the stelai the deceased is shown, often with relatives in attendance (figure 9.17). There is now much more of an emphasis on the family group rather than the individual. A handshake may be exchanged, a rather ambiguous gesture, presumably of farewell but which nevertheless promises a future reunion. Some fourth-century grave stelai were enormous and eventually they were banned in 317/16 BC by Demetrios of Phaleron, whom the Macedonians had installed as governor of Athens. In the Hellenistic period small marble or limestone columns were the most common type of grave marker in Athens. The grave goods were also quite simple, often slender oil flasks known as unguentaria.

A trend for greater extravagance can be seen elsewhere in the fourth century, most spectacularly in Macedonia and Caria. Restraint had never been an obvious Macedonian characteristic. In late sixth- and fifth-century graves at Sindos near Thessaloniki, the dead were buried with gold masks, exquisite jewelry, helmets, swords and spears, bronze and silver vessels, and model furniture made of iron and bronze. A fourth-century tomb at Derveni contained a magnificent gilded bronze krater decorated with a Dionysiac revel. There had been a tradition of burial under tumuli at Vergina since the Early Iron Age. The fourth century saw the construction of the aptly named Great Tumulus which was over 12 meters high and 110 meters in diameter. When this was excavated in 1976–79 three tombs were found. The earliest is a rectangular chamber tomb, roofed with stone slabs, which measures 3.50 by 2.09 meters inside. This had been robbed but the walls were painted and depict the abduction of Persephone by Hades, the god of the underworld. The second tomb had a barrel-vaulted roof which would have provided better support for the massive weight of the tumulus (figure 9.18). The entrance of the tomb is flanked by Doric half-columns, above which there is a triglyph frieze and a painted panel with a superb hunt scene. The marble door leads into an antechamber, 4.46 meters wide and 3.36 meters deep. Through another marble door is the main chamber which measures 4.46 by 4.46 meters. The main chamber had evidently been built first and the antechamber was added later. Both were covered with a thick layer of plaster. Unexpectedly, the tomb was found intact. In a marble sarcophagus at the back of the main chamber there was a solid gold box which contained the cremated remains of a middle-aged man, wrapped in a purple cloth, and a gold wreath of oak leaves and acorns. He had been buried with a gilded silver diadem, a helmet, an iron corslet trimmed with gold, a gold and ivory ceremonial shield, three pairs of greaves, two swords, and six spears. A couch decorated with ivory figures had evidently been placed in front of the sarcophagus and a wooden table on which there was equipment for a banquet: silver cups, jugs, flasks, a krater, and a strainer. An iron tripod and various bronze vessels were provided so that the dead man could have hot water when he bathed.

On one side of the antechamber there was another marble sarcophagus, inside which was a similar but smaller gold box with the cremated remains of a woman, wrapped in purple and gold cloth, and an exquisite gold diadem. The finds in the antechamber included a gold wreath, a pair of gilded greaves, a gold bow and arrow case, two spears, a pectoral, and ten alabastra for perfumed oil. It has been suggested that some of the weapons may have belonged to the man in the main chamber. That he was a Macedonian ruler seems certain, given the size of the tomb, the superb

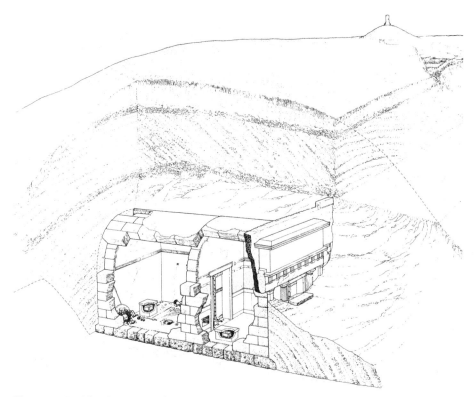

**Figure 9.18**   The Great Tumulus at Vergina

quality of the grave goods, and the presence of the diadem. He could be Philip II, the father of Alexander the Great, who was assassinated in 336 BC. As Alexander was buried in Egypt, the other possibility is Philip III Arrhidaios who died in 317 BC. If the dead man is Philip II, the woman in the antechamber may be Cleopatra, his last wife. Alternatively, this could be Eurydike, the wife of Philip III.

The third tomb in the tumulus also had a painted facade and consisted of a barrel-vaulted chamber and antechamber but was not quite as large. A silver jug on a rectangular stand in the main chamber contained the cremated remains of a youth. A gold wreath had been placed around the neck of the jug. More silver vessels lay on the floor of the chamber: cups, bowls, and dishes for food and drink. There were weapons as well. The identity of the youth is uncertain but he was presumably a member of the royal family, possibly Alexander IV, the posthumous son of Alexander the Great by his Iranian wife Roxane, who was murdered in 311 or 310 BC.

These royal tombs confirm that Vergina was Aigai where Macedonian kings were traditionally buried, even after Pella became the capital around 400 BC. The tombs also started a trend. In Macedonia and elsewhere in Greece many more barrel-vaulted tombs were constructed in the Hellenistic period. They often have decorated facades which can be extremely elaborate, as in the case of the Tomb of the Judgement at Lefkadia, but would not have been visible once the tomb was buried under a

**Figure 9.19**    Reconstruction of the Mausoleum at Halikarnassos

tumulus. Some of the tombs were painted inside as well and have marble furniture. Unfortunately most have been robbed but there is an emphasis on the military prowess of the men and on the provision of equipment for banquets, which is reminiscent of the Vergina tombs and also the graves at Sindos much earlier.

Macedonian tombs were certainly impressive but for sheer size they do not match the colossal Mausoleum at Halikarnassos (modern Bodrum in Turkey). Mausolos, who died in 353 BC, ruled Caria on behalf of the king of Persia. Work on the tomb must have started before his death and it was completed by his wife Artemisia who was also his sister. There is a detailed description of the tomb by Pliny (*Natural History* 36. 30–1), which is fortunate because it was completely demolished by the Knights of St John when they built the castle of St Peter at Bodrum. Much of the sculpture was broken up and made into lime. All that remains in situ is the platform in which the tomb chamber was located. This was robbed in 1522 but Mausolos had apparently been wrapped in gold cloth and buried in a marble sarcophagus. A sacrificial deposit was found at the foot of the staircase which led down to the chamber. On the platform was a high podium which measured 38 by 32 meters (figure 9.19). On top of this were 36 Ionic columns, which supported a stepped pyramid, crowned by a four-horse chariot. The total height of the tomb was around

42 meters. Pliny records that four of the most famous Greek sculptors worked on the Mausoleum: Skopas, Bryaxis, Timotheos, and Leochares (some sources name Praxiteles instead of Timotheos). They presumably supervised teams of craftsmen since there was an extraordinary amount of sculpture. Battles, animal hunts, lions, and portrait figures decorated the podium, the colonnade, and the pyramid. An earlier tomb, the Nereid Monument from Xanthos in Lycia, which is dated 390–380 BC and has been reconstructed in the British Museum, is equally flamboyant. The Mausoleum subsequently influenced the design of many Hellenistic monumental tombs, such as the Lion Tomb at Knidos and the Belevi Mausoleum near Ephesos. The Carians and the Lycians were not Greeks but they were familiar with Greek architecture and this provided a format they adapted to create tombs which were heroic in style and scale. The result was a cultural hybrid, unquestionably Near Eastern in spirit but with a Greek veneer.


## Conclusions

Is there more of a preoccupation with death when a society is under stress? The expansion of settlement in the Early Bronze Age must have caused conflicts over land ownership, particularly in the islands where resources were more limited. Cemeteries may have been viewed as a symbol of ancestral property rights. At first differences in wealth and status were not made explicit but the appearance of high-quality grave goods suggests competition for power. These divisions can be seen in the cemetery at Mochlos and intensify on Crete immediately before the first palaces were constructed. We would then expect even grander tombs, and the Chrysolakkos at Mallia is undoubtedly impressive. However, in the Protopalatial period the dead were still buried collectively. Possibly there was a belief that the community should take precedence over the individual. The political instability in Greece at the start of the Late Bronze Age provoked a different response. Funerals were an occasion when status was emphasized and rights of succession were asserted. Once power was consolidated, grave goods were less ostentatious, though a tholos tomb like the Treasury of Atreus at Mycenae scarcely epitomizes restraint. The use of tombs for successive generations of the same family must have engendered a sense of security which was shattered by the events at the end of LH IIIB. This precipitated a loss of confidence, and practices became much more diverse as communities re-established their identity. In due course personal achievement was given greater prominence once again. It is not clear whether the elite in Athens imposed restrictions on the way that funerals were conducted but the situation changed in the eighth century when more children were buried alongside adults, presumably in groups of family graves. If this reflected a new sense of civic solidarity, the aristocratic extravagance of the seventh and sixth centuries is a symptom of the political crisis that Athens experienced then. Democracy did curb this competitive instinct for a time but by the end of the fifth century the dead were once again commemorated in style, if not quite on the scale that Mausolos envisaged.

We can only speculate whether beliefs about death were also fluid. However, the funeral rites did remain remarkably consistent. Inhumation was the standard practice until the end of the Bronze Age. The position of the skeleton, whether contracted or extended, may have had some significance initially, though less so by the Late Bronze Age. Many skeletons had been deliberately disturbed. As the dead were often buried collectively, the explanation could be the need to make more room. The remains of previous inhumations were therefore periodically moved aside or placed in an ossuary. Yet we find tombs with no skeletons in situ and it seems that a second funeral formed part of the sequence of ceremonies, perhaps when the dead person was believed to have completed his or her journey and joined the ancestors. It is a rite which was established in the Neolithic period and was widely practiced until the Early Iron Age. The provision of grave goods is a constant feature of funerals. As we have already seen, they often reflect the social persona of the deceased and there may be an emphasis on status. They also make provision for hunger and thirst. Oil symbolizes purification and figurines offered protection.

Does the introduction of cremation in the Early Iron Age represent a break with earlier traditions? It was not a completely new practice but there had been few cremations previously. Beliefs had perhaps changed, yet the fact that many communities did not use cremation exclusively suggests that the choice of rite depended on social considerations as well. Because of the preference for individual burial, graves were not reopened as often and the second funeral was curtailed. Perhaps this altered perceptions about a liminal phase between life and death. Nevertheless, we can connect the rituals depicted on the larnakes from Tanagra with the prothesis scenes on Early Iron Age pottery. The procession to the graveside must have been conducted in a similar way. The funeral feast and the commemorative ceremonies no doubt perpetuated earlier practices as well. There was an essential continuity.

## Bibliographical notes

On the archaeology of death and burial generally see Parker Pearson 1999. There is a discussion of Neolithic burials in Cavanagh and Mee 1998, which also covers the whole of the Bronze Age in mainland Greece, and in Perlès 2001. For the Early Bronze Age in the Cyclades see Doumas 1977, Barber 1987, and Broodbank 2000. Watrous 2001 provides a period-by-period account of Early Minoan and Protopalatial Crete. Branigan 1993 is a detailed study of the tholos tombs. Soles 1992 and Vavouranakis 2007 focus on the tombs in the east of Crete. For Archanes see Sakellarakis and Sakellaraki 1997. Cavanagh and Lagia 2010 analyze the burials from Kouphovouno. For the shaft graves and the early Mycenaean period see Dickinson 1977 and Rutter 2001. Voutsaki 1995 assesses the evidence for social and political change. Preston 2004 discusses the warrior graves at Knossos. Gallou 2005 reconstructs Mycenaean funeral practices. Cavanagh and Mee 1995 describe the larnakes from Tanagra. The Late Bronze–Early Iron Age transition is reviewed in Dickinson 2006. Snodgrass 1971 and Lemos 2002 discuss the eleventh and tenth centuries;

Coldstream 1977 covers the ninth and eighth centuries. For Knossos see Coldstream and Catling 1996. Morris 1987 and 2000 examines the developments in eighth- and seventh-century Athens. Kurtz and Boardman 1971 provide an overview of the Archaic and Classical periods. Classical funeral practices are described by Garland 1985. Morris 1992 and Houby-Nielsen 1995 focus on sixth- and fifth-century Athens. For Vergina see Andronikos 1993 and Gill 2008 on the identity of those who were buried in the tombs there. Fedak 1990 discusses the architecture of Hellenistic monumental tombs, Miller 1993 is a detailed account of Macedonian tombs, and Jeppesen 1997 pieces together the Mausoleum at Halikarnassos.

# CHAPTER 10

# Religion

## Introduction

Many of the people whose beliefs will be examined in this chapter would have found our concept of religion difficult to grasp. They did not consciously make a distinction between activities which we would label as sacred or secular. The reconstruction of their beliefs will therefore be a major challenge, especially on the basis of the archaeological evidence and even when there are texts available. The identification of a particular location as a shrine or sanctuary is not always certain. Even if cult activity is indicated, we cannot necessarily determine how rituals were performed, what they signified or who was worshiped. Nevertheless, some sense of the role of religion in society may become apparent: the extent of community involvement, the level of investment by elites or the state, whether practices varied or were consistent.

## Neolithic and Early Bronze Age Figurines

Evidence of cult activity in the Neolithic period is decidedly limited. The most plausible shrine is at Nea Nikomedeia in southern Macedonia. The houses in this Early Neolithic settlement were grouped around a much larger structure in which there were high-quality greenstone axes, hundreds of unused flint blades, clay roundels, and five terracotta figurines. The theory that this was a shrine is mainly based on the presence of the figurines, which could have featured in communal ceremonies. However, it is uncertain whether they were actually worshiped.

*Greek Archaeology: A Thematic Approach*   By Christopher Mee
© 2011 Christopher Mee

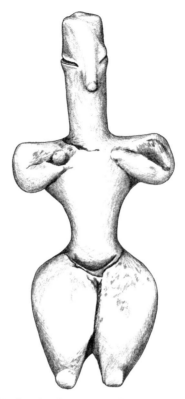

**Figure 10.1**   Early Neolithic figurine from Nea Nikomedeia

Figurines were common in Neolithic Greece, particularly in Thessaly and Macedonia. Most were made of terracotta and some of stone, shell, or bone. Wood may also have been used but is not as resilient. The majority of the figurines were anthropomorphic and most were female, though gender is not always indicated and may sometimes have intentionally been left indeterminate. The earliest figurines were quite schematic and when they do become more naturalistic there is an emphasis on certain parts of the body, especially the hips and thighs (figure 10.1). Facial features tend to be rather abstract, with slit eyes and a pinched-out nose. They stand, sit, crouch, or squat, often with their arms raised or folded over their chests, though a range of different poses and gestures can be seen.

Where the figurines were found potentially tells us about their function but it is clear that many had been discarded after they were used. Most come from domestic contexts in and around houses. Some were near hearths and ovens or in storage areas. Very few were buried with the dead, so there is no obvious connection with beliefs about an afterlife. The figurines have been interpreted as deities and in particular as images of a mother goddess. Alternatively they are believed to be fertility symbols or to represent ancestors. Another suggestion is that they were simply toys. What the figurines signified no doubt varied and therefore their use, whether in

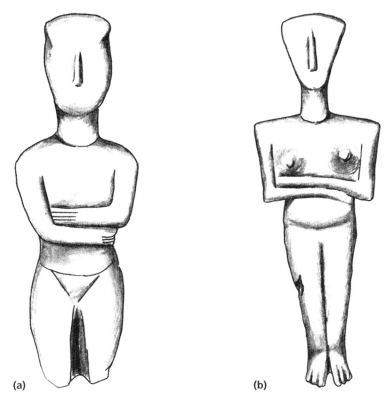

(a)  (b)

**Figure 10.2a & b**  Early Cycladic figurines (National Museums Liverpool, World Museum)

ceremonies, magic, instruction, or play. It has been pointed out that figurines were much more common in the north than the south of Greece. Possibly the higher population density in Thessaly and Macedonia increased the need for collective rituals which reinforced social solidarity.

In the Early Bronze Age there was some continuity in the way that figurines were used, especially in northern Greece. However, in the Cyclades a new set of practices evolved. Most of the figurines were made of marble and come from cemeteries. These developments can be traced back because marble figurines have been found in the Late Neolithic settlement at Saliagos and terracotta figurines in the cemetery, though not actually in the graves, at Final Neolithic Kephala. Many of the EC I figurines were highly stylized with long necks, short arms, and square hips. Later in the period more naturalistic figurines appear. Characteristic of EC II is the folded-arm type (figure 10.2a & b). The head is tilted back slightly and given a prominent nose. Breasts are sometimes indicated and the arms are folded over the body, usually the left above the right. The pubic triangle is often incised, the knees are flexed, and the feet point down. The figurines could not stand unless they were supported in some way. They range in size from 10 to 150 cm and average around 30 cm. Traces of paint are preserved on a number of the figurines and this is how anatomical details such as the eyes and hair, body decoration, and jewelry were depicted. Those folded-arm figurines which have any sexual features are almost always female. There were also some male figurines, in particular musicians and warriors.

An extraordinarily high proportion of Cycladic figurines have been excavated illicitly. Most of those which do have a proper context were found in cemeteries. As some had been broken and repaired, they were evidently in use before they were buried. Only around 10 percent of graves contained figurines and it is clear that they symbolized high social status. Given their value, it is remarkable that so many figurines come from Dhaskalio Kavos on the small island of Keros. Unfortunately the site has been ransacked by looters but hundreds of broken figurines and marble vessels were left there. Excavation has now shown that this "special deposit" is not a badly disturbed cemetery. The figurines and vessels were deposited after they had been deliberately broken, as part of a ritual at which people from many of the islands were present. Like Delos later, Dhaskalio Kavos may have been a pan-Cycladic sanctuary.

Inevitably there is no consensus about the interpretation of the figurines. One suggestion is that the larger examples were cult images and the smaller ones represented the devotees who took part in rituals. It is surely significant that so many were buried with the dead. Scratches were painted on the faces of some of the figurines, presumably to denote their role as mourners at the funeral. Perhaps the figurines also embodied beliefs about ancestry and descent. They are occasionally shown as pregnant, though the slim proportions do not emphasize fertility so much as sexuality. Their function may well have depended on the particular context.

Cycladic-style figurines have also been found in tombs on Crete, and this raises the possibility of shared practices or beliefs. It seems that cemeteries became a focus for ritual activities which may have been connected with ancestral property rights. Perhaps it was also thought that the dead could intercede on behalf of the community with the powers which controlled the natural world. We certainly get a sense of collective involvement in these rituals and in this respect they set a precedent for the sanctuaries in the Cretan countryside.

## Cretan Rural Sanctuaries

As the name suggests, peak sanctuaries were on or near the summit of mountains. The presence of votive figurines confirms the sanctity of these sites. Around 25 have been identified, mainly in the center and east of Crete. The peak sanctuary on Jouktas has EM II finds and may be the earliest. By MM I–II there was cult activity at all of the sites but many went out of use in MM III and only six or eight still functioned in LM I. These sanctuaries were not necessarily located on the highest peaks. The main consideration was that they could be seen from and overlooked the settlement with which they were associated, while many were also intervisible.

**Figure 10.3**   Peak sanctuary on a rhyton from the palace at Zakro

Although the elevation of some of the sanctuaries is over 1,000 meters, they were not inaccessible. The climb up from the settlement would typically have taken an hour or so. Often they were near upland pastures and it may have been felt that the exploitation of this liminal zone required divine sanction.

No structures have been found at most of the sites, which were therefore defined by natural features of the bedrock. It is the sanctuaries which were still in use in MM III–LM I that have architecture, particularly Jouktas where a row of five rooms faces an altar and a chasm 10 meters deep. On a stone rhyton from the palace of Zakro a sanctuary is depicted set in a rocky landscape (figure 10.3). The wild goats and the tree blown over by the wind imply that this is high up. In front of the sanctuary is a wall crowned by horns of consecration which encloses a court with an altar. The shrine is at the back of the court up a flight of steps.

The terracotta figurines from peak sanctuaries often represent men or women whose gestures suggest that they must be worshipers (figure 8.3). There are also votive limbs, sometimes deformed, which were presumably dedicated in the hope of a cure. The number of animal figurines could reflect concerns about the safety and welfare of livestock, though some may be token sacrifices. Pottery is common and shows that food and drink were consumed. High-quality dedications include bronze figurines and weapons, gold jewelry, stone vessels, and libation tables, some of which have Linear A inscriptions.

At Atsipades, one of the few peak sanctuaries which have been excavated, around 5,000 figurines were found. Many had been broken, perhaps deliberately, and left in clefts in the rock. It seems that large numbers of people gathered on the lower terrace and feasted, since there were sherds from cups, dishes, and jars here. The main focus of the cult was on the upper terrace where various ritual vessels were concentrated. Ash layers have been noted at several peak sanctuaries. Food may have been cooked on these fires, which would explain the presence of animal bones at Jouktas and some other sites. Figurines were apparently thrown into the flames as well. No doubt individuals sometimes visited peak sanctuaries but the main ceremonies were communal events. We do not know how often they took place or in whose honor because none of the figurines can be identified as the deity or deities worshiped in the sanctuaries.

Crete has hundreds of caves formed by erosion of the limestone mountains. In the Neolithic period the dead were often buried in caves or rock shelters. This practice continued in the Early Minoan period, especially in the center and east of the island. There may have been cult activity as well but this is not definitely indicated until MM I at Amnisos, Kamares, Psychro, and the Idaean cave. Sacred caves were fewer in number than peak sanctuaries, though more have a LM III phase. Although some of the caves were easily accessible, others were remote and would have taken hours to reach. The Kamares cave is visible from Phaistos but over 1,500 meters up and the Idaean cave is at a similar elevation, above the snowline in winter.

The depth of the caves obviously varies but many have chambers with no natural light. The darkness combined with the cool atmosphere and resonant acoustics would have heightened the sensory experience for those involved in the ceremonies and could have contributed to an altered state of consciousness. The consumption of wine was evidently part of the ritual in some of the caves, and perhaps other psychoactive substances. Votives had often been placed around stalagmites or in fissures in the rock. There are not as many terracotta figurines in cave sanctuaries and they do not include any limbs. Bronze figurines are more common and also weapons, particularly at Arkalochori and Psychro. In some caves the cult centered on particular stalagmites which may have been visualized as aniconic images of the tutelary deity. This does not tell us much about the identity of the deity, though we do have a clue in the case of the cave at Amnisos, which was the Classical sanctuary of Eileithyia, a goddess of childbirth, whose name occurs as Eleuthia in a Linear B text from Knossos.

There were also sacred enclosures in the countryside. The sanctuary at Kato Syme was by a spring, 1,130 meters up on the southern slopes of Mount Dikte. The cult had started by MM II and continued until the Roman period when Hermes and Aphrodite were worshiped here, though they need not have been the original deities. In the Neopalatial period a massive enclosure wall was constructed around an open-air podium. Fires had been lit in the enclosure and animals—sheep, goats, cattle, and agrimia—were sacrificed here. The heads of some of these animals had evidently been placed in the ashes of the fires. Miniature vessels, goblets, chalices, and

**Figure 10.4**  Isopata gold ring (Herakleion Museum)

conical cups were used in the cult. The finds from the sanctuary also include hundreds of stone libation tables, some with Linear A inscriptions, terracotta bull figurines, and bronze votives. As there is no settlement nearby, it has been suggested that Kato Syme was a regional or possibly an island-wide cult center.

Anemospilia is below the peak sanctuary on Jouktas and not far from Archanes. The shrine here was built in MM IIB and destroyed, apparently by an earthquake, in MM IIIA. It consists of three rooms which open off a corridor. At the back of the east room was an altar. The central room was full of pottery and two terracotta feet were also found here. It is thought that they were attached to the wooden body of a statue. A skeleton lay in the doorway of the central room and there were three more skeletons in the west room. They may all have been victims of the earthquake but a more dramatic theory proposes that one of the three individuals, a male aged about 18, had been sacrificed. His body was on a low platform and a bronze spearhead near his legs would be the weapon which was used to kill him.

Cult scenes set in the countryside are shown on a number of Minoan gold rings and sealstones. On a ring from Isopata four women dance in a meadow (figure 10.4). A much smaller figure at the top must be a goddess whose presence has been invoked by the performance. Two of the dancers raise their arms in homage as she descends from the sky. A tree set in a small enclosure often appears in these scenes and is touched or violently shaken by the frenzied worshipers (figure 10.5).

**Figure 10.5**    Gold ring from Mycenae (Athens, National Archaeological Museum)

## Religion in the Cretan Palaces and Towns

It is suspected that there was official involvement in rural cult activity in the Neopalatial period. This would explain the structures and the higher quality of the votives in some of the sanctuaries. Were the palaces also responsible for the fact that so many peak sanctuaries went out of use? Can we detect a move to centralize religion?

The first palaces undoubtedly had a ceremonial role, since the central and west courts were an integral feature of their design and provided open spaces where large numbers of people could gather. The west court at Phaistos was crossed diagonally by a raised path. This ran up to terraced steps on which spectators must have stood. Items of cult equipment were found in some of the rooms on the east side of the court and there may have been a shrine located here. The west court at Knossos has similar raised paths which possibly marked out processional routes (figure 3.3). In the Neopalatial period a theatral area with steps on two sides was built at the point where several of these paths meet at the north end of the court. The religious ceremony depicted on a miniature fresco from Knossos evidently took place in the west court because the raised paths are shown. Women dance sedately in front of a crowd of spectators who look toward a shrine or altar.

The west court was a public space, accessible from the palace and the town. The central court was more secluded and would therefore have been reserved for ceremonies which required some privacy. Evans believed there was a shrine on the west side of the central court at Knossos. Sealed in two cists in a room behind this were

(a)                                    (b)

**Figure 10.6a & b**   Faience figurines from the Temple Repositories at Knossos (Herakleion Museum)

objects which may have come from the shrine. It seems that they were put here after a fire in MM III or LM IA. Pieces of figurines made of faience were found, two of which have been restored (figure 10.6a & b). One of the women has snakes around her waist, arms, and head. The other, who is slightly smaller, brandishes her snakes. The larger woman has been identified as a goddess and the smaller as a priestess. However, they are both dressed in the same way, have elaborate headdresses, and handle snakes which look venomous. A more likely interpretation is that both women represent goddesses or priestesses, perhaps in the guise of goddesses. The snakes could symbolize regeneration, the underworld, the countryside, or even the household. As ever there is some uncertainty, but we can be confident that these figurines were used in religious rituals.

Double axes were incised on the pillars in two of the other rooms in this block. As the double ax is one of the most common Minoan cult symbols, possibly linked with sacrifice, the pillars may have been venerated. It is conjectured that the basins set in the floor on either side of one of the pillars were for libations. West of the central court at Mallia is a room with two pillars. Double axes, stars, and tridents were incised on the pillars which are aligned with a structure in the court identified as an altar. The room just off the main hall in the Royal Villa at Knossos is one of the most impressive of these pillar crypts. However, there is no evidence that rituals were performed here and the question of a Minoan pillar cult remains unresolved.

Also on the west side of the central court at Knossos is the throne room block (figure 3.4). The main reason why it is believed that the ceremonies held here were religious is the lustral basin opposite the throne. These are quite a common feature in Cretan palaces and villas. A short flight of steps leads down into the room which is partially screened off by a balustrade. Evans described these rooms as lustral basins because he concluded that they were used for ritual purification. Initiation ceremonies would be another possibility but sometimes the location, for example in House Da at Mallia (figure 4.7), makes a purely religious or ritual function implausible. The alternative view, that lustral basins were bathrooms, seems more likely in this instance. The lustral basin in the west wing of the palace at Zakro is next to a small room with benches. As items of cult equipment were found here and in an adjacent room, this may have been a shrine. East of the central court is a sacred well in which votives had been deposited. At Mallia and Phaistos there were rooms with benches, and a case can again be made for some form of ritual activity.

Given the uncertainty about where and how the Cretans practiced their religion, what they believed is inevitably speculative. Some of the Linear B tablets from Knossos do list deities to whom dedications were made. Of course these texts date from the period when the Mycenaeans were in control of the palace and they presumably introduced the worship of Zeus, Poseidon, Ares, and Hermes, but there are also a number of deities whose names are not Greek and who may be Cretan. The iconographic evidence suggests that goddesses dominated the Minoan pantheon but just as many gods appear in the Linear B tablets. This was definitely a polytheistic and possibly quite adaptable religion.

Whatever the role of the palaces had been, their destruction must have had an impact on cult practices and beliefs. There is continuity and yet a different emphasis. Some of the rooms in the palace at Knossos were reused in LM III and one became the Shrine of the Double Axes (figure 10.7). Pottery was found on the floor by the entrance and on the low step around a tripod altar. At the back of the room was a bench and on this were horns of consecration, another common cult symbol which could represent a sacrificed bull, though this is not certain. Also on the bench were five terracotta figurines, one of which must be a goddess who is accompanied by worshipers or attendants. Similar goddess figurines, modeled in the same way and with upraised arms, have been found in bench sanctuaries elsewhere on Crete. One at Gazi has poppies in her crown, cut so that opium could be extracted. Narcotics would obviously have helped to induce visionary experiences. The goddess with upraised arms was still revered in LM IIIC, especially at east Cretan sites such as Karphi.

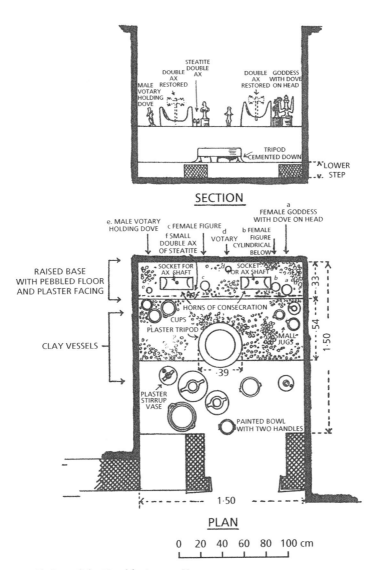

**Figure 10.7** Shrine of the Double Axes at Knossos

## Cretan Converts?

The Cretans who had settled on the island of Kythera founded a peak sanctuary at Ayios Georgios, which overlooks Kastri. The dedications include many bronze figurines, mainly of worshipers, as well as stone vessels, one of which has an inscription in Linear A. These are the type of high-quality votives found in the peak sanctuaries which continued in use in the Neopalatial period and emphasize the commercial importance of Kythera.

The situation at Akrotiri on Thera is rather different, since this was not a Cretan settlement. So it is significant that there was a lustral basin in Xeste 3, one of the finest houses (figure 4.11), particularly because the frescoes here and in the room directly above have religious themes. On the wall of the lustral basin are three women, one of whom has cut her foot. They face an altar or shrine topped by horns of consecration. In the fresco on the first floor, women gather saffron crocuses which they place at the feet of a seated female, flanked by a griffin and a monkey, who is evidently a goddess. Some of the women have their hair cut short and are clearly girls. If these scenes are connected, the most likely interpretation is that the rooms in Xeste 3 were used for initiation ceremonies.

There is an individuality in the ritual practices at Akrotiri, despite the Cretan influence, which is also reflected in the temple at Ayia Irini on Kea. This has been partially destroyed by the sea but had at least six rooms. Pieces of over 50 terracotta figures were found in the temple. The largest are life-size and represent women dressed in the Minoan fashion with their breasts exposed. Although the clay is rather coarse, they were once painted. They may have been arranged so that they formed a procession or danced in line, which would suggest that they were worshipers.

Cretan religious scenes and symbols also appear in Early Mycenaean Greece, for example on the gold ring from Mycenae discussed above (figure 10.5). It is possible that trees were shaken violently as part of ceremonies on the mainland. However, the attraction of this ring could well have been the intrinsic value of the metal, which was enhanced by the fine workmanship. We cannot be sure that the owner understood what this scene meant. The ring was a status symbol, not an article of faith. Evidence for cult activity in this period on the mainland is limited, though there are LH I–II sacrificial deposits and votives in the sanctuary of Apollo Maleatas at Epidauros. Cemeteries were more of a focus for ritual initially.

## Mycenaean Religion

A circular structure in the main court of the palace at Tiryns, directly opposite the entrance of the megaron, may well be an altar. The great hearth in the center of the megaron dominates the room and was obviously more than just a source of heat (figure 3.6). By the hearth at Pylos there was a tripod altar and several miniature vessels. Two circular depressions in the floor at the side of the throne were possibly for liquid libations. A banquet scene was painted on one of the walls and this can be linked with a sacrificial procession in the vestibule in which men and women flank an enormous bull (figure 10.8). The ruler must have presided over the ceremonies in the megaron and the feasts which were held in the palace. Some of the meat consumed on these occasions came from cattle and deer which had evidently been sacrificed. The carcasses were dismembered and then the bones were burned, presumably so that the gods could have their share.

A number of Linear B tablets mention festivals. One in honor of Poseidon was held at the sanctuary of *pa-ki-ja-ne*, literally the place of slaughter, which has not

**Figure 10.8**  Reconstruction of the fresco in the vestibule of the palace at Pylos

been identified but was in the vicinity of Pylos. Tablet Tn 316 also records shrines
of Zeus, Hera, and Hermes at *pa-ki-ja-ne*, as well as less familiar deities of whom
Potnia, the mistress, was the most important since she is mentioned first. The tablets
list the gifts which each of the deities received, a gold goblet and a woman in the
case of Potnia, a gold dish and a man for Zeus. Given the name of the sanctuary, it
is possible that these men and women were sacrificed or they may have served the
deity in some way. The tablets indicate the level of official involvement in these
festivals and also the extensive religious duties and powers of the ruler.

The cult center at Mycenae is on the south side of the citadel and was linked with
the palace by a processional way (figure 8.13). The four main shrines were built on
different levels because of the slope (figure 10.9). They were constructed in LH IIIB
and repaired after an earthquake. Then at the end of LH IIIB a fire destroyed the
cult center. In one of the rooms in Tsountas House is a horseshoe-shaped altar, with
an installation for libations on one side. A stone platform in the court in front of
the room may be another altar. The Megaron has a rectangular hearth and below
this is the Temple which opens off a court with a circular altar. There is a platform
in the center of the main room and benches at the back, in front of a triangular
alcove. A terracotta figurine and a tripod altar were in situ on one of the benches.
A flight of steps leads up to a small storeroom where more figurines were found.
This had been sealed, perhaps after the earthquake. The figurines include a number
of coiled snakes which could imply Cretan influence, though it is not clear what
they signified (figure 10.10c). Possibly they were the attendants or familiars of the
deity. At least 20 of the figurines, which range in size from 35 to 70 cm, are female
or of indeterminate sex (figure 10.10a). They are rather crudely modeled and were
certainly intended to look grotesque. This would suggest that they represented
deities but it has been pointed out that the pose of some of these figurines is one
of supplication, while others hold an ax or hammer, so they may be cult celebrants.
A smaller figurine seems a more likely deity, perhaps a goddess of fertility since she
cups her breasts.

A female figurine with upraised arms from the adjacent shrine complex, known
as the Room with the Fresco, is rather similar (figure 10.10b). Also found here was

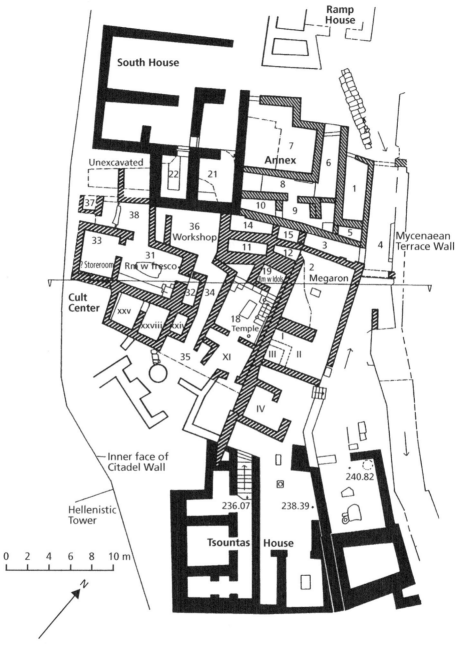

**Figure 10.9** Plan of the cult center at Mycenae

(a)

(b)

(c)

**Figure 10.10a–c**   Female and snake figurines from the cult center at Mycenae

a fine ivory head of a male which had evidently been attached to a body made
of some other material and possibly represents a god. There was a hearth in
the center of the main room and an altar in the far corner. The fresco was on the
wall behind the altar and depicts two females, one with a sword and one with a
spear, who are presumably goddesses. Between them are two shadowy figures. A
third woman lower down holds sheaves of corn and could be another goddess or

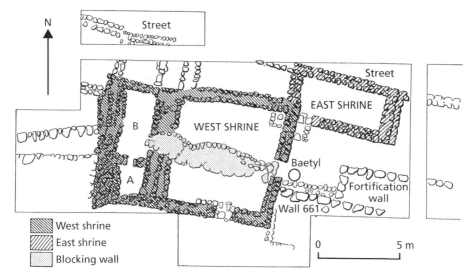

**Figure 10.11**    Plan of the sanctuary at Phylakopi

a priestess. After the earthquake the fresco was whitewashed and the shrine apparently went out of use.

The cult center is not particularly conspicuous and the shrines were modest in size. They were not built in the way we would expect at a site where the architecture is generally so impressive. Despite the link with the palace, a separation of political and religious authority could be indicated here. The shrine in the lower citadel at Tiryns is also set apart from the palace and this raises questions about official control of cult activity. The sanctuary at Ayios Konstantinos on Methana was well away from any major Mycenaean center and the figurines, which include helmeted riders on horseback, chariot groups, and oxen, emphasize how much variation there is.

We would expect different practices at Phylakopi on Melos, since this was a Cycladic town, even if there were close ties with mainland Greece. The sanctuary is on the south side of the site, some distance from the megaron which may have been the administrative center (figure 2.5). The West Shrine was constructed first in LH IIIA and consisted of a main room, approximately 6 meters square, with two entrances, one of which was subsequently blocked (figure 10.11). In front of the shrine was a paved court with a bench and a round stone baetyl. The East Shrine, a rectangular room 4.80 by 2.20 meters, was built in LH IIIB1. Then in LH IIIC both shrines were destroyed. Some renovation work was undertaken and parts of the sanctuary remained in use until later in LH IIIC.

The most important of the finds (figure 10.12a–c) is a terracotta female figurine 45 cm high, which had been stored in one of the rooms at the back of the West Shrine, and it seems likely that she is a goddess. Three male figurines had apparently fallen from a platform in the northwest corner of the main room. They could be votaries, though the largest, which is 35 cm high, may represent a god. The many

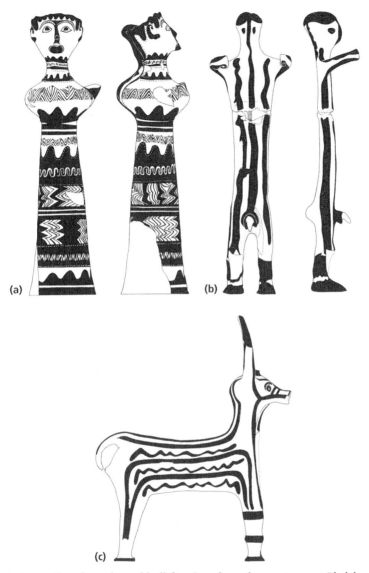

(a)

(b)

(c)

**Figure 10.12a–c**   Female, male, and bull figurines from the sanctuary at Phylakopi

animal figurines from the two shrines include a number of hollow terracotta bulls
Despite certain differences the sanctuary at Phylakopi does have much in common
with mainland shrines. However, Cretan influence seems minimal, given the absence
of horns of consecration and double ax symbols. Generally we see a clear division
between Minoan and Mycenaean ritual practices. The individuality of each sanctuary also suggests that each community had a quite distinctive set of religious beliefs.
Yet there were some shared forms of expression, notably the small female figurines
found in so many Mycenaean settlements, cemeteries, and shrines (figure 10.13).

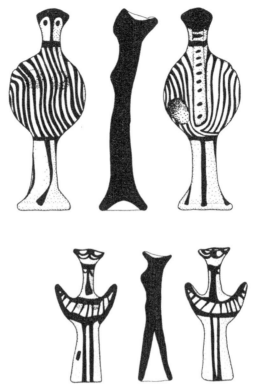

**Figure 10.13**   Phi and psi figurines (National Museums Liverpool, World Museum)

## Religion after the Palaces

After the destructions at the end of LH IIIB the cult center at Mycenae was not rebuilt, though a new shrine was constructed in the lower citadel at Tiryns. The Phylakopi sanctuary was repaired and also the Ayia Irini temple. At the Amyklaion in Laconia, where cult activity started in late LH IIIB or early LH IIIC, many female figurines were dedicated, as well as wheel-made bulls and smaller animals. A large female head may have come from a cult image. Kalapodi in Phocis is another shrine which was established early in LH IIIC, around an open altar on a terrace where food and drink were evidently consumed. Obviously the destruction of the palaces must have had an impact on Mycenaean religion. Nevertheless, there is continuity in LH IIIC and the impression is of a gradual transformation in the way that individuals and communities interacted with the gods.

Similarly on Crete, despite the upheavals which resulted in a move to more defensible sites in LM IIIC, many of the shrines were still bench sanctuaries with figurines of the goddess with upraised arms. At Karphi there were at least five of these sanctuaries. Kavousi-Vronda only has one shrine but more than 30 goddess figurines were found here. An element of competition between groups within these communities is suspected. It is also possible that the Kavousi shrine served a number of settlements. Certainly the sanctuary at Kato Symi is considered to be a regional cult center where people gathered for sacrificial feasts.

## Early Iron Age

At Kato Symi there is evidence of cult activity in the tenth century. The sanctuary may have become a center for initiation ceremonies which were later held in honor of Hermes and Aphrodite. The continuity here is not so obvious elsewhere on Crete because many of the upland settlements with bench sanctuaries were now abandoned. Some new shrines appear, notably Temple A at Kommos which was built in the ruins of the Minoan harbor town. A similar link with the past can be seen in the location of other Cretan sanctuaries. This development may have been politically motivated, perhaps as part of a process of territorial expansion.

In mainland Greece, even more than on Crete, the eleventh century was a period when settlement was disrupted. Inevitably this affected the level of activity at most sanctuaries and Mycenaean-style figurines finally disappeared. There was not a complete break because a number of the deities listed in the Linear B texts—Artemis, Dionysos, Hera, Hermes, Poseidon, and Zeus—were worshiped later and sacrifices were performed in the same way as at Pylos. Nevertheless, Kalapodi is one of the few sanctuaries where continuity can be demonstrated. At the Amyklaion the gap may have been quite brief but the dedications do change when the cult was reinstated.

Olympia would become one of the major Greek sanctuaries. There was a Mycenaean settlement, though no definite evidence of any ritual activity until the later eleventh century associated with a layer of ash. Crudely made animal figurines and bronze dress pins were some of the earliest votives. The sanctuary at Isthmia was also founded around this time. Layers of burnt bone, ash, and pottery suggest that animals were sacrificed and this was followed by a communal meal. Accessibility may have been one of the main reasons why the sanctuary was located at Isthmia. People from across the region could meet here and no doubt the sacrifices and feasts provided their leaders with an opportunity to make an impression. The practice of religion at these early Greek sanctuaries clearly had a social dimension.

In the tenth and ninth centuries the number of sanctuaries and the quality of the votives steadily increases, especially at Olympia. The bronze tripod cauldrons (figure 6.22) and horse figurines, with their aristocratic connotations, indicate that certain sanctuaries had become a focus for high-status dedications. The appeal of Olympia was that the sanctuary drew worshipers from across the Peloponnese, so any display of wealth here would have the widest possible impact. However, sanctuaries were not the only ritual context exploited by elites because this was also a period when funerals were often an occasion for ostentatious expenditure, particularly in the case of the man and woman who were buried in the "Heroon" at Lefkandi. As there is no evidence of cult activity, this was not a hero shrine, though the dead were clearly venerated if not worshiped.

**Figure 10.14**   View across the Argive plain from the Heraion

## The Eighth Century

In the eighth century religion becomes much more visible and this is seen as a direct consequence of the political developments which created the Greek city state or polis. Religion provided a sense of identity and social cohesion for the citizens of a polis. Sanctuaries represented the community, and the increased scale of activity reflects this. The Acropolis is a classic example of a state sanctuary in the center of a city. From her prominent position on the citadel, Athena could watch over her devotees. Some sanctuaries were on the edge of a city, such as that of Artemis Orthia in Sparta, which is down by the River Eurotas, a naturally marginal location. Those sanctuaries identified as regional centers, such as Isthmia, were often sited away from the communities they served and this would have emphasized their political neutrality. Yet there were also sanctuaries which symbolized control of the country-side. The main sanctuary of Argos was the Heraion which is on the other side of the plain, 8 kilometers from the city (figure 10.14). It is possible that this had origi-nally been a regional sanctuary for the Argolid but was then taken over by Argos, perhaps in the late eighth century when a massive terrace wall was constructed in a style reminiscent of Mycenaean fortifications. A great procession crossed the plain for the festival of Hera, which ritually unified the city and the sanctuary. Once they reached the temple, the Argives had a fine view of their territory. The mountains behind also placed the sanctuary at the frontier between the cultivated landscape and a wilder world. The sanctuary of Hera on Samos was linked with the city by a

sacred way which ran across the plain. The site of the sanctuary is a marshy river
basin by the sea, which is certainly atmospheric if not especially conspicuous. There
was also a sacred way between Athens and Eleusis for the procession which set out
from the city to take part in the mysteries at the sanctuary of Demeter. As Eleusis
had once been independent, this procession reconfirmed the union with Athens.

A similar process of assimilation can be seen in Laconia, where the Spartans
adopted the Hyakinthia at Amyklai as one of their main state festivals. They also
founded sanctuaries in the countryside, and cult activity is definitely attested at two
of these sites in the eighth century, the Menelaion and Tsakona. The view from both
of these sanctuaries is impressive and they were located where they would be very
visible. In a sense they mark out Spartan territory but curiously there was no expansion in rural settlement at the time this sacred landscape was created.

The Menelaion was the sanctuary of Menelaos, the mythical ruler of Sparta, and
his errant wife Helen. One reason why this site was chosen was surely the Mycenaean
settlement here. The Homeric epics had inspired an interest in the past but this hero
shrine had a contemporary relevance. Although their claim on Menelaos must have
been rather tenuous, the Spartans saw themselves as his heirs, the rightful rulers of
Laconia. Votive deposits have also been found in Mycenaean tombs, mainly in the
Argolid, Messenia, and Attica. This may have been an act of propitiation, perhaps
because the tomb was opened accidentally. However, some tomb cults started in the
eighth century and continued until the Hellenistic period. In the tholos tomb at
Menidi in Attica, Geometric, Archaic, and Classical pottery and terracotta figurines
had been left in the fill of the dromos. Some of the tholos tombs at Mycenae were
also visited and their size must have made a deep impression. Yet chamber tombs
attracted just as much attention, particularly at Prosymna, which is linked with the
Argive Heraion, and at Volimidia in Messenia where there were animal sacrifices as
well as votives. We do not have any indication who was honored in this way. A
Classical sherd from Grave Circle A at Mycenae is simply inscribed "for the hero."
In some cases these tomb cults may have centered on a specific local hero or anony-
mous ancestors whose support could be enlisted in claims over land ownership.

Sacrifice was the principal act of worship in a Greek sanctuary. Although there
were bloodless sacrifices, the victim was usually an animal—a sheep, goat, pig, or
bull. The altar was where the sacrifice took place (figure 10.15). After the victim had
been killed, some of the meat and fat was burned for the gods. The rest of the meat
was cooked and generally eaten in the sanctuary. Because of the importance of
sacrifice, the altar was the focal point of the sanctuary. The sacred space, the temenos
of the god, would also be demarcated in some way. Many sanctuaries never had a
temple but over the course of the eighth century they do start to appear. The temple
was the house of the god or goddess, personified by his or her cult statue and therefore permanently present in the community. Most of the early cult statues were
apparently made of wood and have not survived. Descriptions stress how simple
they were, like a plank in the case of the statue of Hera on Samos.

Some of the early temples were equally rudimentary. The temple of Hera
at Perachora was approximately 8 meters in length and 3.50 meters wide with a

**Figure 10.15**    Reconstruction of the eighth-century altar in the sanctuary of Hera on Samos

semicircular apse. Terracotta models from the sanctuary may represent this temple (figure 10.16). If so, it evidently had a shallow porch with twin columns and the interior was lit by windows as well as the door. The walls must have been of mud-brick and the roof was presumably thatched. A similar apsidal structure under the Archaic temple of Apollo at Eretria could be an early eighth-century predecessor. There is a theory that this imitated the bay hut which was reputedly the first temple of Apollo at Delphi. Later in the eighth century the Eretrians provided Apollo with a much larger temple, 35 meters in length. The temple of Hera on Samos was more or less the same size but rectangular rather than apsidal (figure 10.17). The base of the cult statue was positioned so that the view of the goddess would not be obscured by the central row of columns which supported the roof. Doubts have been expressed about the existence of the columns around the outside of the temple.

An architectural sequence could be set out, whereby temples became progressively larger and more elaborate. Yet early in the tenth century the "Heroon" at Lefkandi had already anticipated many of the features which we see much later. It was apsidal, at least 47 meters in length, and even had a portico of wooden posts (figure 3.7a & b). As the "Heroon" was dismantled and covered by an enormous tumulus after 25 years or so, it could not have been copied directly, though similar structures may have remained visible. The first temple of Artemis at Ephesos was rectangular and had a peristyle of wooden columns. Consequently it looks like a seventh-century temple but is in fact dated around the middle of the eighth century. Clearly there were general trends and also independent initiatives.

The amount of pottery found in sanctuaries is a good indication of the increased level of activity in the eighth century. Much of this was used for the feasts which were such an integral part of religious festivals and would have been one of the few

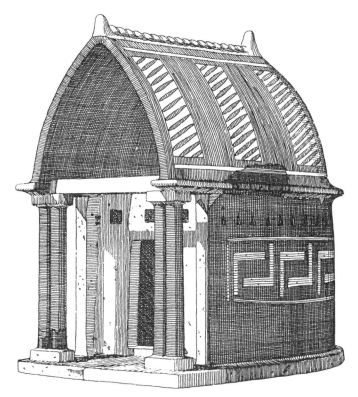

**Figure 10.16**  Temple model from Perachora

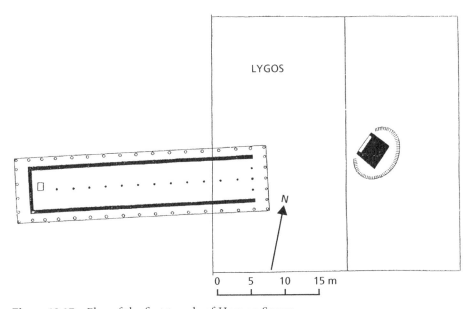

**Figure 10.17**  Plan of the first temple of Hera on Samos

occasions in the year when many of those who attended ate meat. Given the amount of wine that was consumed, pottery was no doubt broken accidentally and then discarded. However, there may have been a belief that it should be left within the sanctuary anyway as a commemoration of the ceremony. The pottery stressed the communal aspect of participation in a festival, whereas votives were more individualistic.

Dedication of votives became a common practice in the eighth century. At Olympia there were terracotta and bronze figurines of animals, some of which may have been sacrificial substitutes. Many of the figurines were evidently made at the sanctuary and sold to visitors. The bronze tripod cauldrons are particularly impressive, larger than before with decorated legs and high circular handles. Their size reflects an element of competition between aristocrats, which is appropriate because tripods were often awarded as prizes at the funeral games of heroes, notably for the chariot race which Achilles held in honor of his friend Patroklos (*Iliad* 23.264). The tripod cauldrons at Olympia may have been dedicated by victors or possibly competitors in the games. The Greeks later fixed on 776 BC as the date of the first Olympic games and they believed that extra events were added later in the century, when the sanctuary did attract a greater number of dedications.

More weapons and armor were dedicated at the end of the eighth century. Jewelry also makes up a higher proportion of the votives, especially in sanctuaries of Hera, Athena, and Artemis. Perhaps women now took a more prominent role in religion. Personal items such as weapons and jewelry had previously been buried with the dead and their appearance in sanctuaries does represent a change of practice. There were still rich graves but sanctuaries offered a much more conspicuous location for self-promotion, with the additional benefit that this could be presented as an act of piety on behalf of the community.

## The Archaic Period

Some sanctuaries attracted a more exotic range of dedications in the seventh century. Many imported items from Egypt and the Near East have been found in the Heraion on Samos. This is a reflection of the extensive trade contacts which the Samians had established. Merchants who had successfully completed a journey overseas no doubt believed that their goddess should be rewarded. Foreign visitors may also have felt that it was prudent or politic to follow suit. The fact that these votives were exotic would have increased their value, especially those which had an obvious religious significance. They certainly influenced the way that the Greeks visualized their gods. The sanctuary of Hera at Perachora also has a rich array of seventh-century votives. The presence of Near Eastern and Italian imports ties in with the commercial interests of Corinth, which controlled the sanctuary. Nevertheless it is curious that there should have been so much investment in such a marginal shrine. The Corinthians may have wanted to claim the Perachora peninsula as part of their territory and thereby secure the sea lanes on which they depended. However, the votives do seem quite personal and suggestive of more private concerns. Perhaps the relative seclusion of the sanctuary was exploited by groups who wished to promote their own sense of identity. Religion provided a mechanism for integration at different social levels.

There was an early seventh-century temple in the city of Corinth. In a significant departure from previous practice, the roof was covered with terracotta tiles rather than thatch. As these tiles were large and heavy, more substantial roof timbers would have been needed. The walls also had to be strengthened to support the weight. A combination of cut blocks of poros limestone and mudbrick was used, held together by a timber framework. Although we do not know the dimensions of the temple, which was completely dismantled in the sixth century, it would certainly have been impressive. Around the same time the Corinthians also built a temple in the sanctuary at Isthmia. The walls were at least partially constructed of stone, which was stuccoed and painted. The temple may have had a peristyle of wooden columns, seven at the ends and 18 on each side, though this has been questioned. The temple of Apollo at Thermon is dated around 630 BC. Behind the main room was a porch or opisthodomos, a feature of many later Greek temples (figure 10.18a & b). It is generally restored with a peristyle of five by 15 wooden columns, which supported a frieze of terracotta panels. Some of these were painted with scenes from myth in a style which is reminiscent of Corinthian pottery. Terracotta antefixes in the form of human heads covered the ends of the tiles and some of the exposed woodwork was protected by decorative revetments.

The developments in the design of mainland Greek temples were taken further early in the sixth century with the construction of the temple of Artemis at Corcyra, the wealthy Corinthian colony on Corfu (figure 10.19a & b). This was 21.94 by 47.50 meters and had a peristyle of eight by 17 columns. The interior was laid out with a porch, the main room had two rows of columns and behind this was either an opisthodomos or a shrine. The columns supported a plain architrave and above this a frieze of triglyphs and metopes. Sculpture filled the pediments at either end of the temple with the gorgon Medusa, a giant figure over 3 meters high, in the center. This was power architecture, and monumentality becomes the medium through which cities expressed their sovereignty. The temple of Artemis is also one of the earliest examples of the Doric order, which is defined on the basis of the type of column capital and frieze. It is possible that some of the seventh-century temples were Doric but, because wood rather than stone was used for the columns, this is not certain.

There has been considerable speculation about the origins of the Doric order. The column on the relief above the Lion Gate at Mycenae has a similar type of capital and could still be seen, so a link with the heroic past may have seemed appropriate. Some of the features of wooden temples were translated into stone, even though they were structurally unnecessary. Perhaps this reflects an element of conservatism, which would imply that the development of the Doric order was a gradual process. Alternatively, the experiments with the use of stone in the temples at Corinth and Isthmia could have led to the creation of a new architectural

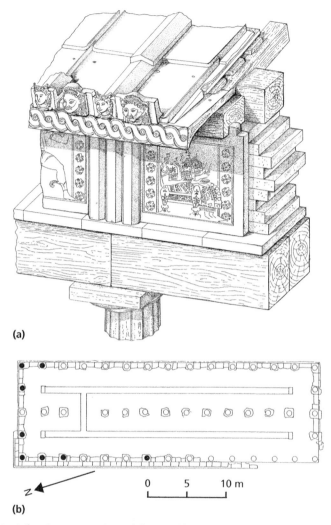

**(a)**

**(b)**

**Figure 10.18a & b**   Reconstruction of the entablature and plan of the temple of Apollo at Thermon

vocabulary which drew, rather eclectically, on earlier traditions. The conversion to stone did take time. The temple of Hera at Olympia was also built in the early sixth century and originally had wooden columns. These were gradually replaced but one still remained in the second century AD when Pausanias visited Olympia. However, the massive monolithic columns of the mid sixth-century temple of Apollo at Corinth show why stone was preferred (figure 10.20).

Monumentality was taken to another level on Samos and at Ephesos. Construction of a new temple of Hera on Samos was completed around 560 BC (figure 10.21). This measured 48.33 by 93.45 meters and had a double peristyle. There

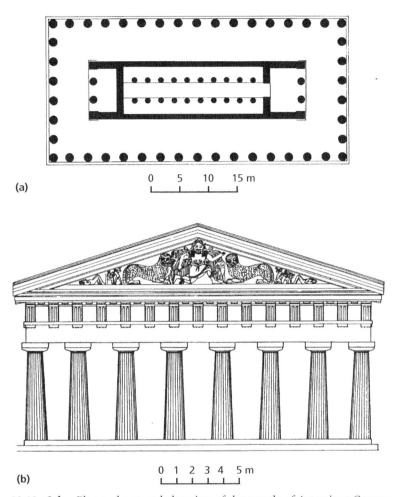

(a)

(b)

**Figure 10.19a & b**   Plan and restored elevation of the temple of Artemis at Corcyra

were two more rows of columns in the porch and the main room. The temple of Artemis at Ephesos was started soon after the Heraion and is even larger, 55.10 by 109.20 meters. The peristyle consisted of two rows of eight columns at the front, nine at the back, and 21 on each side. The main room may have been left open to the sky. These are two of the earliest Ionic temples. The columns of the Artemision, which were approximately 12 meters high, have the characteristic volute capitals and bases (figure 10.22). Ionic was a much more flexible architectural style than Doric and could not really be described as an order in the sixth century. Near Eastern and Egyptian influence can clearly be seen in the way that the Heraion and the Artemision were designed and built. As Samos was involved in the settlement at Naukratis, it is quite possible that the techniques required to quarry, transport, and lift blocks of stone which weighed as much as 40 tons were learned in Egypt.

**Figure 10.20** Temple of Apollo at Corinth

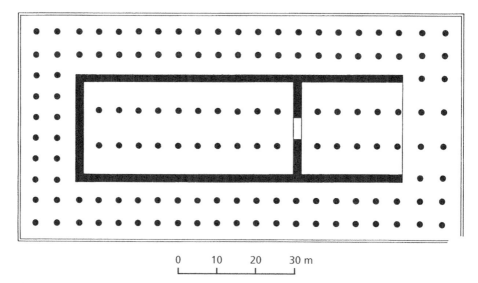

0    10    20    30 m

**Figure 10.21** Plan of the third temple of Hera on Samos

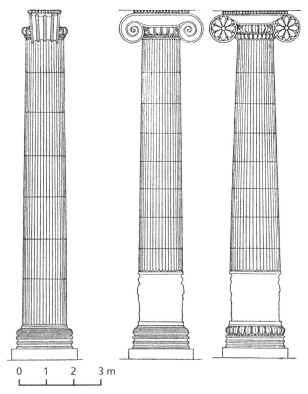

0    1    2    3 m

**Figure 10.22**   Columns of the temple of Artemis at Ephesos

The fact that the Greeks could construct such colossal temples does not of course explain why they chose to do so. Samos and Ephesos were neighbors and rivals, so there was undoubtedly an element of competition in this architectural extravaganza. They may also have wanted to assert their independence in the face of the threat posed by the Lydians in particular. It is therefore ironic that Kroisos, the king of Lydia, financed the completion of the Artemision after he captured Ephesos. In the second half of the sixth century the temple of Hera was dismantled, possibly because the marshy ground had subsided, and work started on a replacement which measured 55.16 by 108.63 meters. Polykrates, the powerful tyrant of Samos, must have seen this as an opportunity to enhance his reputation, though the temple was still unfinished when he died.

The Greeks who settled in Italy and Sicily soon established sanctuaries, though not much is known about their temples until the early sixth century when they started to make more use of stone. The Syracusans built a Doric temple of Apollo with sturdy columns set so close together that the capitals almost touched. There may have been some initial uncertainty about the quality of the local stone. The temple had two rows of columns at the front which is quite common in Sicily. The Doric order in the west differs in a number of respects. This could have been a

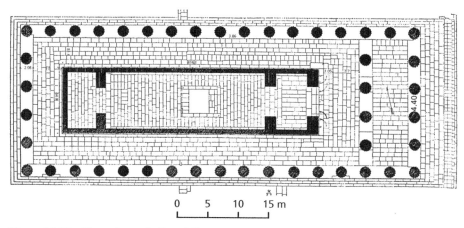

**Figure 10.23**   Plan of temple C at Selinous

conscious decision to replicate the architectural style which had become established back in Greece but in a way that was clearly distinctive. However, the peers with whom these polities interacted most closely were their more immediate neighbors, the other colonies in particular, as well as the Phoenicians, Sicilians, and Italians. They had the resources to undertake the construction of some of the most impressive Archaic temples. At Selinous temple C was built on the acropolis above the city in the mid sixth century (figure 10.23). It measured 23.80 by 63.75 meters, had a peristyle of six by 17 columns, double at the front, and an adyton instead of an opisthodomos behind the main room. Temple D soon followed and then, in a sanctuary east of the river, temple F, which had screen walls between the columns of the peristyle, presumably to block the view of the interior. Temple G was started in the late sixth century and, at 50.07 by 110.12 meters, matched the Heraion and Artemision for size but was still incomplete when the Carthaginians sacked Selinous in 409 BC. In a sanctuary west of the city were two rather more modest sixth-century temples, one of which was dedicated to Demeter. The temple of Hera at Poseidonia on the west coast of Italy is remarkably well preserved and is unusual because the peristyle consists of nine by 18 columns. Their proportions and the wide capitals suggest a mid sixth-century date. Around 500 BC another temple, possibly of Athena, was built on the north side of the city. This has a more conventional peristyle of six by 13 columns. However, the columns inside, in front of the porch, were Ionic and also some of the decorative details.

There was considerable experimentation by the architects who designed the temples in the west and they had an opportunity to showcase some of these innovations, such as their use of intricately decorated terracotta revetments, because a number of the colonies built treasuries at Olympia and Delphi. A panhellenic sanctuary was the obvious place for these prestigious dedications. The games at Olympia brought competitors and spectators together from across the Greek world but Delphi was even more cosmopolitan. In the late seventh or early sixth century a

**Figure 10.24**    Reconstruction of the Siphnian treasury at Delphi

federation known as the Amphictyony had taken over control of the sanctuary from the local community. The first Pythian games were held in 591/0 or 586/5 BC and Delphi was firmly established as a panhellenic sanctuary. The role of the oracle was a major factor in this. It was consulted by states on fundamental policy issues, as well as by individuals who included Near Eastern rulers, most notably Kroisos. Herodotos (1.50–51) describes some of the extraordinary gifts which he sent, such as a gold bowl which weighed almost a quarter of a ton and a silver bowl with a capacity of 5,000 gallons.

A fire destroyed the temple of Apollo at Delphi in 548 BC but reconstruction work was delayed because the sanctuary authorities were dependent on subventions and could not finance the project. Eventually an exiled Athenian family, the Alkmaionids, did complete the temple and used marble instead of poros limestone at the front, which ensured that in return they were given the support of the oracle. States seem to have been more generous when their dedications were readily identifiable. Around 525 the Siphnians donated some of the profits from their gold and silver mines to build a treasury. This had female statues instead of Ionic columns in the porch, a superbly sculpted frieze, and pediments (figure 10.24). A remarkable cache of sixth-century votives was buried under the sacred way, apparently after a fire. There were pieces of three gold and ivory statues, as well as a life-size silver bull.

Many sanctuaries were now populated by marble statues of young men and women, kouroi and korai (figure 9.15). It is not clear who they represent. They do not have the characteristic attributes of gods and goddesses, such as a bow in the case of Apollo, and they were evidently not an idealized image of the donor, since many of the korai on the Acropolis were dedicated by men. Perhaps they symbolized the type of youthful perfection which aristocrats so admired. They certainly stand out as the indulgence of a privileged class. Most votives were much more modest. The introduction of the one-piece mold from the Near East resulted in the mass production of terracotta figurines. Lead votives could also be made cheaply, and over 100,000 were excavated in the sanctuary of Artemis Orthia in Sparta. Although it seems unlikely that everyone left a dedication every time they visited a sanctuary, this had obviously become a regular means of communication between individuals and the gods.

## The Fifth Century

The Greeks believed that their victories over the Persians in 480–479 BC had been divinely inspired and a monument was set up at Delphi by the cities who had fought against Xerxes. Also in 480, the Carthaginians invaded Sicily but were defeated at the battle of Himera by Gelon of Syracuse and Theron of Akragas. Gelon celebrated this victory with two temples, one at Himera and one in Syracuse which is now the cathedral. Theron used Carthaginian prisoners to construct the massive temple of Olympian Zeus at Akragas, which measured 110.09 by 52.74 meters and was the largest Doric temple as well as the most idiosyncratic (figure 10.25). There were screen walls between the columns and the architrave was supported by Atlas figures 7.65 meters high.

The temple of Zeus at Olympia was built in 470–457 BC and also commemorated a military victory, by the city of Elis, which controlled the sanctuary, over nearby Pisa. Inter-state rivalry was responsible for many of the most impressive works of art and architecture, which generally took the form of dedications. The temple of Zeus had a peristyle of six by 13 Doric columns and was laid out canonically with a porch, main room, and opisthodomos (figure 10.26). The sculpture of the pediments and metopes defines the early Classical style and the cult statue was later acknowledged as one of the wonders of the ancient world. It was made by the Athenian sculptor Pheidias in a workshop at Olympia and depicted Zeus seated on a throne. The statue was colossal, over 12 meters high, and consisted of a wooden frame to which ivory veneer was attached for the flesh and gold for the drapery.

Pheidias was responsible for the chryselephantine cult statue of the goddess Athena in the Parthenon as well. This was the centerpiece of the temple, which was under construction by 447 BC and was completed in 432. The Parthenon was conceived by Perikles as a symbol of Athenian political power and was funded by the tribute which the subject cities paid, theoretically for the upkeep of the fleet. It also recalled past glories because the plan was based on a temple which had been started after the battle of Marathon in 490 but was destroyed by the Persians when they captured Athens in 480. It is not clear why the Athenians waited 30 years before

0    5    10    15 m

**Figure 10.25**    Reconstruction of the temple of Zeus at Akragas

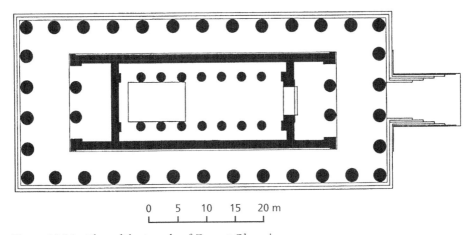

0    5    10    15    20 m

**Figure 10.26**    Plan of the temple of Zeus at Olympia

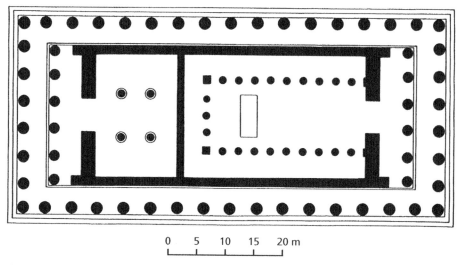

Figure 10.27   Plan of the Parthenon

they replaced this older Parthenon. Doubts have been expressed about an oath which the Greeks supposedly swore that temples should be left in ruins as a reminder of Persian impiety. The platform of the earlier temple was reused for the Parthenon which differed in one significant respect in that eight columns were set at each end rather than the customary six (figure 10.27). Consequently the interior of the temple was wider and this provided more space for the cult statue of Athena. The gold on the statue reportedly weighed over 1000 kg but could be stripped off and melted down in a crisis, which would have left the virgin goddess rather overexposed. Annual inventories also listed the many other treasures stored in the temple. It was built entirely of marble and has 17 columns on each side. The cult statue stood on the base in the east room, framed by columns. The function of the smaller west room has never been resolved. The pediments showed the birth of Athena at one end and her contest with Poseidon at the other. The metopes depicted the battle between the gods and the giants and the victories of the Greeks over the Amazons, centaurs, and Trojans. A continuous frieze ran around the central part of the temple, set so high up that it could not easily be seen. There has been considerable debate about the subject of the frieze but the standard view is that it shows the procession at the climax of the Panathenaic festival.

No temple would ever match the Parthenon for the quality of the architecture and sculpture. It was audaciously extravagant, and yet two more temples of Athena were constructed on the Acropolis later in the fifth century. The Ionic Erechtheion housed the ancient olive-wood statue of Athena and cults associated with the mythical history of Athens. In form and function the Parthenon and the Erechtheion were quite different yet complementary. The temple of Athena Nike celebrated the role of the goddess in the military victories of the city—perhaps rather prematurely given the disasters that soon followed. It was also Ionic and therefore provided a

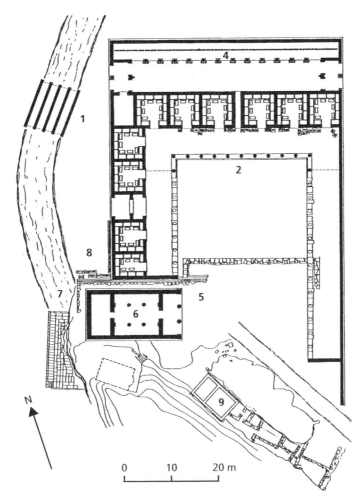

**Figure 10.28**    Plan of the sanctuary of Artemis at Brauron

visual contrast with the adjacent Doric Propylaia, the monumental entrance of the sanctuary. The well-preserved temple of Hephaistos in the Agora was built around the same time as the Parthenon. It was one of four which were evidently designed by the same architect, since they have a number of features in common. The other three temples were in the countryside at Sounion in the sanctuary of Poseidon, at Rhamnous in the sanctuary of Nemesis, and at Acharnai or Pallene. There is some uncertainty about the location of this fourth temple because it was dismantled in the first century and re-erected in the Agora. The Telesterion, the hall of initiation in the center of the sanctuary at Eleusis, was also rebuilt in the late fifth century and a stoa was constructed in the sanctuary of Artemis at Brauron around three sides of an open court (figure 10.28). The rooms behind the Doric portico have off-center doors, which indicate that couches were placed against the walls, and presumably this was where sanctuary officials dined when the Brauronia festival was celebrated. There must have been state investment in these construction projects which consolidated the integration of the Athenian polis as a religious community.

In the early years of the Peloponnesian War, Athens was devastated by the plague, which spread rapidly in the city because of the refugees who fled from the countryside when the Spartans invaded. This may have prompted the introduction of the cult of Asklepios from Epidauros in 421/420 BC. A god who could heal the sick would obviously have been welcomed. His sanctuary was on the south slope of the Acropolis and, unusually, was set up by a private individual called Telemachos. The wooden structures which he built were replaced in the fourth century by a stone temple and stoa. Those who came to be cured slept in the stoa. They hoped that Asklepios would appear in a dream and suggest how their illness should be treated. No doubt the god was richly rewarded if they recovered.

## The Fourth Century and the Hellenistic Period

The main sanctuary of Asklepios was at Epidauros, where he was certainly worshiped by the early fifth century. As a result of the growth in his popularity, the sanctuary expanded in the fourth century (figure 10.29). Epidauros was not a particularly wealthy city and relied on donations to cover the construction costs. Inscriptions give details of the way that the work was subcontracted and it is clear that progress could be slow if the flow of funds was disrupted. The temple of Asklepios (1) was rather modest, 11.76 by 23.06 meters with a peristyle of six by 11 Doric columns, though the cult statue was made of gold and ivory. Behind the temple is a circular structure known as the Thymele (2). This was 20 meters in diameter and had 26 Doric columns around the outside. Inside there were 14 Corinthian columns which enclosed a black and white marble floor. It was possible to climb down into the foundations through a hole in the center of the floor. The fact that Asklepios was a hero who died and then became a god could explain this link with the underworld. Also in the central part of the sanctuary was the abaton (3), a stoa where the sick slept after they had sacrificed and purified themselves. Inscriptions record some of the miraculous cures that followed this ritual. The surgical instruments found in the sanctuary indicate that more conventional forms of medicine were also practiced here. As well as the visits by individuals who came for treatment, Epidauros hosted a major festival of Asklepios and facilities for this were developed in the fourth century. The large peristyle court on the south side of the sanctuary (4) was originally interpreted as a gymnasium but a number of the rooms have off-center doors and no doubt the meat from the sacrificial victims was served here. A stadium (5) was built for the athletic events which formed part of the festival and a magnificent theater for the musical contests.

Similarly in Athens a new stadium was constructed for the Panathenaic games and the theater of Dionysos was provided with stone seats which could hold around 15,000 spectators. At Olympia there were few modifications made in the sanctuary

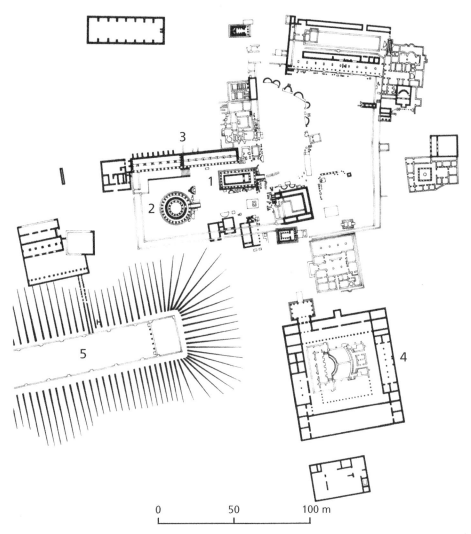

**Figure 10.29**   Plan of the sanctuary of Asklepios at Epidauros

of Zeus in the fourth and third centuries, apart from the circular Philippeion in which statues of the Macedonian royal family were displayed. However, a large gymnasium complex, palaistra, and guesthouse were built west of the Altis.

Pausanias (8.45) regarded the temple of Athena Alea at Tegea as the finest in the Peloponnese "in size and construction." It was built around 340 BC and the architect was the sculptor Skopas. The Doric columns of the peristyle have the slender proportions which are characteristic of the fourth century. Engaged columns lined the cella, Corinthian below and Ionic above (figure 10.30). This combination of the three orders may have been inspired by the temple of Apollo Epikourios at Bassai and is replicated in the temple of Zeus at Nemea which is dated around 330 (figure 10.31).

**Figure 10.30**    Reconstruction of the cella of the temple of Athena at Tegea

**Figure 10.31**    Temple of Zeus at Nemea

**Figure 10.32**    Temple of Athena at Priene

The Greek cities of Asia Minor now commissioned some of the most spectacular temples. The late fourth-century temple of Athena Polias was prominently positioned on a terrace in the center of Priene (figure 10.32). It was designed by Pythios and effectively created a new template for the Ionic order. Around the same time work started on a replacement for the sixth-century temple of Artemis at Ephesos which had burned down in 356 BC. The new temple was colossal, 51.44 by 111.48 meters, with columns 17.65 meters high, three rows at the front and two rows at the sides and back. It is not obvious from the sad remains that this was one of the wonders of the ancient world but fortunately the temple of Apollo at Didyma is much better preserved (figure 10.33a & b). On a seven-stepped platform, 51.13 by 109.34 meters, there was a double peristyle of 11 by 21 columns 19.70 meters high, the tallest of any Greek temple. This enclosed an open court with a shrine which may mark the site of a sacred spring. Construction was under way by 300 BC but the temple was never completed. The temple of Artemis at Sardis was almost as large, 45.73 by 99.16 meters, and is also unfinished.

The Doric temple of Athena Polias at Pergamon is a remarkably modest 12.27 by 21.77 meters, though it was set within a spacious court framed by stoas (figure 2.12). The altar of Zeus on a terrace just below the temple is much more flamboyant (figure 10.34). It was built by Eumenes II in the early second century and consisted

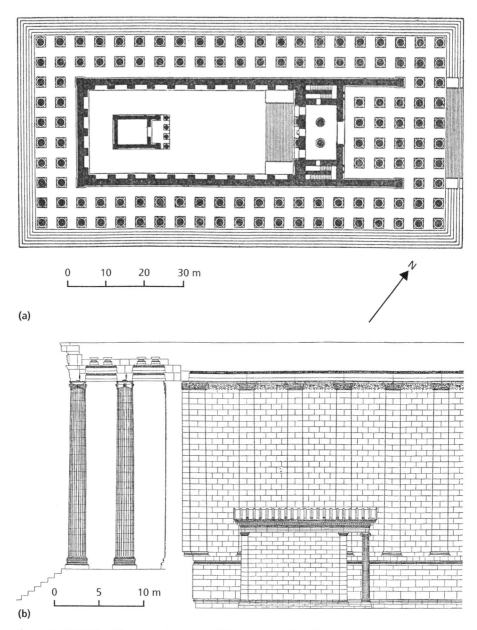

**(a)**

0    10    20    30 m

N

**(b)**

0    5    10 m

**Figure 10.33a & b**  Plan and elevation of the temple of Apollo at Didyma

of an enormous stepped platform, 36.44 by 34.20 meters, on which there was a high podium decorated with a sculpted frieze. This depicted the battle between the gods and the giants in the vividly expressive Hellenistic baroque style. Like the sculpture of the Parthenon, which is echoed in some of the figures on the frieze, the victory of the gods over the monstrous giants symbolized the military triumphs of

**Figure 10.34**   Reconstruction of the altar of Zeus at Pergamon

Pergamon. On top of the podium, enclosed by an Ionic colonnade, was the actual altar. Religion still provided a medium for grand gestures.

## Conclusions

Greek religion was multifaceted. A regional dimension can be seen in the way that Olympia and Delphi became panhellenic sanctuaries. At the same time religion defined the polis as a community and created a sense of identity. A sanctuary such as Perachora could serve a particular group, and religion was obviously personal as well. Because religion operated at these different levels, there would have been tensions and change was inevitable. Nevertheless, religion is inherently conservative, and we should expect some continuity. The practice of religion was disrupted at the end of the Bronze Age yet many of the same gods were still worshiped later and sacrifices were performed in much the same way.

In the Early Bronze Age tombs were the main focus of ritual activity. It was not until the Middle Bronze Age that sanctuaries became a feature of the Cretan landscape and a concept of sacred space was articulated. Although the Minoan palaces did have a ceremonial role, religion was rooted in the countryside in the peak and cave sanctuaries. Their marginal location suggests that there was a need to negotiate with the forces of nature. A similar concern is implicit in those later Greek sanctuaries which were on the edge of a wilder world but they were also an expression of territoriality. Sacred space could easily become secularized.

There may always have been a connection between sanctuaries and sacrifice. The figurines at Dhaskalio Kavos had been deliberately broken and therefore effectively killed. The animal bones found at peak sanctuaries could be sacrificial. At Kato Syme the evidence is even clearer. The fact that the heads of the victims had been placed in the ashes ties in with the deposits of burnt bones from cattle and deer at Pylos.

This tradition was maintained in the Early Iron Age and became the core element of Classical ritual. The corollary of animal sacrifice was meat for feasts, and commensality was an integral component of Greek religion, attested in Cretan rural sanctuaries and the Mycenaean palaces, at Kalapodi and Isthmia. By the Classical period a major festival could bring together thousands of worshipers.

There is often a process of elaboration in the way that sanctuaries developed. Elite investment is suspected in many of the rural sanctuaries which remained in use on Crete in the Neopalatial period, although the Mycenaeans do not seem to have indulged their taste for the grandiose. Greek temples started modestly but soon took on a more monumental character. As the rivalry between cities intensified, they became a conspicuous and yet appropriately pious symbol of success. The same spirit of competition is evident in dedications. The tripod cauldrons at Olympia marked the start of a trend. When weapons and jewelry appeared in sanctuaries rather than graves, the link with personal achievement and status was made explicit. Cities celebrated military victories with treasuries and groups of statues.

Terracotta figurines were the most common type of votive in Greek sanctuaries and continue a practice which originated in the Neolithic period. Of course the fact that clay was readily available and easily modeled is the main reason why so many figurines were produced. They also provided a flexible medium of communication through which hopes and concerns could be transmitted. They represent the voice of the individual in collective acts of worship.

## Bibliographical notes

On the complexities of the archaeology of religion, see Insoll 2004. Talalay 1993, Papathanassopoulos 1996, Perlès 2001, Bailey 2005, and Mina 2008 discuss Neolithic figurines; Barber 1987, Broodbank 2000, Sherratt 2000, and Hoffman 2002 examine the Early Cycladic evidence. Renfrew et al. 2007 report on the recent survey and excavations at Dhaskalio Kavos. Marinatos 1993 is a good overview of Minoan religion. Rutkowski 1986 provides a detailed account of Cretan cult sites and Moss 2005 is also useful. Peatfield 1990 and 1992, Jones 1999, and Kyriakidis 2005 focus on peak sanctuaries. See Tyree 2001 for sacred caves, Lebessi and Muhly 1990 for Kato Syme, and Sakellarakis and Sakellaraki 1997 for Anemospilia. A number of the papers in Hägg and Marinatos 1987 examine the role of the Cretan palaces, and Gesell 1985 also covers town shrines. Sakellarakis 1996 discusses the peak sanctuary at Ayios Georgios on Kythera, Marinatos 1984 the evidence of cult activity at Akrotiri on Thera, Caskey 1986 the temple at Ayia Irini on Kea, Niemeier 1990 the religious scenes on Early Mycenaean gold rings, and Lambrinoudakis 1981 the sanctuary at Epidauros. For religious ceremonies, feasts, and sacrifices in Mycenaean palaces see Wright 1994 and 2004, Bendall 2004, Halstead and Isaakidou 2004, and Stocker and Davis 2004. Whittaker 1997 discusses aspects of Mycenaean shrines generally, Moore and Taylour 1999 and French 2002 the cult center at Mycenae, and Renfrew 1985 the sanctuary at Phylakopi. Cult activity in Greece and Crete in the period after the palaces is reviewed by Morgan 1999, d'Agata 2001 and 2006, and Dickinson 2006. De Polignac 1995 considers the location of Greek sanctuaries; for Laconia see Catling 2002. There is a detailed analysis of tomb and hero cults in Antonaccio 1995 and of early temples in Mazarakis Ainian 1997. The different types of votives are discussed by Coldstream 1977 and Morgan 1993. Kyrieleis 1993 summarizes the early history of the Heraion on Samos. For the seventh-century temples at Corinth and Isthmia, see Rhodes 2003 and Gebhard 1993. Coulton 1977 traces the development of Greek temple design and Barletta 2001 the origins of the orders. The architecture of the temples is well described in Lawrence and Tomlinson 1996 and Spawforth 2006. Tomlinson 1976 is a general account of Greek sanctuaries; Bommelaer 1991 is excellent on Delphi, Hurwit 1999 on the Acropolis, and Tomlinson 1983 on Epidauros. For Greek religion more generally see Bruit Zaidman and Schmitt Pantel 1992, Price 1999, and Mikalson 2005.

# Timeline

| | | | | | |
|---|---|---|---|---|---|
| 6700–5800 | Early Neolithic | Introduction of agriculture | Village communities | Nea Nikomedeia | First use of pottery |
| 5800–5300 | Middle Neolithic | | | Sesklo | |
| 5300–4500 | Late Neolithic | | | Dimini | |
| 4500–3200 | Final Neolithic | | | | |
| 3200–2700 | Early Bronze I | Spread of settlement in southern Greece and the islands | | | First use of metals Copper metallurgy |
| 2700–2200 | Early Bronze II | | Corridor houses | Lerna, Lithares, Myrtos | |
| 2200–2000 | Early Bronze III | | | | |
| 2000–1900 | Middle Bronze I | Settlement expansion on Crete, contraction in Greece and the islands | First Minoan palaces | Knossos, Phaistos, Mallia | |
| 1900–1800 | Middle Bronze II | | | Kolonna, Asine, Lerna | |
| 1800–1700 | Middle Bronze III | | Second palaces Shaft graves at Mycenae | Gournia, Ayia Triada, Akrotiri, Phylakopi, Ayia Irini | Peak and cave sanctuaries on Crete |
| 1700–1600 | Late Bronze I | | Destruction of Minoan sites | | |

| Date | Period | Settlement / developments | Sites | Sanctuaries / architecture | Technology / art |
|---|---|---|---|---|---|
| 1600–1400 | | Settlement expansion in Greece | | | |
| 1400–1300 | Late Bronze II | Mycenaean palaces | Mycenae, Tiryns, Pylos Nichoria | Mycenaean cult centers | |
| 1300–1200 | Late Bronze III | | | | |
| 1200–1050 | | Destruction of Mycenaean palaces; Depopulation in Greece; Remote sites occupied on Crete | Karphi | | Iron metallurgy |
| 1050–900 | Protogeometric | | Athens, Lefkandi | Cult at Olympia and Isthmia | |
| 900–850 | Early Geometric | Rise of polis | Smyrna | Increase in the number of sanctuaries | |
| 850–760 | Middle Geometric | Settlement expansion and an increase in the population | | | |
| 760–700 | Late Geometric | Colonization starts in Italy and Sicily | Zagora | Temples at Perachora, Eretria, Samos | Orientalization in art |
| 700–600 | Archaic | Colonization in the Black Sea | | Temples at Corinth, Isthmia, Thermon | |
| 600–480 | | Increase in rural settlement | Athens, Metapontion | Monumental temples at Corcyra, Corinth, Samos, Ephesos, Syracuse, Selinous | |
| 480–400 | Classical | Planned towns | Miletos, Piraeus | Olympia, Akragas Parthenon | |
| 400–323 | | | Halieis, Olynthos, Priene, Chersonesos | Epidauros, Tegea, Nemea, Priene, Mausoleum | |
| 323–146 | Hellenistic | Expansion into Asia; Decrease in number of rural sites in Greece | Vergina, Pella, Alexandria, Antioch, Pergamon, Ai Khanoum; Eretria, Delos | Ephesos, Didyma, Pergamon | |

# Glossary

| | |
|---|---|
| **acropolis** | the citadel of a town or city |
| **alluviation** | sediment deposited by rivers |
| **amphora** | a two-handled storage vessel |
| **andron** | the dining room of a Greek house |
| **archon** | literally ruler, the holder of high office in a Greek city |
| **aryballos** | a container for perfumed oil |
| **ard** | a simple type of plough |
| **boule** | the council of a Greek city with responsibility for state affairs |
| **bouleuterion** | the place where the boule met |
| **cella** | the main room of a temple |
| **chora** | the territory of a polis/city state |
| **cist grave** | a slab-lined grave |
| **dromos** | the entrance passage of a tomb |
| **ekklesia** | the assembly of adult male citizens in a Greek city |
| **gypsum** | white evaporite mineral used in construction |
| **hectare** | 10,000 square meters |
| **hoplite** | a heavy-armed infantryman |
| **hydria** | a water jug |

| | |
|---|---|
| **kore** | an Archaic female statue used as a dedication or grave marker |
| **kouros** | an Archaic male statue used as a dedication or grave marker |
| **krater** | a vessel in which wine and water were mixed |
| **larnax** | a terracotta coffin |
| **lekythos** | an oil flask |
| **lustral basin** | a sunken room in Cretan palaces and villas |
| **maquis** | a type of Mediterranean scrub vegetation |
| **megaron** | a rectangular structure with a porch and one or more rooms set behind this |
| **niello** | powdered sulphides of copper and silver heated to produce a bluish-black plastic compound |
| **odeion** | a roofed concert or lecture hall |
| **oikos** | a house or a chamber in a house |
| **palaistra** | a peristyle structure used for athletic and educational activities |
| **pastas** | a room which opens off the court of some Greek houses |
| **pastoralism** | livestock husbandry |
| **peltast** | a light-armed soldier |
| **pentekonter** | a 50-oared galley |
| **phrygana** | a type of Mediterranean scrub vegetation |
| **pithos** | a large storage jar |
| **polis** | a Greek city state |
| **prytaneis** | literally presidents, in Athens the members of the boule who were on duty |
| **skyphos** | a two-handled drinking vessel |
| **stele** | a stone slab used as a grave marker or for public inscriptions |
| **stirrup jar** | an oil container |
| **symposion** | a male drinking party |
| **taphonomic** | of the process whereby materials are transformed into the archaeological record |
| **tell** | an artificial settlement mound |
| **tholos** | a circular structure |
| **trireme** | a warship with three banks of oars |
| **tyrant** | an individual who seized power and ruled unconstitutionally |

# References

Adam, J.-P., 1982. *L'architecture militaire grecque* (Paris: Picard)

Alcock, S. E., 1994. Breaking up the Hellenistic world: survey and society. In I. Morris (ed.), *Classical Greece: Ancient Histories and Modern Archaeologies* (Cambridge: Cambridge University Press) 171–90

Alcock, S. E., J. F. Cherry, and J. L. Davis, 1994. Intensive survey, agricultural practice and the classical landscape of Greece. In I. Morris (ed.), *Classical Greece: Ancient Histories and Modern Archaeologies* (Cambridge: Cambridge University Press) 137–70

Alcock, S. E. and J. F. Cherry (eds), 2004. *Side-by-Side Survey: Comparative Regional Studies in the Mediterranean World* (Oxford: Oxbow Books)

Anderson, J. K., 1993. Hoplite weapons and offensive arms. In V. D. Hanson (ed.), *Hoplites: The Classical Greek Battle Experience* (London: Routledge) 15–37

Andreou, S., M. Fotiadis, and K. Kotsakis, 2001. The Neolithic and Bronze Age of northern Greece. In T. Cullen (ed.), *Aegean Prehistory: A Review* (Boston: Archaeological Institute of America) 259–327

Andronikos, M., 1993. *Vergina: The Royal Tombs and the Ancient City* (Athens: Ekdotike Athinon)

Antonaccio, C. M., 1995. *An Archaeology of Ancestors: Tomb Cult and Hero Cult in Early Greece* (Lanham: Rowman and Littlefield)

Antonaccio, C. M., 2005. Excavating colonization. In H. Hurst and S. Owen (eds), *Ancient Colonizations: Analogy, Similarity and Difference* (London: Duckworth) 97–113

Arafat, K. and C. Morgan, 1989. Pots and potters in Athens and Corinth: a review. *Oxford Journal of Archaeology* 8: 311–46

Arafat, K. and C. Morgan, 1994. Athens, Etruria and the Heuneburg: mutual misconceptions in the study of Greek–barbarian relations. In I. Morris (ed.), *Classical Greece: Ancient Histories and Modern Archaeologies* (Cambridge: Cambridge University Press) 108–34

Ault, B. A., 2005. *The Excavations at Ancient Halieis 2. The Houses: The Organization and Use of Domestic Space* (Bloomington and Indianapolis: Indiana University Press)

---

Ault, B. A. and L. C. Nevett (eds), 2005. *Ancient Greek Houses and Households: Chronological, Regional and Social Diversity* (Philadelphia: University of Philadelphia)

Bailey, D. W., 2005. *Prehistoric Figurines: Representation and Corporeality in the Neolithic* (London: Routledge)

Barber, R. L. N., 1987. *The Cyclades in the Bronze Age* (London: Duckworth)

Barletta, B. A., 2001. *The Origin of the Greek Architectural Orders* (Cambridge: Cambridge University Press)

Bendall, L., 2004. Fit for a king? Hierarchy, exclusion, aspiration and desire in the social structure of Mycenaean banqueting. In P. Halstead and J. C. Barrett (eds), *Food, Cuisine and Society in Prehistoric Greece* (Oxford: Oxbow) 105–35

Betancourt, P. P., 1985. *The History of Minoan Pottery* (Princeton: Princeton University Press)

Biers, W. R., 1992. *Art, Artefacts and Chronology in Classical Archaeology* (London and New York: Routledge)

Blegen, C. W. and M. Rawson, 1966. *The Palace of Nestor at Pylos in Western Messenia I: The Buildings and their Contents* (Princeton: Princeton University Press)

Boardman, J., 1975. *Athenian Red-Figure Vases: The Archaic Period: A Handbook* (London: Thames and Hudson)

Boardman, J., 1980. *The Greeks Overseas: Their Early Colonies and Trade* (London: Thames and Hudson)

Boardman, J., 1989. *Athenian Red-Figure Vases: The Classical Period: A Handbook* (London: Thames and Hudson)

Boardman, J., 1991. *Athenian Black-Figure Vases: A Handbook* (London: Thames and Hudson)

Bommelaer, J.-F., 1991. *Guide de Delphes: Le Site* (Paris: École française d'Athènes)

Branigan, K., 1993. *Dancing with Death: Life and Death in Southern Crete c. 3000–2000 BC* (Amsterdam: Hakkert)

Branigan, K., 1999. The nature of warfare in the southern Aegean during the third millennium BC. In R. Laffineur (ed.), *Polemos: le contexte guerrier en Égée à l'Âge du Bronze* (Liège: Université de Liège) 87–93

Broodbank, C., 2000. *An Island Archaeology of the Early Cyclades* (Cambridge: Cambridge University Press)

Broodbank, C., 2004. Minoanisation. *Proceedings of the Cambridge Philological Society* 50: 46–91

Bruit Zaidman, L. and P. Schmitt Pantel, 1992. *Religion in the Ancient Greek City* (Cambridge: Cambridge University Press)

Bruneau, P. and J. Ducat, 2005. *Guide de Délos* (Paris: École française d'Athènes)

Cadogan, G., 1976. *Palaces of Minoan Crete* (London: Methuen)

Cadogan, G., E. Hatzaki, and A. Vasilakis (eds), 2004. *Knossos: Palace, City and State* (London: British School at Athens)

Cahill, N., 2002. *Household and City Organization at Olynthus* (New Haven: Yale University Press)

Cahill, N., 2005. Household industry in Greece and Anatolia. In B. A. Ault and L. C. Nevett (eds), *Ancient Greek Houses and Households: Chronological, Regional and Social Diversity* (Philadelphia: University of Philadelphia) 54–66

Cambitoglou, A., J. J. Coulton, J. Birmingham, and J. R. Green, 1971. *Zagora 1: Excavation of a Geometric Settlement on the Island of Andros* (Sydney: Sydney University Press)

Cambitoglou, A., A. Birchall, J. J. Coulton, and J. R. Green, 1988. *Zagora 2: Excavation of a Geometric Town on the Island of Andros* (Athens: Archaiologiki Etaireia)

Camp, J. McK., 1986. *The Athenian Agora: Excavations in the Heart of Classical Athens* (London: Thames and Hudson)

Camp, J. McK., 2001. *The Archaeology of Athens* (New Haven: Yale University Press)

Carman, J., and A. Harding (eds), 1999. *Ancient Warfare: Archaeological Perspectives* (Stroud: Sutton)

Carradice, I., 1995. *Greek Coins* (London: British Museum Press)

Carter, J. C., 2003. *Crimean Chersonesos: City, Chora, Museum and Environs* (Austin: Institute of Classical Archaeology, University of Texas at Austin)

Carter, J. C., 2006. *Discovering the Greek Countryside at Metaponto* (Ann Arbor: University of Michigan Press)

Caskey, M. E., 1986. *Keos II. The Temple at Ayia Irini I: The Statues* (Princeton: American School of Classical Studies at Athens)

Casson, L., 1995. *Ships and Seamanship in the Ancient World* (Baltimore: Johns Hopkins University Press)

Catling, R. W. V., 2002. The survey area from the Early Iron Age to the Classical period. In W. G. Cavanagh, J. Crouwel, R. Catling, and G. Shipley (eds), 2002. *Continuity and Change in a Greek Rural Landscape: The Laconia Survey II* (London: British School at Athens) 151–256

Cavanagh, W., 1999. Revenons à nos moutons: surface survey and the Peloponnese in the Late and Final Neolithic period. In J. Renard (ed.), *Le Péloponnèse: archéologie et histoire* (Rennes: Presses Universitaires de Rennes) 31–65

Cavanagh, W., 2004. WYSIWYG: settlement and territoriality in southern Greece during the Early and Middle Neolithic periods. *Journal of Mediterranean Archaeology* 17: 165–89

Cavanagh, W. G., J. Crouwel, R. Catling, and G. Shipley (eds), 1996. *Continuity and Change in a Greek Rural Landscape: The Laconia Survey II* (London: British School at Athens)

Cavanagh, W. G., J. Crouwel, R. Catling, and G. Shipley (eds), 2002. *Continuity and Change in a Greek Rural Landscape: The Laconia Survey I* (London: British School at Athens)

Cavanagh, W. G. and A. Lagia, 2010. Burials from Kouphovouno, Sparta, Lakonia. *Mesohelladika*. In A. Touchais, G. Touchais, S. Voutsaki, and J. Wright (eds), *Mesohelladika: The Greek Mainland in the Middle Bronze Age* (Athens: École française d'Athènes) 415–31

Cavanagh, W. G. and C. Mee, 1995. Mourning before and after the Dark Age. In C. Morris (ed.), *Klados: Essays in Honour of J. N. Coldstream* (London: Institute of Classical Studies) 45–61

Cavanagh, W. G and C. Mee, 1998. *A Private Place: Death in Prehistoric Greece* (Jonsered: Paul Åströms Förlag)

Cavanagh, W. G., C. Mee, and P. James, 2005. *The Laconia Rural Sites Project* (London: British School at Athens)

Cherry, J. F., 1986. Polities and palaces: some problems in Minoan state formation. In C. Renfrew and J. F. Cherry (eds), *Peer-Polity Interaction and Socio-Political Change* (Cambridge: Cambridge University Press) 19–45

Cherry J. F. and J. L. Davis, 2001. Under the sceptre of Mycenae: the view from the hinterlands of Mycenae. In K. Branigan (ed.), *Urbanism in the Aegean Bronze Age* (Sheffield: Sheffield Academic Press) 141–59

Cherry, J. F., J. L. Davis, and E. Mantzourani (eds), 1991. *Landscape Archaeology as Long Term History: Northern Keos in the Cycladic Islands from Earliest Settlement until Modern Times* (Los Angeles: Institute of Archaeology, University of California at Los Angeles)

Cherry, J. F., D. Margomenou, and L. E. Talalay (eds), 2005. *Prehistorians around the Pond: Reflections on Aegean Archaeology as a Discipline* (Ann Arbor: Kelsey Museum of Art)

Chryssoulaki, S., 1999. Minoan roads and guard houses—war regained. In R. Laffineur (ed.), *Polemos: le contexte guerrier en Égée à l'Âge du Bronze* (Liège: Université de Liège) 75–84

Cline, E. H. 1994. *Sailing the Wine-Dark Sea: International Trade and the Late Bronze Age Aegean* (Oxford: Tempus Reparatum)

Cline, E. H. and D. Harris-Cline (eds), 1998. *The Aegean and the Orient in the Second Millennium* (Liège: Université de Liège)

Coldstream, J. N., 1968. *Greek Geometric Pottery* (London: Methuen)

Coldstream, J. N., 1977. *Geometric Greece* (London: Ernest Benn)

Coldstream, J. N. and H. W. Catling (eds), 1996. *Knossos North Cemetery: Early Greek Tombs* (London: British School at Athens)

Connolly, P., 2006. *Greece and Rome at War* (London: Greenhill)

Conophagos, C. E., 1980. *Le Laurium antique et la technique grecque de la production de l'argent* (Athens: Ekdotike Hellados)

Coulton, J. J., 1977. *Greek Architects at Work: Problems of Structure and Design* (London: Elek)

Craddock, P. T., 1995. *Early Metal Mining and Production* (Washington: Smithsonian Institution Press)

Crouwel, J. H., 1981. *Chariots and Other Means of Land Transport in Bronze Age Greece* (Amsterdam: Allard Pierson)

Cunningham, T. and J. Driessen, 2004. Site by site: combining survey and excavation data to chart patterns of socio-political change in Bronze Age Crete. In S. E. Alcock and J. F. Cherry (eds), 2004. *Side-by-Side Survey: Comparative Regional Studies in the Mediterranean World* (Oxford: Oxbow Books) 101–13

d'Agata, A. L., 2001. Religion, society and ethnicity on Crete at the end of the Late Bronze Age: the contextual framework of LM IIIC cult activities. In R. Laffineur and R. Hägg (eds), *Potnia: Deities and Religion in the Aegean Bronze Age* (Liège: Université de Liège) 345–54

d'Agata, A. L., 2006. Cult activity on Crete in the early Dark Age: changes, continuities and the development of a "Greek" cult system. In S. Deger-Jalkotzy and I. S. Lemos (eds), *Ancient Greece: From the Mycenaean Palaces to the Age of Homer* (Edinburgh: Edinburgh University Press) 397–414

d'Agostino, B., 2006. The first Greeks in Italy. In G. R. Tsetskhladze (ed.), *Greek Colonisation: An Account of Greek Colonies and Other Settlements Overseas* (Leiden: Brill) 201–37

Darcque, P., 2005. *L'habitat mycénien: formes et fonctions de l'espace bâti en Grèce continentale à la fin du IIe millénaire avant J-C* (Athens: École française d'Athènes)

Davis, J. L. (ed.), 1998. *Sandy Pylos: An Archaeological History from Nestor to Navarino* (Austin: University of Texas Press)

Davis, J. L., 2001. The islands of the Aegean. In T. Cullen (ed.), *Aegean Prehistory: A Review* (Boston: Archaeological Institute of America) 19–94

Davis, J. L., 2008. Minoan Crete and the Aegean islands. In C. Shelmerdine (ed.), *The Cambridge Companion to the Aegean Bronze Age* (Cambridge: Cambridge University Press) 186–208

Davis, J. L., S. E. Alcock, J. Bennet, Y. G. Lolos, and C. W. Shelmerdine, 1997. The Pylos Regional Archaeological Project, part I: overview and the archaeological survey. *Hesperia* 66: 391–494

Day, P. M. and R. C. P. Doonan, 2007. *Metallurgy in the Early Bronze Age Aegean* (Oxford: Oxbow Books)

Day, P. M. and D. E. Wilson, 1998. Consuming power: Kamares Ware in Protopalatial Knossos. *Antiquity* 72: 350–8

Deger-Jalkotzy, S., 1999. Military prowess and social status in Mycenaean Greece. In R. Laffineur (ed.), *Polemos: le contexte guerrier en Égée à l'Âge du Bronze* (Liège: Université de Liège) 121–31

Deger-Jalkotzy, S., 2006. Late Mycenaean warrior tombs. In S. Deger-Jalkotzy and I. S. Lemos (eds), *Ancient Greece: From the Mycenaean Palaces to the Age of Homer* (Edinburgh: Edinburgh University Press) 151–79

Deger-Jalkotzy, S., 2008. Decline, destruction, aftermath. In C. Shelmerdine (ed.), *The Cambridge Companion to the Aegean Bronze Age* (Cambridge: Cambridge University Press) 387–415

de Polignac, F., 1995. *Cults, Territory and the Origins of the Greek City-State* (Chicago: University of Chicago Press)

Dickinson. O., 1977. *The Origins of Mycenaean Civilisation* (Göteborg: Paul Åströms Förlag)

Dickinson, O., 1994. *The Aegean Bronze Age* (Cambridge: Cambridge University Press)

Dickinson, O., 2006. *The Aegean from Bronze Age to Iron Age* (London: Routledge)

Domínguez, A. J., 2006a. Greeks in Sicily. In G. R. Tsetskhladze (ed.), *Greek Colonisation: An Account of Greek Colonies and Other Settlements Overseas* (Leiden: Brill) 253–357

Domínguez, A. J., 2006b. Greeks in the Iberian peninsula. In G. R. Tsetskhladze (ed.), *Greek Colonisation: An Account of Greek Colonies and Other Settlements Overseas* (Leiden: Brill) 429–505

Doumas, C., 1977. *Early Bronze Age Burial Habits in the Cyclades* (Göteborg: Paul Åströms Förlag)

Doumas, C., 1983. *Thera: Pompeii of the Ancient Aegean* (London: Thames and Hudson)

Driessen, J., I. Schoep, and R. Laffineur (eds), 2002. *Monuments of Minos: Rethinking the Minoan Palaces* (Liège: Université de Liège)

Ducrey, P., 1986. *Warfare in Ancient Greece* (New York: Schocken)

Ducrey, P., I. Metzger, and K. Reber, 1993. *Eretria fouilles et recherches VIII: le quartier de la Maison aux Mosaïques* (Lausanne: École suisse d'archéologie en Grèce)

Dyson, S. L., 2006. *In Pursuit of Ancient Pasts: A History of Classical Archaeology in the Nineteenth and Twentieth Centuries* (New Haven and London: Yale University Press)

Evely, R. D. G., 2000. *Minoan Crafts, Tools and Techniques: An Introduction* (Jonsered: Paul Åströms Förlag)

Evely, D., H. Hughes-Brock, and N. Momigliano (eds), 1994. *Knossos: A Labyrinth of History* (London: British School at Athens)

Fedak, J., 1990. *Monumental Tombs of the Hellenistic Age: A Study of Selected Tombs from the Pre-Classical to the Early Imperial Era* (Toronto: University of Toronto Press)

Fisher, N. and H. van Wees, 1998. *Archaic Greece: New Approaches and New Evidence* (London: Duckworth)

Forsén, J., 1992. *The Twilight of the Early Helladics: A Study of the Disturbances in East-Central and Southern Greece Towards the End of the Early Bronze Age* (Jonsered: Paul Åströms Förlag)

Forsén, J. and B. Forsén, 2003. *The Asea Valley Survey: An Arcadian Mountain Valley from the Palaeolithic Period until Modern Times* (Stockholm: Svenska Institutet i Athen)

Foxhall, L., 1998. Cargoes of the heart's desire: the character of trade in the archaic Mediterranean world. In N. Fisher and H. van Wees (eds), *Archaic Greece: New Approaches and New Evidence* (London: Duckworth) 295–309

Foxhall, L., 2007. *Olive Cultivation in Ancient Greece: Seeking the Ancient Economy* (Oxford: Oxford University Press)

French, E., 2002. *Mycenae: Agamemnon's Capital* (Stroud: Tempus)

Galanidou, N. and C. Perlès (eds), 2003. *The Greek Mesolithic: Problems and Perspectives* (London: British School at Athens)

Gale, N. H. (ed.), 1991. *Bronze Age Trade in the Mediterranean* (Jonsered: Paul Åströms Förlag)

Gallou, C., 2005. *The Mycenaean Cult of the Dead* (Oxford: Archaeopress)

Garland, R., 1985. *The Greek Way of Death* (London: Duckworth)

Gates, C., 2003. *Ancient Cities: The Archaeology of Urban Life in the Ancient Near East and Egypt, Greece and Rome* (Abingdon: Routledge)

Gebhard, E. R., 1993. The evolution of a pan-Hellenic sanctuary: from archaeology towards history at Isthmia. In N. Marinatos and R. Hägg (eds), *Greek Sanctuaries: New Approaches* (London: Routledge) 154–77

Gesell, G. C., 1985. *Town, Palace and House Cult in Minoan Crete* (Göteborg: Paul Åströms Förlag)

Gill, D. W. J., 1994. Positivism, pots and long-distance trade. In I. Morris (ed.), *Classical Greece: Ancient Histories and Modern Archaeologies* (Cambridge: Cambridge University Press) 99–107

Gill, D. W. J., 2008. Inscribed silver plate from Tomb II at Vergina: chronological implications. *Hesperia* 77: 335–58

Graham, J. W., 1987. *The Palaces of Crete* (Princeton: Princeton University Press)

Greco, E., 2006. Greek colonisation in southern Italy: a methodological essay. In G. R. Tsetskhladze (ed.), *Greek Colonisation: An Account of Greek Colonies and Other Settlements Overseas* (Leiden: Brill) 169–200

Grove, A. T. and O. Rackham, 2001. *The Nature of Mediterranean Europe: An Ecological History* (New Haven and London: Yale University Press)

Hägg, R. (ed.), 1997. *The Function of the "Minoan Villa"* (Stockholm: Svenska Institutet i Athen)

Hägg, R. and N. Marinatos (eds), 1987. *The Function of the Minoan Palaces* (Stockholm: Svenska Institutet i Athen)

Halstead, P., 1992a. Dimini and the "DMP": faunal remains and animal exploitation in Late Neolithic Thessaly. *Annual of the British School at Athens* 87: 29–59

Halstead. P., 1992b. The Mycenaean palatial economy: making the most of the gaps in the evidence. *Proceedings of the Cambridge Philological Society* 38: 57–86

Halstead, P., 1996. The development of agriculture and pastoralism in Greece: when, how, who and what? In D. R. Harris (ed.), *The Origins and Spread of Agriculture and Pastoralism in Eurasia* (London: University College London Press) 296–309

Halstead, P., 1998–99. Texts, bones and herders: approaches to animal husbandry in Late Bronze Age Greece. In J. Bennet and J. Driessen (eds), *A-Na-Qo-Ta: Studies Presented to J. T. Killen* (Salamanca: Ediciones Universidad de Salamanca) 149–89

Halstead, P., 2000. Land use in postglacial Greece: cultural causes and environmental effects. In P. Halstead and C. Frederick (eds), *Landscape and Land Use in Postglacial Greece* (Sheffield: Sheffield Academic Press) 110–28

Halstead, P. 2001. Mycenaean wheat, flax and sheep: palatial intervention in farming and its implications for rural society. In S. Voutsaki and J. Killen (eds), *Economy and Politics in the Mycenaean Palace States* (Cambridge: Cambridge Philological Society) 38–50

Halstead, P., 2006. Sheep in the garden: the integration of crop and livestock husbandry in early farming regimes of Greece and southern Europe. In D. Serjeantson and D. Field (eds), *Animals in the Neolithic of Britain and Europe* (Oxford: Oxbow) 42–55

Halstead, P. and V. Isaakidou, 2004. Faunal evidence for feasting: burnt offerings from the Palace of Nestor at Pylos. In P. Halstead and J. C. Barrett (eds), *Food, Cuisine and Society in Prehistoric Greece* (Oxford: Oxbow) 136–54

Hansen, J. M., 1988. Agriculture in the prehistoric Aegean: data versus speculation. *American Journal of Archaeology* 92: 39–52

Hansen, M. H. and T. Fischer-Hansen, 1994. Monumental political architecture in Archaic and Classical Greek *poleis*: evidence and historical significance. In D. Whitehead (ed.), *From Political Architecture to Stephanus Byzantius* (Stuttgart: Franz Steiner) 23–90

Hanson, V. D., 1993. Hoplite technology in phalanx battle. In V. D. Hanson (ed.), *Hoplites: The Classical Greek Battle Experience* (London: Routledge) 63–84

Healey, J. F., 1978. *Mining and Metallurgy in the Greek and Roman World* (London: Thames and Hudson)

Hemelrijk, J. M., 1991. A closer look at the potter. In T. Rasmussen and N. Spivey (eds), *Looking at Greek Vases* (Cambridge: Cambridge University Press) 233–56

Hiller, S., 1999. Scenes of warfare and combat in the arts of the Aegean Late Bronze Age: reflections on typology and development. In R. Laffineur (ed.), *Polemos: le contexte guerrier en Égée à l'Âge du Bronze* (Liège: Université de Liège) 319–28

Hoepfner, W. and G. Brands (eds), 1996. *Basileia: Die Paläste der hellenistischen Könige* (Mainz am Rhein: Von Zabern)

Hoepfner, W. and E.-L. Schwandner, 1994. *Haus und Stadt im Klassischen Griechenland* (Munich: Deutscher Kunstverlag)

Hoffman, G. L., 2002. Painted ladies: Early Cycladic II mourning figures. *American Journal of Archaeology* 106: 525–50

Hope Simpson, R. and D. K. Hagel, 2006. *Mycenaean Fortifications, Highways, Dams and Canals* (Sävedalen: Paul Åströms Förlag)

Horden, P. and N. Purcell, 2000. *The Corrupting Sea: A Study of Mediterranean History* (Oxford: Blackwell)

Houby-Nielsen, S. H., 1995. "Burial language" in Archaic and Classical Kerameikos. *Proceedings of the Danish Institute at Athens* 1: 129–92

Howgego, C., 1995. *Ancient History from Coins* (London: Routledge)

Hunt, P., 2007. Military forces. In P. Sabin, H. van Wees, and M. Whitby (eds), *The Cambridge History of Greek and Roman Warfare I: Greece, the Hellenistic World and the Rise of Rome* (Cambridge: Cambridge University Press) 108–46

Hurwit, J. M., 1999. *The Athenian Acropolis: History, Mythology and Archaeology from the Neolithic Era to the Present* (Cambridge: Cambridge University Press)

Iakovidis, S., 1969. *Perati: To Nekrotapheion* (Athens: Archaiologiki Etaireia)

Iakovidis, S., 1983. *Late Helladic Citadels on Mainland Greece* (Leiden: Brill)

Isaakidou, V., 2006. Ploughing with cows: Knossos and the secondary products revolution. In D. Serjeantson and D. Field (eds), *Animals in the Neolithic of Britain and Europe* (Oxford: Oxbow) 95–112

Insoll, T., 2004. *Archaeology, Ritual and Religion* (London: Routledge)

Isager, S. and J. E. Skydsgaard, 1992. *Ancient Greek Agriculture: An Introduction* (London: Routledge)

Jameson, M. H., 1992. Agricultural labour in ancient Greece. In B. Wells (ed.), *Agriculture in Ancient Greece* (Göteborg: Paul Åströms Förlag) 135–46

Jameson, M. H., C. N. Runnels, and T. H. van Andel, 1994. *A Greek Countryside: The Southern Argolid from Prehistory to the Present Day* (Stanford: Stanford University Press)

Jeppesen, K., 1997. The Mausoleum at Halikarnassos: sculptural decoration and architectural background. In I. Jenkins and G. B. Waywell (eds), *Sculptors and Sculpture of Caria and the Dodecanese* (London: British Museum Press) 42–8

Johnson, M. and C. Perlès, 2004. An overview of settlement patterns in eastern Thessaly. In J. F. Cherry, C. Scarre, and S. Shennan (eds), *Explaining Social Change: Studies in Honour of Colin Renfrew* (Cambridge: McDonald Institute for Archaeological Research) 65–79

Johnston, A., 1991. Greek vases in the marketplace. In T. Rasmussen and N. Spivey (eds), *Looking at Greek Vases* (Cambridge: Cambridge University Press) 203–31

Jones, D. W., 1999. *Peak Sanctuaries and Sacred Caves in Minoan Crete: A Comparison of Artifacts* (Jonsered: Paul Åströms Förlag)

Jones, J. E., 1984–5. Laurion: Agrileza, 1977–1983: excavations at a silver-mine site. *Archaeological Reports* 31: 106–23

Jones, J. E., A. J. Graham and L. H. Sackett, 1973. An Attic country house below the cave of Pan at Vari. *Annual of the British School at Athens* 68: 355–452

Jones, R. E., 1986. *Greek and Cypriot Pottery: A Review of Scientific Studies* (London: British School at Athens)

Kassianidou, V. and A. B. Knapp, 2005. Archaeometallurgy in the Mediterranean: the social context of mining, metallurgy and trade. In E. Blake and A. B. Knapp (eds), *The Archaeology of Mediterranean Prehistory* (Oxford: Blackwell) 215–51

Kayafa, M., 2006. From Late Bronze Age to Early Iron Age copper metallurgy in mainland Greece and offshore Aegean islands. In S. Deger-Jalkotzy and I. S. Lemos (eds), *Ancient Greece: From the Mycenaean Palaces to the Age of Homer* (Edinburgh: Edinburgh University Press) 213–31

Kern, P. B., 1999. *Ancient Siege Warfare* (Bloomington: Indiana University Press)

Kilian-Dirlmeier, I., 1997. *Alt-Ägina IV,3: Das mittelbronzezeitliche Schachtgrab von Ägina* (Mainz: von Zabern)

Knappett, C., 1999. Tradition and innovation in pottery forming technology: wheel throwing at Middle Minoan Knossos. *Annual of the British School at Athens* 94: 101–29

Kraay, C. M., 1976. *Archaic and Classical Greek Coins* (London: Methuen)

Kurtz, D. and J. Boardman, 1971. *Greek Burial Customs* (London: Thames and Hudson)

Kyriakidis, E., 2005. *Ritual in the Bronze Age Aegean: The Minoan Peak Sanctuaries* (London: Duckworth)

Kyrieleis, H., 1993. The Heraion at Samos. In N. Marinatos and R. Hägg (eds), *Greek Sanctuaries: New Approaches* (London: Routledge) 125–53

Laffineur, R. and P. P. Betancourt (eds), 1997. *TEXNH: Craftsmen, Cratftswomen and Craftsmanship in the Aegean Bronze Age* (Liège: Université de Liège)

Laffineur, R. and E. Greco (eds), 2005. *Emporia: Aegeans in the Central and Eastern Mediterranean* (Liège: Université de Liège)

Lambrinoudakis, V. K., 1981. Remains of the Mycenaean period in the sanctuary of Apollo Maleatas. In R. Hägg and N. Marinatos (eds), *Sanctuaries and Cults in the Aegean Bronze Age* (Stockholm: Svenska Institutet i Athen) 59–65

Lawrence, A. W. 1979. *Greek Aims in Fortification* (Oxford: Clarendon Press)

Lawrence, A. W. and R. A. Tomlinson, 1996. *Greek Architecture* (New Haven and London: Yale University Press)

Lebessi, A. and P. Muhly, 1990. Aspects of Minoan cult: sacred enclosures. The evidence from the Syme sanctuary (Crete). *Archäologischer Anzeiger* 1990: 315–36

Lemos, I., 2002. *The Protogeometric Aegean: The Archaeology of the Late Eleventh and Tenth Centuries* BC (Oxford: Oxford University Press)

Lemos, I., 2005. The changing relationship of the Euboeans and the East. In A. Villing (ed.), *The Greeks in the East* (London: British Museum) 53–60

Loader, N. C., 1998. *Building in Cyclopean Masonry* (Jonsered: Paul Åströms Förlag)

Lohmann, H., 1992. Agriculture and country life in Classical Attica. In B. Wells (ed.), *Agriculture in Ancient Greece* (Göteborg: Paul Åströms Förlag) 29–57

Luke, J., 2003. *Ports of Trade, Al Mina and Geometric Greek Pottery in the Levant* (Oxford: Archaeopress)

Marinatos, N., 1984. *Art and Religion in Thera: Reconstructing a Bronze Age Society* (Athens: Mathioulakis)

Marinatos, N., 1993. *Minoan Religion* (Columbia: University of South Carolina Press)

Mazarakis Ainian, A., 1997. *From Ruler's Dwellings to Temples: Architecture, Religion and Society in Early Iron Age Greece (1100–700 BC)* (Jonsered: Paul Åströms Förlag)

MacDonald, C. F., E. Hallager and W.-D. Niemeier (eds), 2009. *The Minoans in the Central, Eastern and Northern Aegean: New Evidence* (Athens: Danish Institute at Athens)

McDonald, W. A. and G. R. Rapp (eds), 1972. *The Minnesota Messenia Expedition: Reconstructing a Bronze Age Regional Environment* (Minneapolis: University of Minnesota Press)

McDonald, W. A., W. D. E. Coulson, and J. Rosser, 1983. *Excavations at Nichoria in Southwest Greece III: Dark Age and Byzantine Occupation* (Minneapolis: University of Minnesota Press)

McDonald, W. A. and C. G. Thomas, 1990. *Progress into the Past: The Rediscovery of the Mycenaean Civilisation* (Bloomington and Indianapolis: Indiana University Press)

McDonald, W. A. and N. C. Wilkie, 1992. *Excavations at Nichoria in Southwest Greece II: The Bronze Age Occupation* (Minneapolis: University of Minnesota Press)

McGrail, S., 2001. *Boats of the World from the Stone Age to Medieval Times* (Oxford: Oxford University Press)

Mee, C., 2007. The production and consumption of pottery in the Neolithic Peloponnese. In C. Mee and J. Renard (eds), *Cooking up the Past: Food and Culinary Practices in the Neolithic and Bronze Age Aegean* (Oxford: Oxbow) 200–24

Mee, C., 2008. Mycenaean Greece, the Aegean and beyond. In C. Shelmerdine (ed.), *The Cambridge Companion to the Aegean Bronze Age* (Cambridge: Cambridge University Press) 362–86

Mee, C. and H. A. Forbes (eds), 1997. *A Rough and Rocky Place: The Landscape and Settlement History of the Methana Peninsula, Greece* (Liverpool: Liverpool University Press)

Mikalson, J. D., 2005. *Ancient Greek Religion* (Oxford: Blackwell)

Miller, S. G., 1993. *The Tomb of Lyson and Kallikles: A Painted Macedonian Tomb* (Mainz: Von Zabern)

Mina, M., 2008. Carving out gender in the prehistoric Aegean: anthropomorphic figurines of the Neolithc and Early Bronze Age. *Journal of Mediterranean Archaeology* 21: 213–39

Möller, A., 2000. *Naukratis: Trade in Archaic Greece* (Oxford: Oxford University Press)

Molloy, B., 2008. Martial arts and materiality: a combat archaeology perspective on Aegean swords of the fifteenth and fourteenth centuries BC. *World Archaeology* 40: 116–34.

Moore, A. D. and W. D. Taylour, 1999. *Well Built Mycenae Fascicule 10: The Temple Complex* (Oxford: Oxbow Books)

Morel, J.-P., 2006. Phocaean colonisation. In G. R. Tsetskhladze (ed.), *Greek Colonisation: An Account of Greek Colonies and Other Settlements Overseas* (Leiden: Brill) 358–428

Morgan, C., 1993. The origins of pan-Hellenism. In N. Marinatos and R. Hägg (eds), *Greek Sanctuaries: New Approaches* (London: Routledge) 18–44

Morgan, C., 1999. *Isthmia VIII: The Late Bronze Age Settlement and Early Iron Age Sanctuary* (Princeton: American School of Classical Studies at Athens)

Morgan, C., 2009. The Early Iron Age. In K. A. Raaflaub and H. van Wees (eds), *A Companion to Archaic Greece* (Chichester: Wiley-Blackwell) 43–63

Morgan, C. and J. J. Coulton, 1997. The *polis* as a physical entity. In M. H. Hansen (ed.), *The Polis as an Urban Centre and as a Political Community* (Copenhagen: Det Kongelige Danske Videnskabernes Selskab) 87–144

Morgan, C. and T. Whitelaw, 1991. Pots and politics: ceramic evidence for the rise of the Argive state. *American Journal of Archaeology* 95: 79–108

Morris, I., 1987. *Burial and Ancient Society: The Rise of the Greek City-State* (Cambridge: Cambridge University Press)

Morris, I., 1991. The early polis as city and state. In J. Rich and A. Wallace-Hadrill, *City and Country in the Ancient World* (London: Routledge) 25–57

Morris, I., 1992. *Death Ritual and Social Structure in Classical Antiquity* (Cambridge: Cambridge University Press)

Morris, I., 2000. *Archaeology as Cultural History: Words and Things in Iron Age Greece* (Oxford: Blackwell)

Morris, I., 2004. Classical archaeology. In J. Bintliff (ed.), *A Companion to Archaeology* (Malden: Blackwell) 253–71

Morris, I., 2009. The eighth-century revolution. In K. A. Raaflaub and H. van Wees (eds), *A Companion to Archaic Greece* (Chichester: Wiley-Blackwell) 64–80

Morrison, J. S., J. F. Coates and N. B. Rankov, 2000. *The Athenian Trireme: The History and Reconstruction of an Ancient Greek Warship* (Cambridge: Cambridge University Press)

Moss, M. L., 2005. *The Minoan Pantheon: Towards an Understanding of its Nature and Extent* (Oxford: British Archaeological Reports)

Mountjoy, P. A., 1986. *Mycenaean Decorated Pottery: A Guide to Identification* (Göteborg: Paul Åströms Förlag)

Mountjoy, P. A., 1993. *Mycenaean Pottery: An Introduction* (Oxford: Oxford University Committee for Archaeology)

Mountjoy, P. A. and M. J. Ponting, 2000. The Minoan thalassocrcay reconsidered: provenance studies of LH IIA/LM IB pottery from Phylakopi, Ayia Irini and Athens. *Annual of the British School at Athens* 95: 141–84

Mussche, H. F., 1974. *Thorikos: A Guide to the Excavations* (Brussels: Comité des fouilles belges en Grèce)

Myers, J. W., E. E. Myers, and G. Cadogan (eds), 1992. *The Aerial Atlas of Ancient Crete* (Berkeley: University of California)

Mylonas Shear, I., 1987. *The Panagia Houses at Mycenae* (Philadelphia: University of Pennsylvania)

Nevett, L. C., 1999. *House and Society in the Ancient Greek World* (Cambridge: Cambridge University Press)

Nielsen, I., 1999. *Hellenistic Palaces: Tradition and Renewal* (Aarhus: Aarhus University Press)

Niemeier, W.-D., 1990. Cult scenes on gold rings from the Argolid. In R. Hägg and G. C. Nordquist (eds), *Celebrations of Death and Divinity in the Bronze Age Argolid* (Stockholm: Svenska Institutet i Athen) 165–70

Noble, J. V., 1988. *The Techniques of Painted Attic Pottery* (London: Thames and Hudson)

Nordquist, G. C., 1987. *A Middle Helladic Village: Asine in the Argolid* (Uppsala: Uppsala University)

Nowicki, K., 2000. *Defensible Sites in Crete, c. 1200–800 BC* (Liège: Université de Liège)

Ober, J., 1985. *Fortress Attica: Defence of the Athenian Land Frontier, 404–322 BC* (Leiden: Brill)

Oliver, G. J., 2007. *War, Food and Politics in Early Hellenistic Athens* (Oxford: Oxford University Press)

Osborne, R., 1987. *Classical Landscape with Figures: The Ancient Greek City and its Countryside* (London: George Philip)

Osborne, R., 1989. A crisis in archaeological history? The seventh century BC in Attica. *Annual of the British School at Athens* 84: 297–322

Osborne, R., 1996. *Greece in the Making, 1200–479 BC* (London: Routledge)

Osborne, R., 1998a. *Archaic and Classical Greek Art* (Oxford: Oxford University Press)

Osborne, R., 1998b. Early Greek colonisation? The nature of Greek settlement in the West. In N. Fisher and H. van Wees (eds), *Archaic Greece: New Approaches and New Evidence* (London: Duckworth) 251–69

Owens, E. J., 1991. *The City in the Greek and Roman World* (London: Routledge)

Palaima, T. G., 1999. Mycenaean militarism from a textual perspective. Onomastics in context: *lāwos, dāmos, klewos*. In R. Laffineur (ed.), *Polemos: le contexte guerrier en Égée à l'Âge du Bronze* (Liège: Université de Liège) 367–78

Palaima, T. G. and C. Shelmerdine, 1984. *Pylos Comes Alive: Industry and Administration in a Mycenaean Palace* (New York: Fordham University)

Palyvou, C., 2005. *Akrotiri Thera: An Architecture of Affluence 3500 Years Old* (Philadelphia: INSTAP Academic Press)

Papadopoulos, J. K., 2003. *Ceramicus Redivivus: The Early Iron Age Potters' Field in the Area of the Classical Athenian Agora* (Princeton: American School of Classical Studies at Athens)

Papathanassopoulos, G. A., 1996. *Neolithic Culture in Greece* (Athens: Goulandris Foundation)

Pare, C. F. E., 2000. Bronze and the Bronze Age. In C. F. E. Pare (ed.), *Metals Make the World Go Round: The Supply and Circulation of Metals in Bronze Age Europe* (Oxford: Oxbow Books) 1–38

Parker, A. J., 1992. *Ancient Shipwrecks of the Mediterranean and the Roman Provinces* (Oxford: Tempus Reparatum)

Parker Pearson, M., 1999. *The Archaeology of Death and Burial* (Stroud: Sutton)

Peatfield, A., 1990. Minoan peak sanctuaries: history and society. *Opuscula Atheniensia* 17: 117–31

Peatfield, A., 1992. Rural ritual in Bronze Age Crete: the peak sanctuary at Atsipadhes. *Cambridge Archaeological Journal* 2: 59–87

Peperaki, O., 2004. The House of Tiles at Lerna: dimensions of social complexity. In J. C. Barrett and P. Halstead (eds), *The Emergence of Civilisation Revisited* (Oxford: Oxbow Books) 214–31

Perlès, C., 2001. *The Early Neolithic in Greece* (Cambridge: Cambridge University Press)

Popham, M. R., P. G. Calligas and L. H. Sackett, 1993. *Lefkandi II: The Protogeometric Building at Toumba. Part 2: The Excavation, Architecture and Finds* (London: British School at Athens)

Preston, L., 2004. Final Palatial Knossos and Postpalatial Crete: a mortuary perspective on political dynamics. In G. Cadogan, E. Hatzaki, and A. Vasilakis (eds), *Knossos: Palace, City and State* (London: British School at Athens) 137–45

Price, S. R. F., 1999. *Religions of the Ancient Greeks* (Cambridge: Cambridge University Press)

Pullen, D. J., 1986. A "House of Tiles" at Zygouries? The function of Early Helladic monumental architecture. In R. Hägg and D. Konsola (eds), *Early Helladic Architecture and Urbanization* (Göteborg: Paul Åströms Förlag) 79–84

Pullen, D. J., 2008. The Early Bronze Age in Greece. In C. Shelmerdine (ed.), *The Cambridge Companion to the Aegean Bronze Age* (Cambridge: Cambridge University Press) 19–46

Pyke, G. and P. Yiouni, 1996. *Nea Nikomedeia I: The Excavation of an Early Neolithic Village in Northern Greece 1961–1964* (London: British School at Athens)

Rasmussen, T., 1991. Corinth and the Orientalising phenomenon. In T. Rasmussen and N. Spivey (eds), *Looking at Greek Vases* (Cambridge: Cambridge University Press) 57–78

Reber, K., 1998. *Eretria Ausgrabungen und Forschungen X: Die klassischen und hellenistischen Wohnhäuser im Westquartier* (Lausanne: École suisse d'archéologie en Grèce)

Reber, K., 2007. Living and housing in Classical and Hellenistic Eretria. In R. Westgate, N. Fisher, and J. Whitley (eds), *Building Communities: House, Settlement and Society in the Aegean and Beyond* (London: British School at Athens) 281–8

Reed, C. M., 2003. *Maritime Traders in the Ancient Greek World* (Cambridge: Cambridge University Press)

Rehak, P. and J. Younger, 2001. Neopalatial, Final Palatial and Postpalatial Crete. In T. Cullen (ed.), *Aegean Prehistory: A Review* (Boston: Archaeological Institute of America) 383–473

Renfrew, C., 1985. *The Archaeology of Cult: The Sanctuary at Phylakopi* (London: British School at Athens)

Renfrew, C., C. Doumas, L. Marangou, and G. Gavalas (eds), 2007. *Keros, Dhaskalio-Kavos: The Investigations of 1987–88* (Cambridge: McDonald Institute for Archaeological Research)

Renfrew, C. and M. Wagstaff (eds), 1982. *An Island Polity: The Archaeology of Exploitation in Melos* (Cambridge: Cambridge University Press)

Renfrew, J., 1973. Agriculture. In D. R. Theocharis (ed.), *Neolithic Greece* (Athens: National Bank of Greece) 147–64

Rice, P. M., 1987. *Pottery Analysis: A Sourcebook* (Chicago: University of Chicago Press)

Ridgway, D., 1992. *The First Western Greeks* (Cambridge: Cambridge University Press)

Rihll, T. E., 2001. Making money in Classical Athens. In D. J. Mattingly and J. Salmon (eds), *Economies beyond Agriculture in the Classical World* (London: Routledge) 115–42

Rihll, T. E., 2007. *The Catapult: A History* (Yardley: Westholme)

Rhodes, R. F., 2003. The earliest Greek architecture in Corinth and the 7th-century temple on Temple Hill. In C. K. Williams and N. Bookidis (eds), *Corinth, the Centenary, 1896–1996* (Princeton: American School of Classical Studies) 85–94

Robb, J. E. and R. H. Farr, 2005. Substances in motion: Neolithic Mediterranean "trade." In E. Blake and A. B. Knapp (eds), *The Archaeology of Mediterranean Prehistory* (Oxford: Blackwell) 24–45

Robertson, M., 1992. *The Art of Vase-Painting in Classical Athens* (Cambridge: Cambridge University Press)

Robinson, D. M. and A. J. W. Graham, 1938. *Excavations at Olynthus VIII: The Hellenic House* (Baltimore: Johns Hopkins University Press)

Roy, J. 1996. The countryside in classical Greek drama and isolated farms in dramatic landscapes. In G. Shipley and J. Salmon (eds), *Human Landscapes in Classical Antiquity: Environment and Culture* (London: Routledge) 98–118

Runnels, C., 2001. The Stone Age of Greece from the Palaeolithic to the advent of the Neolithic. In T. Cullen (ed.), *Aegean Prehistory: A Review* (Boston: Archaeological Institute of America) 225–58

Rutkowski, B., 1986. *The Cult Places of the Aegean* (New Haven and London: Yale University Press)

Rutter, J., 2001. The prepalatial Bronze Age of the southern and central Greek mainland. In T. Cullen (ed.), *Aegean Prehistory: A Review* (Boston: Archaeological Institute of America) 95–155

Sakellarakis, Y., 1996. Minoan religious influence in the Aegean: the case of Kythera. *Annual of the British School at Athens* 91: 81–99

Sakellarakis, Y. and E. Sakellaraki, 1997. *Archanes: Minoan Crete in a New Light* (Athens: Ammos)

Sekunda, N., 2007. Land forces. In P. Sabin, H. van Wees, and M. Whitby (eds), *The Cambridge History of Greek and Roman Warfare I: Greece, the Hellenistic World and the Rise of Rome* (Cambridge: Cambridge University Press) 325–57

Shanks, M., 1996. *Classical Archaeology of Greece: Experiences of the Discipline* (London and New York: Routledge)

Shaw, J. W., 1987. The Early Helladic II corridor house: development and form. *American Journal of Archaeology* 91: 59–79

Shefton, B. B., 1994. Massalia and colonization in the north-western Mediterranean. In G. R. Tsetskhladze and F. de Angelis (eds), *The Archaeology of Greek Colonization* (Oxford: Oxford University School of Archaeology) 61–86

Shelmerdine, C. W., 2001. The palatial Bronze Age of the southern and central Greek mainland. In T. Cullen (ed.), *Aegean Prehistory: A Review* (Boston: Archaeological Institute of America) 329–81

Shelmerdine, C. W., 2008. Background, sources and methods. In C. Shelmerdine (ed.), *The Cambridge Companion to the Aegean Bronze Age* (Cambridge: Cambridge University Press) 1–18

Shepherd, G., 1995. The pride of most colonials: burial and religion in the Sicilian colonies. *Acta Hyperborea* 6: 51–82

Shepherd, G., 2005. Dead men tell no tales: ethnic diversity in Sicilian colonies and the evidence of the cemeteries. *Oxford Journal of Archaeology* 24: 115–36

Sherwin-White, S. and A. Kuhrt, 1993. *From Samarkand to Sardis: A New Approach to the Seleucid Empire* (London: Duckworth)

Sherratt, S., 1994. Commerce, iron and ideology: metallurgical innovation in $12^{th}$–$11^{th}$ century Cyprus. In V. Karageorghis (ed.), *Cyprus in the $11^{th}$ Century BC* (Nicosia: A. G. Leventis Foundation and the University of Cyprus) 59–107

Sherratt, S., 2000. *Catalogue of Cycladic Antiquities in the Ashmolean Museum: The Captive Spirit* (Oxford: Oxford University Press)

Siganidou, M. and M. Lilimpaki-Akamati, 1996. *Pella* (Athens: Ministry of Culture)

Snodgrass, A. M., 1964. *Early Greek Armour and Weapons from the End of the Bronze Age to 600 BC* (Edinburgh: Edinburgh University Press)

Snodgrass, A. M., 1971. *The Dark Age of Greece: An Archaeological Survey of the Eleventh to the Eighth Centuries BC* (Edinburgh: Edinburgh University Press)

Snodgrass, A. M., 1980a. *Archaic Greece: The Age of Experiment* (London: Dent)

Snodgrass, A. M., 1980b. Iron and early metallurgy in the Mediterranean. In T. A. Wertime and J. D. Muhly (eds), *The Coming of the Age of Iron* (New Haven and London: Yale University Press) 335–74

Snodgrass, A. M., 1987. *An Archaeology of Greece: The Present State and Future Scope of a Discipline* (Berkeley: University of California Press)

Snodgrass, A. M., 1989. The coming of iron in Greece: Europe's earliest Bronze/Iron transition. In M. L. Stig Sørensen and R. Thomas (eds), *The Bronze Age–Iron Age Transition in Europe* (Oxford: British Archaeological Reports) 22–35

Snodgrass, A. M., 1991. Archaeology and the study of the Greek city. In J. Rich and A. Wallace-Hadrill (eds), *City and Country in the Ancient World* (London: Routledge) 1–23

Snodgrass, A. M., 2006a. Heavy freight in Archaic Greece. In A. M. Snodgrass, *Archaeology and the Emergence of Greece* (Edinburgh: Edinburgh University Press) 221–33

Snodgrass, A. M., 2006b. The "hoplite reform" revisited. In A. M. Snodgrass, *Archaeology and the Emergence of Greece* (Edinburgh: Edinburgh University Press) 344–59

Snodgrass, A. M., 2007. Greek archaeology. In S. E. Alcock and R. Osborne (eds), *Classical Archaeology* (Malden: Blackwell) 13–29

Soles, J. S., 1992. *The Prepalatial Cemeteries at Mochlos and Gournia and the House Tombs of Bronze Age Crete* (Princeton: American School of Classical Studies)

Soles, J. S., 2003. *Mochlos IA: Mochlos Period III, Neopalatial Settlement on the Coast: The Artisans' Quarter and the Farmhouse at Chalinomouri* (Philadelphia: INSTAP Academic Press)

Souvatzi, S. G., 2008. *A Social Archaeology of Households in Neolithic Greece: An Anthropological Approach* (Cambridge: Cambridge University Press)

Sparkes, B. A., 1991. *Greek Pottery: An Introduction* (Manchester: Manchester University Press)

Spawforth, A., 2006. *The Complete Greek Temples* (London: Thames and Hudson)

Stocker, S. R. and J. L. Davis, 2004. Animal sacrifice, archives and feasting at the Palace of Nestor. In J. C. Wright (ed.), *The Mycenaean Feast* (Princeton: American School of Classical Studies) 59–75

Stos-Gale, Z. A. and N. H. Gale, 2003. Lead isotopic and other isotopic research in the Aegean. In K. P. Foster and R. Laffineur (eds), *Metron: Measuring the Aegean Bronze Age* (Liège: Université de Liège) 83–101

Strauss, B., 2007. Naval battles and sieges. In P. Sabin, H. van Wees, and M. Whitby (eds), *The Cambridge History of Greek and Roman Warfare I: Greece, the Hellenistic World and the Rise of Rome* (Cambridge: Cambridge University Press) 223–47

Talalay, L. E., 1993. *Deities, Dolls and Devices: Neolithic Figurines from Franchthi Cave, Greece* (Bloomington and Indianapolis: Indiana University Press)

Tang, B., 2005. *Delos, Carthage, Ampurias: the Housing of Three Mediterranean Trading Centres* (Rome: Bretschneider)

Tartaron, T. F., 2008. Aegean prehistory as world archaeology: recent trends in the archaeology of Bronze Age Greece. *Journal of Archaeological Research* 16: 83–161

Theocharis, D. R., 1973. *Neolithic Greece* (Athens: National Bank of Greece)

Tomlinson, R. A., 1976. *Greek Sanctuaries* (London: Elek)

Tomlinson, R. A., 1983. *Epidauros* (Austin: University of Texas Press)

Tomlinson, R. A., 1992. *From Mycenae to Constantinople: The Evolution of the Ancient City* (London: Routledge)

Tournavitou, I., 1995. *The "Ivory Houses" at Mycenae* (London: British School at Athens)

Travlos, J., 1980. *Pictorial Dictionary of Ancient Athens* (New York: Hacker)

Trümper, M., 2007. Differentiation in the Hellenistic houses of Delos: the question of functional areas. In R. Westgate, N. Fisher, and J. Whitley (eds), *Building Communities: House, Settlement and Society in the Aegean and Beyond* (London: British School at Athens) 323–34

Tsetskhladze, G. R., 1994. Greek penetration of the Black Sea. In G. R. Tsetskhladze and F. de Angelis (eds), *The Archaeology of Greek Colonization* (Oxford: Oxford University School of Archaeology) 111–35

Tylecote, R. F., 1987. *The Early History of Metallurgy in Europe* (London: Longman)

Tyree, E. L., 2001. Diachronic changes in Minoan cave cult. In R. Laffineur and R. Hägg (eds), *Potnia: Deities and Religion in the Aegean Bronze Age* (Liège: Université de Liège) 39–49

Tzavella-Evjen, H., 1985. *Lithares: An Early Bronze Age Settlement in Boeotia* (Los Angeles: Institute of Archaeology, University of California at Los Angeles)

Vallet, G., F. Villard, and P. Auberson, 1983. *Mégara Hyblaea 3: guide des fouilles: introduction à l'histoire d'un cité coloniale d'occident* (Rome: École française de Rome)

Vanschoonwinkel, J., 2006. Mycenaean expansion. In G. R. Tsetskhladze (ed.), *Greek Colonisation: An Account of Greek Colonies and Other Settlements Overseas I* (Leiden: Brill) 41–113

van Wees, H., 2004. *Greek Warfare: Myths and Realities* (London: Duckworth)

van Wijngaarden, G. J., 2002. *Use and Appreciation of Mycenaean Pottery in the Levant, Cyprus and Italy (1600–1200 BC)* (Amsterdam: Amsterdam University Press)

Vavouranakis, G., 2007. *Funerary Landscapes East of Lasithi, Crete, in the Bronze Age* (Oxford: Archaeopress)

Vickers, M. J. and D. W. J. Gill, 1994. *Artful Crafts: Ancient Greek Silverware and Pottery* (Oxford: Clarendon Press)

Voutsaki, S., 1995. Social and political processes in the Mycenaean Argolid: the evidence from the mortuary practices. In R. Laffineur and W.-D. Niemeier (eds), *Politeia: Society and State in the Aegean Bronze Age* (Liège: Université de Liège) 55–64

Wachsmann, S., 1998. *Seagoing Ships and Seamanship in the Bronze Age Levant* (London: Chatham)

Waldbaum, J. C., 1999. The coming of iron in the eastern Mediterranean: thirty years of archaeological and technological research. In V. C. Pigott (ed.), *The Archaeometallurgy of the Asian Old World* (Philadelphia: University Museum, University of Pennsylvania) 27–57

Wallace, S. A., 2003. The changing role of herding in the Early Iron Age of Crete: some implications of settlement shift for economy. *American Journal of Archaeology* 107: 601–27

Walter, H. and F. Felten, 1981. *Alt-Ägina III,1: Die vorgeschichtliche Stadt. Befestigungen, Häuser, Funde* (Mainz: von Zabern)

Warburton, D. A. (ed.), 2009. *Time's Up: Dating the Minoan Eruption of Santorini* (Athens: Danish Institute at Athens)

Warren, P., 1972. *Myrtos: An Early Bronze Age Settlement in Crete* (London: British School at Athens)

Warren, P., 2004. Terra cognita? The territory and boundaries of the early Neopalatial Knossian state. In G. Cadogan, E. Hatzaki, and A. Vasilakis (eds), *Knossos: Palace, City and State* (London: British School at Athens) 159–68

Warren, P. and V. Hankey, 1989. *Aegean Bronze Age Chronology* (Bristol: Bristol Classical Press)

Watrous, V., 2001. Crete from earliest prehistory through the Protopalatial period. In T. Cullen (ed.), *Aegean Prehistory: A Review* (Boston: Archaeological Institute of America) 157–223

Watrous, L. V., D. Hadzi-Vallianou, and H. Blitzer, 2004. *The Plain of Phaistos: Cycles of Social Complexity in the Mesara Region of Crete* (Los Angeles: Cotsen Institute of Archaeology, University of California at Los Angeles)

Wells, B. (ed.), 1996. *The Berbati-Limnes Archaeological Survey, 1998–1990* (Jonsered: Paul Åströms Förlag)

Wheeler, E. L., 2007. Land battles. In P. Sabin, H. van Wees, and M. Whitby (eds), *The Cambridge History of Greek and Roman Warfare I: Greece, the Hellenistic World and the Rise of Rome* (Cambridge: Cambridge University Press) 186–223

Wheeler, T. S. and R. Maddin, 1980. Metallurgy and ancient man. In T. A. Wertime and J. D. Muhly (eds), *The Coming of the Age of Iron* (New Haven and London: Yale University Press) 99–126

Whitby, M., 1998. The grain trade of Athens in the fourth century BC. In H. Parkins and C. Smith (eds), *Trade, Traders and the Ancient City* (London: Routledge) 102–28

Whitelaw, T., 1983. The settlement at Fournou Korifi Myrtos and aspects of Early Minoan social organisation. In O. Krzyszkowska and L. Nixon (eds), *Minoan Society* (Bristol: Bristol Classical Press) 323–45

Whitelaw, T., 2001a. From sites to communities: defining the human dimensions of Minoan urbanism. In K. Branigan (ed.), *Urbanism in the Aegean Bronze Age* (Sheffield: Sheffield Academic Press) 15–37

Whitelaw, T., 2001b. Reading between the tablets: assessing Mycenaean palatial involvement in ceramic production and consumption. In S. Voutsaki and J. Killen (eds), *Economy and Politics in the Mycenaean Palace States* (Cambridge: Cambridge Philological Society) 51–79

Whitelaw, T., 2004a. Estimating the population of Neopalatial Knossos. In G. Cadogan, E. Hatzaki, and A. Vasilakis (eds), *Knossos: Palace, City and State* (London: British School at Athens) 147–58

Whitelaw, T., 2004b. Alternative pathways to complexity in the southern Aegean. In J. C. Barrett and P. Halstead (eds), *The Emergence of Civilisation Revisited* (Oxford: Oxbow Books) 232–56

Whitelaw, T., 2007. House, households and community at Early Minoan Fournou Korifi: methods and models for interpretation. In R. Westgate, N. Fisher, and J. Whitley (eds), *Building Communities: House, Settlement and Society in the Aegean and Beyond* (London: British School at Athens) 65–76

Whitley, J., 2001. *The Archaeology of Ancient Greece* (Cambridge: Cambridge University Press)

Whittaker, H., 1997. *Mycenaean Cult Buildings: A Study of their Architecture and Function in the Context of the Aegean and the Eastern Mediterranean* (Bergen: The Norwegian Institute at Athens)

Wiencke, M. H., 2000. *Lerna IV: The Architecture, Stratification and Pottery of Lerna III* (Princeton: American School of Classical Studies at Athens)

Wiener, M. H., 1990. The isles of Crete? The Minoan thalassocracy revisited. In D. A. Hardy, C. G. Doumas, J. A. Sakellarakis, and P. M. Warren (eds), *Thera and the Aegean World III.1* (London: Thera Foundation) 128–61

Wilson, D., 2008. Early Prepalatial Crete. In C. Shelmerdine (ed.), *The Cambridge Companion to the Aegean Bronze Age* (Cambridge: Cambridge University Press) 77–104

Winter, F. E., 1971. *Greek Fortifications* (London: Routledge and Kegan Paul)

Wright, J. C., 1994. The spatial configuration of belief: the archaeology of Mycenaean religion. In S. E. Alcock and R. Osborne (eds), *Placing the Gods: Sanctuaries and Sacred Space in Ancient Greece* (Oxford: Oxford University Press) 37–78

Wright, J. C., 2004. A survey of evidence for feasting in Mycenaean society. In J. C. Wright (ed.), *The Mycenaean Feast* (Princeton: American School of Classical Studies at Athens) 13–58

Wright, J. C., 2008. Early Mycenaean Greece. In C. Shelmerdine (ed.), *The Cambridge Companion to the Aegean Bronze Age* (Cambridge: Cambridge University Press) 230–57

Wright, J. C., J. F. Cherry, J. L. Davis, E. Mantzourani, S. B. Sutton, and R. F. Sutton, 1990. The Nemea Valley Archaeological Project: a preliminary report. *Hesperia* 59: 579–659

# Index

*Greek Archaeology: A Thematic Approach*   By Christopher Mee
© 2011 Christopher Mee

Printed and bound by CPI Group (UK) Ltd, Croydon, CR0 4YY
04/08/2021
03078339-0001